Introduction to TESOL

Introduction to TESOL

Becoming a Language
Teaching Professional

Kate Mastruserio Reynolds, Kenan Dikilitaş, and Steve Close

WILEY Blackwell

Registered Office(s)
John Wiley & Sons, Inc., 111 River Street, Hoboken, NJ 07030, USA
John Wiley & Sons Ltd, The Atrium, Southern Gate, Chichester, West Sussex, PO19 8SQ, UK

Editorial Office
9600 Garsington Road, Oxford, OX4 2DQ, UK
For details of our global editorial offices, customer services, and more information about Wiley products visit us at www.wiley.com.

Library of Congress Cataloging-in-Publication Data
A catalogue record for this book is available from the Library of Congress

Paperback ISBN: 9781119632696; ePub ISBN: 9781119632719; ePDF ISBN: 9781119632733.

Cover image: © Catherine Falls Commercial/Getty Images
Cover design by Wiley

Set in 10/12 pt STIXTwoText by Integra Software Services Pvt. Ltd, Pondicherry, India

SKY10030207_092921

To all the newcomers to teaching and our daughter, Maddy,

"Every great dream begins with a dreamer. Always remember, you have within you the strength, the patience, and the passion to reach for the stars to change the world."

– Harriet Tubman

Kate Mastruserio Reynolds and Steve Close

To all the teachers shaping the future of children with education and to my son, Derin,
"A good teacher is like a candle—it consumes itself to light the way for others."

– Mustafa Kemal Atatürk

Kenan Dikilitaş

Contents

Acknowledgments

We would like to acknowledge the contributions of countless professionals in the field of TESOL from whom we have had the privilege of learning. Thank you to all of our students and colleagues who we have had the good fortune to collaboratively construct our understandings and grow academically alongside.

A big thank you to the following educators who contributed their insights and voices to this text. Your voices beautifully illustrated the intentional instruction and assessment practices you employ and your dedication to English learners. English language learners worldwide benefit because of your professionalism!

- Ami Christensen
- Angela Bell
- Benardo Tupas Panzo
- Connie "Alia" Mitchell
- Elizabeth Kitzmann
- Jing Jing "Summer" Jiao
- Kara Shore
- Katie Lembra
- Mari Bodensteiner
- Matthew Ventiri

No text can be written without the support and patience of one's family and friends, and cookies. We would like to say thank you specifically to those who have heard the word "book" too many times this year.

- Maddy Reynolds
- Molly Vogt
- Sherry Draeger
- Our friends and families

Introduction

This textbook is an introduction to the profession of TESOL (teachers of English to speakers of other languages) from a bird's eye point of view. We wanted newcomers to feel welcomed to the profession through an exploration of the breadth and scope of the field. We believe that newcomers will feel connected through understanding the knowledge base, skills, beliefs, and attitudes that TESOL educators have.

This is a descriptive textbook, which will help any prospective TESOL educator understand the interdisciplinary knowledge base that TESOL professionals share as well as the opportunities and subfields within the discipline. It is meant for educators who are hoping to learn more about TESOL or who are considering entering the field. It covers almost all areas of TESOL in a readable manner for students who are inclined to enter the field or teachers who are already in the field without formalized teacher preparation. It presents an opportunity to understand the numerous specializations and niches in the field that can be explored in TESOL. For example, one could teach first grade students bilingually in Egypt, foreign language instruction of English in Russia, academic second language writing at universities in English-speaking contexts, or research language patterns employed cross-culturally by different genders.

The major goal of this text is to share essential facts while providing basic information about contexts for teaching, our learners and their goals, professional organizations, linguistics, second language acquisition theories, instructional practices, and professional development. It is designed to help those interested in TESOL situate and commence their studies and research, and orient them so they know where to find resources, how to engage in the profession, and how to grow over the course of a career. It spans English as a second language (ESL) and English as a foreign language (EFL) contexts as the authors are experienced teacher educators in both contexts. We hope it helps all readers identify where to enter the profession in ways that are inspiring and interesting.

This book provides multiple perspectives on teaching and learning a second language, and uses language that new TESOLers can understand, thereby building basic knowledge about the field of TESOL. We hope to offer guidance for the newcomer from the perspective of this is what TESOL educators do and why. Not every instructional or assessment practice works for every student in every context, so it is our intention to provide information about the choices educators can make and align them with potential future contexts and learner populations. We intend our guidance to be descriptive of instructional and assessment practices, without prescribing them

Introduction to TESOL: Becoming a language teaching professional, First Edition. Kate Mastruserio Reynolds, Kenan Dikilitaş, and Steve Close.
© 2022 John Wiley & Sons, Inc. Published 2022 by John Wiley & Sons, Inc.

as the only way to approach these instructions and assessments. We hope that everyone who reads this book will find the ideas suggested to be stimulating. We hope, too, that readers will be creative in their teaching and learning and share their innovations with the field, so it continues to develop in the rich manner it has.

The learning theory that informs our perspectives on learning and teaching is Constructivism. Constructivism is the theory that individuals construct, or transform, their understandings of meanings and concepts through learning experiences (von Glasersfeld, 2005). This language is used throughout the text. However, we recognize that many of the practices, for example, teaching language skills or developing lesson plans, spring from Bloom's mastery learning model (1976). This text, therefore, is a hybrid of both educational perspectives.

In an odd way, this text is a love letter to a field of study, TESOL, second language learning, and English language learners (ELLs). In total, we have been studying and teaching in the field of TESOL for 80 years. That sort of dedication reveals a deep commitment to our ELLs and teacher candidates as well as the subject, the profession, and the processes involved in principled second language teaching and learning. It is our sincere hope that we convey in this text the wonderful, fascinating complexities and diversity of the field and inspire you to join us to engage professionally as a lifelong teacher-learner. We hope you find your niche within TESOL, so you can be the next generation of TESOL leaders.

References

Bloom, B. (1976). *Human characteristics and school learning*. McGraw-Hill.

von Glasersfeld, E. (2005). Introduction: Aspects of constructivism. In C. T. Fosnot (Ed.), *Constructivism: Theory, perspectives, and practice* (2nd ed.) (pp. 3–7). Teachers College Press.

Part One

The Field of TESOL

1

What Is TESOL?

This chapter will introduce TESOL as a field showing the various contexts and populations for English language instruction. It will highlight the domains that provide insight into how to teach, assess, and research in English as a second language. This chapter will provide basic acronyms needed by English language instructors in TESOL to situate their work and learn more about it. Proficiency levels, which describe levels of language development, will be presented. Finally, the interdisciplinary nature of TESOL and specializations within the field will be discussed.

Learning Outcomes

At the conclusion of this chapter, you will be able to:

- compare and contrast the unique attributes of different contexts of English language learning
- define common acronyms in the field
- apply knowledge of proficiency levels to lesson planning, delivery, and instruction
- connect the disciplines that inform the study of second/additional language learning
- describe the interdisciplinary nature of TESOL
- discuss the specializations of professionals in the field

In this vignette, you will read about two locations where English is taught and how the context influences the instruction. Observe the differences and reflect upon how you envision your future English language teaching or which example mostly closely aligns with your current instructional setting and practices.

TESOL Voices

Diverse Learners, Diverse Settings

In Kobe, Japan at Aitoku Gakuen Junior/Senior High School, uniformed ninth-grade students enter their English as a foreign language (EFL) class. Both the teacher, who speaks Japanese and English, and the teacher assistant, a native

---

Introduction to TESOL: Becoming a language teaching professional, First Edition. Kate Mastruserio Reynolds, Kenan Dikilitaş, and Steve Close.
© 2022 John Wiley & Sons, Inc. Published 2022 by John Wiley & Sons, Inc.

English speaker from Australia, greet the students in English as they enter the classroom. The teacher prepares her lesson by arranging the necessary paperwork and bringing up a video about air pollution in Japan. The teacher assistant engages the students in casual social conversation about how they feel, how their weekend was, and what they are up to personally. The students seem a bit embarrassed, but try to respond to the questions as well as they can. Some students respond in full sentences and provide some details about their lives; others provide one-word answers and look down to avoid more questions. Once the teacher begins the class, she reviews the meanings of the key vocabulary they are learning. Students provide definitions and examples of the vocabulary during a quick game, competing to see how many their team can get correctly in 2 min. After the vocabulary review, the students watch an 8-min video in English on air pollution in Japan. While they watch, they are asked to identify key information presented in the video. Next, they individually read an article about air pollution in English. Some students raise their hands to ask questions about a word or phrase and the teacher or teaching assistant approaches them to answer quietly. The teacher leads the whole class in discussion about the article by asking comprehension and opinion questions. She says, for example, "What is the greatest cause of air pollution today? How do you think you can reduce air pollution?" Students raise their hands to respond and several contribute their ideas of how they can reduce air pollution. Then, the teacher gives them a group project to investigate more ways people can reduce air pollution. Students are given small posters to describe and illustrate with their findings. Students will present their posters to the class.

At Citrus Park Elementary in Tampa, Florida, United States, a third-grade mixed class of native English speakers and English language learners (ELLs) listen to directions about their science experiment on erosion. First, they should discuss their prediction with their partner of what they think will happen when they drip the water into each tin. Both tins have a small incline. One tin has only loose soil at the top of the tin; the other has roots attached to the tin with the same amount of loose soil on top. Students are instructed to write down the prediction for the team after they discuss it. Next, they begin the experiment by dripping water using an eyedropper from a small beaker into two baking tins. The classroom fills with chatter as students give suggestions about where and how to drop the water. Some exclamations can be heard as the loose soil side creates an avalanche of loose soil in the bottom of the tin with only one dropper full of water. The students write down their observations on a graphic organizer. Next, they move to the roots and soil tin and begin dripping their water. They note in their graphic organizer that only a little of the soil erodes through the roots. The teacher circulates and reminds them to reread their predictions and check to see if they predicted correctly. They write in their graphic organizer whether their prediction was correct. They reflect on the experiment and discuss why they think the water eroded faster without roots. The teacher asks students to take their pans to the sink area, where they place the soil and roots in different buckets and the emptied trays in the sink. Once they are seated, the teacher asks the students what they predicted, observed, and what resulted. They discuss the reasons for the differences and connect this experiment to the erosion of a mountain.

> In Melbourne Adult Migrant English Program (AMEP) in Melbourne, Australia, 12 adults ranging from 23 to 51 enter their English language class after leaving their children at the associated childcare center nearby. They are present to learn basic English language skills for participating in their jobs and conducting personal business in the community. Most of the students speak Mandarin or Arabic, but some are native speakers of Urdu or Vietnamese. One characteristic they all have in common is they are recent immigrants to Australia. Some of them arrived due to humanitarian reasons (e.g., political unrest, famine, or war); others for economic opportunities. They are greeted warmly by name by a teacher and three tutors and take their individual folder from the cabinet. Tutors sit down close by individuals or pairs and begin working with them. Each individual or small group is working on a different topic and level. In one pair, a tutor is presenting new vocabulary of items in a grocery store. The two older women say the vocabulary word aloud after the teacher. In a small group, the tutor is helping the students in a guided reading on conducting a job search. One student sits at a computer and takes an exam on business English terminology. The last group work with the teacher who is helping them with the academic reading skill of making inferences. Their class will last roughly 2 hr this evening, so they can pick up their children and return home at a reasonable hour.

All of these examples represent some of the variations of English teaching contexts and instruction. In each of these contexts, the learner population will be different. We will next talk about the acronyms used in the field and how they describe populations of learners; however, while we start here, we would like you to imagine the students in these different locales and keep the learners and learning at the forefront of your mind while reading.

The World of TESOL Through Acronyms

TESOL, in the simplest definition of the term, is teaching English to people who do not speak English as a first language. In this sense, the term TESOL is an umbrella term for many other related concepts. These related concepts are typically represented in acronyms.

Individuals encountering the field of TESOL are often struck by the number of acronyms associated with our community. These acronyms, while plentiful and a bit overwhelming, provide insiders with shortcuts to arrive at understandings quickly and demonstrate who is knowledgeable about the field and who is current in their understandings.

While some of the acronyms indicate the population who is studying and what their studies emphasize, others provide key information about context. The initial acronyms encountered are distinctions between the study of language (e.g., ESL, ELL, EFL, ELT, and EIL) (see Table 1.1) and the study of teaching language (e.g., TESL, TEFL, and TESOL) (see Table 1.2). Acronyms for the study of language start with E for

Table 1.1   Common acronyms to describe the study of English language

Acronym	Meaning	Context
ESL	English as a second language	Study of English in contexts where the language used outside of the classroom is English
ESOL	English to speakers of other languages	Study of English in contexts where the language used outside of the classroom is English
EFL	English as a foreign language	Study of English in contexts where the language used outside of the classroom is not English. Often the language employed outside of the classroom is the students' primary language
EIL	English as an international language	Study of English as it is used internationally. It may imply use among individuals who may not be native speakers or bound to traditional native speaker norms
ELL	English language learning	This term does not imply context, but has been adopted frequently in the United States

Table 1.2   Acronyms for the study of how to teach ESL/EFL/EIL/ELL

Acronym	Meaning	Context
TESL	Teaching English as a second language	Teaching English to students in second language contexts (i.e., where the language used outside of the classroom is English)
TESOL	Teaching or teachers of English to speakers of other languages	Teaching English to students in second language contexts (i.e., where the language used outside of the classroom is English)
TEFL	Teaching English as a foreign language	Teaching English to students in foreign language contexts (i.e., where the language used outside of the classroom is not English). Often the language employed outside of the classroom is the students' primary language
ELT	English language teaching	Teaching English internationally. This term does not imply context

English, whereas those for teaching the language begin with T for teaching. The distinction they demonstrate is the study of the language is for individuals who wish to learn or improve their English language skills, while the study of teaching the language is for individuals who desire to teach others the language.

The teachers may be former students of English language who have mastered a degree of proficiency in the language, or individuals who were born in bilingual or multilingual settings and had the advantage of learning two or more languages from birth, or native monolingual English speakers. All these pathways to the teaching of English are valued in TESOL and provide their future language students with insights they have gleaned from their pathway into the field. For example, the native speaking teacher may have a native accent, but nonnative speakers often have grammatical and linguistic insights from their studies native speakers do not possess.

The most common acronyms in the field to describe the study of English language by individuals who speak one or more other languages are ESL, EFL, EIL, and ELL.

There are other acronyms for the study of English, such as VESL (vocational English as a second language), and content-based (CBI), sheltered instruction observation protocol (SIOP), which we will discuss later in the text.

ESL stands for *English as a second language*. It refers to language learning contexts, or locations, in which the majority of inhabitants speak English. Some English-dominant speaking countries spring to mind quickly, such as Australia, Canada, New Zealand, the United Kingdom, and the United States. In the field of TESOL, a shared value is that there is no "best" version of English; British English is not inherently better than the other variations of English. These countries have traditionally been considered the generators of patterns or norms of English language use. However, as the number of the speakers of English has increased over years, the English spoken by non-English speakers has also changed. This topic, World Englishes, will be covered in more detail in upcoming chapters.

Representing the different forms of English

In recent years, there has been a tendency to legitimize the English spoken by people coming from different first language (L1) backgrounds, which also implies that English as a second language and its dissemination is not necessarily kept under the control of countries speaking it as a first language such as England and America.

Other countries have many speakers of English because they were former colonies of an English-dominant country, but may also have many other languages spoken in the country (e.g., India, Nigeria, Pakistan, and the Philippines). There are many individuals in India, for example, who have spoken English all of their lives and who speak some of the 22 major languages spoken there. Interestingly, Indian English has elements of the native languages of the people infused into their English. This infusion affords flair and flavor to their language use. Additionally, Indian English speakers generate new patterns of language use in vocabulary, grammar, and pronunciation that are not necessarily influenced by their first language(s).

The acronym ESL implies certain perspectives. It suggests that students only speak one language when they might speak more than one. TESOL professionals often speak of "second language acquisition" to mean the process of learning or acquiring a second or additional language. Professionals in the field have suggested that we should use the term English as an additional language, which can be seen in some writings. In this text, you will see both terms employed.

Other issues exist with the use of "second language" as well. In the past, students learning another language often needed to travel to the target language country to practice their language with native speakers in order to develop a high degree of language proficiency. With the ease of global communication on the internet, students may have access to English in formerly unprecedented ways. They have access to newspapers, magazines, blogs, movies, music, and chatrooms with native English models of language. This access breaks down the distinction between "second and foreign language" contexts to some degree.

In spite of the issues noted above, ESL remains a widely used acronym. Many professionals use the term and keep these caveats in mind.

Heterogeneous or homogeneous learner populations

In some classrooms, there may be students who speak many different languages. For example, in New South Wales, Australia, there are 239 different languages spoken in the public schools as of 2018 (CESE Bulletin, 2018). Students may speak Chinese, Arabic, Vietnamese, Tagalog, Samoan, or Greek. We call this a heterogeneous class due to the different languages.

In other language settings, there may be classes with students who all speak the same language. This class composition is called a *homogeneous* population, because they share a similar first language. These distinctions are important, because the types of activities a teacher may use differ if they all share a language.

Generally, there are more *heterogeneous* class compositions in second language settings and more homogeneous groups in foreign language contexts. However, there are always exceptions to this pattern.

ESOL stands for *English to speakers of other languages*. The contexts for ESOL are similar to ESL—contexts where the language used outside of the classroom is English. This acronym was introduced to explicitly alleviate a problem, which was that the acronym ESL implied studying English as a "second," not "additional," language. ESOL implies students may speak more than one other language.

ESOL was adopted by several U.S. states in their laws and by TESOL International Association and its affiliates in their names. For example, Washington Association for the Education of Speakers of Other Languages (WAESOL) (https://waesol.org) and Peru Teachers of English to Speakers of Other Languages (http://www.perutesol.org).

EFL represents English as a foreign language. It describes the study of English in contexts where the language used outside of the classroom is not English. Often the language employed outside of the classroom is the students' primary language. For example, the study of English in countries such as China, Japan, Saudi Arabia, Thailand, Ukraine, and the United Arab Emirates.

There are some inherent issues with the use of EFL. EFL is one of the older acronyms to describe the study of English. With the use of the world "*foreign*," it has a negative connotation of otherness or oddity. In the field of TESOL, we hope to bridge cultural differences, so emphasizing otherness is counterproductive.

Despite the anachronistic nature of some of these acronyms, they do provide a clear distinction in context, which provides insiders with information about the amount of language practice and practice opportunities, and duration and type of instruction. For example, in Japan, elementary school children have English class for a couple of hours per week in which they learn basic vocabulary for families, food, hobbies through games and song. By middle and high school, students have English class daily, in which they learn speaking, listening, reading, and writing through choral drills, oral presentations, readings, interactive activities, and games. Much of the learning is about memorization and repetition. The classroom formats generally revolve around the teacher. The teacher asks a question and calls upon a student, for example. We call this teacher-centered interaction. For example, students in Japan may access outside-of-class opportunities to develop their oral language skills on the internet, but interaction within the community in English is not necessary, and often not even possible. Because of this and other factors, Japanese English learners tend to struggle with their oral language proficiency. This example is not intended to demonize the instruction of English in Japan. Actually, there are many exciting, culturally congruent practices employed by knowledgeable educators in Japan. These are generalizations to illustrate associations common with the EFL setting only. Although these are generalizations, generalizations are valuable at times.

English as an international language

EIL stands for *English as an international language*. It describes the study of English as it is used internationally. The term recognizes the use of English as a "lingua franca" or common language for communication. The concept of lingua franca will be further discussed in Chapter 4. EIL implies that English is used among individuals who may not be native speakers or bound to traditional native-speaker language norms. The contexts associated with EIL are in multilingual settings such as large, international cities (e.g., Hong Kong, Macau, Singapore, Doha, and Dubai) or on the internet.

The use of English in these contexts may generate new language patterns or norms that have more to do with efficient communication and clarity than with traditional or formal English language use; however, speakers are typically successful in their communication. Kate had frequently interaction with speakers of diverse languages while living in Doha, Qatar, where roughly 88% of the population is from outside the country (Demographics of Qatar, 2019). Many individuals were from nearby countries in the Middle East and Asia, but also from the Philippines and Malaysia. The official language of Qatar is Arabic. English is also employed there as an international language, because it is a commonly learned language and many people have learned some of it. Street names were often not marked, so it was often necessary to negotiate at length with cab drivers about where to go, and how to get to a particular location. Communication between Kate and a cab driver depended in large part on each speaker's knowledge of the area and abilities in Arabic for the street names and oral English. Many language shortcuts were taken to ensure that they understood each other and had the same location in mind. These types of interactions, if frequent, create new language patterns.

Language extinction, linguistic imperialism, and language policy

In locations worldwide, the native languages of communities are becoming extinct, meaning there are no new speakers of the language due to the increased usage of other languages. Often these other languages are English, French, Portuguese, and Spanish. To demonstrate the decreasing use of indigenous languages, Oré and Diaz (2019) report that, "Brazil, the region's most linguistically diverse country, runs the risk of losing a third of its 180-plus languages by 2030. In Mexico, almost two thirds of its 68 languages are on the brink of disappearance. This trend repeats in Argentina, Bolivia, Colombia, Chile, Ecuador, Paraguay, Peru and Central America"

(Oré & Diaz, 2019). The growth of English as a lingua franca is a contributing factor in language extinction.

Increasingly, people who do not have any intention of living or working in an English-speaking country need to be able to speak English for work and other purposes, so they opt to learn it. On one hand, that is a good for the employment prospects of TESOL professionals; on the other, it means that some native languages and/or indigenous languages are not maintained in some contexts. For example, a refugee to the United States from Guatemala who speaks Quechua and Spanish would learn English in the United States. That individual may also use Spanish, since it is a common language there. Furthermore, that individual might choose not to speak Quechua to their children. If the children of this individual learn to speak English and Spanish, the result is that there are fewer speakers of Quechua. This is how languages die out over time.

As a whole, the current extinction of languages worldwide can be traced back to the imperialism in the 16th to 19th centuries. Phillipson (1992) and Canagarajah (2003) linked the dominance of English worldwide and the rise of English as a lingua franca to the imperialistic endeavors of Britain in places such as, India, Hong Kong, Nigeria, and the United States in Guam, the Philippines, and Puerto Rico. When these colonizing forces took control of these locations, English became the language of power and knowing the language of those in power was an advantage; however, with the upsurge of English, the native languages declined. Moreover, the colonizers' values and ideologies were promoted during the instruction of English in these locations. *Linguistic imperialism* is the promotion of one dominant language to the exclusion of others and the furtherance of the cultural values and ideologies associated with the dominant language.

The practice of linguistic imperialism varies in intensity and intent. A community may be forced simultaneously to learn the language of a colonizing force and to consciously suppress the native language. This was the case in many of the satellite nations of the former Soviet Union and Native American nations of the United States. Other cases of linguistic imperialism are less intentional and hegemonic (i.e., the social, cultural, and linguistic sway applied by a dominant group). For example, in India, where there are 121 languages spoken, the arrival of English meant that those who communicated only in non-English languages were at a distinct disadvantage; therefore, people opted to learn English. In this case, the British teachers did promote British culture, values, and Western ideologies with the instruction of English.

From a critical theory perspective, it is vital for TESOL professionals to be aware of the issues around the dominance of English worldwide, and embrace the variations in English and local language use. Teachers can do this by showing respect for students' home languages and cultures, being cautious about promoting the cultural values or ideologies associated with the countries where English is spoken (i.e., norm-generating), asking parents to read in their native language(s) to their children at home, promoting learning of languages other than English, and supporting educational policies that clearly encourage the maintenance of other languages. It is in this manner that TESOL professionals can serve language learners in various contexts, reduce linguistic imperialism, and support native languages of students.

ELL stands for *English language learning*. It has come to mean the study of English as another language. This term does not imply any particular context, but has been adopted frequently in the United States, particularly in the public K–12 schools. It has some positive connotations, because it places the focus on learning. This acronym emphasizes the study of language, but it shares an abbreviation of ELL, which can mean English language learner, a phrase which refers to the students studying English. Depending on the situation, this difference may be problematic. Other English professionals, those who teach English composition (writing) or literature to native English speakers, have vocalized some concern about the term, too, arguing that they also teach English language learning, but with a different population and focus. Others find the term to be redundant. All in all, it is considered a less problematic term than ESL and many educators use it.

Some other common acronyms that you will encounter in the field are NL, TL, L1, L2, NS, and NNS. Juanita is a native speaker (NS) of Spanish in Mexico. We can say Spanish is her native language (NL) or first language (L1). She is learning English as an additional language. In this case, English is the target language (TL) or second language (L2). She studies with Ms. Milagros, who is a nonnative speaker (NNS) of English. These common acronyms will be used throughout this textbook, so you may want to commit them to memory.

Differentiating the focus from language teaching to preparing language teachers

Anyone who has tried to look up teaching English by "ESL" will be familiar with the difficulties associated with the use of ESL versus TESL or EFL versus TEFL. Not only do they look similar, but also their meanings are sometimes confused. Generally, if it has a "T" at the beginning of the acronym, it means teaching English as a second/foreign language (TESL/TEFL) and is used to describe the preparation to become a teacher of ESL/EFL. The emphasis is on the *teaching* of the subject. Applying this rule, the acronym "TESOL" then indicates teaching or teachers of English to speakers of other languages. Two professional organizations, TESOL International Association (www.tesol.org) and International Association of Teachers of English as a Foreign Language (IATEFL) (www.iatefl.org), have the T in their acronyms, but are used to describe the processes of teaching and learning of English in differing contexts.

Another common acronym for teacher preparation is ELT for English language teaching. This term is often employed in the United Kingdom and other countries closely associated with Britain; for example, countries in the European Union and former colonies of Britain, such as Hong Kong and India. ELT is used as an inclusive term, which does not highlight context. It is considered an overarching term, which is a positive characteristic. Another positive characteristic is that the use of it reduces all of the acronyms. A con for the use of the term is that it is not precisely descriptive for insiders.

In some contexts, you may observe the use of TESOL or Applied Linguistics employed interchangeably. The reasons that these terms can be used interchangeably stem from the early emergence of the field in 1946. As the field was beginning to be established and was initially defining itself, it was concerned with research-based foreign language teaching (including English to nonnative speakers) (https://www.

linguisticsociety.org/resource/applied-linguistics). The field has continued to define itself and the parameters of study. Currently, according to the Association Internationale de Linguistique Appliquée (n.d.) or International Association of Applied Linguistics, the field of "Applied Linguistics is an interdisciplinary and transdisciplinary field of research and practice dealing with practical problems of language and communication that can be identified, analyzed or solved by applying available theories, methods and results of Linguistics or by developing new theoretical and methodological frameworks in Linguistics to work on these problems" (https://aila. info). In other words, the fields share interests in research on both second/additional language acquisition/learning and language teaching.

One minor difference between TESOL and Applied Linguistics is that TESOL focuses on English, whereas Applied Linguistics is concerned with the learning/acquisition of any second or additional language. For example, learning Italian in Italy if you do not speak Italian as a native speaker.

While it may appear overwhelming to newcomers to have so many diverse acronyms, their use has a practical application. The various acronyms help identify the population and context of instruction. They also indicate an orientation to the field to be inclusive and representative of learners and their backgrounds. It is best considered as shorthand or code for simplifying discussions among colleagues.

Questions for reflection

- Why do you think the field has developed so many acronyms? Do you think they help professionals share important information about their contexts or do you think they are simply jargon? Why?
- Which contexts do you foresee you will work in during your career?
- How might proficiency levels be somewhat correlated to particular contexts? To what degree might this be true? What would be the exceptions to this relationship?

Being Proficient and Levels of Proficiency

TESOL educators describe the ability of a learner to communicate in oral and written language as their proficiency. While people outside of the discipline may use the terms "fluent" and "fluency," TESOL educators tend to use these terms in very specific instances. Most of the time, we use the term proficiency, because it allows us to show the degree to which a person is able to communicate. For example, Kenan is highly proficient in English. Kate is moderately proficient in French, and Steve is moderately proficient in French and minimally proficient in Russian.

Organizations such as the American Council of Teachers of Foreign Languages (ACTFL), World-Class Instructional Design and Assessment (WIDA), and the Council of Europe (Common European Framework or CEFR) have developed scales to describe learners' abilities in specific language skills (i.e., speaking, listening, reading, and writing) or in general.

ACTFL Proficiency Scales

The ACTFL Oral Proficiency Guidelines were the first of their kind in 1982, and influenced other scales over time. ACTFL (2012) has a scale that starts with novice, intermediate, and then moves along to advanced and superior (for more information, see https://www.actfl.org/resources/actfl-proficiency-guidelines-2012). ACTFL is used by many world language educators. The scales in different language skills illuminate what the learners should be able to do at each level of proficiency (see Figure 1.1). For example, in speaking, a learner at the beginning level can use formulaic language to greet someone.

WIDA proficiency indicators

WIDA has six levels of proficiency (see Figures 1.2 and 1.3) that range from 1 as the lowest and 6 as the most advanced (Board of Regents of the University of Wisconsin System, 2012). The WIDA proficiency level descriptors separate interpretative (i.e., reading/listening) modes from expressive (i.e., writing/speaking modes) and differentiate abilities at the word, sentence, and discourse levels (i.e., paragraph or essay). In the 2020 edition, they have also included categories of language functions common in the classroom: Narrate, Inform, Explain, and Argue.

The WIDA team also developed "can do" descriptors that help educators understand what ELLs can do in speaking, listening, reading, and writing in social, instructional, and academic language. These descriptors were developed for kindergarten, first grade, and grade clusters of 2–3, 4–5, 6–8, and 9–12. They can be used to guide lesson plan

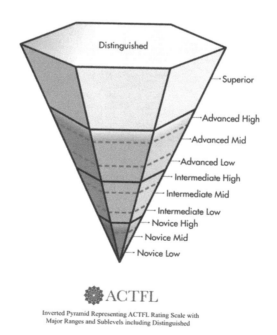

Inverted Pyramid Representing ACTFL Rating Scale with
Major Ranges and Sublevels including Distinguished

Figure 1.1 ACTFL Proficiency Scale. Used with permission from ACTFL.

WIDA Performance Definitions - Speaking and Writing Grades K–12

Within sociocultural contexts for language use…		
Discourse Dimension	**Sentence Dimension**	**Word/Phrase Dimension**
Linguistic Complexity	**Language Forms and Conventions**	**Vocabulary Usage**
Level 6 - Reaching English language learners will use a range of grade-appropriate language for a variety of academic purposes and audiences. Agility in academic language use is reflected in oral fluency and automaticity in response, flexibility in adjusting to different registers and skillfulness in interpersonal interaction. English language learners' strategic competence in academic language use facilitates their ability to relate information and ideas with precision and sophistication for each content area.		
At each grade, toward the end of a given level of English language proficiency, and with instructional support, English language learners will produce…		
Level 5 Bridging • Multiple, complex sentences • Organized, cohesive, and coherent expression of ideas characteristic of particular content areas	• A variety of complex grammatical structures matched to purpose • A broad range of sentence patterns characteristic of particular content areas	• Technical and abstract content-area language, including content-specific collocations • Words and expressions with precise meaning across content areas
Level 4 Expanding • Short, expanded, and some complex sentences • Organized expression of ideas with emerging cohesion characteristic of particular content areas	• Compound and complex grammatical structures • Sentence patterns characteristic of particular content areas	• Specific and some technical content-area language • Words and expressions with expressive meaning through use of collocations and idioms across content areas
Level 3 Developing • Short and some expanded sentences with emerging complexity • Expanded expression of one idea or emerging expression of multiple related ideas across content areas	• Simple and compound grammatical structures with occasional variation • Sentence patterns across content areas	• Specific content language, including cognates and expressions • Words or expressions with multiple meanings used across content areas
Level 2 Emerging • Phrases or short sentences • Emerging expression of ideas	• Formulaic grammatical structures • Repetitive phrasal and sentence patterns across content areas	• General content words and expressions • Social and instructional words and expressions across content areas
Level 1 Entering • Words, phrases, or chunks of language • Single words used to represent ideas	• Phrase-level grammatical structures • Phrasal patterns associated with familiar social and instructional situations	• General content-related words • Everyday social and instructional words and expressions

Figure 1.2 WIDA performance definitions—speaking and writing. Used with permission from WIDA.

WIDA Performance Definitions - Listening and Reading Grades K–12

Within sociocultural contexts for processing language…		
Discourse Dimension	**Sentence Dimension**	**Word/Phrase Dimension**
Linguistic Complexity	**Language Forms and Conventions**	**Vocabulary Usage**
Level 6 - Reaching English language learners will process a range of grade-appropriate oral or written language for a variety of academic purposes and audiences. Automaticity in language processing is reflected in the ability to identify and act on significant information from a variety of genres and registers. English language learners' strategic competence in processing academic language facilitates their access to content area concepts and ideas.		
At each grade, toward the end of a given level of English language proficiency, and with instructional support, English language learners will process…		
Level 5 Bridging • Rich descriptive discourse with complex sentences • Cohesive and organized, related ideas across content areas	• A variety of complex grammatical structures • Sentence patterns characteristic of particular content areas	• Technical and abstract content-area language • Words and expressions with shades of meaning across content areas
Level 4 Expanding • Connected discourse with a variety of sentences • Expanded related ideas characteristic of particular content areas	• Complex grammatical structures • A broad range of sentence patterns characteristic of particular content areas	• Specific and some technical content-area language • Words or expressions with multiple meanings across content areas
Level 3 Developing • Discourse with a series of extended sentences • Related ideas specific to particular content areas	• Compound and some complex grammatical constructions • Sentence patterns across content areas	• Specific content-area language and expressions • Words and expressions with common collocations and idioms across content areas
Level 2 Emerging • Multiple related simple sentences • An idea with details	• Compound grammatical structures • Repetitive phrasal and sentence patterns across content areas	• General content words and expressions, including cognates • Social and instructional words and expressions across content areas
Level 1 Entering • Single statements or questions • An idea within words, phrases, or chunks of language	• Simple grammatical constructions (e.g., commands, Wh- questions, declaratives) • Common social and instructional forms and patterns	• General content-related words • Everyday social, instructional and some content-related words and phrases

Figure 1.3 WIDA performance definitions—listening and reading. Used with permission from WIDA.

development that is grade-level appropriate, so educators can provide supports and activities suitably geared for ELLs.

The proficiency level descriptors combine with the modes and levels of discourse (i.e., word, sentence, and paragraph(s)), language function at the six grade-level clusters, so that informed educators can design purposeful and targeted lessons (see the WIDA 2020 edition for details and examples).

The ACTFL and WIDA scales do not necessarily align one to one. At level 1 of WIDA, an ELL might be able listen to and understand yes/no questions with support. WIDA performance definitions are used in a majority of U.S. states and increasingly in international schools throughout the world.

Council of Europe Framework proficiency scale

Council of Europe Framework (CEFR) has six levels of proficiency that are correlated to the ACTFL Proficiency Scale (Council of Europe, n.d.). The CEFR scale ranges from Basic (A level) to Independent (B level) and Proficient User (C level) of the language. At each level is a lower and upper tier indicated by 1 or 2. At the most basic level is A1 (see Table 1.3). A language learner at A1 would be able to hold basic

Table 1.3 Council of Europe Framework

Proficient User	C2	Can understand with ease virtually everything heard or read. Can summarize information from different spoken and written sources, reconstructing arguments and accounts in a coherent presentation. Can express him/herself spontaneously, very fluently and precisely, differentiating finer shades of meaning even in more complex situations.
	C1	Can understand a wide range of demanding, longer texts, and recognize implicit meaning. Can express him/herself fluently and spontaneously without much obvious searching for expressions. Can use language flexibly and effectively for social, academic and professional purposes. Can produce clear, well-structured, detailed text on complex subjects, showing controlled use of organizational patterns, connectors and cohesive devices.
Independent User	B2	Can understand the main ideas of complex text on both concrete and abstract topics, including technical discussions in his/her field of specialization. Can interact with a degree of fluency and spontaneity that makes regular interaction with native speakers quite possible without strain for either party. Can produce clear, detailed text on a wide range of subjects and explain a viewpoint on a topical issue giving the advantages and disadvantages of various options.
	B1	Can understand the main points of clear standard input on familiar matters regularly encountered in work, school, leisure, etc. Can deal with most situations likely to arise whilst travelling in an area where the language is spoken. Can produce simple connected text on topics which are familiar or of personal interest. Can describe experiences and events, dreams, hopes & ambitions and briefly give reasons and explanations for opinions and plans.
Basic User	A2	Can understand sentences and frequently used expressions related to areas of most immediate relevance (e.g., very basic personal and family information, shopping, local geography, employment). Can communicate in simple and routine tasks requiring a simple and direct exchange of information on familiar and routine matters. Can describe in simple terms aspects of his/her background, immediate environment and matters in areas of immediate need.
	A1	Can understand and use familiar everyday expressions and very basic phrases aimed at the satisfaction of needs of a concrete type. Can introduce him/herself and others and can ask and answer questions about personal details such as where he/she lives, people he/she knows and things he/she has. Can interact in a simple way provided the other person talks slowly and clearly and is prepared to help.

Used with permission from Council of Europe.

conversations about themselves with help. The CEFR is used in Europe and many international contexts.

Proficiency scales do not necessarily indicate how long each level will take, with the exception of the CEFR. Some levels will not be achieved by some learners. Learners may also stagnate or step down on the scale without effort to improve their language abilities.

As you read this text, you will find many references to language proficiency levels. These will be general references, unless otherwise noted.

TESOL Is Highly Interdisciplinary

The discipline of TESOL draws upon other fields to inform their perspectives. For example, research from psychology provides important contributions on how children and adults grow, think, and learn, how first languages are acquired, and how the brain stores and processes information. From anthropology, we learn about culture, cultures, and cross-cultural interaction. From linguistics, we understand more about the structures, sounds, meanings, functions, and uses of language. The intersection of psychology and linguistics enhances understanding of the neurological processing of linguistic information in the brain. The field of foreign/world language teaching contributes insights into proficiency levels, traditional and interactive language methods, and assessment practices. From communications, we draw strategies of oral communication in formal talks and presentations as well as studies in cross-cultural and intercultural communications. English composition studies provide insights into the learning and teaching of writing to native speakers, writing genres and structures, patterns of written discourse, sentence-level written grammar, and argumentation. The various fields of teacher education, such as literacy, curriculum and instruction, educational diversity studies, and instructional assessment, offer insights into the instruction and assessment of reading by native speakers, curriculum development, academic content learning, lesson planning, lesson delivery, assessment design and interpretation, educational institutions, and culturally responsive instruction.

The TESOL specialist combines knowledge from all of these areas with second language acquisition theory (how people acquire/learn additional languages as well as the personal, sociocultural, and linguistic influences on the processes). The TESOL specialist applies this information to appropriate instructional planning, delivery, and assessment for ELLs at all ages from nursery school to university.

The discipline also interacts with academic content areas (i.e., subjects of literature, math, science, and social studies/history) as well as subjects considered "special topics" in the schools (i.e., music, art, and physical education). When TESOL specialists combine academic fields, this is called content-based ESL instruction (CBI) or sheltered content instruction, while in the European context this content and language integration is referred to as content and language integrated learning (CLIL), which is discussed in Part Two. CLIL holds both content and language as dual instructional goals integrating them equally to support simultaneous development of both knowledge bases.

Vocational content areas are studied by ELLs for professional purposes, such as aviation, law, business, engineering, design, tourism studies, etc. This intersection of vocational content and language study is English for specific purposes (ESP). You will find ESP courses listed as Business English or Legal English in adult education or university language programs.

Should I use the term second language acquisition or second language learning?

You may hear TESOL professionals use the phrases interchangeably or generally, meaning undertaking the development of an additional language. The two terms offer small, but meaningful distinctions for a TESOL professional. If you hear TESOL professionals discuss second language *learning* specifically, it means the study of English as an additional language in academic settings. Whereas, the use of second language *acquisition* specifically refers to situations in which individuals "pick up" a language in naturalistic settings, such as in conversations with friends, watching television, and/or reading for pleasure.

This distinction is one reason that language educators endeavor to create meaningful communication opportunities in the classroom that replicate natural conversational settings. If the language learning in classroom settings is more meaningful and authentic, it will be more useful and memorable for the learners.

Roles and Specializations of TESOL Professionals

The discipline of TESOL includes language teaching, teacher preparation and research, but also roles in developing curriculum, writing books and instructional materials and assessments, consulting, serving as a resource teacher, and leading and directing language programs.

TESOL has several unique areas of specialization and professional interest. A TESOL professional may choose a special focus in their work, which is one advantage of the field. This allows educators in the field to employ their unique strengths and build knowledge and skills in areas of individual interest, rather than focusing solely on language acquisition. Each specialization is specific to a context and learner population. For example, there are assessment organizations that specialize in the development of standardized tests on language proficiency for ELLs, such as the Test of English as a Foreign Language (TOEFL), International English Language Testing System (IELTS), Test of English for International Communication (TOEIC), and ACCESS tests. Individuals who work for Educational Testing Services (ETS), for example, who owns the TOEFL exam, focus on the design and implementation of testing questions and exams. They investigate the timing of questions and computer-adaptive test technology.

Teaching

Specialists may have teaching roles in public or private elementary, middle, and high schools, as well as community colleges and universities in second and foreign language contexts. Educators tend to specialize in an age group or subject matter. For example, an educator may focus on young learners who are learning to read in their primary language while learning to speak, listen, and read in English. At high school, an educator may teach world history bilingually. University-level TESOL educators may work with international exchange students who seek language development or academic degrees or those who were born in an English-speaking country and need support in reading and writing in academics. Others may focus on adult immigrant or refugee learners at a community college who need English for survival in their new culture. *Survival English* focuses on basic communication skills such as language for interacting when shopping, banking, renting/buying lodging, or securing employment, for instance.

Specialists teach different sizes and styles of classes: one-on-one, small-size classes of 6–20, medium classes of 25–30 students, or large classes of up to 50 in some settings. Some TESOL educators are "floating teachers," who travel from school to school in a district to provide English language instruction. Some TESOL educators work exclusively online providing one-on-one instruction via distance education. TESOL educators may teach in English immersion, sheltered content, or bilingual classes.

Specialists may work for businesses with corporate language courses for employees or at private language schools. A huge, international corporation with headquarters in Cincinnati, Ohio, offers employees from their international locations intensive courses to enhance their English communication, so employees can collaborate better. Private language schools are privately owned companies that can range in size from small to large corporations. A private language school in Arequipa, Peru, teaches teens and adults oral English for use in their academic and professional lives.

To teach at public K–12 schools in many contexts, professionals need to hold a bachelor's degree and a teaching license, certification, or other credential appropriate to the country. Depending on the setting, there may be other requirements. To teach English at community colleges and universities, the minimum credential is not a teaching license or certification, but a Master's degree in TESOL.

To teach online, at private language schools, or in international corporations, the minimum credential varies. For the most part, individuals will need a bachelor's degree and possibly a Certificate in Teaching English to Speakers of Other Languages (CELTA) or TEFL certificate. The CELTA certificate is a short-duration, intensive teacher preparation credential offered mainly in the United Kingdom and the European Union (EU). The CELTA certificate is widely respected in the field and yields highly capable instructors.

A TEFL certificate is typically granted by private companies, language schools, or universities. These certificates are valued internationally by hiring committees seeking instructors for private language schools. Individuals often confuse the TEFL certificate with a teaching license or teaching certification for a U.S. state.

Generally, individuals earn a TEFL certificate in a short-duration program in person or online. In this case, short-duration can mean 30–60 hr of instruction, but it can be as much as 180 hr. However, if the TEFL certificate is granted by a university, it is often for much more time and higher quality coursework. As a rule of thumb, the quality of teacher preparation is in direct correlation to the number of hours and the quality of the program. As consumers, individuals must make choices as to program duration, quality, and reputation that will help them develop in the profession.

Administration

The need to understand and be able to work with the unique backgrounds, skill sets, and needs of ELLs is great, so leadership roles are available to TESOL professionals. Often, TESOL educators have grown into leadership roles in public schools over time, serving as instructional coaches, team leaders, or district-level program administrators. As team leaders and instructional coaches, these individuals collaborate with other teachers to ensure high-quality academic instruction for ELLs while providing support for general educators in how to work with ELLs and their families. They may provide leadership for other TESOL educators in new developments in research and practices or offer district-level workshops and professional development opportunities for TESOL and/or general educators. District-level administrators often have instructional mentoring and guidance responsibilities, but they also interpret regional or state-level policy and mandates, evaluate and choose curricula, proctor standardized tests, and report student academic and/or language achievement on reports to national educational bureaus or ministries.

Another avenue in administration open to TESOL professionals is intensive English program (IEP) administration in universities. In second language contexts, IEPs offer courses to international exchange students studying for degrees or study abroad. These individuals organize all parts of the language program offered to ELLs including organizing curriculum at differing levels, ensuring consistent and quality instructional delivery, proctoring pre- and post-course/program assessment, ordering books and materials, arranging cultural excursions, handling all issues associated with student visas, arranging housing, marketing their program, and recruiting students.

Some TESOL professionals move into governmental roles. These professionals may work in national-level offices, bureaus, or ministries of education or state to organize international scholar exchange, oversee grant programs for teacher preparation or student exchange, research educational achievement of ELLs, develop laws, policy and guidelines around the teaching and learning of English, develop curriculum, and engage in soft diplomacy through the sharing of culture. For example, a TESOL educator might find opportunities in ministries of education in China or Japan to write curricula, textbooks, or standards.

Professors as teacher educators and researchers

While some TESOL professionals work with teachers in the public schools as instructional coaches, others prepare future teachers in the role of professor. Professors of TESOL must have a doctoral degree in TESOL or Applied Linguistics. However, in some settings an individual may instruct teachers with a Master's degree in the field. Professors engage in teaching future teachers and investigating all perspectives of education and language related to ELLs. For example, individuals teach and research aspects of second language learning/acquisition theories and processes, linguistics, intercultural communication, race and ethnicity, educational systems, teaching, learning and assessment of academic or vocational subjects, speaking, listening, reading, writing, grammar, vocabulary, and pronunciation. Without the contributions of teacher educators and researchers, the field would not have core principles to provide a foundation for instruction.

Curriculum and assessment development and materials writing

Many teachers strive to engage their students by creating new materials and activities for their classes. In some cases, the materials they develop can be the basis for a book, which would become a helpful resource for other educators. Educators interested in writing and sharing their ideas may become well-known authors in the field and make a living creating textbooks and resources.

Publishers are often looking for knowledgeable and creative materials writers to develop textbooks. Some of the most common publishers in TESOL are Cengage Learning, Pearson ELT, Wiley, Cambridge University Press, Oxford University Press, TESOL International Association, Macmillan, Heinemann, Ballard-Tighe and University of Michigan Press. There are smaller publishing houses that supply important materials for professionals, such as Multilingual Matters and Domino Publishing. These publishers provide textbooks and readers for pre-kindergarten through university in various areas of study. They also offer resource materials for the classroom, such as manipulatives and games. Some organizations create software and applications as well for language study (e.g., Dyned, Rosetta Stone) or for teachers' use (e.g., www.lessonwriter.com).

Educators who are interested in the development of tests, exams, and assessments can work for organizations who develop different types of exams. Some examples of assessment organizations are IELTS and WIDA. The IELTS is a standardized test of English language proficiency focusing on the language needed for communication in academic or work settings. WIDA is an organization that created a series of assessments to evaluate ELLs' language proficiency in academics to determine if they need language study and support in pre-K–12 schools. Educators working in this area write test items, such as reading passages and comprehension questions or writing prompts. They may also assess how well a test question distinguishes the highest and lowest levels of performance.

Consulting

At times, publishers and testing organizations need knowledgeable educators to consult with them in the development of a textbook or exam. School districts need the guidance of experts as well. Some educators become vital resources for publishers, testing organizations, and schools working as independent consultants. Educational consultants may evaluate textbooks and provide a written review of the strengths and weaknesses of a textbook before publication. School districts invite consultants to observe classes, provide workshops or long-term professional development on a new educational development or methodology, or engage in data analysis for program evaluation or redesign.

Contributions of TESOL and Applied Linguistics in Education

The field of TESOL/Applied Linguistics has influenced education worldwide. Research into the teaching and learning of additional languages has permeated teacher preparation programs all over the world. Research into the authentic use of language in conversations has shown how conversations are structured and how people take turns, which can be used to inform the teaching of speaking and listening skills in the language classroom. Research into the ways that teachers talk to their classes and what ELLs need in order to develop their language has yielded highly interactive classes, in which students practice speaking and listening, reading and writing to each other as opposed to listening to teachers lecture.

One important contribution of TESOL to education in general is based on research that differentiates social and academic language (Cummins, 1979, 2008). In teacher education programs, teachers are learning to teach ELLs the language they need for academic achievement in their general education classrooms (a.k.a., mainstream classrooms). This research has influenced standards of instruction for pre-K–12 schools, such as the Common Core State Standards, in that teachers are now taught to model academic language use and create opportunities for students to identify patterns of academic language use in science, math, history, and language arts.

Questions for reflection

- Which professional roles do you wish to fill during your career? What skill sets are necessary for each of these roles?
- Each of the roles that TESOL educators can specialize in provides different opportunities and benefits for the individual. Which role(s) are you interested in exploring?
- Try to consider your own preferences when thinking about a specialization. Are there areas of TESOL education that do not appeal to you at all?

Chapter Conclusions

As professionals in TESOL, we should recognize that generalizations exist for a reason, while at the same time, understanding that each individual student is unique and has followed a unique route. It is important to keep in mind the generalization and determine through inquiry which ones may or may not pertain in a particular situation.

Discussion Questions

1 Which acronyms that describe English language study are you familiar with? Which ones are new to you? Which one(s) do you think you will use the most and why?
2 Do you think the distinctions used to describe the study of English and the teaching of English are important? Why or why not? What are the problems with these distinctions?
3 Which fields have the greatest and which the least influence on the field of TESOL in your opinion?
4 What roles of TESOL professionals appeal to you? Would you engage in any outside of teaching language?

Tasks

1 Reflect on your path to the field and your future goals. Draw a timeline of your path from when you first learned of the field and where you hope to go with your study.
2 Research one academic article related to ELLs and/or TESOL that has been published in the past year in these disciplines (anthropology, communications, education, linguistics, psychology, sociology). What topic did the article address? What were the findings? How did it relate to ELLs/TESOL? Compare and contrast your findings with those of your classmates.

Further Reading/Read and Discuss

Read about World Englishes:
Kachru, B. (1992). World Englishes: Approaches, issues and resources. *Language Teaching*, 25, 1–14
Kachru, B. B. (2012). World Englishes: Overview. In C. A. Chapelle (Ed.), *The Encyclopedia of Applied Linguistics*. Blackwell. https://doi.org/10.1002/9781405198431. wbeal1349
Read about linguistic imperialism:
Yuting, L., & Hyun, J. (2015). Linguistic imperialism. In F. V. Tochon (Ed.), *Language education policy studies* (online). University of Wisconsin—Madison. Retrieved from: www.languageeducationpolicy.org/21stcenturyforces/linguisticimperialism.html (accessed March 4, 2021).

References

American Council on the Teaching of Foreign Languages (ACTFL). (2012). *ACTFL proficiency guidelines 2012*. American Council on the Teaching of Foreign Languages.
Association Internationale de Linguistique Appliquée or International Association of Applied Linguistics. (n.d.). *Welcome*. https://aila.info (accessed March 4, 2021).
Board of Regents of the University of Wisconsin System. (2012). *WIDA's 2012 amplification of the ELD standards (Publication)*. WIDA Consortium.
Canagarajah, A. S. (2003). *Resisting linguistic imperialism in English teaching*. Oxford University Press.
Centre for Education Statistics and Evaluation (CESE). (2018). *Schools: Language diversity in NSW*. CESE Bulletin. New South Wales Government. https://www.cese.nsw.gov.au/publications-filter/schools-language-diversity-in-nsw-2018 (accessed March 4, 2021).
Council of Europe. (n.d.). *Global scale—Table 1 (CEFR 3.3): Common reference levels*. https://www.coe.int/web/common-european-framework-reference-languages/table-1-cefr-3.3-common-reference-levels-global-scale (accessed March 4, 2021).
Cummins, J. (1979). Cognitive/academic language proficiency, linguistic interdependence, the optimum age question and some other matters. *Working Papers on Bilingualism Toronto*, (19), 197–202.

Cummins, J. (2008). BICS and CALP: Empirical and theoretical status of the distinction. In N. Hornberger (Ed.), *Encyclopedia of language and education* (pp. 487–499). Springer.

Demographics of Qatar. (2019, October 6). https://en.wikipedia.org/wiki/Demographics_of_Qatar

Oré, D., & Diaz, L. (2019, July 27). In 21st century, threats 'from all sides' for Latin America's original languages. *Reuters*. https://www.reuters.com/article/us-latam-indigenous-language/in-21st-century-threats-from-all-sides-for-latin-americas-original-languages-idUSKCN1UN04W (accessed March 4, 2021).

Phillipson, R. (1992). *Linguistic imperialism*. Oxford University Press.

World-Class Instructional Design and Assessment (WIDA). (2012). *2012 amplification of the WIDA English language development standards*. Board of Regents of the University of Wisconsin System.

World-Class Instructional Design and Assessment (WIDA). (2020). *WIDA English language development standards framework, 2020 edition kindergarten—Grade 12*. Board of Regents of the University of Wisconsin System.

2

How Is TESOL an Academic Profession?

In this chapter, you will view the profession from a bird's eye view while learning about the instructional contexts and professional development opportunities for preparation to teach ESL/EFL/ELT. You will learn about professional engagement in the field of TESOL/Applied Linguistics, which will be highlighted against a back-drop of the history and development of the field. You will encounter how profession-als in TESOL engage in the role of advocacy for their language learners and profession.

Learning Outcomes

At the conclusion of this chapter, you will be able to:

- describe different instructional contexts for teaching English and for teacher prepa-ration to work in a TESOL environment
- identify the international and regional professional organizations that you could join and their history and contributions to the field
- justify your membership in international and regional professional organizations based on the benefits they provide
- devise a professional development plan for yourself
- justify engaging in advocacy for the profession and learners and lend your support through advocacy activities

A colleague attended an international convention, which she describes in the vignette. Notice the breadth of topics and her enthusiasm about the experience. Reflect upon what sessions you may be interested in attending.

TESOL Voices

The Convention Extended and Enhanced Teacher Preparation

I attended my first TESOL International Association Convention in 2009 in Denver, Colorado, as an undergraduate student with only a couple years of theoretical

---

Introduction to TESOL: Becoming a language teaching professional, First Edition. Kate Mastruserio Reynolds, Kenan Dikilitaş, and Steve Close.
© 2022 John Wiley & Sons, Inc. Published 2022 by John Wiley & Sons, Inc.

classroom knowledge and encouragement from my advisor, who was very active in the TESOL community. I was assured an engaging, fun experience and the reality certainly did not disappoint.

Coming from a smaller university with an intimate TEFL program, the TESOL convention was my first real-world glimpse into the breadth and diversity of the field. I remember the feeling of amazement the first time I paged through the conference guide and saw the variety of sessions and workshops being offered in just a few days. The range of interest sections and topics was impressive and exciting. There was so much more than I expected, and the scope of fields affiliated with TESOL instantly broadened. There were sessions about peacekeeping and conflict resolution, public policy, linguistics, and technology in addition to the hundreds of sessions about pedagogy—lessons, best practices, and opportunities to hear about practical classroom experiences. As a student with very little hands-on experience in the field, these sessions were insightful and offered authentic applications of textbook and classroom-learned theories and practices. Attending the conference proved to enhance of my education as well as a connection to the professional realm. The community is welcoming, and I never felt out of place or too unqualified to be there.

I continued attending after gaining teaching experience, eventually submitting my own proposals and participating as a co-presenter in collaborative sessions with fellow classmates and colleagues. In addition to local and state conferences, I have found the convention to be a touchstone for staying current with advancements in the international field. It has been one of the best ways to connect with teachers and advocates to share and learn new resources and ideas.

Kara Shore
Instructor

Our Professional Roots

While second language learning has been occurring since different language speakers first interacted, the field recognizes two major milestones in our origins. The history of second/foreign language teaching begins with instruction in the classics of Greek and Latin in 1750 (Howatt & Smith, 2014). The second major milestone was the commencement of formal academic study of second language acquisition in the 1960s (Ellis, 2014). Many programs of TESOL/Applied linguistics date to the early 1960s as well and grew from university programs of modern languages and linguistics (Modern Language Association, n.d.). While TESOL teacher preparation programs may be found in university English or linguistics departments, they may also be located in departments of education of modern/world languages.

Since the mid-1960s when TESOL was emerging as a professional area of scholarship and teaching, the field has grown in the number of educators working in the field, but also in terms of breadth and impact. The numbers of individuals teaching English worldwide are difficult to determine. What can be determined is the number of members of the two leading professional development organizations. TESOL International Association reports 13,300 members and International Association of Teachers of English as a Foreign Language (IATEFL) indicates membership of over 4,000 in 2016 (Hill, 2019), although many more professionals work in the field despite not being part of these professional development associations.

The diverse areas of study in our discipline illustrate the broad focus of research, teaching, and assessment. Initially, TESOL's primary areas of interest were linguistics, language learning processes, and language skill instruction (i.e., grammar, pronunciation, speaking, listening, reading, and writing). These areas continue to be discussed and developed through new ways to engage learners and an expansion in our understandings of the nature of language learning. The field has grown in many different directions over the years. Focuses include investigations into language learning processes in various contexts and the influences of identity, anxiety, and cultural factors impact on learners' language learning, participation, and motivation inform our teaching. The study of the qualities of language learners who excel at language learning ("good language learners") yielded instructional practices in explicit teaching of language learning strategies that help learners remember new language, analyze their language use, cope with anxiety, and compensate for lack of a vocabulary word. Discussion of equity in work environments resulted in educators supporting nonnative English-speaking teachers. A study of the nature of authentic language use led to development of the "communicative competencies," which we use to guide our learning objectives. Later, authentic language was analyzed in huge corpuses (i.e., databases) with computerized search mechanisms that allowed us to isolate words or phrases to see how they were used in spoken or written language. Now, textbooks utilize this information when authors select high-frequency vocabulary for study as opposed to words that *might* be used.

While the field continues to expand in breadth and depth, TESOL/Applied Linguistics is contributing to education worldwide in significant ways. Developments in TESOL/Applied Linguistics are applied in the instruction of world languages (i.e., Arabic, Chinese, and Spanish). General educators in many countries now have an awareness of the differences between language used in social interaction and that used in academic interaction. This information has helped educators become more aware of the language demands of their academic subject, so they may make learning more accessible for all learners and not just ELLs. World-Class Instructional Design and Assessment (WIDA) developed "can do" indicators in their initial proficiency guidelines, which many educators now employ in classes to share learning objectives with students.

Questions for reflection

- Did you think the field was older or younger? Why?
- Why is it important when the field became professional and began researching?

Teacher Preparation in TESOL

Teacher preparation in TESOL can be obtained from universities, private businesses, and professional organizations. Which type of preparation that individuals choose is based on the individual's goals, prior learning, and opportunity. The preparation required for work in a particular academic setting tends to be linked to salary, benefits, work environment and treatment, and job satisfaction, although there are exceptions. The requirements to work in any of the settings discussed in the next sections depend on the location, so there are exceptions to all of these generalizations. For example, a native speaker of English can find a job at a private language school in China with relative ease; perhaps without even having a university degree. Still, with this ease come some complications and difficulties that most people would prefer to avoid.

Teacher education in the field of TESOL is strongly recommended for work in the field due to the specialized body of knowledge needed by TESOL educators. For example, TESOL educators need to have a good working knowledge of linguistics (i.e., semantics, syntax, phonology, pragmatics, and lexis), second language acquisition, methods of language instruction (i.e., speaking, listening, reading, writing, grammar, pronunciation, vocabulary, and spelling), methods of instruction that combine academic subjects and language, curriculum design, materials development, culture(s), and assessment. They need to be able to plan and deliver lessons for language learning, collaborate with other educators and ELLs' families, create and proctor language assessments, reflect on the effectiveness of lessons, and work supportively with ELLs. The subsequent chapters will offer more depth and insights into these knowledge and performance areas.

Working in pre-K–12 public schools

Teachers are needed from preschool to high school to serve as English teachers in both EFL and ESL settings. English is taught from elementary school in China and Japan, along with many other countries. In second language contexts, such as Australia and the United States, English learners may be citizens born in the country who speak a different language at home, or the students may be immigrants or refugees. Citizens who speak another language begin preschool with their peers and need teachers who can make them comfortable in the environment and modify the instructional activities so they can comprehend and participate. For example, teachers may highlight key vocabulary in spoken and written form. Immigrants and refugees can arrive at any age, so they could enter an English-medium school in grades 4, 7, or 10, when they would need to learn the language quickly in order to learn their grade-level academic subjects. One approach to instruction is to combine grade-level subjects with the language English learners need while providing instructional support and comprehensible instruction.

Knowing how to work with English learners with different background experiences, linguistic and academic needs requires knowledge and preparation. Professional education licensure, also known as teacher certification or endorsement, is usually governed by bureaus, departments, or ministries of education (terms vary by countries). Professional licensures are typically required for instruction in public pre-K–12 schools. An ESL/EFL/ELT educator typically holds a bachelor's degree in education,

English literature/composition, linguistics, or core academic subjects, such as math, science, or history, in addition to teacher preparation coursework (i.e., courses including educational theory, methods, and assessment). The teacher preparation coursework depends on the requirements of the bureaus, departments, or ministries of education and the university. In some rare cases, individuals may take teacher licensing exams if they hold a bachelor's degree, but no teacher education coursework, to obtain their teaching credential (e.g., the State of Texas allows licensure by exam).

Work at universities and community colleges

In order to work at a university or community college, generally individuals need to have a bachelor's and a Master's degree. The preferred Master's degrees are in TESOL or Applied Linguistics. Teacher licensure is not necessarily required.

In some EFL contexts, a Certificate in Teaching English to Speakers of Other Languages (CELTA) is also accepted in lieu of a Master's degree in TESOL. A CELTA is a teacher preparation offered by Cambridge English. The CELTA is a teacher credential for new teachers who wish to teach EFL and who are educated to the level of entry into college, speak English at the Common European Framework of Reference (CEFR) C1 level or higher (for more information about the CEFR, see https://www.coe.int/en/web/common-european-framework-reference-languages/reference-level-descriptions).

Individuals working at community colleges generally work with learners of 17 years old and up. Community college ELLs may be older adults who have immigrated to an English-speaking country or who are interested in developing their English skills for personal or professional reasons. At community colleges, many classes are adult learners who are beginners with the language. The ages of the learners vary widely. A topic of study for an evening class could be "going grocery shopping" and learning the vocabulary for different foods. Students may practice dialogues they could have with the cashier or bag person. They could learn expressions for making a request for a specific grocery item.

Some ELLs at community colleges wish to hone their English skills for eventual university study. In these ESL classes, students who tend to be closer to the traditional college age would learn about academic reading and writing in order to improve their academic language skills, for instance. They would learn new vocabulary about a reading topic, for example, online privacy. Then, they would have prereading activities, such as discussing how much they share of their personal life online and why. The teacher would ask the students to read the passage in different ways, such as silent reading or guided readings. Students would have discussions after the article to confirm their understandings and then they would revisit the reading in extension activities, such as discussing how much online privacy should our governments protect and how.

Individuals working at universities work with resident ELL students matriculated into the university or those who are international students and will not matriculate, but only study in an exchange or other short-duration program (i.e., 6 weeks to 1 year). Often international students study in intensive English programs (IEPs) where they will learn with other international students who share the same proficiency level (i.e., beginner, intermediate, and advanced), and learn in courses that integrate speaking, listening, reading and writing, grammar, vocabulary, and pronunciation. They may also learn more about the host country and culture through excursions and seminars. The goals of international students are to develop their English for success in their academic courses or for their future occupations and to learn more about their host culture.

For those language learners who are matriculated, the most common needs are in academic reading and writing, although some universities have more extensive programs. An example of a credit-bearing academic reading and composition class is English 101 (composition). In these classes, the goal is to develop learners' literacy skills, so they develop their academic reading and writing skills for future university success. Students learn to analyze readings through a critical lens and respond in writing to, for example, persuade, explain, compare/contrast, or debate.

Many community colleges are adopting innovative teaching modalities to help ELLs. For example, accelerated linked courses give ELLs the opportunity to study English and a "content area" (interpersonal communication, sociology, history) in two separate, but linked classes. Both instructors work together, overlapping their material in a way that gives students an opportunity to earn credit for multiple courses simultaneously.

Teaching ESL/EFL/ELT at community college and university is a professional position. Opportunities at this instructional level vary by country. These positions are typically competitive to obtain. They may be short-duration or long-term contracts. Often in EFL settings, there are other fringe benefits, such as housing, insurance, round-trip flights, and visa assistance.

Work at private language schools

Private language schools are schools owned and operated by private individuals or corporations. There are private language schools in virtually all countries, with both EFL and ESL settings. They range in size from small family-owned businesses to large, widely known corporations, such as Berlitz. They are outside of the public school system and, therefore, do not have to comply with the same governmental regulations as public schools.

Many students enroll in private language schools for study after work or school hours. Their study at the private language school gives more instruction to extend learners' proficiency level and build their confidence. Courses tend to be focused on students' goals and needs. For example, adult students may study intensively to improve their proficiency score on the International English Language Testing System (IELTS) exam (https://www.ielts.org/en-us), so they may be promoted at work or obtain a new position. Classes tend to be smaller with interaction in speaking, listening, reading, and writing in English as the focus of instruction; however, grammar and vocabulary will also play a role.

Private language schools require different types of qualifications. It is difficult to provide a rule of thumb for the types of qualifications because, depending on the size and quality of the private language school, expectations vary. Some small private language schools may not require any specific qualification. On the other hand, we know of excellent small, family-owned private language schools that require a bachelors' degree and a TEFL certificate, whereas others may only require a bachelors' degree. Large private language schools will most likely require a bachelors' degree and a TEFL certificate or CELTA at the minimum.

TEFL certificates may be obtained through private language schools, who will then employ their graduates, online or from universities. The quality of these TEFL certificates can normally be determined from the duration of the TEFL certificate program and the reputation of the organization. Many online TEFL certificates offer a course of study over 120 hr of instruction. Universities tend to have courses of study with approximately 30–50 semester credits or 90–150 hr of instruction, but the courses are more rigorous.

Newcomers to the field need to be aware of two potentially problematic areas of working with private language schools. First, small, private language schools may not be established, long-standing institutions. They may have operational challenges that employees might experience. The treatment employees may receive may not align with their expectations. For example, many colleagues have reported being asked to go on a "visa run," which is a round trip outside of the country, so that they can continue to work while holding a tourist visa. By doing so, the private language school does not have to help their educators obtain a work permit/visa. Promises made may not always be kept. It is important to research prior to accepting a position. Second, it has been reported that some of the job postings for private language schools are fraudulent and are designed to obtain the applicant's name, social security number/personal identification number, passport number, passport image, and/or money. TESOL educators need to ensure that the school that they are considering is a legitimate business and must be cautious about sharing personal information or sending money to a school.

Work in tutoring or one-on-one teaching and online teaching

Tutoring or one-on-one teaching has long been a reliable standby for many TESOL instructors starting out. Instructors post advertisements to attract students for one-on-one instruction focused on the level, goals, and interests of the particular student. Tutoring has found a niche in the online world where opportunities for teaching one-on-one online have exploded in the past 10 years.

Typical one-on-one instruction begins with an assessment of the student's language abilities to determine what should be the emphasis of instruction. The student's interests and goals are factored into the establishment of instructional objectives. For example, many students wish to have one-on-one tutoring to develop their conversational skills in a less embarrassing, more personal environment. Instructors create individual lessons and participate in conversational exchanges with the student.

Unless an instructor was employed at an online English language learning corporation that would attract students and collect funds, making a living at one-on-one teaching would require an educator to hustle to find students, develop lessons and assessments, and conduct the business end of the instruction.

Online instruction has become an avenue for some individuals wishing to teach ESL/EFL/ELT. Instructors can find online teaching opportunities through universities, private language schools, or corporations. Some of these organizations have no brick-and-mortar classrooms. In these environments, an instructor can teach students one-on-one or in small groups, who range from children to adults. Classes are usually not mixed age groups though, since instructional choices for one group would not be appropriate for another. The computer interface that connects the instructor to student(s) may be Zoom, Skype, or Google hangouts, a classroom management system (e.g., Blackboard, Desire to Learn, or Canvas), or a platform designed specifically by the organization. Instructional approaches would be different for a group of several people. Instruction online to small groups tends to emphasize reading, listening, and writing. Speaking occurs between the teacher and students, but there may be platforms that allow for students to interact easily with each other.

Online instruction and tutoring tend to be hourly work and wages are based upon the educational background of the individual. For most online companies, an instructor needs at least a bachelors' degree, but a TEFL certificate or CELTA would increase the likelihood of being hired and higher wages received. It is possible to tutor without any particular credential or teaching preparation, but mistakes can be made and learners may not excel as they should.

Other work environments

Aside from the traditional venues an instructor may work in, TESOL professionals can pursue other options. Large, international corporations with business in many countries hire English language teachers to help employees develop their English skills to enhance corporate communications or comply with governmental regulations. Some governmental entities hire English language professionals to teach English to allow work in English when the individuals speak different native languages. For example, customs agents, nuclear power plant employees, and judges need to be able to communicate with individuals in English. An example of both corporations and governmental entities requiring English language instruction are pilots, navigators, and air traffic controllers, who must speak English to interact with all those flying. In the United States, TESOL professionals have been hired to teach English in prison too. Finally, religious and not-for-profit organizations (such as the Literacy Volunteers of America) also offer English classes for children and adults.

Each of these nontraditional ESL/EFL/ELT instructional environments has unique benefits and drawbacks. For each of these instructional environments, the contract, wages, duration, size of the class, instructional materials and resources, and instructional practices will vary.

Questions for reflection

- Which professional setting is the most attractive to you and why? Why would other settings not appeal to you?
- Do you think your willingness and interest in working in other settings might evolve and change over time?

Professional Development in TESOL

Many TESOL educators starting in the field begin with academic preparation. Others start their work by accepting a position to teach English through volunteering, serving a mission, or teaching while studying abroad. Still others start their work by helping the English learner or learners at their school when there is not a certified teacher. There are as many routes into the field as there are roots of a tree. No matter how we commence our work in English language teaching, we all need to learn, to collaborate, to have guidance, to have support and affirmation, to grow, and to remain stimulated intellectually. Teaching should be exciting. Kate shares this expression with her student teachers, "When you are bored teaching, your students are 100 times more bored." For us, there has been no lack of opportunities for professional growth and intellectual engagement because we engage with professional organizations in the field. We are all lifelong learners.

We cannot grow in isolation. Professional engagement allows us to continue to grow after our formal education is completed. We gather new information that builds upon what we already know and from different people and perspectives. We can problem solve and hone our abilities through interaction with peers. We also have opportunities to share our knowledge and experience with others, which benefits all involved. Engaging with colleagues in professional organizations and communities of practice provides opportunities to grow in knowledge and experience in teaching English.

Kate remembers the first conference she attended as being quite exciting because of the hundreds of avenues to explore. She was like a kid in a candy shop with so many decisions to make. So many avenues to choose. Should I choose the sessions on pragmatics in the ESL classroom or pronunciation for beginners? What books have been recently produced for writers at the intermediate proficiency level? The experience helped her generate new ideas of how to engage learners and what and how to teach.

For Kenan, it was a great opportunity to be part of an international organization's home for English language teachers, teacher trainers and educators, and researchers. He felt privileged to contribute to the development of others and learn from interaction with them as to what can be done to improve the field and how this can be done. We all grow professionally in communities of practice that offer various facilities to improve our communication with people from other countries and gain new insights into our professional practices and area of research. Kenan recognizes three main insights that he gained in such TESOL communities, which include:

- constant exposure to and interaction with volunteers who provide professional guidance;
- free and intensive learning in communities where every member is dealing with different domains and aspect of the same field; and
- ongoing professional development that requires multiple opportunities to engage in tasks that are shared, developed, and sustained to cultivate identity and nurture our professional vision.

Beyond the learning, collaboration, and support we receive from participation, when we engage professionally, it legitimizes us as an ESL/EFL/ELT professional. Other educators and individuals we encounter often recognize our commitment and engagement as a sign of our professionalism. Finally, many individuals start in the field as teachers and over time grow professionally into more specialized career paths. For example, they may become interested in preparing teachers to teach ESL/EFL or in writing ESL/EFL textbooks. Below are some of the organizations that help individuals to develop their skills and progress throughout their careers.

Influential Professional Development Organizations

In 1966 and 1967, respectively, TESOL International Association and IATEFL launched (Alatis, n.d.; IATEFL, n.d.). Over the past 50 years, study of ESL/EFL learning, teaching, and assessment has occurred in conjunction with these and myriad other professional organizations. In this section, we will provide descriptions of the most influential professional organizations in TESOL so that you will become familiar with these professional resources.

IATEFL (https://www.iatefl.org)

IATEFL is a professional organization founded in 1967 with the goal of "linking, developing, supporting English language professionals worldwide" (IATEFL, n.d.). The organization has a wide reach in Europe and parts of the Middle East and Asia, and even live streams keynote speakers from its conference to 60,000 English language teachers worldwide. The IATEFL conference is held annually in April and attracts approximately 2,500 attendees. The association hopes to support EFL teachers in all parts of the world.

IATEFL is operated by eight trustees who are members and volunteers of the association. Hundreds of volunteers also participate in the governance of the association by volunteering on committees, which are organized by topics such as conference proposals, digital learning, conference organization, scholarships, and membership. Members of IATEFL elect to participate in special interest groups (SIGs). These SIGs allow members to investigate a particular topic related to their work. For example, IATEFL SIGs include Business English, English for Specific Purposes, Global Issues, Learner Autonomy, Learning Technologies, Literature, Materials Writing, Pronunciation, Research, Teacher Development, and Young Learners and Teenagers.

In addition to the annual conference, SIGs offer online webinars and events in various countries. EFL teachers and educators can attend local or regional events or participate online to learn more about the topic and develop their professional network.

TESOL International Association (TESOL, https://www.tesol.org)

TESOL International Association (TESOL) became a professional organization for teachers of English as a second/foreign language in 1966. The organization is run by an executive director, president, and board of directors who work with a core team of not-for-profit business and education professionals and organizational members who volunteer on professional councils and governance committees.

TESOL's mission is to advance "...the expertise of professionals who teach English to speakers of other languages in multilingual contexts worldwide. We accomplish this through professional learning, research, standards, & advocacy" (TESOL International Association, n.d.). TESOL has affiliates in more than 70 countries worldwide from Albania to Venezuela (see more at https://www.tesol.org/connect/tesol-affiliate-network/worldwide-affiliate-directory), which are operated in an independent manner.

TESOL serves members who teach in public and private prekindergarten to high schools, and adults in community colleges, universities, and language schools. It also serves consultants, materials writers, researchers, and teacher educators (those who prepare teachers).

Its professional development offerings include an annual convention held in North America, online courses, seminars and webinars, academies, institutes, and symposiums. The annual convention draws between 6,000 and 10,000 international participants and offers hundreds of sessions on areas such as culture, digital learning, oral language, materials development, program administration, literacy, assessment, vocabulary, and grammar. The convention has ample opportunities for networking and learning about textbooks and other publications in the field.

TESOL academies are intensive topic-focused workshops held worldwide. These academies are usually requested and developed by a school district, school, or group of individuals (e.g., affiliate) on a specific topic. Their institutes are 2-day workshops on a wide variety of topics of interest to teachers. The TESOL symposiums are 1-day programs related to a topic identified by a regional affiliate with a keynote speaker and face-to-face interaction.

TESOL offers online certificate programs, such as the TESOL Core Certificate Program, the TESOL Certificate: Advanced Practitioner, and the Developing an Online Teaching Program. These certificates are not teaching licenses or endorsements that are issued by governmental offices; rather, they are additional credentials to extend one's professional knowledge and skills.

TESOL advances the profession through publications of journals on research and practice (e.g., *TESOL Quarterly*, *TESOL Journal*), electronic newsletters (i.e., *TESOL Connections*), and books (e.g., *Integrating Language and Content*, *Pedagogy and Practice for Online English Language Teacher Education*, *Transforming Practices for the Middle School Classroom*, and *Standards for Initial TESOL pre-K–12 Teacher Preparation Programs*).

TESOL supports research in second language teaching, learning, and assessment through mini-grants and the TESOL/the International Research Foundation for English Language Teaching (TIRF) Research Symposium.

Finally, TESOL engages in advocacy for the profession and for ELLs through its annual Advocacy and Policy Summit. Professionals convene in the Washington, DC area and learn about how to advocate with governmental representatives and to understand the shifting landscape of laws pertinent to education, language learning, and learners.

British Council (https://www.britishcouncil.org)

The British Council began its work in 1934 as a charitable and diplomatic tool of the United Kingdom. According to the British Council's 1940–1 Annual Report, its goal was "to create in a country overseas a basis of friendly knowledge and understanding of the people of this country, of their philosophy and way of life, which will lead to a sympathetic appreciation of British foreign policy, whatever for the moment that policy may be and from whatever political conviction it may spring" (British Council, n.d.). The mission of the British Council is "promoting a wider knowledge of [the UK] and the English language abroad and developing closer cultural relations between [the UK] and other countries" (British Council, n.d.). With its broad outreach goals, the British Council today has educational resources for students wishing to learn English, for educators who teach English as a foreign language. Furthermore, it has projects in the arts, culture, science, technology, and community development.

Offices of the British Council are located in over 100 locations worldwide. Its presence appears most prevalent in Africa, Central Asia, East Asia, Europe, and the Middle East. You can find its offices in countries such as:

- Africa (e.g., Algeria, Cameroon, Kenya, Libya, Mozambique, Rwanda, Sierra Leone, Uganda, Zambia, and Zimbabwe);
- Central America (e.g., Caribbean, Colombia, Mexico);
- South America (e.g., Argentina, Brazil, Chile, Peru, Uruguay, Venezuela);
- East and Southeast Asia (e.g., China, Hong Kong, Indonesia, Japan, Singapore, and Thailand);
- Central and South Asia (e.g., Afghanistan, Azerbaijan, India, Nepal, Pakistan, and Uzbekistan);
- Europe (e.g., Albania, Austria, Belgium, Bulgaria, Croatia, Czech Republic, Estonia, France, Germany, Greece, Ireland, Italy, Malta, Norway, Poland, and Ukraine); and
- The Middle East (e.g., Bahrain, Iraq, Lebanon, Kuwait, Qatar, Saudi Arabia, United Arab Emirates, and Yemen).

The organization aims to serve educators in foreign language contexts teaching kids, teens, and adults in public and private schools. Professional tutors also enhance their knowledge and skills through their professional development opportunities. In 2018–19, the British Council taught English to nearly 420,000 students and provided professional development opportunities to 77,000 English teachers (British Council, 2019).

The British Council aims to assist teachers of English to speakers of other languages by offering professional development opportunities (e.g., face-to-face and online courses, workshops, and conferences). It has booklets on assessing learning, managing the lesson, and taking responsibility for professional development. In addition to offering CELTA courses, it has courses for TESOL professionals on getting started; engaging with learning technologies, cyber well-being, and digital literacies; understanding teaching for tests; understanding and engaging learners with listening, pronunciation, grammar, reading, speaking, vocabulary, and writing; and general ESL/EFL/ELT instructional methods.

It also supports ESL/EFL teachers by providing online and print resources (i.e., research books and articles), curricula, lesson plans, activities, reading passages, songs, and poems. For example, it has curricula on general interest topics such as the environment, famous authors, beginning language, and cultures. For kids, there are lessons and materials on topics such as the alphabet, friendship, food, family, holidays, and the body. The lesson topics for teens include cycling, tattoos, animation, and bullying. For adults, there are lessons on beauty, left-handedness, money, happiness, and international cities.

WIDA (https://wida.wisc.edu)

WIDA has become an influential organization for individuals teaching English since its inception in 2003. WIDA comprises two consortia: WIDA Consortium, which is made up of 41 U.S. states and territories, and WIDA International School Consortium, a network of over 400 international schools worldwide. In these locations, WIDA works with educational leaders, school districts, public and private schools, and pre-K–12 educators on assessment and professional development.

WIDA's mission is to "advance academic language development and academic achievement for children and youth who are culturally and linguistically diverse through high quality standards, assessments, research and professional learning for educators" (WIDA, n.d.). To achieve that goal, the organization offers language standards, proficiency descriptors, and assessments of academic English for use in screening, placing, and guiding instructors of ELLs (see Chapter 1). The WIDA standards span five areas:

Standard 1: Social and Instructional Language;
Standard 2: Language of Language Arts;
Standard 3: Language of Mathematics;
Standard 4: Language of Science; and
Standard 5: Language of Social Studies.

WIDA provides professional development opportunities for educators in using their standards in curricular and lesson planning and developing instructional techniques in areas, such as creating a welcoming environment for ELLs, teaching academic vocabulary, and teaching for comprehension. Its self-paced e-workshops range in topics from engaging newcomer multilingual learners to developing language for learning in math, foundational concepts, and leading for equity.

WIDA has influenced education practices worldwide with its "can do" descriptors, which highlight what a language learner can do with speaking, listening, reading, and writing when they are at a specific grade and proficiency level. For example, a student in grades 4–5 at proficiency level 3 can explain clear sequential procedures to peers and compare data or information (WIDA, 2016) (for more detail, see https://wida.wisc.edu/teach/can-do/descriptors).

Initially, WIDA developed a standardized assessment of ELLs' academic language based on the standards, called the ACCESS test. The organization later developed placement-screening assessments. It conducts professional development for educators wishing to help ELLs prepare for the assessment and those interested in learning to administer it.

WIDA offers a conference in October annually in various cities in North America for educators to learn from each other about WIDA's resources. Internationally, it offers institutes, symposiums, and workshops. School districts and schools can arrange for a WIDA-prepared facilitator to conduct a workshop on topics such as differentiation, classroom action research, educator collaboration, formative language assessment, and purposeful lesson planning.

National and regional organizations

Other professional organizations TESOL and Applied Linguistics educators engage with are based on their specific interests, needs, and location/learner population. Here are some other organizations you may consider for professional development opportunities.

Organizations emphasizing foreign language perspectives

- American Council of Teachers of Foreign Languages (ACTFL, https://www.actfl. org)—ACTFL is oriented to the teaching of world languages such as Chinese, Spanish, or Russian. As you now know, English is the foreign language in some locations. The organization is known for developing the first proficiency guidelines to determine an individual's speaking ability in the target language. It has subsequently developed writing proficiency guidelines as well. It offers professional development such as an annual convention in November, oral proficiency interview (OPI) test preparation for teachers, publications, and advocacy engagement. The OPI test proctor preparation is thorough and highly valued by education programs. It has books on topics such as assessing language performance and language processing in our brains. The organization is also engaged with advocacy to raise public awareness of the benefits of additional language learning; on the website you can find advocacy resources and position statements.
- Council of Europe (https://www.coe.int/en/web/portfolio/home)—The Council of Europe created a set of proficiency guidelines that are employed widely throughout Europe, the Middle East, and South America. The proficiency guidelines are called the Common European Framework of Reference for Languages: Learning, Teaching, and Assessment (CEFR). Professionals in areas that utilize the CEFR will refer to learners' proficiency levels simply by the level (A, B, C) and stage (A1, A2, B1, B2, C1, and C2). The CEFR helps instructors to orient their lessons to the proficiency level(s) of their students. You can read more about the CEFR at https://www.coe. int/en/web/common-european-framework-reference-languages/level-descriptions. The Council of Europe also offers tools for developing curricula, designing programs with reference to the CEFR, aligning instruction to the CEFR, and research to better understand language teaching and learning. Many other schools, school districts, and language schools utilize the CEFR and have developed resources that work within the CEFR, which can be found online.

Organizations emphasizing second language perspectives

- Center for Applied Linguistics (CAL, https://www.cal.org)—CAL is "a nonprofit organization promoting access, equity and mutual understanding for linguistically and culturally diverse people around the world" (CAL, 2019). With the broad mission to work on topics related to both ELLs and world language learners, the organization conducts and distributes research on all topics related to the study, instruction, and assessment of additional languages. For example, it has projects on heritage language learners of English, parent engagement, cultural orientation, academic learning of ELLs, vocabulary instruction, and language policy. Resources it provides include brief reports and digests (free and downloadable), books, and teacher preparation materials on video. On the website, you will also find links to over 100 organizations and foundations related to learning/teaching/assessing language and understanding culture.
- The Office of English Language Acquisition (OELA, https://www2.ed.gov/about/offices/list/oela/index.html)—OELA is part of the US Department of Education.

Its goal is to "provides national leadership to help ensure that English Learners and immigrant students attain English proficiency and achieve academic success" (OELA, 2020). OELA also strives to support heritage language learners and bilingual, multicultural learners. It offers reports and research to help educators and lawmakers to guide educational policy decisions in additional to providing free tool kits for teachers working with English learners, families, and newcomer ELLs. OELA works closely with the National Clearinghouse for English Language Acquisition (NCELA, https://www.ncela.ed.gov), which funds and disseminates educational research on second language acquisition and learning. NCELA offers an online searchable library with over 20,000 resources that range from curricula to classroom materials and reports, fact sheets, and multimedia products. OELA offers an annual conference for recipients of the National Professional Development grants, which fund teacher preparation to work with ELLs and research on second language acquisition and learning.

- Colorín Colorado (www.colorincolorado.org)—Colorín Colorado is a relative newcomer to the field, but the organization has had a substantial impact on teachers of ELLs by offering practical, readily accessible instructional materials for immediate classroom use. Their goal is to provide resources for educators and parents on their bilingual (Spanish–English) website. For TESOL professionals, they offer streaming videos, articles, and resources that branch from ELL strategies and best practices to the specific practices themselves (e.g., lesson planning for ELLs includes selecting vocabulary, using graphic organizers, prereading a text, and writing content and language objectives), for example. In the ELL strategies and best practices section alone, there are nine overarching topics each with several concepts to be explored. The organization provides free book lists for different age groups, webcasts, and videos. Its resource library includes toolkits, policy information, research reports, and web resources. It also has recommendations for parents who are trying to help their child to read, supporting their child in their learning process, learning at home, raising bilingual children, and making informed choices when their child needs extra support.

Organizations emphasizing bilingual and multilingual instruction

- Center for Advanced Research on Language Acquisition (CARLA, http://carla.umn.edu/index.html) CARLA is a leader in research on multilingual and multicultural learning. It freely shares the results of its research and action projects with educators through working papers (i.e., reports), databases, archives, and bibliographies. The resources it offers about acquiring new languages focus on content-based instruction, immersion, less commonly taught languages, and proficiency assessment. It has tech integration modules with training modules teachers can explore to increase their technology usage in L2 classes. Its virtual assessment center includes a virtual item bank that has test questions for seven different languages by proficiency level and language skill, which are valuable to any educator of L2s.
- The National Association for Bilingual Education (NABE, http://nabe.org)—NABE is a leading organization focusing on bilingual language and multicultural instruction. The organization is primarily centered on the North American context, but does have four international affiliates. The organization offers an annual conference

in February, symposiums, and institutes. The symposiums are organized like a mini conference, whereas the institutes resemble workshops. A recent topic of the symposiums and institutes was dual language instruction, for example. It offers publications on bilingual research and instructional practices and promotes bilingual materials for language learners. It is known for the advocacy work it did with the Seal of Biliteracy, which is awarded to schools, districts, or educational offices. The Seal of Biliteracy recognizes students who have attained proficiency in two or more languages by high school graduation. In creating this award, NABE led to positive recognition of the value of bilingualism.

Governmental resources

Every country/region has its own approach to language teaching and learning in their schools. In some locations, instructional choices are more centralized, with a ministry of education who makes curriculum, textbook, and assessment decisions. In these settings, the ministry communicates these decisions to schools and teachers. Depending on the setting, teachers may have opportunities for choice among recommended options. In other settings, teachers have no choice regarding what, how, or with what to teach and assess. In other locations, instructional choices are decentralized, so that regional and local educational institutions can make instructional decisions on curricula, texts, and assessments that work with the learners in their setting.

It is important to learn as much as possible about the work environment beforehand, in order to predict how much flexibility will be allowed in instruction and assessment. It is also important to know how the education system is designed, in order to access the proper resources and guidelines on instruction and assessment. In China or Qatar, for example, it is necessary to follow the ministry of education policies, procedures, and resources. Teachers can go to the ministry for instructional resources, guidelines, and professional development. In the United States, educators can go to state departments of education for this sort of professional information and assistance.

A general education organization

- The Association for Supervision and Curriculum Development (ASCD, www.ascd.org)—ASCD is an organization that offers professional development resources for general education, but it has also produced some influential resources for teaching ELLs. It has an annual conference, many books and articles, and online professional development opportunities. For example, it offers texts on collaborating with ELLs' Latinx families, working with multicultural and ELL newcomers, and research-based instruction of ELLs.

Professional Development Plan

Teacher candidates may have their first experiences with engaging in professional development during their teacher preparation program. At the end of their program, they are encouraged or required to write a professional development plan. These plans may be formal or informal in nature.

The rationale for developing a professional development plan is that the teacher establishes goals for their continued learning, so they grow in areas of interest and need. These plans are born from the belief that we all are lifelong learners and need to engage in the enhancement of our knowledge and skills over time.

Professional development plans may include engagement in a professional organization, reading a book on a particular topic, participating in workshops or webinars, or conducting research. The organization of a professional development plan is essentially a linear plan of topics to explore, a timeframe for the activity, and a source for the learning (e.g., reading a book, attending a webinar). A good professional development plan is realistic and meaningful to the individual writing it. They should not be considered busy work or an exercise that just needs to be completed or they do not have any lasting value.

Questions for reflection

Think of the areas you wish to learn more about as you read this book. Which areas would you like to explore further? How will you explore the topic? What will your source(s) of information be? When do you hope to do this? We recommend that you keep track of these thoughts and rough out a plan for yourself to guide your continued professional learning. In particular, ask yourself:

- Which professional organization is the most appealing to you? What does it offer that appeals to you?
- How might you become involved in a professional organization at this stage in your career?
- What would be the pros and cons of professional engagement at this point in your career?

Volunteerism and Service Mindset

One of the easiest ways to develop professionally is to volunteer with a professional organization. It may seem counterintuitive that you will learn as you contribute your perspectives and understandings to the field, but it in fact works. In this vignette, notice how the writer started with minor, achievable volunteer roles that slowly develop into noteworthy and important opportunities. Kenan was a volunteer in IATEFL in member,

---

Volunteering in professional organizations goes back for me to when I began advocating for the creation of a TESOL club in graduate school, where I helped to start a TESOL club. This club led members to work together to attend our first TESOL International Convention in Orlando in 1997. The following year we went to Seattle, where I began my job search, which led to where I am now (i.e., administering a large EFL program after years of teaching EFL).

Throughout my career, I have always looked back at that time as a good experience. It helped me when I applied to start the Riyadh Chapter of the Kingdom of Saudi Arabia Association of Language Teachers (KSAALT) TESOL in Saudi Arabia in

2009. This experience taught me about event management, recruiting members, and a long list of activities that are involved in volunteering to run a chapter for a teacher's association. In addition to volunteering my time through professional development activities, I also volunteer my time as a reviewer of conference abstracts for several associations like TESOL International and the American Evaluation Association. All of these activities have helped me to develop and grow as a professional in the field of TESOL and higher education.

Another way that I have volunteered my time for TESOL is by becoming a TESOL/ Council for the Accreditation of Educator Preparation (CAEP) Reviewer. I have enjoyed this tremendously as it has allowed me to learn more about what other programs are doing to raise the quality of English language teachers. I have continued to try to give back to the field in order to support better practices for TESOLers around the world.

Connie Mitchell
Prince Sultan University

---

international conference organizer, and coordinator capacities, particularly in research SIGs. Engagement helped Kenan hone and practice his acculturation into the field of teaching and teacher education as well as developing further intercultural communication skills. Learning opportunities also went beyond this since he was involved in many joint authorships for short articles, journal publications, and book editing, which offered not only instrumental benefits to create output, but also professional development by nurturing his educator and researcher identity. He also expanded his professional network in which he felt connected to the leading names in TESOL and engaged in discussions and projects in different capacities. He highlighted the enriching and empowering elements that he enjoyed during that time and the lingering effect of this affiliation on his ability to contribute to the micro- and macro-level developments in the field. He also initiated a number of voluntary online training courses for teachers and educators across the world within the community, which broadened his vision of language teaching and language teacher education. Being able to access the international contexts of teaching and learning in other geographies cultivated abilities, such as developing curriculum for teachers in underprivileged regions and mentoring teacher researchers. Development as a teacher, teacher educator, and researcher in such communities is a process that one can achieve not as a solitary engagement, but as social and ongoing investment in learning. He sees professional learning in these supportive communities as an identity-changing experience, which offers a powerful change and development.

Kate started volunteering with the TESOL International Association in 1998 as a conference volunteer. She assisted in the employment clearinghouse and met other educators and employers. She learned about the qualifications and expectations for finding positions in Asia, North and South America, and the Middle East. She learned about the employers' qualities, benefits, and negotiating contracts. At roughly this timeframe, Kate volunteered as the text review column editor for the Ohio TESOL Newsletter. She obtained desk copies from publishers and provided them to individuals who would review and evaluate them. She worked with authors by providing feedback on their reviews so they could craft reviews that were informative and useful for practice. Kate developed her writing and editorial skills while developing relationships with peers and learning about the texts and materials being published. This knowledge helped her in choosing her own textbooks and collaborating with colleagues in the future. These voluntary roles served as a springboard for more opportunities on the Professional Development Committee and Convention Planning Chair for 2013 for TESOL International.

Kate continues her voluntary activities with her regional affiliate of TESOL; currently she is on the Board of Washington State English to Speakers of Other Languages (ESOL) and with TESOL International Association as the Teacher Educator Interest Section, Chair Elect. She learns more about the language learners of Washington State and the resources developed by educators in Washington. In her work in the TEIS, she has the opportunity to work with colleagues to develop convention proposals, webinars, and newsletters for teacher educators. Each year, working with these experts on the proposals and eventual convention sessions keeps Kate current in the developments in research and teaching, so she can use this information in her teaching.

Steve was a "trailing spouse" in Ukraine, and began teaching for Cambridge English on a volunteer basis. He worked with Ukrainian nationals who were employed by large international companies, teaching them both conversational and business English. Eventually, this grew into a paid position with the school. Steve also taught English at a state university in Uzbekistan, earning the same wages as the university's other professors (approximately US$30 per month). While in Uzbekistan, Steve volunteered in local organizations for teaching English.

Through these examples, we hope you can see the benefits of volunteering in terms of developing your professional network, building your knowledge and practices of teaching and assessment, and extending other professional skill sets (e.g., writing, editing, evaluating).

Some emerging professionals are often concerned about how to get involved or the amount of time volunteering requires. Getting involved is simpler than it may appear at the outset. When joining a professional organization, opportunities are announced to members for volunteering in the organization's activities. Individuals volunteering at conferences do not necessarily need to have many skill sets, so it is possible to begin with tasks that are comfortable and familiar; other opportunities require individuals to write a paragraph-long biographical statement of professional experience or qualifications; still others require a more thorough application process. It is important to start in a comfortable place.

The amount of time for volunteering is directly related to the role or task. Some tasks require only a couple of hours, while other tasks take a couple hours over weeks. Since these are voluntary roles, others in the organizations understand that volunteers may hold a full-time job and have other life obligations. Above all, we need to keep in mind that the time committed yields positive outcomes for our professional lives and for the field. We gain much more than we contribute.

Professional Recognition and Advocacy

Perhaps it is due to the comparative youth of the field of TESOL or perhaps it is based on misconceptions about second language teaching and learning, but educators in the field often encounter a lack of understanding of second language learners, learning, and teaching. This lack of understanding is both within the society and in pre-K–16 education systems. TESOL professionals engage with the public and other educators through advocacy on issues related to our learners, their learning, and teaching ESL/EFL/ELT.

Advocacy about ELLs and remedial coursework for language study

The lack of understanding affects the experience and treatment of ESL/EFL/ELT learners. For instance, at universities worldwide, ELLs are often placed in English composition courses at lower levels than their peers, which are considered remedial. Coursework for ELLs in English composition courses in these instances is at lower levels (English 098 or 099), because some university educators believe that ELLs should have the English language skills of a native speaker prior to participating in first-year English composition or English 101. In this scenario, the perception is that ELLs need to fix an issue before they can proceed into regular coursework. Learning in two languages should be considered *additive*, meaning ELLs are working in two languages, which is a more complex intellectual process. A growing perception in college-level teaching is that ELLs should be taught first-year English courses modified for them, so they can proceed academically alongside their peers. In other areas, ELLs must take community college or foundation program English courses before they can proceed into their academic study. When ELLs need to take lower-level or additional courses prior to other study, this adds an additional course to their education, which makes their degree longer and more costly.

Advocacy about ELLs and submersion/immersion

In many K–12 settings, general educators and administrators make decisions about the education of ELLs based on misconceptions about second language learning and teaching. A pervasive belief persists that second language learners only need to be immersed in the language in the classroom to develop language skills. TESOL educators often share resources and research to illuminate the experiences of so-called immersion for ELLs. *Submersion* is used by TESOL professionals instead of immersion to describe how linguistically and academically overwhelming and incomprehensible the experience is when instruction is unmodified. *Immersion*, to a TESOL professional, means engaging ELLs with language and possible content (depending on program) at their proficiency level while supporting them in the second language acquisition process. TESOL professionals also discuss with general educator colleagues the inequity of not engaging ELLs with the language at their proficiency level and the rates at which they fall behind their peers in academic learning if instruction is unmodified. Advocacy in one's profession can be one-on-one discussions with colleagues.

Advocacy about ELLs and academic learning

Other pervasive myths that affect ELLs and which TESOL professionals strive to clarify and remedy through advocacy and research are (a) instruction strategies for including ELLs in general education courses is simply good teaching, and (b) ELLs can acquire English in 1–2 years of study. First, appropriate inclusive instruction for ELLs recognizes the language demands and expectations of learning both social and academic language. *Social language* is the oral and written language we use to establish, maintain, and conclude interpersonal relationships. For example, we may greet someone in passing in the office by saying, "Hey! How are you? Haven't seen you around in a while." Alternatively, you could say, "Long time, no see." At a library, we might inquire about the availability of a book by saying to the librarian, "Hi. I'm looking for the book, *A Tale of Two Cities*, by Dickens. When will it be back?" Social language can be speaking to someone in person, on the phone, or texting with abbreviations and emojis. According to Cummins' (1979) research, it takes 1–3 years to acquire social language.

Cummins distinguished social from academic language. Academic language is the language we use to engage with academic learning. For example, in history classes, books, and documentaries, one hears and reads many descriptions of historical time periods, such as the feudal period. The lives of the wealthy elites, the crafts people, and the agricultural laborers would be described. For historical descriptions, we need to know many adjective forms, past tense verbs, among other language. Science fields have descriptive language as well. For instance, they may describe different attributes of animals or plants. The language demands for academic learning can be subject specific and cognitively demanding; therefore, Cummins indicated that it takes between 5 and 7 years to acquire academic language. It could take up to 10 years, if the learning was interrupted by moving from place to place or other events that caused them to change schools or be away from school for a period of time. TESOL educators have advocated so strongly on these topics that general educators now take teacher preparation courses on working with ELLs and the concepts have permeated the standards of various disciplines.

Advocacy about ELLs and special education referrals

Another cause for advocacy is ELLs and special education referrals. English language learners are more likely to be referred to special education than native-speaking peers due to a lack of understanding on the part of educators about the processes and challenges of learning an additional language simultaneously with an academic subject (de Valenzuela et al., 2006). Through advocacy, TESOL professionals volunteering with TESOL International Association developed a position statement to help protect ELLs from being placed in the wrong educational setting (TESOL International Association, March 2007).

Advocacy about qualifications for teachers of ESL/EFL/ELT

TESOL educators encounter other misunderstandings about the body of knowledge and skills needed to work successfully with ELLs, which affect our professional treatment as well. A common myth in the public arena is that to teach a language one need only be a speaker of it. This myth implies that educators do not need any formal preparation to teach English. One basic example to dispel this myth is that in any ESL/EFL/ELT course the teacher needs to be able to explain the differences in form, meaning, and use of regular past tense and past progressive verbs. Professional preparation is required to understand the forms and the differences, present the forms, develop lessons on the forms with activities and materials, and assess learning of them. This is only one micro example of many that illustrates the body of knowledge and skill that

TESOL educators need to develop to teach ESL/EFL/ELT, and, therefore, professionals with this knowledge should be treated professionally.

Advocacy about professional recognition

Due to the prevalent myths and misconceptions about second language teaching and learning, TESOL educators frequently report a lack of professional recognition and respect among their educational peers (TESOL International Association, June 2008). This is visible on university campuses when IEPs are not located in academic departments, and ELLs do not receive language credit for speaking in two languages or studying English at university, for example. It can be observed when K–12 classrooms are assigned that are not on par with the general education classes; TESOL educators sometimes need to hold ESL/EFL/ELT classes in the library, or even worse in hallways and stairwells. In EFL settings, individuals are hired to teach English based solely on being a native speaker, for instance. Situations like this are inequitable and TESOL professionals and professional organizations strive to advocate for parity for ELLs and the field.

Local, regional, and national communities' beliefs influence leaders to make laws related to program design, instruction, placement, and assessment of ELLs. At times, lawmakers and leaders are informed by professionals and professional organizations who cite research and practice. Situations do occur that prohibit a program model, such as bilingual instruction, or change the language of instruction for a university. Engagement in professional organizations helps us advocate for equitable and evidence-based educational programs, instruction, placement, and assessment for ELLs.

TESOL International Association's teacher education standards include the expectation that TESOL professionals engage in advocacy. Standard 5 states, "Candidates demonstrate professionalism and leadership by collaborating with other educators, knowing policies and legislation and the rights of ELLs, advocating for ELLs and their families, engaging in self-assessment and reflection, pursuing continuous professional development and honing their teaching practice through supervised teaching" (TESOL International Association, 2019, p. 11). To that end, the organization offers an annual Advocacy Summit in the Washington, DC area, in which participants learn about laws relevant to ELLs in the United States as well as strategies for advocating to lawmakers and advocacy resources (see https://www.tesol.org/advance-the-field/advocacy-resources).

Questions for reflection

- Do you think it is important for TESOL professionals to advocate for their learners? Why or why not?
- How might you include advocacy in your current or future work?
- How might you engage others in order to support ELLs and the profession?

Chapter Conclusions

TESOL has grown significantly over the years, both in number of educators, and in sophistication of techniques. Like most academic fields, TESOL hosts a variety of approaches, opinions, and methodologies. However, recent developments in the field have done much to unify the overall philosophy of the field and to consolidate the concept of what we do, how we do it, and how we can best prepare those who plan to enter the field. Unlike many academic fields, TESOL offers a broad range of ways for educators to begin teaching and begin applying what they have learned. At present, TESOL is seen by many academics as a "service discipline," which exists only to serve the needs of more established disciplines. However, as this chapter has shown, TESOL is a field of study comparable with other academic disciplines, which continues to grow in terms of knowledge and resources, and has a sense of coherence and unity among the professionals within the field.

Discussion Questions

1 In what context are you interested in working in the future? What aspects of the context intrigue you? What else do you need to learn to work in that context?
2 Knowing a bit about the history and breadth of the field, which areas are you most interested in exploring further? What area has this information focused your attention on and why?
3 Why would you want to engage in professional development early in your career? Why would that benefit you?
4 Which professional organizations are you most interested in joining and why?

Tasks

1 What teacher preparation do you have or want? How does it or will it help you to obtain your desired teaching position? Is there another credential you want to seek out as a result of reading this chapter?
2 What should you do to avoid the job scams mentioned? How will you protect yourself?
3 Design a professional development plan to outline which professional organization you would like to join, what you hope to learn, and how you plan to grow professionally over the next 5–8 years.
4 Survey educators informally online or at your school. How do educators in other fields perceive the discipline of TESOL? Why are there challenges to professional recognition and respect in your opinion?

Further Reading/Read and Discuss

Read about teaching one-to-one in:
Wilberg, P. (2002). *One to one: A teachers' handbook*. Heinle/Thomson.
Read about teacher development in:
Richards, J. C. (2000). *Beyond training*. Cambridge University Press
Read about language teacher professional organizations:

Elsheikh, A., Coombe, C., & Effiong, O. (Eds.) (2018). *The role of language teacher associations in professional development.* Springer.
Read about professional development in:
Candall, J., & Christison, M. A. (Eds.). (2016). *Teacher education and professional development in TESOL: Global perspectives.* Routledge.

References

Alatis, J. E. (n.d.). *The early history of TESOL.* https://www.tesol.org/about-tesol/association-governance/tesol's-history/the-early-history-of-tesol (accessed March 5, 2021).

British Council. (n.d.). *Our history.* https://www.britishcouncil.org/about-us/history (accessed March 5, 2021).

British Council. (2019). *Annual accounts and reports 2018–19.* https://www.britishcouncil.org/about-us/how-we-work/corporate-reports/annual-report-2018-19 (accessed March 5, 2021).

Center for Applied Linguistics. (2019, September 20). *Homepage.* www.cal.org (accessed March 5, 2021).

Cummins, J. (1979). Cognitive/academic language proficiency, linguistic interdependence, the optimum age question and some other matters. *Working Papers on Bilingualism*, 19, 121–129.

de Valenzuela, J. S., Copeland, S. R., Qi, C. H., & Park, M. (2006). Examining educational equity: Revisiting the disproportionate representation of minority students in special education. *Exceptional Children*, 72(4), 425–441.

Ellis, R. (2014). Instructed second language acquisition. In M. A. Celce-Murcia, D. Brinton, & M. A. Snow (Eds.), *Teaching English as a second or foreign language* (pp. 31–45). National Geographic Learning and Heinle Cengage Learning.

Hill, N. R. (2019). *Content analysis of members' interest, participation, and use of a virtual community of practice associated with intensive English programs.* Theses and Dissertations (All). 1754. https://knowledge.library.iup.edu/etd/1754 (accessed March 5, 2021).

Howatt, A. P. R., & Smith, R. (2014). The history of teaching English as a foreign language, from a British and European perspective. *Language & History*, 57(1), 75–95. https://doi.org/10.1179/1759753614Z.00000000028

International Association of Teachers of English as a Foreign Language (IATEFL). (n.d.). *History of IATEFL.* https://www.iatefl.org/about (accessed March 5, 2021).

Modern Language Association. (n.d.). *MLA history.* https://www.mla.org/About-Us/About-the-MLA/MLA-Archives/Time-Lines/MLA-History (accessed March 5, 2021).

Office of English Language Acquisition, Language Enhancement, and Academic Achievement for Limited English Proficient Students (OELA). (2020, February 12). *Home page.* https://www2.ed.gov/about/offices/list/oela/index.html (accessed March 5, 2021).

TESOL International Association. (n.d.). *Mission and values.* https://www.tesol.org/about-tesol/association-governance/mission-and-values (accessed March 5, 2021).

TESOL International Association. (2007, March). *Position statement on the identification of English language learners with special education needs* [Policy statement]. https://www.tesol.org/docs/pdf/8283.pdf?sfvrsn=2&sfvrsn=2 (accessed March 5, 2021).

TESOL International Association. (2008, June). *Position statement on the status of, and professional equity for, the field of teaching English to speakers of other languages* [Policy statement]. https://www.tesol.org/docs/pdf/11222.pdf?sfvrsn=2&sfvrsn=2 (accessed March 5, 2021).

TESOL International Association. (2019). *Standards for initial TESOL pre-K–12 teacher preparation programs*. TESOL.

WIDA. (n.d.). *Mission and history.* https://wida.wisc.edu/about/mission-history (accessed March 5, 2021).

WIDA. (2016). *WIDA can do descriptors: Key uses edition, grades 4–5.* WIDA Consortium.

3

With Whom and Where Do Those Prepared in TESOL Work?

In this chapter, you will explore the contexts and settings where TESOL educators work, and the variations of program models that occur in response to cultures, population, and needs. You will encounter concepts related to culture and the classroom.

Learning Outcomes

At the conclusion of this chapter, you will be able to:

- describe the variety of English teaching across the world with reference to cultural and ideological considerations
- compare and contrast cultural patterns and communication styles and their impact in the classroom
- pinpoint main arguments in English language teaching related to diverse contexts of learning and teaching
- link contextual features with program delivery model

Do you want to be a global trekker or stay close to home? In this vignette, a colleague discusses how he has managed to live internationally while teaching English in several locations.

TESOL Voices

My International Teaching Journey

My teaching journey has literally taken me around the world, and may even take me back to where I more or less started in the United States. Nonetheless, my journey started in Tottori, Japan, as an assistant language teacher (ALT) in 1995. I was utterly unprepared for what I was about to face. My primary role was mostly as a human tape-recorder, especially as the focus was on grammar translation and passing tests, but most of all I was a "barrel monkey," mostly having fun. Nonetheless, as entertaining as this situation was, I felt that I needed further grounding in both the theory and practice of teaching, or I would continue to be no more than a glorified entertainer.

   Thus, I decided to seek further education at the School for International Training (SIT), and it opened my eyes to how much I didn't know. It was both exciting and

---

Introduction to TESOL: Becoming a language teaching professional, First Edition. Kate Mastruserio Reynolds, Kenan Dikilitaş, and Steve Close.
© 2022 John Wiley & Sons, Inc. Published 2022 by John Wiley & Sons, Inc.

filled me with terror. It seemed like everyone knew more than me, a lot more than me. However, I eventually made up the gap, very much so during my certification track practicum, practical experience teaching, spent at Brattleboro Union High School under the mentorship of Ana G., a graduate of SIT herself.

Despite having both obtained tenure in New Jersey and bought a home, the events of the 2008 recession had other plans for me. I was wandering again to a distant shore; in this case, it was to Qatar, an emirate in the Middle East. Qatar was not the planned destination. In truth I was originally aiming to return to Japan, but Qatar offered the best financial opportunity. Qatar was an interesting mix of a focus on learning and teaching toward designated assessments, and an honest desire to learn to communicate in order to play an active role in a larger international community where English was the primary means of communication. Qatar was also my first real opportunity to play a significant role in developing a curriculum that had an effect on literally thousands of lives.

Once again events beyond my control set me on the road again, this time back to Japan; however, I was not prepared for the minimal changes to the education system since I had first encountered it as an ALT. Honestly, it was a shock, despite all the improvements I heard about from teachers at Japanese Association for Language Teaching (JALT) conferences where I presented in the summers. The only differences I observed were my perspective: not just as a teacher, but now as a parent with three kids in the public school system. My current role is as an EFL teacher at an international school. The primary focus is on regularly requiring students to study for tests and mock tests. Despite this, I have made the push to focus on the teaching of a Common European Framework of Reference for Languages (CEFR)-based standard of instruction that will allow students simultaneously to prepare for the prescribed assessments and achieve a recognized level of communicative competence.

So, what is next? Honestly, I don't know. While I have set a goal for the school I'm currently with, I also know change is very slow to come to Japan. Additionally, it has been my experience that the reason for this slowness is a fear of change. Therefore, I don't know how long I will stay, as time moves on, and my patience to get people to change grows short. So, I may decide to move back to the United States or somewhere else where change may be more embraced. The field of TESOL, though, has provided me countless opportunities to grow and experience different cultures throughout the world.

Matthew R. Vetrini
Nishinomiya, Japan

With Whom and Where Do Those Prepared in TESOL Work?

Most people think of TESOL only with regard to learning English within countries where English is the not dominant language. However, there are several contexts in which those prepared in TESOL can work as a professional. These include being an English language teacher in other countries than America, England, and Canada where English is the first language. In this section, we introduce the varieties of contexts along with the corresponding roles and identities undertaken in each context.

Teaching is a context-dependent profession that involves a multitude of factors that influence the way teaching occurs. One may not be able to teach English in an East Asian country in exactly the same way as in European countries. This is closely related to the ways in which individuals learn. Although we label these differences contextual, because they arise from the situational circumstances, this perception is based on the ways in which individuals shape their cultures and contexts. Therefore, the "where and with whom" issue is interrelated and inseparable as two sides of a coin. Adaptation to a context as a teacher, especially as a language teacher, takes time and takes place over time as one experiences and reflects on teaching, observes and understands students and other teachers, uses and evaluates the materials, and equally importantly explores and interprets the language learning policies in the national context, often through an international lens.

Cultural patterns

Several ways to describe cultural patterns have emerged from research (Hofstede, 2001; Piller, 2012; Samovar et al., 2010; Scollon et al., 2012). These patterns help educators to understand differing world views/perspectives and approaches to interaction. When discussing cultures, it is easy to overgeneralize or find exceptions to the rule. This discussion is based on generalizations from research, and yet you will find that learners in your classroom do not always exhibit these patterns. Sometimes, too, you will find colleagues or learners who are highly familiar with your culture, so when you bow in greeting, they extend their hand to shake.

1. High context and low context
When Kate was in Ukraine, she was often surprised by the low number of signs in airports, subways, and towns. It was challenging for her to find her way around when most locations were not marked by signs and, when there were signs, they were only in Russian (the extent of Kate's Russian language proficiency is ordering green or black tea and pizza). What Kate was experiencing was the difference between her low-context culture, in which everything is fully spelled out and explained, and high-context cultures, in which individuals rely on personal knowledge and communication within networks. In Ukraine at that time, particularly where Kate traveled, not many outsiders were regularly visiting. Individuals in the culture could navigate their way around based on the information presented. Without a high degree of proficiency to be able to ask for directions, Kate's experience was peppered with adventures in getting lost.

Communication breakdowns can occur between individuals from cultures with these different patterns. In the classroom, instructors might find that students want more of an explanation, or find that too much explanation is pedantic. Instructors should be thoughtful about how much direction to provide, how forthcoming to be, and how students may feel about their communication volume and directness.

2. Monochronic, polychronic, and variably monochronic
Imagine a classroom without interruptions, where you can teach without a knock on the door or announcement. Some cultures promote the reduction of interruptions;

these are called monochronic. They prefer to do one task at a time in an orderly fashion, because there is a time and a place for everything. The opposite style is polychronic, in which there are several tasks occurring at the same time. Variably monochronic is a combination of both styles. Which style are you most familiar with? What would you prefer for your students' learning? The choices you make in answer to these questions may or may not align with your students.

3. Future, present, and past time orientation
Future-oriented societies tend to be optimistic about the future and think they can influence the future through their actions. Individuals from future-oriented cultures tend to be active in planning and completing their goals. Countries tending toward this pattern are the United States and, progressively more, Brazil and Finland.

Present-oriented societies view the past as passed and the future as uncertain, so they prefer to focus on what can be done in the present and shorter-term projects. Cultures that tend toward this pattern are France, Mexican America, Philippines.

Past-oriented societies are concerned with traditional values and patterns. Past-oriented cultures tend to be slow to change deeply rooted cultural patterns. Countries holding this orientation are the United Kingdom, China, India, Japan, and Native American nations.

4. Quantity of time
The perception that time is either limited or infinite is how quantity of time is defined. Cultures that view time as limited tend toward punctuality and being thrifty with time/using time wisely. Cultures that perceive time as plentiful may arrive when they are able to, understand that individuals will arrive later than the designated time, and may ask others to come back the following day. In the classroom, individuals from cultures with plentiful time may turn in homework later than desired or ask for extensions. Those from limited-time perspectives may not appreciate changes to deadlines and perceive changes as lack of organization.

5. Power distance
The relationship between people in power, superior positions, and those in subordinate positions is defined as *power distance*. How much people accept these power differences varies by culture. How much distance there is between those two groups is either flexible or inflexible. In high-power-distance cultures, if a person were to bypass their boss, it is considered insubordination. In low-power-distance cultures, if a person were to do this, it would not be considered a problem. Low-power-distance cultures may even promote a sense that the superior is just part of the team and all members of the team are equal participants in the decision-making process.

In the classroom, the instructor is technically the superior, but students from various cultures may be highly formal and deferential or informal and casual in how they interact with the instructor. Students may wish to be addressed by their title and full name, for example. Others may wish to call their instructor by their first name. If an instructor is more informal than the culture they are teaching in, students may not respect the instructor.

6. Individualism and collectivism

Individualist cultures see individuals as unique. They tend to work independently and are rewarded for individual accomplishments. Setting one's goals and being self-determined in the process of accomplishing them are esteemed. When individuals from individualistic cultures are not recognized for their personal accomplishments, they tend become demotivated. Individualistic cultures include Anglo, Germanic, and Nordic cultures in Europe.

Collectivist cultures tend to focus on group goals and collaborative efforts toward the goals. Individuals are not singled out for commendation; rather, the team is applauded for accomplishments. When individuals from collectivist cultures are identified for recognition without the other members of the group, they may be embarrassed. Collectivist cultures include Arabic, Latin American, eastern and southern Asian, and sub-Saharan African cultures.

In a culturally collectivist classroom, instructors may want to provide groups from collectivist cultures group projects and team competitions in which all members receive the same grade. Also, instructors may find that students want to help each other in class or on assignments, which the instructor may perceive as cheating. For instructors in this situation, clearly outlining whether tasks and assignments are individual or team will help avert problems.

Although the way that one teaches changes depending on the context, teaching styles are, of course, based on the individual educator's own learning background. The educator's learning background is an influential factor in how we see the learning process from our own perspectives and how we let these beliefs and understandings affect our actions, that is, the act of teaching and learning. An individual who has not undertaken formal teacher preparation is more likely to depend on his or her past learning experiences when deciding how to teach and interact with the students in the classroom. Conversely, another who has gone through a formal, step-by-step and systematic teacher preparation program might be aware of the theories of learning, and role of context and learners in teaching. However, it is important to note here that there are instances in which TESOL educators experience challenges working in vastly different contexts where their own beliefs about learning and those of students are in stark contrast.

It is then of critical importance to develop awareness of where and with whom one will work. It can also be eye-opening and rewarding to experience such differences, conflicts, and dissonance (i.e., tensions or clashes) between one's beliefs and those of the learners and colleagues. These experiences serve as learning opportunities and help understand the field of TESOL, and more importantly professional development in one's career if you engage in subsequent reflection and critical discussion based on these experiences.

Individuals do not learn from the experiences themselves, but from reflecting on these experiences, John Dewey argued (Dewey, 1933). This implies that the experiences teaching are valuable mediating resources and processes by which educators can develop critical views about being and becoming an educator. The context and people in the context are the key factors that offer educators opportunities to understand and grow in their profession. Below we offer detailed discussion on the types of context and learners in these contexts.

Questions for reflection

- What do you know of the culture and context of your instruction? How might you learn more?
- Should instructional and assessment practices be congruent with the culture and context? Why or why not?

Critical Pedagogy and Social Justice

Education should be equitable, meaning that students should have access to education and be treated fairly and with respect. In classrooms around the world, this is not always the case. Learners may be overtly or covertly, intentionally or unintentionally discriminated against on the basis of race, gender, religion, language, ability, or sexual orientation.

Types of discrimination and bias

Overt discrimination is the easiest to see and call out, if individuals are empowered to. If a teacher calls a student a disparaging nickname, for example. Covert discrimination, like systemic racism in which there is a culture of discrimination within a given environment, is difficult to see clearly and work against. An individual might observe covert discrimination in a classroom, for example, if only males or only Muslims are called on. Or either group is not called upon.

Most overt discrimination can be classified as "intentional," meaning that an individual who holds power (whether in a classroom or in the general population) undertakes actions that are perceived as offensive, and does so with full understanding of how those actions will be perceived. People who feel comfortable engaging in intentional discrimination are almost always members of privileged communities who expect that others will support their actions. Their discrimination is intended to enforce hierarchies or social strata that they see as normative. Examples of discrimination to enforce hierarchies are the policy of Apartheid in South Africa or the "Separate, but Equal" policy of education in the United States that kept black and white children separate in schools that lasted until the 1960s. An example of discrimination that is normative is when a teacher says, "I need some strong boys to help me move this desk," or "Could one of the girls in the class bring snacks for next week?" That teacher is showing intentional gender bias, accompanied by discrimination.

Some overt discrimination and most covert discrimination fall into the category of "unintentional" discrimination, meaning that an individual who holds power is unaware of the implications of their actions even though they are offensive and discriminatory. While intentional discrimination is generally a direct outcome of an action, unintentional discrimination is often a secondary outcome. Much unintentional discrimination originates in cultural assumptions of "normalcy" and a failure to acknowledge diversity in a population. While the person in power has no intention of enforcing hierarchies, their actions still discriminate against students from marginalized groups. A teacher who asks students to write about how they like their steaks cooked probably has no intention of discriminating against vegetarians, and yet students who do not eat meat may be offended and/or perform poorly on this exercise. Exercises that can be fun and inspiring for the majority of students can be offensive and objectionable for others. When students are offended in this manner, they may feel marginalized and unable to learn in the classroom.

A third category of discrimination is "perceived" discrimination. This generally takes place when a person who holds power engages in an action that has a nondiscriminatory or even antidiscriminatory intent, but which is nonetheless perceived as discriminatory. For example, a teacher might attempt to draw out a student by referring to an aspect of that student's economic or cultural background. Even if the intent is to show respect for the student and to empower them within the classroom, in some cases the student will see the action as offensive. In such cases, it is generally a better idea to focus on perception than on intent.

A bias is prejudice for or against someone, a group, or something. Everyone has biases of some kind. Steve, Kate, and Kenan are prejudiced in favor of education, for example, and against violence. As educators we need to be thoughtful and aware of our own biases and the ways they may affect our students. People are often unaware of their own biases though; this is called unconscious or implicit bias. If you are interested in exploring your own implicit bias, Harvard University has a test in their Project Bias, which you can take online to explore your own (https://implicit.harvard.edu/implicit). According to Suttie (2016), four ways to reduce implicit bias are:

1. Cultivate awareness of your biases.
2. Work to increase empathy and empathic communication.
3. Practice mindfulness and loving-kindness.
4. Develop cross-group friendship in your personal life.

If we do not spend time to reduce implicit bias, we may unintentionally perpetuate injustice.

A related concept is microaggressions. *Microaggressions* are seemingly trivial words and actions that the recipient perceives as offensive. For example, asking a Muslim student if it is difficult to wear a hijab all day or a Sikh to take off his turban.

Privilege

Discrimination often finds its roots in privilege, meaning that those who discriminate against others are not vulnerable to the same sorts of discrimination. In such cases, the person who holds power often lacks empathy for those against whom they discriminate because they have never been in a similar situation. Among the most frequently discussed forms of privilege are "male privilege" and "white privilege." McIntosh (2004), describes white privilege as "an invisible weightless knapsack of special provisions, maps, passports, codebooks, visas, clothes, tools and blank checks" (p. 19) that grant unearned advantages to white people in ways that are unrealized to the individual. An example she offers is, "When I am told about our national heritage or about 'civilization', I am shown that people of my color made it what it is" (2004, p. 20). This example makes clear the unintentional discrimination and how it is perpetuated. Different kinds of privilege exist in countries everywhere. Understanding the context and the degree to which we can voice counter-narratives is important for TESOL educators. When feasible, TESOL educators need to advocate for the disenfranchised or marginalized. "Within the field of education, advocacy as *voicing* is a central theme as teachers speak *up*, speak *with*, and speak *for* their EL students" (Linville & Staehr Fenner, 2019, p. 342, emphasis in original).

Discrimination toward teachers

Teachers may be discriminated against based on race, gender, religion, language, ability, or sexual orientation too. In some locations, students may value a male teacher as opposed to a female teacher, a white teacher as opposed to a teacher of color, or a cisgendered, heterosexual teacher as opposed to a teacher who identifies in the lesbian, gay, bisexual, transgender, queer/questioning, intersex, asexual/ally (LGBTQIA+) community.

Teachers who are nonnative English speakers themselves may also be discriminated against by students or administrators. Students may desire a native English speaker, because they value the native speaker's accent and ability to use complex slang. They do not understand that native English speakers do not know their grammar or the process of learning English in the same way the nonnative English-speaking teacher does. The intuitive nature of a native English speaker's grammar, even if they study grammar, is a different body of knowledge than that of a nonnative English speaker who has studied the grammar enough to develop their proficiency to an advanced level. Administrators look to hire native speakers, because of the perceived intrinsic value of having a native English speaker for their language abilities or to attract students to their language school. Nonnative English-speaking teachers (NNESTs) bring substantial value to the classroom because they understand the learners' positions, the challenges the learners will encounter when learning English, and the grammatical system, for example. Learners also see a model of English language learning in the NNEST. Dee (2005) demonstrated the value of learners seeing a person like themselves in the teacher.

Having an equity stance

Educators today are taught about *social justice*, which describes movements that seek to ensure equal treatment for marginalized or disempowered groups. We can create socially just classrooms, schools, and communities through our words and deeds. As educators we need to take students' and colleagues' statements of discrimination seriously and endeavor to work to make educational environments equitable. It is right and ethical for us to work toward equity for all students and teachers, and promote acceptance and understanding. Having an equity stance means that teachers need to advocate for equity in course and classroom assignments and hiring practices in schools in which they teach. It also means that teachers view everything in their instructional work through a critical lens, called *critical pedagogy*. For example, teachers need to consider equity in lesson planning, group work, materials employed, presentation delivery, calling on students, asking for volunteers, etc. An outstanding example of a teacher employing a critical lens comes from a presentation by a teacher in Qatar who noted that the ELT book he was using had a drawing of a town that students were supposed to use to practice names of buildings (e.g., post office, town hall) and giving directions (e.g., right, left). The drawing had a church in it. The students in his class were all Muslim and might not perceive this as culturally relevant. So, in a stroke of genius, the teacher found a drawing of a mosque and put it on the projector. He pointed out that the drawing in the book had a church, so if students wanted to they could draw in towers or imagine it was a mosque. He indicated that in the activity they would use the word mosque instead of church. The students responded very positively to him and thanked him for it. It is through applying critical pedagogy that educators can make class environments more equitable.

Contexts

U.S. and English-dominant ESL countries (Kachru's inner circle)

The overall context of language teaching and learning can be approached from Kachru's circle-structured model, World Englishes, which categorizes contexts according to whether English is used as a native language. The inner circle, for example, includes countries where English is the primary language, mother tongue, or first language: the United Kingdom, the United States, Australia, New Zealand, Ireland, Anglophone Canada, and South Africa, and some of the Caribbean territories. These countries offer learners from other countries various language acquisition opportunities with intensive and extensive exposure to the living structure and use of language as opposed to those in the books for English language teaching. Learning becomes a social practice, reflecting types of interaction that tend to happen naturally, and which depend on the integration of the learner into a linguistically active environment, whether in a public environment or in the classroom.

Teaching in "Foreign" Language Contexts and in English-dominant Contexts

Native and nonnative issues

In TESOL, native speakers are those who speak English as their first language or those who grew up interacting with English speakers in a country whose dominant language is English. Nonnative speakers are those who learned English as a second/foreign language. Nonnative speakers of English who can be categorized as second language learners are more likely to be exposed to language use in communicative settings. For example, in Nordic countries such as the Netherlands, Sweden, Norway, Finland, or in countries such as India and the Philippines, English is used as the second communicative language by most people, creating room and opportunity for English to be practiced for social functions and work purposes. This leads to acquisition of English in public settings rather than learning in the classroom. On the other hand, foreign language learners are those who learn English in classroom settings through formal instruction and have limited access to language used for daily communication. However, there is a long-standing discrimination against teachers of English who do not speak English as their first language (Medgyes, 1992; Moussu & Llurda, 2008; Braine, 2012), and only a recent trend toward increased appreciation for these educators (Llurda, 2004).

Although discrimination toward educators as persons occurs within education based on individual's nationality and/or language background, professionals in the field of TESOL tend to reject this view. Some argue that English language educators, regardless of their nationality or being either a native speaker or professional user of English, need to be thought of and treated as equals (Medgyes, 1992). This argument is focused on the idea that there are advantages to speaking a language as a native speaker of that language, but that teaching others to use the language is an entirely different matter. Being able to speak a language does not necessarily make anyone a better teacher, but aids in the authentic use of that language while teaching it. Nonnative English-speaking educators can offer authentic language use and constitute a model for learners. Users of English as a foreign or second language will have different pedagogical qualities including:

- understanding learner needs and interests;
- being familiar with the English learning processes and challenges;
- possessing distinctive levels of proficiency of English;
- being aware of the context of teaching; and
- understanding the structures and learning of the grammar and syntax of English.

On the other hand, native speakers of English might lack such unique knowledge about learners, context, needs, and more importantly the language learning process. This does not necessarily mean that they cannot develop such knowledge once they are immersed in the context of teaching. They can do so over time.

English as an international language and English as a lingua franca

Communication between people who have English as their first language and those who do not is referred to as conducted through English as an international language (EIL). For example, an American does business with someone in Malaysia and uses English for communication, in which case the communication language is English as international language. Speaking with native speakers of language might lead to a sense of inferiority, demotivation, and unwillingness to communicate, especially for those who perceive their abilities to speak English as limited. This is not a deficit, but an ability to improve or a mindset to shift. The communication between these individuals can lead to frustration when there is little comprehensible talk for both parties. Native speakers, therefore, could be more tolerant and patient in international contexts where they contact speakers of other first languages who might have difficulty in making what they mean clear.

Interestingly, English is the internationally recognized language of aviation. When a pilot communicates with the air traffic controller in the flight tower to take off or land, they do so in English despite what their native language is. Therefore, many pilots, navigators, and air traffic controllers the world over learn English in addition to their learning of aviation.

The use of English in authentic communicative settings for various purposes by and among speakers of other languages is increasingly common. However, this also affects the linguistic aspects of English used in these settings, including pronunciation, word meanings, word order, and pragmatic use of language. English as a lingua franca (ELF) users appear to map the linguistic features of their own languages onto English, which may help them understand and be understood by speakers of their home language(s), but may cause miscommunication or stigmatization with those who do not share their home language(s). Seidlhofer (2002) describes this as English being a global lingua franca. For example, a Norwegian and a Turk communicate through English since they do not know each other's languages, in which case the language of communication is ELF. Another example is when a Qatari individual gives directions to their Nepali taxi driver.

Questions for reflection

- What is the key difference between lingua franca and international language?
- Have you had relevant experiences of such differences in language use in an international context? How have they helped you develop your understanding of language teaching?
- How can you interpret this difference for your language use?
- How might these concepts help you organize your interaction with others in your profession?

Controversy in the field—who "owns" English?

Crystal (2003) argues that only one-fourth of users of English in the world are L1 speakers of English, which illustrates that more people from diverse L1 backgrounds speak English than native speakers of English. In such contexts, English is more prone to changing and evolving as a different language than the one used in L1 English contexts, such as in England and the United States. This clearly shows that claims regarding "owning" a language like English, which functions as an international or global language, are not valid arguments. This is because the control of a language by countries populated by native speakers has no more relevance than that of countries that use the language as a lingua franca. The only exception to this is when a country seeks to support and control the use of its own language in different countries. The British Council or American embassies in different countries, for example, offer several language and culture programs for local people to improve their English and serve as English language educators or teacher educators in their own countries.

Despite ongoing political claims regarding "correctness" or "proper language," one cannot claim ownership over any language since people can learn any language they want and use any language they know in the international arena. Although there might be restrictions on the language or languages that can be used within the boundaries of countries, particularly in formal settings, this is not possible when people learn and communicate in other languages, especially online. It seems futile to try to control or own languages, since English is increasingly being used and accepted as a language for daily communication in many parts of the world.

How Does Teaching English Differ in Different Contexts?

The facets of context in TESOL

English has been learned and used in many countries and by many individuals whose first languages are different. Language teaching is closely related to the specific context in which an educator is prepared. Context involves classroom context (e.g., learner-specific and culturally related characteristics, materials used, and the curriculum followed) and social context (e.g., languages used in social life, parental expectations, and language policy in the country). Any instruction that excludes the context of teaching and learning might end up with a failure, demotivation, and disengagement from further learning. Therefore, it is critical that educators develop awareness in understanding the role of contextual characteristics that might hamper or foster learning, motivate students, and encourage them to engage actively in the learning process. While context can be interpreted as linguistic context where meaning is created in relation to the special situations in which language is used, we refer to context here as "the broader setting for language teaching," which is displayed in Figure 3.1.

Determining how English is to be taught involves considering the continental, regional, and country setting where the instruction will occur. The first key consideration is which form of English language instruction applies to the area. For example, is the country one in which English is the language outside of the classroom or is there another language used? What are the purposes for individuals to learn English in this location?

Each continent, region, and country has unique cultural influences and beliefs about learning and teaching that affect the instruction of English. For example, in Uzbekistan, learners are expected to be respectful and deferential to the educator. They stand when the educator enters the classroom and remain standing until they are told to sit. They are dismissed when the educator gives the cue. Classroom instruction tends to be direct instruction because the educator is seen as the authority who is

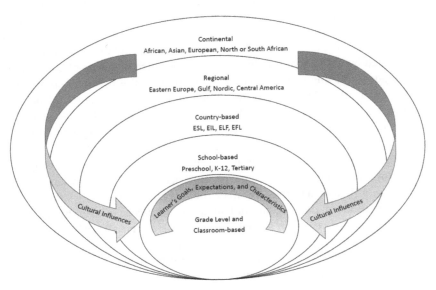

Figure 3.1 Broader settings for language teaching.

entitled to share their knowledge with the students. Educators direct questions to the learners individually and learners are expected to answer. These patterns are rooted in long-standing traditions and expectations of how schooling should occur, regardless of whether they are rooted in current theory or expectations.

Six patterns of differences in cross-cultural communication

1. Communication styles

When individuals from different cultures come into contact, even when they are using the same language, words, and phrases, they may communicate strongly divergent meanings. Understanding of basic concepts may have different nuances, or shades of meaning. Furthermore, the degree of directness/indirectness, assertiveness, and voice volume are dynamics in communication.

 Nonverbal communication, or "body language," comprises facial expressions, eye contact, gestures, and personal space. In some cultures, direct eye contact is considered a challenge. Hand gestures in one culture may be considered rude in another. Facial expressions for emotions may be interpreted in unintended ways. Over the past 30 years, discussions of whether to teach nonverbal communication patterns for the target language culture(s) have occurred in the field. Teaching nonverbal behavior communication patterns and having expectations of eye contact can become problematic in the classroom. Suffice it to say, most TESOL professionals explore with their learners how different cultures treat nonverbal communication. In doing so, they raise learners' awareness, so they may adapt to any future intercultural communication moment.

2. Attitudes toward conflict

Some cultures wish to avoid conflict, while others embrace it. People like Americans see it as an opportunity for growth and learning. Other cultures view it as awkward or demeaning. Some cultures may wish to address conflict indirectly and wish to avoid face-to-face interaction, while others will seek to resolve the conflict in person in a direct fashion.

3. Approaches to completing tasks

Patterns exist in how groups work together to complete a task and relate to notions of time, access to resources, notions of potential rewards, and relationship building. Often in the multicultural classroom, students will need to become familiar with their peers, discuss roles in groups, determine a way to manage their time, and consider availability of resources.

4. Decision-making styles

Consider if you prefer to make individual decisions or desire a group to arrive at a consensus. What you prefer is based on both your personality and your culture. Consensus building is an important tool for many Japanese. Individuals from Latin American and southern Europeans tend to prefer ownership of decision making, whereas in the United States, typically the majority rules.

5. Attitudes about open emotion and personal affairs

The degree of privacy and openness about feelings and personal topics vary among cultures. Some students may feel uncomfortable discussing personal or taboo topics in class. Or students may not feel comfortable about sharing their feelings about a personal experience, particularly one that is painful or upsetting (e.g., refugee experiences, trauma, or immigration story).

6. Approaches to knowledge and beliefs

Cultures arrive at knowledge and beliefs by following differing paths. Some employ striving for perfection or enlightenment through recurrent practice. Others prefer research or problem solving. Some prefer symbolic imagery, traditions passed along through elders, or rhythm as vehicles for learning. A thoughtful educator would create differing learning experiences that utilize different ways of knowing and learning.

All of these patterns are generalizations based on research (DuPraw & Axner, 1997), but they are generalizations. Intercultural interaction will be mitigated based upon race, gender, social class, sexual orientation, among other factors. Educators should strive to learn as much as possible about the culture and individual learners in their classes in order to avoid pitfalls and missteps.

Further, there are politics that influence how language is taught. For example, in some locations there is a concern that English will overtake the use of local languages and the local languages may die out. In these situations, laws are made that influence the instruction of local languages so they are prioritized over the instruction of English. For more reading on endangered languages and language revitalization, visit the Endangered Languages Project (www.endangeredlanguages.com).

The politics of a particular country influence the ways that teaching occur all the way to what happens in the classroom. In P.R. China, the national Ministry of Education (MOE) outlines how teaching should be carried out at all instructional levels. The MOE regulates curriculum, textbooks, and assessments, so throughout China one would see a consistent curriculum and student performance. No matter where you may teach, you would have the same textbook for grade 8 with the same assessment criteria and goals. Other countries organize their educational systems so local educational professionals make decisions about curriculum and instruction. New teachers need to investigate the country they intend to work in to learn as much as they can about the larger educational context before accepting a new position.

Narrowing our scope from the continental to regional and regional to country-based, we can then consider the ways that learning and teaching are influenced at the school and classroom levels. First, the learners' ages and grade levels factor into how to teach and what topics are taught. If a teacher is teaching third grade in Japan, the courses are focused on learning vocabulary through song and hands-on activities (foreign language instruction). If an educator is working at middle school in Australia, students may be acquiring English while learning about the grade-level academics (content-based instruction). An educator at a high school in Wales might be observed teaching formal, academic writing (English for academic purposes). A Turkish student studying at Boğaziçi University in Istanbul, despite having Turkish as a first language, would study all of their courses in English (English as a medium of instruction). If an educator is instructing at a university in Mexico, the learners would be studying topics that allow them to build their social communication skills (foreign language instruction). In Quebec, Canada, educators tend to use both French and English in a bilingual classroom, so that French learners acquire English and English learners acquire French (two-way bilingual education).

Second, in most situations schools have curricula and textbooks. Educators need to learn about these resources and understand how their work fits into the curriculum. When Kate was on a Fulbright in Ukraine in 2007–8, her mentor showed her early on the curricular topics she would need to teach as well as the topics and concepts that were taught before and after. That way, she could rely on the instruction prior to her courses and build on that learning in preparation for the expectations of the next instructional level. When Steve taught in Ukraine, his students attended a university sponsored by an American church organization, and there were limits on what could be included in the curriculum, with some topics being strictly prohibited.

School context

Schools are physical places in which educators and administration create a culture of learning and teaching through the adoption of a particular curriculum. Educators need to know the contextual characteristics of their schools and curricular issues adopted and followed. Individual schools might be categorized in several ways. For example, one category can be age-specific schools such as kindergarten, primary school, secondary school, high schools, and colleges. In each of these age-specific categories, one can find schools adopting different mediums of instruction, such as monolingual schools where students are immersed in English, which is the language of all subjects. Some approaches adopted in immersion settings are content-based instruction (CBI), English for academic purposes (EAP), and English for specific purposes (ESP). Another format in which English is the medium of instruction is in EFL settings when English is taught as a course. Common approaches in these school settings are content and language integrated learning (CLIL) and English as a medium of instruction (EMI). Another school type is bilingual schools, where both languages are used as communicative and instructional language in the school.

The school context in which language teaching is delivered varies depending on age, purpose, level, and content adopted by a particular school. An educator might work at a unique school where language teaching has a special focus and is intensively used as a medium of instruction. Most international schools offer English-medium instruction, which makes it easy for educators to survive without being overwhelmed or blocked by potentially existing linguistic differences and challenges that they might experience. Some schools may not have a specific methodology or model of instruction, which leaves educators free to choose their methodology or model.

Classroom context

The classroom has influences all its own, think of it as the micro level of influences on instruction. Teachers make instructional decisions based on the unique characteristics of the learners in the classroom, the particular purpose of learning, the materials available, and even space constraints. However, educators make many instructional decisions based on second language acquisition theory/principles and methods guide as well.

In language classrooms, students' social and cultural backgrounds make up part of the characteristics of the classroom. They play a key role in ascertaining what and how an instructor can teach, so an educator might need to know in as soon as possible their students' individual characteristics (e.g., introversion/extroversion, motivation, anxiety, interests, and language strengths and weaknesses), goals, and expectations in relation to their families and cultures. Learning has been found to be interlinked with learners' individual differences, which may facilitate learning when considered and hinder it when not.

All cultures have similarities and differences even if they do not appear to on the surface. Likewise, all cultures have influences on language and language use, which may be similar or different to English. For example, in one culture it may be acceptable to argue a point with another person repeatedly until the other person agrees; whereas, another culture may consider repetitions of an argument as annoying, badgering, over-persistent, or aggressive. Therefore, educators need to develop an awareness and understanding of the relationship between language use and culture in order to aid language learners in learning to communicate in their L2. This awareness and understanding also includes not seeing cultural patterns as "wrong" or "improper" from one's own cultural perspective when a linguistic or social behavior is displayed. Rather, these behaviors are to be respected and interpreted appropriately. The development of intercultural awareness is then key to learning English. This will enhance the process of learning of English since the abovementioned factors could be facilitative in the understanding and use of English. In some classrooms, teaching and learning is hindered because of educators' failure to address these less visible, but still prominent culture-specific factors. Therefore, the educator's ability to create a comfortable classroom atmosphere is closely linked to students' profile and cultural background. For example, cultural events and styles can be discussed in English with reference to differences with other cultures and how culture-specific issues influence the use of languages. A meaningful discussion on these differences will generate a content that could engender motivation and authenticity. Therefore, it is important to use intercultural issues as authentic course content in a systematic way and help students adapt to these differences as they learn to communicate. The major aim is not to lead them to assimilation of new culture or promote the values and ideologies of English-speaking countries, but to have a full command of the similarities and differences in order to facilitate appropriate communication. However, being aware of the learners' diverse cultures has not been easy in recent years since students' profiles and backgrounds might even vary within the same community. For example, an educator might find that many of their Arabic-speaking students come from diverse cultures in the Middle East or northern Africa. Addressing contextual diversity has become a necessity for instructors.

Culture influences the roles of teachers and students in learning. In some locations, teachers are supposed to do most of the communicating in the classroom. They present new information and ask learners questions to gauge learners' comprehension. Students may ask questions, too. Educators describe classrooms in which the teacher is the source and the transmitter of knowledge as teacher-centered. More recently, many of these classrooms are adopting teaching practices that emphasize participation and communication. Students may be asked to work with a partner or in a small group to do an activity, task, or project. In this way, the students become the focal point for learning and utilize the language more than in a teacher-centered classroom. In such classrooms, educators develop the roles of being a model, discussion facilitator, rule explainer, instruction prompter, coach, and intensive practice designer who can support and strengthen language learning though systematic engagement in practice and review of new materials. Active and activity-focused classrooms are called student-centered classes.

Newly emerging classroom profiles are causing educators to reconsider their understandings and apply different management styles and techniques. Due to vibrant migration within the world, more and more people have been relocating and settling in different countries where they are immersed in the educational system and find themselves in new classrooms. Due to the increase in student mobility, one can even find classrooms in many places in the world where students have highly diverse social and cultural backgrounds. Educators need to consider these differences while designing their teaching. In a multicultural classroom, the students' expectations of an educator would vary and pose a pressing challenge to an educator's instructional decisions and even influence their material selection and use, let alone the pedagogical in-class tasks and activities, which might involve speaking, discussion, argumentation, digitalization, and collaboration. In some cultures, students are not offered opportunities to engage in interactional and social activities, which might contribute to their tendency to remain silent and shy away from sharing their ideas, even when they have some. Furthermore, students' perceptions of the role and responsibilities of the educator and the educators' language backgrounds influence students' willingness to participate and learn in the setting.

Classroom dynamics in relation to learners has been increasingly important in that each learner has his or her own learning path closely shaped by their cultural values, social norms, and linguistic background. A classroom is not a static setting but has become a multifaceted and multidimensional context, which even goes beyond it. It is also no more a physical entity composed of four walls, but a community composed of diverse students who come together to learn together whether online or face-to-face. Here we mean a digital classroom described as community of learners. Educators today should experience teaching online, distance education, and the use of digital platforms, tools, and materials to enrich their teaching, all of which could be a powerful way of addressing student diversity in expecting a different kind of learning experience.

Questions for reflection

- What metaphor can you develop to describe the concentric circles of context (see Figure 3.1)?
- Why is it important to consider all of the contextual influences from broadest to most specific?

Contextual Factors

As discussed in the opening paragraph of this chapter, context is key to learning and teaching regardless of the type of profession. All kinds of teaching but especially language teaching might be complicated by the contextual differences that are situated in and dependent upon the physical and cultural geography of the place in which the teaching occurs. The context, then, is the collective sum of individual differences composed of a wide range of social factors. The interrelationships among all these factors indirectly influence the process of teaching languages.

Contextual factors also include those in Table 3.1. These factors are the most local and critical for an instructor. The national politics and the attitudes of the community about the language and language learning have direct bearing on whether they view the language as valuable and how much energy students will bring to the learning experience. The students' mobility and opportunities for language use in the community have direct bearing on their investment in learning the language, and how much how fast and how well they learn it. The courses, topics, educators, internet availability, and materials will also influence how you will teach. For example, having the internet and materials available allows a wider range of resources (i.e., readings, activities) and interaction opportunities, such as online epenpals.com, padlet.com, or quizlet.com. Teaching in a resource-challenged setting sometimes interferes with the availability of these sets of resources (or even desks). Figures 3.2–3.4 show some different educational settings.

Table 3.1 Contextual factors related to classrooms and schools.

Materials	Existence of and access to learning materials and resources
Attitudes	Community attitudes regarding the learning of other languages
Educators	Number and competence of trained and professional educators
Courses	Number of hours for courses on learning other languages
Internet	Access to internet to explore countries of other languages
Use	Opportunities to use other languages in the region
Mobility	Opportunities to interact with people from other countries
Policies	National policies for learning other languages

Figure 3.2 Lao elementary school resources.

Figure 3.3 Classroom taken over by goats in Laos.

Figure 3.4 In the Ukrainian classroom, students share resources.

There are more specific context-related situational factors that could fall within this general category, but they could also be idiosyncratic (pertaining to individual inter-pretation) so may not be generalized to all contexts. However, this does not necessarily mean they are not important; on the contrary, they are. Therefore, they need to be analyzed and employed for the advantage of teaching and learning. For example, some instructors like to use songs as teaching materials in their English classes, but there are times when the students in the context of that classroom are not so keen to sing songs that are chosen specifically to appeal to them. The students may react personally to these choices, perhaps perceiving the songs as being related to parents' silencing of their voices in the family, which could render it shaming to sing in the social setting. Attitudes toward songs can also be generational, or ideological. When Steve tried to use traditional Ukrainian folk music in his classes, students told him that those songs represented their parents' values, and that they had a much stronger affiliation with "Christian culture" than "Ukrainian culture." Experiences like these are unique to the context of teaching and should be used as a learning opportunity rather than taken for granted and unquestioningly replaced with a different activity.

Questions for reflection

- Have you experienced such context-related factors situated in your specific context?
- What can you learn from having to work under circumstances including these factors?
- In what ways can you reflect on these contextually situated factors?

Program Models of Instruction

In this chapter, we have been describing the relationship between context and language instruction. We will delve deeper into the program models of instruction. Program models encompass the *why*, the *what*, as well as the *how* we teach the way we do. A program model will include a theoretical framework that describes why instructors teach in this model the way they do. Program models include methods of instruction that describe what subjects (i.e., content) will be taught and how they be taught. Without the theoretical framework, which provides a research-based foundation upon with the instruction is built, and the methods, activities, and techniques used, an educator is without guidance and may approach instruction in a haphazard manner (see Brown, 1994, 2007, Informed Eclectic).

Earlier in this chapter, we mentioned some of the program models. We will investigate program models that focus more on the instruction of language skills or content. Program models that focus on language as the subject of study are EFL, ESL, or English language development (ELD), newcomers' programs, EAP. Those that focus on academic content as the subject of study do so to varying degrees. These models consist of bilingual education, CBI, sheltered instruction, CLIL, and EMI. Program designers/curriculum specialists endorse either bilingualism or English-only immersion, so each of the models listed above will have one of these orientations. For example, EFL, ESL, or ELD programs tend to be immersion, but they may allow for some L1 use; whereas, bilingual education programs develop academic language in two languages, so learners and educators may employ both languages. Consider this scenario bilingual immersion.

Program Models in Which Language Is the Subject Studied

EFL, ESL, or ELD

EFL, ESL, and ELL programs teach learners how to speak, listen, read, and write in English. They interweave these language skills with grammar, vocabulary, pronunciation, and spelling instruction. These courses teach vocabulary sets, such as colors, numbers, family members, clothing, and transportation. The grammar points often begin simply with simple statements, articles, pronouns, present tense, near future and future tense, and proceed to simple past tense and more complex grammar of relative clauses, different past tenses, and shifting tenses. Educators use textbooks or create authentic scenarios for students to practice their grammar or vocabulary in each of the four language skills. Educators also use a variety of fun and engaging activities for language practice. The educators often employ only the target language, English, to present new vocabulary and grammar with audio and visual supports to make the new information comprehensible to the learners, so the learners are immersed in the language. In some cases, though, the instructor may rely on the first language to define complex concepts or ideas or encourage *translanguaging*, when multilingual speakers use any linguistic tool available to them to communicate.

Often, these programs are intended to allow ELLs to develop their basic language skills and provide a foundation of language knowledge that learners can then use in their personal lives, work, or future academics. Since these programs serve learners with little experience in English, learners at the beginning stages of language learning participate in them. In some cases, language learners take intensive courses in language before they can move into academic study in English.

Newcomers' programs

In many second language contexts, due to immigration, migration, and asylum needs, school districts have set up newcomers' programs. Newcomers' programs have been developed in areas where there is a high influx of new language learners who do not have any prior experience learning with or in English. These programs tend to be organized for intensive language learning for a short period of time. For example, learners may be in these programs for 3–9 months prior to moving into the general education classroom. In some contexts, the duration of the program may be longer, but this is not the norm. Interestingly, newcomers' programs tend to accept learners into the program on a rolling basis, meaning that students can enroll at any point in the academic year. This enrollment approach is necessary, because the ELLs may enter the country at any time during the year. The organization of instruction, therefore, is coordinated to welcome the new arrivals and facilitate their integration into the learning context.

Newcomers' programs are designed to focus mainly on the immediate language needs to survive and develop social language skills to establish and maintain social relationships. Some programs at the high school level will include beginning academic language to ease learners' transitions into general education classes. *Survival language* is defined as basic communication skills for asking and answering questions to obtain resources needed for survival in the target language culture. For example, adults might need to know how to find a toilet, obtain, and pay for food at the grocery store, use the subway, rent an apartment, or find a job. Even finding a job these days requires a fair amount of language use when completing applications online and answering the personality questionnaires. For K–12 learners, newcomers' programs focus on an array of personal needs (e.g., ordering food in the cafeteria, obtaining a book, or borrowing a pencil), academic business needs (e.g., asking a question in class, reading the homework directions, or logging into the classroom management system to submit homework), social language (e.g., talking about oneself, giving advice, apologizing, making an excuse), and beginning academic language (e.g., listing, defining, discussing, categorizing).

Newcomers' programs support learners who are new to the second language context, so they do not have the demands of learning the academic subject in general education before they have some language to build upon. In instances where the number of ELLs is much lower, school districts have other approaches to supporting newcomers, such as sheltered content in the general education classroom or pull-out programs.

EAP

Not all language-focused classes are focused on conversational English. *EAP* courses typically do not emphasize the learning of standard conversational English, but they may focus solely on a particular discipline within academia. In these courses, the academic content serves as a topic for language learning only. The topics are not necessarily treated in depth, but used as a source for practicing communication and academic skills. In an EAP course, the goals are developing language skills and academic study skills necessary for success in academic classes. The topics of study are the key distinction. For example, in EAP courses, students will study how to listen for information in an academic lecture by (a) discussing the topic of the lecture to access their schema, (b) learning and practicing new vocabulary that will occur in the lecture, (c) listening to an academic lecture while taking notes, (d) discussing the content of lecture, and (e) writing their opinion of the topic.

EAP programs focus on developing the language skills, such as speaking, listening, reading, and writing, which ELLs will rely on in their academic classes. In these classes, students will study a variety of topics that are aligned with the types of topics found in academic courses; unlike academic courses that are organized around one academic subject, EAP courses include a wide variety of topics from different disciplines. For example, in academic listening textbooks that Kate has used, the topics emanate from history, political science, biology, astronomy, anthropology, business, computer science, environmental studies, and education. The rationale for these different subjects is that the students in EAP courses may go into these courses in the future or major in the subject at university. Furthermore, using assorted topics is considered as a means to motivate and interest learners.

Students in EAP programs tend to learn a range of academic skills that are pertinent in any academic setting; for example, discussing topics, opinions, problems, or beliefs in small groups, giving a formal presentation, writing a formal academic paper, reading textbooks for main ideas and supporting details, and taking notes.

EAP programs are typically organized by proficiency level similar to the American Council of Teachers of Other Languages (ACTFL) Proficiency Scale, with between three and nine levels of courses from beginner and intermediate to advanced. If there are nine levels, each one includes a low, middle, and high stage (see Figure 3.5).

EAP courses are typically found in newcomers' programs at middle or high school or in exchange programs at universities.

Questions for reflection

- Have you studied either a foreign or second language in one of these programs? What were the strengths and weaknesses of the program? How closely did your program mirror the typical model? What was the same and what was different?
- How was the program model aligned with the goals, needs, and abilities of the language learners?

Program Models in Which Academic Subjects and Language Are Studied

CBI

Communicative language teaching is a methodology for authentic and meaningful learning of social language (for more detail, see Chapter 4). Communicative language teaching has been applied to learning the language of school as well. The language of school, or academic language, describes the kind of language that students need to be able to comprehend when listening to lectures, speaking when giving presentations or

Figure 3.5 EAP levels.

working in small groups, reading in their textbooks, or writing their essays. Academic language is specific to the different academic subjects. For example, in history, a typical textbook would contain descriptions of life in the past. Learners read how one event is the cause of another event. They encounter stories, or narratives, from a first- or second-hand perspective. They understand the specific vocabulary of the time being described or how historians communicate using specific terms. The academic language of history, therefore, is distinct from the language used in science and other academic subjects.

The distinction between social language and academic language and their language functions

In 1979–80, Cummins' research made the distinction between social and academic language (Cummins, 1979, 1980). Social language, basic interpersonal and communicative skills, is the language employed in social settings to establish and maintain social relationships. Social language includes both oral conversations and written communications, such as personal text messages. Social language topics range from discussing the weather and telling stories, to giving directions or asking someone to pick up some milk on the way home from work. Socially, we may employ personal, interactional, and imaginative language functions (Halliday, 1975) to greet someone, make an apology, give advice, express opinions or feelings, show agreement, or tell a story, for example.

When we communicate socially, we consider the contextual factors. We choose what language in which to frame a sentence based on the age, gender, and relationship of the person to us. We also think about ethnicity and race and education. Our communication depends upon our relationship to the other individual, so it may be more informal or more formal.

Academic language, or cognitive academic language proficiency, is the ability to use the language of schooling. Academic language is both oral and written. For example, orally we may listen to a lecture, work in a small group on an academic investigation or lab, or present a research project. In terms of written formats, we may read an article, lab report, or a textbook chapter and write an essay or paper, poem or story. Unlike social language, academic language tends to lean toward formal communications, but there are moments of informal academic language use. The kinds of language functions we often engage in when using academic language are:

- regulatory, used to tell others what to do (e.g., "Open your book to page 112");
- heuristic, used to acquire or learn something about the individual's environment (e.g., "What is the difference between a strike-slip and a reverse fault (in geology)?");
- imaginative, used to create an imaginary environment (e.g., creative writing assignment); and
- representational, using language to convey facts and information (e.g., "The difference between a strike-slip and a reverse fault are...").

As Snow (2014) indicates academic language learners acquire the language to be able describe, classify, define, predict, and sequence.

Different program models will emphasize social or academic language depending on the needs and goals of the language learners.

Many schools from kindergarten to university use the second language contexts to teach English while simultaneously learning academic subjects. Learners study the academic language of history in English when learning the history. The CBI approach regards English not as a separate subject to be taught, but as a vehicle to learn content in other subjects such as science, art, math, and other courses. This way English becomes a "subject learning language" as opposed to the common practices in language contexts where English is the subject matter to learn. Content, or the subject matter, here refers to what is in the texts studied. CBI in science can be seen in a passage entitled "the ways in which environmental pollution can be prevented." Through this text, learners are simultaneously accumulating and understanding the academic language associated with science and pollution. The study of language itself can be an academic topic in the text such as "how idioms are used in diverse cultures." In language teaching and learning, the topics are usually created from the language itself; for example, verb tenses that are the topic of the English lessons and the example sentences offered within the instruction are usually about daily life, such as "I haven't seen him for 2 days" to exemplify the functions of the tense.

CBI is an overarching term to describe the integration of content and language learning. Under this umbrella of CBI, there are a couple of other approaches. In North America, the term CBI is common. Likewise, you may hear it described as *sheltered content instruction*, meaning teaching academic subjects while providing accessible language through supports such as explicit vocabulary instruction, models of the concepts and the language, use of graphic organizers, and opportunities to interact with peers to practice the language. Common models of sheltered content instruction are Sheltered Instruction Observation Protocol (SIOP), Guided Language Acquisition Design (GLAD), Cognitive Academic Language Learning Approach (CALLA), and Specifically-Designed Academic Instruction in English (SDAIE). Each of these models describes how to teach academic subjects while supporting learners in the learning of academic language. Many of the instructional strategies in these instructional models are similar and are supported by the same core second language acquisition research.

CBI is not limited to classes that are made up entirely of ELLs. Steve has team-taught courses based on the "I-BEST" model, which links courses in language and a content area (in his case, Communications) to provide support to students who otherwise might not do well in the class. While ELLs are the most common demographic in these classes, they also include students who face cognitive and socio-economic barriers to academic success.

CLIL is commonly practiced in European school contexts, where English language and content is acquired as mutually supportive input. Language is better acquired, because the input in the subject courses includes relevant and familiar content, which might also be interesting and challenging for learning. The linguistic input, which includes words, meanings, and structures, becomes meaningful through the conveyance of information that is essential to school and to life skills as well. CLIL seems to be so broad that everything learned at school is part of language courses and/or content courses, which, for example, include content elements such as numbers (math), water, plants, animals (science), colors (art), etc. CLIL, therefore, offers content-based language acquisition through pedagogical practices. Language and content acquisition are equally emphasized and embedded in the curriculum in terms of goals and outcomes. In CLIL, the instruction is delivered either by an educator who is trained to teach both content and language, or by two teachers, each of whom teaches language or content.

English as medium of instruction

EMI is another concept used to describe contexts in higher education where academic courses in various disciplines are delivered in English, which is not the first language of learners, but the language they learned or acquired. One such EMI university is Boğaziçi University in Istanbul, Turkey.

The primary concern in EMI instruction is that students who are supposed to have advanced levels of proficiency can learn the content of the academic course in English, which is seen as a vehicle to internationalize higher education and provide more international opportunities for learners at the university and in their future occupations. The ability to learn the content of the courses could prepare the students for working in international contexts and studying in other counties. University professors from the academic field deliver these courses, so they are not taught by language instructors.

There are several challenges in this approach, which include the inadequate level of proficiency of the students and of the professors. When language proficiency falls short of conveying nuances of the subject or comprehending the texts to be read, the learning of the content could be diminished. In effect, the language barrier could block content learning since it is not delivered in the first language. Another issue to consider in this approach is the pedagogical support that professors could provide when learners have difficulty in participating in the lesson using their English verbal or writing skills. Finally, some cultures have rejected the idea of learning in EMI, because it creates a barrier for some learners to achieve their academic goals and/or jeopardizes the culture identity. In Qatar, where the Qatar University was an EMI university prior to 2012 (Lindsey, 2015), Qatari citizens felt that their national university was excluding students who spoke Arabic and that requiring a high level of English proficiency for participating in university academic majors was an unfair burden that created a barrier to their degree attainment. The Supreme Education Council of the State of Qatar changed the language of instruction for the university to Arabic for those who would major in business, law, international affairs, mass communications, social sciences, and humanities. The change to Arabic created interesting challenges for university academics, who grappled with subject matter textbooks not written in Arabic, professors who were fluent in English but not Arabic, the lack of Arabic professors in some disciplines, and how internationalized some fields have become (e.g., business, law, education, and many social sciences). The university did retain the use of EMI for medicine, engineering, technology, and the hard sciences.

Other TESOL focuses have generally taken the place of EMI. Nonetheless, EMI universities still exist worldwide and are considered to enhance learners' abilities in vEnglish in their academic discipline, which will help them in their future careers.

> **Questions for reflection**
>
> - Have you learned English though content integration? If so, do you feel you learned enough of the academic subject and language? Do you think you lost or gained anything as a result of the combination?
> - What were the opportunities and challenges in this approach?
> - If you haven't learned English through content before, how do you think you can use content in teaching English? What could be some initial practices you can develop?

English immersion

Immersion is a term that has many facets in the field of TESOL. It may have positive connotations of being surrounded by English, so as to be able to acquire the language in a natural setting. Some learners excel in this kind of situation. However, others may have negative connotations. For example, if one is surrounded by the language and they do not have any linguistic support, they may not have enough language proficiency to be able to make sense of what they are hearing and seeing, which may become overwhelming and paralyze their learning. Within TESOL, educators recognize both connotations, but tend to describe them a bit differently than the general public. We describe the positive immersion situation as immersion, and the negative immersion situation as "sink or swim" or *submersion*, which really conveys the feeling of being left to one's own devices. These models generally focus on those who "swim," but pay less attention to those who "sink."

David Sedaris, in his short story *Me Talk Pretty One Day* describes a French immersion classroom taught in Paris (Sedaris, 2000). He describes a teacher who seemed to actually enjoy the discomfort and struggle that her students endured during the class, and who deliberately made them uncomfortable—much as one would be uncomfortable when thrown into a swimming pool with no knowledge of how to swim. The story covers both sides of immersion, ranging from Sedaris describing a time when he was so despondent about his language abilities that he began buying all of his food from vending machines, to a time when he felt that he truly understood his teacher and communicated back in French, instantaneously, without having to think of what each word meant in English. Sedaris's story is an interesting and humorous description of the potential that immersion classrooms have to transform students, but with a dark undertone acknowledging that not every student in his class was successful.

Immersion can be further described as having access to a high degree of linguistic input, which is the language we can hear or read. According to the work of Krashen (1982, 1985), input is essential to second language acquisition. Without input, and specifically comprehensible input, ELLs cannot acquire the language. Interestingly, though, the input must be comprehensible to the learner, meaning that the learner can understand and comprehend what they are hearing and seeing so they have access to the materials. If the input is incomprehensible, the learner does not have access points into the language, like a climber does not have toe holds on a mountain. In this situation, the ELL cannot acquire the language and may feel overwhelmed, frustrated, or paralyzed.

Language programs of all kinds will provide some degree of immersion in English in order to provide input for second language learning. The degree of English varies according to the context, ELL population, instructional methodology, learning goals, and learners' needs. In some programs, there may be a focus more on English with the instructor speaking English all or nearly all of the class time, and in others the instructor may employ some of the learners' first language (if the learners share a first language). In this next section, we will discuss program models that employ both the first and second languages to varying degrees.

Dual language/bilingual education and multilingual education

Dual language and bilingual education have been in practice in countries that receive immigration such as America and Canada for decades. In the *dual language model*, learners are offered content and literacy courses in two languages, in which case the objective is to make nonnative speakers of English bilingual and biliterate speakers. The process of learning in both languages is proportionate in all domains of the curriculum.

The learner population in bilingual education programs may be (a) ELLs who come to another country at a young age and remain exposed to second language, which is the societal language; or (b) ELLs and those speaking the societal language each learning the others' language. The former is called one-way bilingual education and the latter is called dual language or two-way bilingual education (see Figure 3.6).

In one-way bilingual programs, immigrants develop integrative motivation to be affiliated with the society and develop language skills. However, if they are of school age, and if they must attend school, they need to speak the language of instruction,

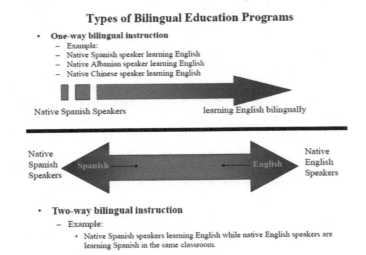

Figure 3.6 Types of bilingual education programs.

which is English in this case, so they are supposed to attend schools where they are supported for language development. There are many ways of achieving this. The main goal of one-way bilingual programs is for the learners to learn English with support from their L1.

The purpose of one-way bilingual programs may be to maintain the learners' first language while learning the second. This variation is called a *maintenance bilingual program* (see Figure 3.7). In these programs, ELLs would receive the majority of instruction in their home language, so they may maintain their abilities to speak, listen, read, and write in their first language. The target language has less of a priority in maintenance bilingual programs.

Another type of bilingual program is the *transitional bilingual program*. In one-way bilingual programs, the ELLs are offered courses in their native language to make sure that they learn the academic content of the courses while they also acquire English. This model is based on the aim that the learners will shift from native language instruction to general education classes delivered in English only. This model aligns with literacy research that showed that learners find it easier to learn to read and write in their L1 and transfer these literacy skills to the L2 than to try to learn to read and write in the L2 only (Cummins, 1994; August et al., 2000; Zaretsky & Schwartz, 2016). Transitional bilingual programs are then a process of developing L1 literacy, keeping the learners learning academic subjects with their grade-level peers while they develop language skills that will help them survive in the school system.

In transitional bilingual programs, depending on the proficiency levels of the learners, the language of instruction is the learner's first language most of the time, with some English interjected. Throughout the duration of the program, the L1 use is gradually reduced by the instructor until the students are using English the vast majority of the time at the conclusion of their program (see Figure 3.8).

In *two-way bilingual programs*, both populations of learners, ELLs and the native English speakers, are each learning the other's language. For example, Chinese speakers learning English and English speakers learning Chinese.

The learners' motivation is also integrative in two-way bilingual programs, meaning they wish to be able to communicate and interact with the target language culture. The

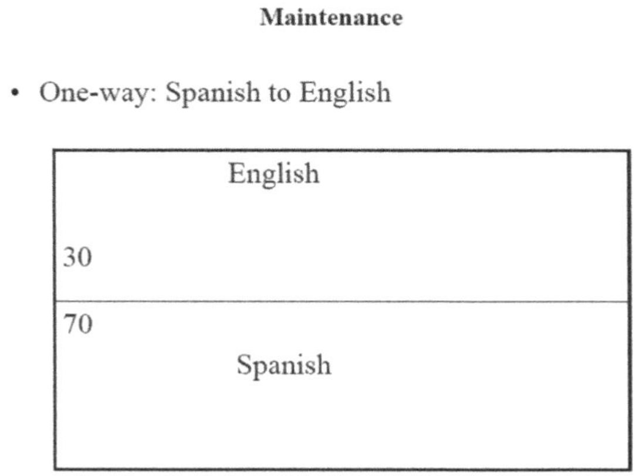

Maintenance

- One-way: Spanish to English

English
30
70 Spanish

Figure 3.7 Maintenance bilingual program example.

Transitional

- One-way: Spanish to English

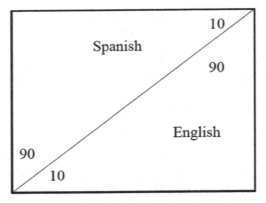

Figure 3.8 Language use in one-way transitional bilingual programs.

Transitional

- Two-way: Spanish to English and Vice Versa

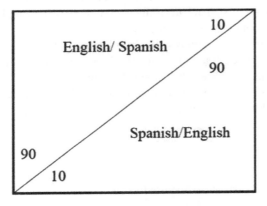

Figure 3.9 Two-way transitional bilingual education programs.

main goal of two-way bilingual programs is to develop bilingual communities in which individuals can communicate in many languages and both languages are valued at the same status. Two-way bilingual programs are typically transitional (see Figure 3.9).

We will delve into two options with more than one educator in a bilingual education class.

One educator with two languages and academic content

This way of conducting bilingual courses is common in CBI that is offered in the second language only. The educators of such courses are often those who studied their major subject in English and developed adequate content knowledge in English too. However, they may not have the pedagogical training that they need to deliver these content courses in English only. These educators are not concerned with language teaching and learning goals since their aim is to teach content in English rather than teaching English with content focus. They might be supplying learners with limited and unsystematic support with learning unknown vocabulary items and genre-specific terms. Such support might usually include giving the meaning of the unknown words in L1 as lists or glossary or describing or defining it in L1.

In courses with one educator, two languages, and academic content, students are proficient enough to follow the content courses delivered in English. The exact situation in such courses may change depending on the context: students might have had an intensive English year before they start CBI programs. They may follow some science content courses such as math, biology, chemistry, or physics in English while most verbal and social courses are offered in L1. One concern with these courses is that the learners' potential inability to understand aspects of the language in which the course is taught might form a crucial impediment to development of content knowledge. Another is the possibility that even the students' *L1* abilities may not be sufficient to allow them to understand the material of the content courses. More specifically, students are usually expected to understand first in their own languages to be able to comprehend it when offered in English. On the other hand, advantages include intensive exposure to the contextually rich language, which students might find meaningful and relevant. For example, when learners see a mathematical formula with a piece of instruction or a follow-up explanation, they might easily relate to the meaning by drawing on the mathematical symbol and grasp the intended meaning. The visuals designed and placed in science course books also offer students a chance for inference of relevant contextual meaning. Therefore, such courses provide many opportunities for acquiring language implicitly and through natural exposure and interaction rather than learning it explicitly through direct instruction and explanation. The former also offers students courses in a way in which they discover meaning without educators' monitoring and assessment, thereby encouraging them to become autonomous language learners alongside the content.

Two educators—one content expert in one language, the other a language specialist in the other language

This bilingual instructional practice requires two educators present in the classroom at the same time. One teaches content, while the other educator uses English to support the learning of the course content. The cooperation between the educators is designed and conducted with a planned flow of the lesson where each of the languages has a function and role to play. One scenario involving this technique would include a content educator in science, who introduces the specific learning content for the first time, coupled with a language educator, who conducts the follow-up tasks and activities in English. This combination generates a classroom context in which meaningful interaction and exposure to interactive use of English are offered continuously. The educators are expected to shift between major and minor roles while synchronously implementing the syllabus. Each educator is supposed to have complementary and supportive roles at each stage of the course flow.

Such a bilingual teaching practice makes two languages continuously active and accessible and contributes to the learning of concepts in two languages, which might also strengthen the acquisition process. On the practical side, the language use is not strictly one language at one time, but two languages are allowed to be used by the learners. They are exposed to input or materials written in both languages. In some cases, they read a text in English and talk about it in their own language, while in another they read in their own languages but present in the second language, English. The key principle in such classrooms is that educators use one of the first and second languages consistently so learners can know to whom to speak which language. In such teaching, learners do not switch from one language to another but shuttle between them to create meaning in its strongest sense. This process of language use is called "translanguaging" (García & Lin, 2017). Translanguaging helps learners, particularly those whose second language is linguistically weaker, to use the stronger native language as a scaffold while learning content in two languages. Considering the learning of the content is closely related to the level of language proficiency, the inability to comprehend what educators are saying in the second language can lead to an irrecoverable knowledge gap in learners. However, when they are allowed to function with two languages while learning in a bilingual classroom, this decreases their psychological stress regarding the language barriers and gives them an opportunity to participate in the lesson without any reservation. When they are not allowed to use the all linguistic resources they have (like both languages), they might shy away from active engagement in the course, thereby having challenges in learning content.

Questions for reflection

- Do you think you could work within simultaneous teaching with two languages?
- Which of the above approaches to bilingual education would better suit your teaching?

Bilingual education: Opportunities and challenges

Bilingual education is a hotly contested instructional methodology and can be contentious in some communities. In a rousing retort, Krashen (1999) responded to the "false assumptions and outright distortions that led to the passage of Proposition 227 in California" in 1998, a legislative move that eliminated bilingual education in favor of "English-only" instruction. Maintenance bilingual programs are not well received in communities whose population feels threatened by having other languages commonly spoken in the community. In these communities, some individuals feel that immigrants and refugees, as well as long-term residents, should respect the target language community and learn to speak the target language quickly in order to assimilate into the community. In these situations, multilingualism and multiculturalism are not community values. Transitional bilingual programs are also vulnerable to lack of community support if the community feels the ELLs are not learning English fast or well enough. Since public education is based on community funding, community attitudes and beliefs have considerable influence on language policy.

Bilingual education programs have their challenges that must be overcome to implement them well. We will focus on three main challenges. First, the number of languages in a school. In many communities, particularly cities, it is common to have more than one L1 spoken by the students. So, in Seattle, according to the Seattle Public Schools, there are 78 different languages spoken, "more than any other zip code in the United States" (Seattle Public Schools, n.d). In a heterogeneous L1 setting such as Seattle, educators cannot implement bilingual programs that emphasize only one L1, because is not equitable. Generally, there are not enough of the same L1 speakers in the same school at the same grade level to implement a bilingual program in heterogeneous L1 settings. Seattle's diverse linguistic population is markedly different from homogeneous L1 settings, such as in Texas or California, where the vast majority of ELLs speak Spanish, which are perfect for bilingual education programs.

Second, finding enough bilingual educators who are at an advanced level of proficiency orally and in writing in both languages and endorsed to teach an academic subject is extremely challenging. Educators need to be advanced speakers and writers of both languages and be able to achieve at advanced or high intermediate levels on tests of spoken and written language in their L2. If a person had a L1 of English, and learned Spanish, for instance, the individual would need to take oral and written proficiency tests in Spanish. The individual would have to obtain their teaching license in a content subject such as English language arts, science, math, history, or elementary education. School districts must be able to find enough highly proficient speakers and writers of both languages who have passed the language tests and who are licensed to teach all the subjects at the different grade levels. It would be difficult to imagine finding enough licensed bilingual educators to make such a system work.

Third, when implementing bilingual education, it is difficult for educators to manage the amount of L1 and L2 they are using in the classroom, let alone the language the learners are using and how often. Some educators put up flags to represent which language is to be used on which day. Others teach one subject in one language, while another subject is taught in another. The least effective way is to translate each sentence said in the target language into the L1 of the students, so that the students do not try to make sense of the information in the target language, but instead wait for the translation.

One solution to some of these challenges is to have more than one educator in each class. In an instructional scenario where there are two educators in-class delivery of content and language can be managed more effectively. If the educator teaching content speaks both languages, s/he is expected to use both languages while teaching. If not, another educator who speaks English, preferably an English educator, cooperates.

Bilingual education has many benefits for learners and society, which may supersede the challenges. Benefits for learners of one-way bilingual programs are multifold. For learners, they have support in their L1 to learn the academic content without falling behind while learning English and they continue to develop their L1 oral and literacy skills, which will aid in L2 learning. Furthermore, bilinguals outperform monolinguals on tests of intelligence in certain cognitive skills, such as metalinguistic awareness, metacognition, creative thinking, problem solving, and abstract reasoning skills (for an excellent summary of this body of research, see Adesope et al., 2010). In other words, bilinguals are smarter in many important areas.

For the community and society, diversity is a valuable commodity. Members of diverse societies tend to be more open-minded and tolerant, because individuals know and care for others from difficult cultures. Members of diverse societies are better informed, because they have better understandings of the world and cultures through their interaction. This knowledge benefits members in their professional lives when they interact globally for business, science, medicine, education, arts, and governmental functions. Diverse societies tend to be more creative and innovative due to the cross-cultural influences. Look at how many different types of food styles you see in London and the creative ways chefs are combining different ethnic foods to create all new cuisines.

Questions for reflection

- Have you learned bilingually? If so, what were the benefits for you? What were the benefits for your community and school?
- Have you observed a bilingual lesson? What are some of the ways that the educator included and balanced both languages? Did the class also include academic content? If so, how did the instructor balance the development of both languages and the academic subject knowledge?
- What do you think are the strengths and weaknesses of bilingual programs? How might the weaknesses be remedied?

Chapter Conclusions

Similar to the French wineries concept of "terroir" that describes all influences from the sky vertically to the earth and horizontally along the earth that influence the flavor of a grape, there are untold numbers of factors that are significant influences on educational choices made when teaching second languages. These factors range from cultural and social to political and practical.

Educators may be familiar with many of these factors when they accept a new position, but others will be learned through experience. It is essential for educators to be as informed as possible about their context for teaching, so they may be as effective and comfortable as possible. When the educator is informed and comfortable in an instructional environment, the language learners experience less cognitive dissonance and are more likely to succeed.

Ultimately, in the language classroom, both the students' and the educators' cultures, goals, and expectations are influenced and interact with context. Both groups bring their home cultures into the classroom interactions, and learn through their own cultural perspectives. Neither culture is inherently better or superior. Culture just exists and influences how we communicate. Language and culture are interwoven, so that we cannot pull them apart. Culture is key to understanding language and learning.

Discussion Questions

1 Share with your peers the context(s) in which you would like to teach and what you know of the context for teaching and learning. Compare and contrast different educational settings for cultural similarities and differences, design of the educational system, and roles and expectations of educators and learners.

2 Which program model would you prefer to work in and why? Which one seems the most effective for second language learning and why? Compare and contrast the different models. Does your choice to work in one model versus another have any relationship to how effective you think it is? If so, why? If not, why not?

3 Discuss your thoughts about the different bilingual program models. Which are the most effective for second language learning? Which are the less effective? Why?

4 How would you adapt to an instructional setting without technology (e.g., the internet, a computer, and a printer)? What steps would you take? What resources would you have to develop/find and how would you do that? Would you be happy working in this kind of setting? If so, why? If not, why not?

Tasks

1 Once you have lived and taught in another context than your home country, do you think you become more aware of context for teaching and learning? More skilled in navigating cultural differences, particularly as they pertain to the classroom? More versatile in your instructional methods? If so, why and how? If not, why not?

2 How might you help influence public perception and discourse about second language learning and teaching? What would be the benefits and drawbacks for engaging in these types of discussions? What skills does one need to be successful in these discussions? What vehicles for influencing others regarding language policy can you think of?

   a. Investigate a learning context, in which you may like to teach.

      i. The country's education system/structure (K–adult)—Describe the programs, options, typical classes, tests, etc. What is this system known for? What is unique about it? How is it similar or different to your home country?

      ii. Curriculum—What do students have to take in terms of courses and topics at which levels? Who decides this? Is there a state- or school-offered curriculum (plan for what to teach when)?

      iii. Standards for language teaching (if applicable)—Standards are expectations for instruction (ACTFL Proficiency Standards, national standards, TESOL Standards, etc.). Standards usually tell educators and stakeholders what the educational priorities and levels are for the system.

      iv. Instructional situation—In the classroom, what does it look like? What is the typical style(s) of teaching (pros and cons of the typical methods/

approaches)? What are the cool aspects of it and the challenging ones? How many students are there per class? What materials are available or needed? Should you know the native language of the students?

v. Cultural factors to consider when teaching.

vi. Educational resources typically available.

Further reading/read and discuss

Read about NNESTs in the NNEST newsletter article from http://nnest.moussu.net/resources.html

Read García and Lin's *Translanguaging* chapter (2017).

Read Krashen's *Condemned without a Trial* (1999).

References

Adesope, O. O., Lavin, T., Thompson, T., & Ungerleider, C. (2010). A systematic review and meta-analysis of the cognitive correlates of bilingualism. *Review of Educational Research*, *80*(2), 207–245.

August, D., Calderón, M., & Carlo, M. (2000). *Transfer of skills from Spanish to English: A study of young learners*. Report for practioners, parents, and policy makers. ED-98-CO-0071. Center for Applied Linguistics.

Braine, G. (2012). Non-native-speaker English teachers. In Carol A. Chappelle (Ed.), *The encyclopedia of applied linguistics* (pp. 1–5). Wiley.

Brown, H. D. (1994). *Principles of language learning and teaching* (3rd ed.). Prentice Hall.

Brown, H. D. (2007). *Principles of language learning and teaching* (5th ed.). Longman.

Crystal, D. (2003). *English as a global language*, 2nd ed. NY: Cambridge.

Cummins, J. (1979). Cognitive/academic language proficiency, linguistic interdependence, the optimum age question and some other matters. *Working Papers on Bilingualism*, No. 19, 121–129.

Cummins, J. (1980). Psychological assessment of immigrant children: Logic or intuition? *Journal of Multilingual and Multicultural Development*, *1*(2), 97–111.

Cummins, J. (1994). Interdependence of first and second language proficiency in bilingual children. In E. Bialystok (Ed.), *Language processes in bilingual children* (pp. 70–89). Cambridge University Press.

Dee, T. S. (2005). A teacher like me: Does race, ethnicity, or gender matter?. *The American Economic Review*, *95*(2), 158–165. http://www.jstor.org/stable/4132809

Dewey, J. (1933). *How we think*. Heath.

DuPraw, M. E., & Axner, M. (1997). *Working on common cross-cultural communication challenges*. PBS Online. https://www.pbs.org/ampu/crosscult.html (accessed March 5, 2021).

García, O., & Lin, A. M. Y. (2017). Translanguaging in bilingual education. In O. García, A. M. Y. Lin, & S. May (Eds.), *Bilingual and multilingual education* (3rd ed., pp. 117–130). Springer.

Halliday, M. A. K. (1975). *Learning how to mean*. Edward Arnold.

Hofstede, G. (2001). *Culture's consequences: Comparing values, behaviors, institutions, and organizations across nations* (2nd ed.). Sage.

Krashen, S. (1982). *Principles and practice in second language acquisition*. Pergamon.

Krashen, S. (1985). *The input hypothesis: Issues and implications*. Longman.

Krashen, S. (1999). *Condemned without a trial: Bogus arguments against bilingual education*. Heinemann.

Lindsey, U. (2015, June). How teaching in English divides the Arab world. *The Chronicle of Higher Education*. https://www.chronicle.com/article/How-Teaching-in-English/230705/?key=TWx2IwI7YXVKNHw1Nm4RaDhQYHNvZU17NnJIbXotbl9XGQ==#st_refDomain=&st_refQuery= (accessed March 5, 2021).

Linville, H. A., & Staehr Fenner, D. (2019). Preparing teacher to be advocates for English learners. In L. C. de Oliveira (Ed.), *The handbook of TESOL in K–12* (pp. 341–356). Wiley-Blackwell.

Llurda, E. (2004). Non-native-speaker teachers and English as an International Language. *International Journal of Applied Linguistics*, *14*(3), 314–323. https://doi.org/10.1111/j.1473-4192.2004.00068.x

McIntosh, P. (2004). White privilege: Unpack the invisible knapsack. In P. S. Rothenberg (Ed.), *Race, class, and gender in the United States: An integrated study* (6th ed.) (pp. 176–180). Worth Publishers.

Medgyes, P. (1992). Native or non-native: Who's worth more? *ELT Journal*, *46*(4), 340–349.

Moussu, L., & Llurda, E. (2008). Non-native English-speaking English language teachers: History and research. *Language Teaching*, *41*(3), 315–348. https://doi.org/10.1017/S0261444808005028

Piller, I. (2012). Intercultural communication: An overview. In C. Bratt Paulston, S. F. Kiesling, & E. S. Rangel (Eds.), *The handbook of intercultural discourse and communication* (pp. 3–18). Wiley-Blackwell.

Samovar, L. A., Porter, R. E., & McDaniel, E. R. (2010). *Communication between cultures* (7th ed.). Wadsworth Cengage.

Scollon, R., Scollon, S. W., & Jones, R. H. (2012). *Intercultural communication: A discourse approach* (3rd ed.). Wiley-Blackwell.

Seattle Public Schools. (n.d.). *Honoring home languages*. https://www.seattleschools.org/departments/english_language_learners/honoring_home_languages (accessed March 5, 2021).

Sedaris, D. (2000). *Me talk pretty one day*. Little, Brown.

Seidlhofer, B. (2002). The shape of things to come? Some basic questions about English as a lingua franca. In K. Knapp & C. Meierkord (Eds.), *Lingua franca communication* (pp. 269–302). Peter Lang Publishing.

Snow, M.A. (2014). Content-based and immersion models of second/foreign language teaching. In M.A. Celce-Murcia, D. Brinton, and M.A. Snow (Eds.), Teaching English as a Second or Foreign Language, 4th ed (pp. 438-454). Boston, MA: National Geographic Learning/ Heinle Cengage.

Suttie, J. (2016, October 28). *Four ways teachers can reduce implicit bias. Greater Good Magazine*. The Greater Good Science Center at the University of California, Berkeley. https://greatergood.berkeley.edu/article/item/four_ways_teachers_can_reduce_implicit_bias (accessed March 5, 2021).

Zaretsky, E., & Schwartz, M. (Eds.). (2016). *Cross-linguistic transfer in reading in multilingual contexts*. John Benjamins Publishing.

Part Two

TESOL Professionals' Knowledge of Linguistics and Second Language Acquisition

4

What Are the Five Areas of Linguistics and How Do They Help TESOL Educators? Why Do TESOL Educators Need a Working Understanding of Linguistics?

This chapter is designed to provide some general definitions of language and categories of language patterns that will be helpful in visualizing how TESOL educators approach linguistic patterns in their instruction. These categories are traditionally considered to be descriptive of language use in practice, so they are grouped as "descriptive linguistics." You will also encounter some essential concepts from language acquisition and linguistic theory. Toward the end of the chapter, information about sociolinguistics and functional linguistics can be found. As you read about these areas, consider how this information helps you as an instructor.

Learning Outcomes

At the conclusion of this chapter, you will be able to:

- articulate reasons that features of an ELL's L1 may impede the learning of a different language
- describe unique features of the language you are teaching that may create challenges for learners
- explain the most basic concepts of linguistics that are present in all languages
- describe the role that linguistics plays in informing language teaching

If you have ever experienced the embarrassing moment of being unable to pronounce a word in another language, and wished you understood L2 pronunciation more, this vignette highlights one educator's process in learning L2 pronunciation and teaching it.

TESOL Voices

Learning About Linguistics Helps Improve Language Learning and Teaching

Many people are intimidated by the pronunciation of French. While it sounds divine, it is not necessarily easy to discern the pronunciation patterns. I learned French in college after having studied Spanish for 2 years in high school and Italian for 1 year in college. The pronunciation of Spanish and Italian were so

---

Introduction to TESOL: Becoming a language teaching professional, First Edition. Kate Mastruserio Reynolds, Kenan Dikilitaş, and Steve Close.

much easier to mimic than French, though, until I identified some patterns and learned about phonology.

Phonology is the study of the sound system of a language. From the first day in my French course, I began comparing and contrasting the sounds I was hearing. The word *eau* in French sounded like *oh* in English. Then I began identifying patterns. In French, there are sounds that are not pronounced at the ends of words, usually, a final -t or -s. So, in this case, it was similar to English's silent *e* ending. However, you do pronounce the final -t or -s when it is followed by an e; for example, in the words *forte* or *framboise*.

As an adult, I had the meta-analytical ability to step back and monitor my own production of French and compare it with the target pronunciation. In my third year of French study, I was required to take a phonetics course, in which I learned about the pronunciation patterns of words and sentences, the intonation and the rhythm. We also learned about the pronunciation of individual consonants and vowels, and coded the sounds, so we could distinguish them. The vowels were pronounced so differently than English ones! I learned the differences between *corps* /kɔʁ/ and *coeur* /kɔœʁ/ in French; between these words there are only minor pronunciation differences, but a major difference in meaning between body and heart.

Later, I became a TESOL professional and began teaching ESL pronunciation for university students. Of course, I had already studied English phonology in my grad program and learned about the patterns of English phonology. Because of the knowledge I had about the sounds of English and the patterns of pronunciation, I could choose the focus of instruction on which consonants and vowels to teach, because they were challenging for my population of ELLs. I could also explain the patterns of intonation for statements and questions, the rises in pitch when a word is the focus of a sentence, and the word stress working within the rhythm of English sentences while also creating that rhythm. I could take my knowledge and transform it into practical examples and create stimulating activities for ELLs to practice those phonological patterns. Without the knowledge of phonology, I wouldn't be able to explain the slight difference between pronouncing an r or an l, an area of frustration for many ELLs. With this knowledge, I am a more informed and effective educator.

Kate Mastruserio Reynolds
Professor
Central Washington University

What Is Language?

According to Sapir (1921), language is "a purely human and non-instinctive method of communicating ideas, emotions and desires by means of voluntarily produced symbols" (p. 8). This has been one of the main definitions over the past century. It highlights that language is possessed and used by humans to communicate and express themselves using arbitrarily formed linguistic forms that are based on sound-meaning matching that evolved over time. To better understand what language is, we review its characteristics, which characterize human language. Language is:

- *arbitrary* in that the relationship between a word and the object or concept is not a reasoned one but a sound-meaning matching that has become habituated through real-time experiences over time;
- *systematic* in that it is produced on the basis of a finite number of rules that allow us to create an infinite number of possible structural linguistic combinations. For example, there are particular rules in phonology (the sound system), morphology (word formation), syntax (the order and arrangement of words within a sentence), lexicon (vocabulary of a language), semantics (meanings of words in isolation), and pragmatics (meaning in context);
- generally *vocal* depending on the active use of sounds human generates;
- *symbolic* in that its sounds or visual orthography convey ideas and concepts that are used to communicate with others; and
- *culture-dependent* in that human language builds on its social culture when generating meaning with language.

While the definition of language might seem obvious, there are in fact many variables that we either take for granted, or do not consider. Generally, we tend to define language according to our own experiences. In fact, postmodern theory of language is based around the belief that the language we use actually *constructs* our reality. We see the world according to how we describe it. For ELLs, learning a new language is more than simply switching vocabulary and grammar. It often involves a revisioning of the world itself. Understanding basic concepts of language from a generalized perspective (what do all languages do?) rather than a comparative one (how are other languages like mine?) can help educators to understand their overall task in the classroom and, more specifically, issues that may arise that have more to do with worldview than verbal or written expression.

What Is Linguistic Knowledge?

Linguistic knowledge refers to a set of rules that allows for creating an infinite number of sentences and, in turn utterances by using a finite number of rules. Linguistic knowledge is in essence the knowledge that newly born babies acquire by exposure to initial interaction with parents and/or babysitters who look after them. This set of knowledge is composed of more or less the same content in all speakers of the same languages. Chomsky calls this competence, which is universally found in human genes and can be transformed, thereby leading to the acquisition of the specific language being exposed in the social environment. A baby is born potentially and genetically ready to acquire any language on earth as long as s/he is adequately exposed to it within an interactive social environment. This shows the close relationship between human genes containing linguistic knowledge and the role of context of interaction in the community. Linguistic knowledge must then be composed of all the universally applicable basic linguistic principles that enable such geographically free language acquisition. In addition to this, being able to speak other languages even after one has been learned depends on such principles since we all learn other languages with reference to the first language, which facilitates our understanding of the concepts and rules in other languages.

Creative aspect of linguistic knowledge

Language knowledge allows us to generate new and novel ways to express ourselves. It allows us to be able to produce phrases by purposefully combining words, sentences by appropriately combining phrases, as well as longer discourses by creatively combining sentences. This way, we can produce original sentences that we have never heard or produced, which makes us creative users of linguistic knowledge. This view, claimed by Chomsky, accounts for the fact that language is not a response behavior to a stimulus (as proposed in behaviorism). We can use the same linguistic form to mean or imply another meaning. For example, some words have multiple senses (especially body organs—face, hand, head, etc.) or meanings depending on the context of use. Some phrases might have several other meanings depending on how, where, and when they are articulated. One-on-one correspondence then could inhibit the potential rich language use in terms of meaning-making processes. The reusability (the same form having multiple linguistic functions) of linguistic forms is also what makes language creative. Therefore, we can make use of our linguistic knowledge and generate an infinite number and variety of linguistic forms, which differ in length, content, and meaning.

Universal grammar

According to Chomsky, human beings are born with an innate capacity to learn language(s) they are exposed to. As discussed in the previous section, the universally representative linguistic knowledge is more specifically described as universal grammar (UG), a dominant linguistic theory from the 1950s to the 1990s introduced by Chomsky (1976, 1980, 1981). UG as a theory mainly argues that humans are endowed with a specific linguistic faculty that is richly structured and these rich details are encoded in the genes and transmitted via DNA to the other generations. Some linguists attempt to unravel these universal properties and principles that come by birth and that characterize all languages spoken on earth.

Competence vs. performance

The linguistic knowledge we introduced earlier is also known as competence: knowledge that is statically available in the human mind. Competence as an implicit system of rules is what enables human to acquire language and develop linguistic abilities to communicate with others. It is the ingredient or abstract knowledge that is to be used to create language systems in our minds. It is what we know about language.

The form of this knowledge that we see is called performance. Performance is how competence has been transformed practically into usable knowledge for the purpose of communication. Performance represents a person's actual use of language—what they can do with language.

This distinction, while it has its critics, can be valuable to talk about what ELLs know about language in comparison with how they use it.

How are first languages acquired?

Linguistics describes not only the linguistic knowledge possessed by speakers of a particular language, but also the linguistic input available in an environment: both these resources influence the particular linguistic patterns acquired and how they are acquired. It is now well established that babies without any significant neurological or physical irregularity can acquire their spoken L1 in a short time with relative ease. They are merely immersed in a linguistic environment and pick up language without teaching by people in the immediate environment. They follow a similar pattern in developmental stages of acquisition, starting with one-word production combined into simple sentences with missing articles and prepositions, for example. They move on to more complex expressions, finishing the majority of their L1 acquisition by the age of 6 years. Yet they master the complex structure and build a comprehensive lexicon with relative ease.

In TESOL, many professionals believe that second languages are acquired, or picked up, in the same way as the first language and they believe that acquisition and learning are different processes. Others believe that the processes of L2 acquisition and learning are similar. We will explore that more in Chapter 5.

Questions for reflection

- How do you believe language is structured in the brain? Do you agree with Chomsky about UG?
- What are your beliefs? Are first and second language acquired in the same manner?

The Areas of Linguistics and Their Application in the L2 Classroom

Imagine entering a classroom to teach second language learners. In order to be prepared to explain how language works and why, as well as answer learners' questions about language use, we need to be informed about systems of language. TESOL educators need basic knowledge of linguistics for three main reasons.

First, language is a patterned, structural system that has a particular way of functioning, which first needs to be understood. It is a familiar scenario that teachers whose L1 is the language they teach, known as native speakers, may not know the systematic structure of their language, so they may be challenged to explain particular rules and how they work. While they can intuitively say whether sentences are acceptable or not, they may be unable to judge the sentence's grammaticality. They may not be able to give linguistic explanations unless they have been prepared to do so.

Second, language patterns can be taught. Knowledge of language, for example, will help teachers explain structures, meanings, and language functions to students using relevant language by giving proper examples as models. All language teaching resources include example sentences or discourses in the form of reading passages, dialogues, sample paragraphs, and instructions. These passages are purposefully written to showcase how language is used and facilitate students' language learning. Teachers need to be able to understand language structures at different levels and from different perspectives, so as to convey the intricate variations of English to students.

Third, language is a living and dynamic structure that is used by individuals coming from diverse cultural and linguistic backgrounds. Language usage and patterns evolve over time within regions and different communities. One reason for the numerous irregularities in English grammar is the interactions of English with speakers from other languages (e.g., Anglo-Saxon, Latin, and French) in history.

An awareness of the evolving nature of language helps TESOL educators to understand that English learned and used around the world is influenced by multiple factors, which might result in differences in usage. There are multiple "Englishes" throughout the world and even within specific countries, just as there are multiple dialects and accents in any language.

These three reasons illustrate that when teaching languages TESOL educators need knowledge of linguistics and how language works as a system, instead of only being able to speak a language. As you read in Chapter 3, context of ELT is multivariate. Around the world, there are distinctive usages of English of which TESOL educators need to be aware so that they can justify and explain when needed. For learners, misunderstandings can arise as a result of linguistic concepts (and ensuing perspectives on larger issues) and educators should be aware of these deep-seated principles as they might occur in the thinking of students.

Areas of Linguistics

Linguistics is a field in and of itself, and exhaustive explanations of all of the principles used within the field would require a complete text. Therefore, we have chosen specific concepts and principles that have direct bearing on ELT, and attempted to describe them at the most basic level. In this chapter, we will provide a brief description of each area of linguistics as it pertains to ELT.

Phonology

Phonology is the study of the sounds of a given language. It describes the way sounds function within a given language and operates at the level of sound systems and abstract sound units. Those who study phonology are concerned with segments and suprasegmentals. Segments are the phonemes or sounds of a language and how these sounds interact when placed together. We typically call these consonants and vowels in English. Suprasegments are the patterns of words, sentences, and utterances. Suprasegments include intonation, rhythm, word stress, prominence/sentence stress, thought groups, and connected speech.

Spelling and sounds

English has a *deep orthography*, which means that spelling and sounds differ to a great extent. There is a less direct relationship between the spelling of the words and their pronunciations. Therefore, a reader must learn the arbitrary or unusual pronunciations of words. The orthography (spelling) of words is misleading, especially in English. One sound can be represented by several different combinations of letters. For example, all of the following words contain the same vowel sound: h*e*, bel*ie*ve, L*ee*, C*ae*sar, k*ey*, am*oe*ba, loudl*y*, mach*i*ne, p*eo*ple, and s*ea*.

Other languages are characterized by a *shallow orthography* in that the words are pronounced as they are written/spelled to a large extent. There is almost a direct or one-to-one correspondence between the form of the word and the way it sounds.

The International Phonetic Alphabet (IPA) was constructed to provide linguists a shared alphabet, so all linguists could be specific in their references to sounds (Table 4.1). It provides common symbols for the same sounds used in a variety of languages, which makes it easier to see how words with different spellings are pronounced. The symbols used in this alphabet can be used to represent all sounds of all human languages. TESOL educators memorize all of these symbols in order to be able to explain different sounds, and identify the word a learner is actually pronouncing in comparison with commonly accepted pronunciations of it. Also, most foreign language dictionaries use the IPA, so it is a useful tool to understand how words sounds when you have not heard them pronounced before.

Knowing the sounds of a language is only a small part of phonology though. It is also important to know that one word can be changed into another by simply changing one sound in the word. Consider the differences between the words *time* and *dime*. The words are identical except for the first sound. The /t/ and /d/ sounds can therefore distinguish words and are called *contrasting sounds*. They are distinctive sounds in English, and all distinctive sounds are classified as *phonemes*. Sounds are indicated in print by writing them with a slash before and after as you see above.

Table 4.1 International Phonetic Alphabet.

International Phonetic Alphabet for English pronunciation									
P	**Pet**	d	**Din**	h	**Heat**	ʌ	**Cut**		
B	**Bin**	n	**Neat**	l	**Leak**	aj	**Sight**		
M	**Mine**	s	**Seat**	r	**Reek**	ɔj	**Toy**		
F	**Feet**	z	**Zeal**	j	**You**	ɪ	**Pit**		
V	**Vet**	č	**Check**	w	**With**	ɛ	**Bet**		
Θ	**Thigh**	ǰ	**Jim**	i	**Heel**	ʊ	**Goose**		
Ð	**Thy**	ʌ̆	**Which**	e	**Bait**	ɔ	**Awe**		
Š	**Shill**	k	**Kiss**	u	**Boot**	a	**Bar**		
Ž	**Azure**	g	**Give**	o	**Coat**	ə	**Sofa**		
T	**Tick**	ŋ	**Sing**	æ	**Bat**	aw	**Cow**		

Consonants

The production of any speech sound involves the movement of air. Air is pushed through the lungs, larynx (vocal folds), and vocal tract (the oral and nasal cavities). Air is passes through the mouth or nose and is influenced in the making of sounds by the parts of the vocal tract that it is guided by. They are classified according to *voicing, aspiration, nasal/oral sounds, places of articulation*, and *manners of articulation*.

Voicing is whether the vocal cords vibrate or not. The sound /s/ is called voiceless because there is no vibration, and the sound /z/ is called voiced because the vocal cords do vibrate when uttered. Place your hand on your throat and say these sounds to see the difference in the vibration.

Only three sounds in English have *aspiration*, the sounds /b/, /p/, and /t/. An extra puff of air is pushed out when these sounds begin a word or stressed syllable. Hold a piece of paper close to your mouth when saying the words pin and spin. You should notice extra air when you say pin. Aspiration is indicated in transcription with a superscript h, as in /p^h/.

Nasal sounds are produced when the velum (the soft palate located in the back of the roof of the mouth) is lowered and air is passed through the nose and mouth. Oral sounds are produced when the velum is raised, and air passes only through the mouth.

As air passes through the mouth or nose, it is influenced in the making of sounds by the parts of the vocal tract that impact it. These areas are known as *articulators* and the locations are *places of articulation* (Table 4.2).

The manner of articulation describes how the air being released is restricted. For example, a *stop* is when the air is completely obstructed as in /b/ and /p/. A *fricative* is when the air is only partially obstructed, so there is friction as in the sounds /f/ and /v/. An *affricate* is a momentary stop of airflow with a quick release as in *ch* or *j*. A glide is unrestricted airflow with little or no obstruction, which must occur with a vowel as in /w/ or /y/. And a *liquid* is a partial obstruction without friction as you hear in /l/ or /r/.

The concepts of voicing, places, and manner of articulation can be combined along with the consonant they form. You can see in Table 4.3 that each of the consonants in English is listed. You will also notice that there are empty cells in the table, because English does not include a consonant made in that way.

Table 4.2 Places of articulation.

Place of articulation	How the sounds are made
Bilabial	Lips together
Labiodental	Lower lip against front teeth
Interdental	Tongue between teeth
Alveolar	Tongue near alveolar ridge on roof of mouth
Palatal	Tongue on hard palate
Velar	Tongue near velum
Glottal	Space between the vocal folds

Table 4.3   Consonants—places and manners of articulation

		Bilabial	Labiodental	Interdental	Alveolar	Palatal	Velar	Glottal
Stop (oral)	Voiceless	p			t		k	
	Voiced	b			d		g	
Nasal (stop)	Voiceless							
	Voiced	m			n		ŋ	
Fricative	Voiceless		f	θ	s	š		h
	Voiced		v	ð	z	ž		
Affricate	Voiceless					č		
	Voiced					ǰ		
Glide	Voiceless							h
	Voiced	w				j	y	
Liquid	Voiceless							
	voiced				l	r		

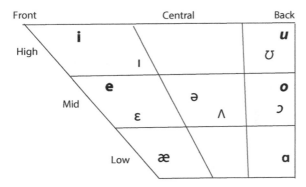

Figure 4.1 Locations of articulators for vowel sounds.

TESOL educators use this information about forming consonants to help explain to students how consonant sounds are made in English.

Vowels

Vowels are produced by a continuous airstream and all are voiced. They are classified according to the height of the tongue, the part of tongue involved, and the position of the lips. The tongue can be high, mid, or low, and the part of the tongue used can be front, central, or back (see Figure 4.1).

Only four vowels are produced with rounded lips and only four vowels are considered *tense* instead of *lax*. The sound /ɑ/ would be written as a low back lax unrounded vowel. Many languages also have vowels called diphthongs, a sequence of two sounds, vowel + glide. Examples in English include *oy* in boy and *ow* in cow. In addition, vowels can be nasalized when they occur before nasal consonants. A diacritic mark [~] is placed over the vowel to show this. The vowel sounds in *bee* and *bean* are considered different because the sound in *bean* is nasalized.

Syllables

Speech sounds are organized or sequenced as a unit, which is called a *syllable*. Syllables are major components or "building blocks" of words. They influence the rhythm of a language, its prosody, its poetic meter, and its stress patterns.

A typical structure of a syllable is a syllable nucleus (most often a vowel) and optional initial and final margins (typically, consonants). For example, the word *older* is composed of two syllables: *ol* and *der*. Syllables are not dependent on meaning and functions. They show how words are segmented when pronounced.

Minimal pairs

Minimal pairs are words with different meanings that have the same sounds except for one. These contrasting sounds can either be consonants or vowels. The words *pin* and *bin* are minimal pairs, because they are exactly the same except for the first sound. The words *read* and *rude* are also exactly the same except for the vowel sound.

Locations of phonemes in words

When TESOL educators discuss the position of phonemes in words, they often refer to their location. The phonemes can be at the front or *initial*, middle or *medial*, and at the end or *final*. The reason for this is that sounds in each position may have slight differences in pronunciation in these three locations.

Free variation

Some words in English are pronounced differently by different speakers. This is most noticeable among American English speakers and British English speakers, as well as dialectal differences. This is evidenced in the ways *neither*, for example, can be pronounced. American English pronunciation is [niðər], while British English pronunciation is [najðər]. With such clear differences even among speakers of English as their L1, TESOL educators accept all variations in pronunciation of a word.

Questions for reflection

- Were you surprised to see the phonetic coding in the IPA and how it works to assign one sound to one symbol? Would this information have helped you learn in the past? Would you have wanted to study it?
- In what ways do you think information about phonology and phonetics will have an impact on your teaching and ELLs' learning?

Syntax

Syntax is also known as word order in sentences. The arrangement of words or syntax helps convey meaning. Overall, it is the study of sentence structure and of the architectural structure of words, phrases, and clauses to form sentences. Different languages have different syntactic word orders. For example, while most languages begin a sentence with a subject, a few others start with objects. Fronting a syntactic element highlights the information, especially in English.

There is universal syntactic knowledge that pertains to all languages. All speakers:

- have mental grammar, which is the core knowledge of language content;
- possess *finite* linguistic knowledge but create *infinite* number of sentences;
- use linguistic knowledge creatively; and
- create and understand sentences they have never heard or created before.

Syntactic structure: Constituents and word order

Syntax is concerned with how words are combined to form constituents, meaningful linguistic units, which form sentences. Language is a structured system, composed of regularities in structure. Constituents are phrases that are formed on the basis of smaller rules. For example, "The boy helped the dog" has three main constituents "the boy," "helped," and "the dog," while "The," "boy," "helped," "the," and "dog" are simple words without any linguistic rules applied on them.

Constituents are basically identified as the structures that answer wh- questions. For example, we can ask the following sentences to the sentence above:

1. Who helped the dog?
   a. The boy.
2. Who did the boy help?
   a. The dog.
3. What did the boy do?
   a. Helped the dog.

English, for example, is a configurational language, which means the subject position is an obligatory element that must be filled. In the following sentences you can see that even if the subject does not refer to an entity, one must fill its position. "It" in "It is very nice to see you" is a placeholder here and does not refer to an entity, whereas "It" in "It is a very nice book" refers to the book. A sentence like "Is very nice to see you" would be ungrammatical as an English sentence, though the equivalent meaning of the same sentence in Turkish would be a perfectly grammatical sentence since Turkish is a non-configurational language in which subjects can be dropped; it would be ungrammatical if the pronominal *it* were added. This Turkish–English example shows that a principle about the subject position in sentences can have two parameters, dropped or pro drop.

There are interesting aspects of syntax in English that can be learned to increase awareness of grammar. The most basic syntax pattern for statements is subject, verb, object (SVO) (for more information on syntax patterns, see Chapter 8).

A teacher might also rely on such knowledge when they need to offer explicit knowledge about grammar to their students. For example, we often find ambiguity in meaning, which arises partly due to the linear order of sentence structure. Rather than classifying these as "errors," it may be helpful to view them as an outcome of linguistic differences between the L1 and L2 of the student.

Questions for reflection

- Syntax is a large body of knowledge. What else would you like to learn about rules for English syntax?
- In what ways do you think information about syntax will have an impact on your teaching and ELLs' learning?

Morphology

Morphology refers to how words are internally structured. The study of morphology investigates the various linguistic units within words and how they are combined to form words. It deals with the basic building block of words, which is a *morpheme*, and how they are combined and recombined to generate meaningful words.

A morpheme is the smallest unit that can carry meaning. It can be as small as a letter that changes the meaning of a word. For example, if you add an *s* to *tree*, you get multiple *trees*, so the meaning was changed from one to many by adding the *s*. *Morphology* is a word composed of two morphemes: *morph-* meaning form or shape and *-ology* meaning study of. The word *word* is composed of one morpheme that cannot be further divided into meaningful forms. So morphemes are atomic linguistic units of language that are meaningful on their own.

Types of morphemes

Roots

A root is the smallest meaningful base of a word without any affixes (prefixes or suffixes), but it is a base to which we can add affixes to generate other words. For example, *talk* is a root to which you can add inflectional morphemes to create words for grammaticality such as *talk, talks, talked,* and *talking.* Roots can stand alone without any other forms attached to them. They have meanings on their own. For example, *boy, child, coffee, woman, desert, time,* and *water* are all root words.

Affixes

An *affix* is a general category assigned to morphemes that are attached to roots. No affixes can stand alone. There are four types of affix, prefix, suffix, infix, and circumfix, but we will only discuss the two that you will discuss in your ELT classes.

1. Prefix

A prefix precedes a root. These include pre-,re-,un-, etc.

unlock	indecent	demotivate	preschool
undo	refocus	discourage	postgraduate

2. Suffix

A suffix follows a root, such as -ly,-er,-ist,-ing,-ment,-ed, etc.

kindly	waitress	books	attached
useful	reading	oxen	broken

Roots, stems, and bases

A stem is the part of the word to which an affix has not yet been attached. Whatever part of the word exists before any morphemes (-s,'s, -s, -ing, -ed, -en, -er, -est) are attached is called the stem (see Table 4.4).

On the other hand, a base is any part of the word to which any kind of affix can be attached. For example, *book* can be a base because both the derivational morpheme (-*let*) and inflectional morpheme (-s) can be attached to it. It is now clear that all roots are bases, while stems are the form of a word before any inflectional morphemes are attached.

Questions for reflection

- What aspects of morphology do you find the most intriguing?
- How does the study of meanings of word parts work with other areas of linguistics?
- How might you employ information about morphology in your teaching?

Table 4.4 Roots, stems, and inflected words.

Roots	Stems	Inflected words
Boy	Boy	Boys
Drive	driver	Drivers
Write	Writer	Writers

Semantics

Semantics is the study of linguistic meaning of morphemes, words, phrases, and sentences. Semantics can be split into two areas of concentration: *lexical semantics*, which is concerned with the meaning of words and the meaning relationships among words, and *phrasal semantics or sentential semantics*, which deals with the meaning of the syntactic units larger than a word. There is also a separate domain of linguistics that also deals with meaning, *pragmatics*, which is concerned with how context and other factors affect meaning (see p. XX in this chapter).

Speakers of a language agree upon particular meanings of words and this makes it possible for them to communicate with each other. It is these meanings that also make it possible for people to create larger units of meanings. The basic meanings of words are acquired in close relation to the semantic properties that each word or morpheme has. It is actually these semantic properties that children acquire. For example, when we hear a sentence such as the following one, "The children chanted to hear their voices echo against the mountain," we automatically understand that the *children* are *human*, and the *echo* and *mountain* are not *alive*. We also know that *chanted* is a verb used to describe how people *sing*, but that the mountain will not respond meaningfully, it will only *echo*.

It is then easily said that each word that has a meaning and carries semantic properties that make their meaning different from that of another word. For example, the verb *assassinate* is different from the verb *kill*, because the former implies an important person has been killed, while the latter does not have the same semantic property. It can be said that all content words (e.g., nouns, verbs, adjectives, and adverbs) have semantic features that make them possess a special meaning that another word does not have. That is why it is hard to find *perfect synonyms* as each word might have a different semantic feature.

Individual words have core meanings or senses. Fluent speakers negotiate differences between similar words with ease. Nevertheless, the differences are subtle, and the fact that they are clear to us as teachers does not mean that they are clear to learners.

Lexical relationships

Lexical items or words are related to one another in different ways. Table 4.5 illustrates possible relationships that words can have.

Again, these are distinctions that most of us learned at an early age and which no longer strike us at a conscious level. For ELLs, these distinctions must be consciously called out. The generalized concepts seen in the table are present in all languages, but can be difficult to negotiate when being taught in a language other than the L1.

Sentence meaning

In English, the order of placement of words within a sentence governs that sentence's meaning. Sentences are formed through the combination of phrases, which are made of function words (e.g., prepositions, determiners, pronouns, quantifiers) and content words (e.g., nouns, adjectives, adverbs, verbs). The ordering of phrases implies a

Table 4.5 Lexical relationships between words.

Relationships	Descriptions	Examples
Homonym	Different words pronounced the same but with different meanings	Too, to, two; bear vs. bare
Polysemy	A word having more than one sense	Face (person, clock, building)
Heteronym	Words spelled the same with different pronunciation	Bass (guitar) vs. bass (fish)
Homograph	Words spelled the same but that have different meanings	Bear (tolerate) vs. bear (animal)
Synonym	Words that sound different but have the same or almost the same meaning	Pail vs. bucket
Antonym	Words that are opposite in meaning. They may be gradable or relational	Tall/short
Complementary (ungradable)	Words that mean just the opposite, and which cannot be graded in degree	Dead/alive; present/absent
Gradable pair	Two antonyms related in such a way that more of one is less of the other	warm/cool
Marked vs. unmarked	In a gradable pair of antonyms, the word that is not used in questions of degree	How *tall* are you? *How *short* are you?
Relational antonyms	Two antonyms may have just the opposite meaning rather the negated version of each other	Give and receive; Teach and learn
Hyponyms	Words belonging to the same semantic class and that are included in a wider class	Red, white, blue are hyponyms of color
Metonyms	Words used instead of another with which they are associated	The White House—American government
Retronyms	An expression that would once have been redundant, but which societal or technological changes have made nonredundant	Silent movie, snail mail, whole milk

logical connection between ideas, even if the words themselves do not. For example, Chomsky provides the example sentence "Colorless green ideas sleep furiously" to illustrate sentence meaning.

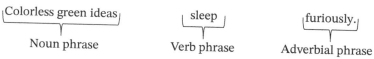

Colorless green ideas — Noun phrase   sleep — Verb phrase   furiously. — Adverbial phrase

Although this sentence is *syntactically* correct, it does not make sense *semantically.* Semantically, it does not work, because it is green, so it cannot be colorless. Likewise, ideas are abstract and therefore cannot have a color or sleep.

colorless[-color] and green [+color] do not match.
ideas [+abstract] [-color] [-inanimate] so it cannot be color [+color] nor can it sleep.

Therefore, a sentence can be grammatical, but not necessarily meaningful. This is known as the *principle of compositionality*, which means that the meaning of a phrase/sentence depends on *both* the meaning (semantics) of its words and how those words are combined structurally (syntax). While the concept of "synthetic grammar" (word order implies a particular meaning) is found in many languages, it is not universal. Nor does the order of words imply the same meaning in all languages that use synthetic grammar.

Meaningfulness

At the level of the sentence, meaning is constructed through a series of steps that fluent speakers understand intuitively and automatically to the extent that they flow together with no need to be cognizant of them as independent steps. However for ELLs, these steps need to be addressed individually, and the educator must be aware that focusing on one aspect of meaningfulness while glossing over others may be confusing to learners. The following aspects of language are used by fluent speakers, often without any recognition of the degree of shared understanding that makes them understandable.

Semantics: Sense and nonsense

Semantics governs the meaning of words in context, specifically how words relate to one another within a sentence. There are sentences that appear to conform to the rules of syntax, but they cannot be semantically correct because of issues with the logical progression of the ideas. The example provided by Chomsky, "Colorless green ideas sleep furiously," is not semantically correct as the semantic properties of the noun phrases (NPs) are in contrast. Semantics can also govern connections between concepts that are distant from one another in a sentence, as in Mark Twain's example of a sentence spoken by Artemus Ward: "I once knew a man in New Zealand who had not a tooth in his head ... and yet that man could beat a drum better than any man I ever saw" (Twain, 1963, p. 188). Again, the clash between two concepts within the sentence, toothlessness and beating a drum, makes the statement semantically incorrect even though it conforms to the rules of syntax.

Metaphors

Metaphor has a nonliteral, indirect meaning created by the users of language through the similarities of two seemingly unrelated concepts. It is also a product of a creative and imaginative mind.

Metaphor is a figure of speech that makes an *implicit comparison*, as in "a sea of troubles" or "All the world's a stage" (Shakespeare & Furness, 1963). While those who grow up with a language may take metaphors for granted, understanding them because they are familiar with individual instances, the same cannot be said of ELLs. Consider the difficulties English speakers would have with metaphors in other languages. In Russian, the phrase "krysha payehala" literally means "the roof is running." As a metaphor, it is understood by virtually all Russian speakers as referring to someone who has lost their mental faculties. Many metaphors work in similar ways—universally understood by the L1 population, but meaningless to language learners unless the implicit meaning is explained.

Idioms

Idioms are expressions whose meanings are unrelated to the meaning of its parts, but they are conventionally understood. Some metaphors are idiomatic, but there are also idioms that are not metaphors. Idiom is seen as part of linguistic knowledge because speakers of a language know very well that a word or phrase being used does not convey a literal meaning, but instead, a figurative one. In the case of idiom, the *principle of compositionality* is violated, because the form of words in idioms has no literal connection to the meaning. For example,

> *Let your hair down* = relax.
> *Put his foot in his mouth* = say something to upset or embarrass someone else.
> *Snap out of it* = get out of a bad/unhappy mood through a quick effort.

One of the more challenging aspects of idiom is that it is constantly changing, and is sometimes meaningful only to a select community. Consider the following list of terms in relatively chronological order that idiomatically conveyed the idea that something was *good* or *acceptable*: *the bee's knees, keen, groovy, cool, hot, gnarly, wicked, sick.* As with metaphor, ELLs will need to have these idiomatic expressions explained. And it is safe to assume that if you, as an educator, understand an idiomatic expression used by people the age of your students, they have probably already moved on to a new one. For more on idiomatic use of language, see Liontas' *Idiomaticity: A Riddle Wrapped in a Mystery Inside an Enigma* (2018).

Lexical ambiguity

A word can have more than one sense, which creates double meanings when used in a sentence. Analyze the following words that have more than one sense (Table 4.6).

In each of these examples, the various meanings have little to do with each other. Often, too, the specific meaning of the word is determined from the context in which it is used. If not enough context is present, a sentence can be highly ambiguous.

Table 4.6 Words with multiple meanings.

Words	Senses
Crab	To direct an aircraft into a crosswind
	To scurry sideways like a crab
	To fish for crab
	To complain
Fly	An insect
	A zipper on a pair of pants
	A baseball hit into the air with a bat
	Beautiful (idiomatic)
Bank	Financial bank
	River bank
	A shot in the game of pool
Batter	A mixture of ingredients used to make cake
	A player in the game of baseball
	To assault violently

Ambiguity in language makes it necessary for educators to be patient and sympathetic, as ELLs can feel that they have learned a particular word, only to find that it has many other possible meanings. Most educators will acknowledge this difficulty and encourage learners by acknowledging that they understand "a" meaning, but not the particular one that suits the current context.

Analytic sentences

This type of a sentence is known as containing true information because of the words in it. For example, "a widow is a woman whose husband is dead" or "a bachelor is an unmarried man" ensures the truth of the meaning. Such sentences do not require reliance on the real-world information. They contain information for the truth of the meaning in the sentence. They can be useful in a teaching context as they simultaneously demonstrate syntax, meaning, and form, and explain a particular rule or convention in L2. They can be used in a variety of contexts, for example, in explaining a metaphor with a sentence like "In the 1960s, when people said the word 'bad,' they actually meant 'good.'"

Contradictory sentences

Contradictory sentences are those whose meanings are not true as a result of the words within them. For example, "a triangle has four sides" and "the sky is green" are false, because the words in them make it clear that a triangle cannot have four sides like a square. The language used in the sentences falsifies the meaning in contradictory sentences. These can be used to great advantage in the classroom, as they require that learners use their analytical skills to sort out the rhetorical meaning of the sentence while they are learning vocabulary and grammar. Imagine a sentence like "The lines at the airport are always very short." Most students will recognize this as a false statement, and one would hope that they would point this out while the example is being discussed in class. If not, it is relatively easy to rephrase the sentence as a question.

Synthetic sentences

Synthetic sentences describe a "factual" or "observable" phenomenon that can be verified, but which may require the use of information not available to the learner. The truth in such sentences is judged by reference to the external world. They can be true or false not because of linguistic issues, but because of accurate description of the world. They require profound knowledge of the context of the utterance. When one says, "My uncle lives in London," we need to check the extralinguistic world to decide on the truth of it. While they may be taken at face value by learners, they do afford an opportunity for discussion, and for clarification of meaning within sentences that use metaphor, idiom, or ambiguity. For example, a student in a classroom might hear the phrase "The Mississippi is the longest river in America." While this is verifiable, it is not necessarily true. A learner might respond that the Amazon is longer than the Mississippi, and that "South America" is still "America." Exercises like this reveal some of the idiomatic uses found in the L1 within a particular area, and can activate the schema of learners who have the knowledge to be able to question the external verification of the sentence's truth.

Knowledge of semantics helps TESOL educators discuss meanings of sentences and relationships between words in sentences.

Questions for reflection

- Were you surprised how semantics works? Which aspects were you most intrigued by?
- In what ways do you think information about semantics will have an impact on your teaching and ELLs' learning?

Pragmatics

Pragmatics is based on the idea that context governs the meaning of a particular utterance, and that it is necessary to understand not only what was stated, but when, where, by whom, how the speaker and interlocutor are related, and so on. Take a term like "bless." It has a clear meaning, and yet different contexts change that meaning drastically. If someone in a church says "God bless you," it has a religious significance. If someone says "Bless you" in response to a sneeze, the meaning is not at all religious and has more to do with respecting a person's health. Contexts can also be regional. For example, if someone from the Deep South of the United States says, "Bless your heart," the meaning is certainly not religious, nor is it respectful. As with the other examples provided in this chapter, literal meanings frequently take a back seat (pardon my idiom) to contextual ones. In pragmatics, contexts can be divided into two types, *linguistic context* and *situational context*.

Linguistic context

Linguistic context is the text mentioned before or after the phrase or sentence to be interpreted. It is related to the textual features that make up the spoken or written language. Linguistic context helps interpret the language independent of the world only by analyzing the grammatical devices, such as when we read a pronoun, for example, *he*, we look back (anaphoric reference) or forward (cataphoric reference) to identify who the pronoun "he" refers to.

Discourse or communication through spoken or written text often in longer expanses of text relates to linguistic context. There are four traditional modes of discourse: narration (stories), description, exposition, and argument. Each of these modes of discourse implies formats and patterns typical of the mode.

Linguistic context and discourse interact in the ways that longer expanses of text are linked together or have cohesion as you observed in the earlier referential pronoun usage example. Grammatical cohesive devices, such as referential pronouns, constitute a grammatical relationship between the sentences to create a coherent and cohesive text that is meaningful. There are four major means to create cohesion and coherence in a text: reference, substitution, ellipsis, and conjunction. Below, you will see explanations of the four major types with examples.

- Reference works by referring forward or back in the discourse. There are four subcategories.
  - Pronominal:
    - *My mother* retired last year.
    - *She* has been spending her spare time on painting since then.
  - Demonstrative:
    - The committee *decided* that a new bridge should be built in the city.
    - *This decision* was also approved by the prime minister.
  - Definite article "the":
    - Orhan Pamuk wrote *a book* on the history of İstanbul.
    - *The book* sold in Turkey as well as in other countries.
  - Comparative:
    - Some students wrote their essays *in half an hour*.
    - But some spent *less* time.
- Substitution works by replacing a previously mentioned word with another.
  - There are many *cities* I like to visit.
  - The most remarkable *one* is Paris.
- Ellipsis works by deleting or removing unnecessary parts of the discourse, because it has been previously mentioned. There are three kinds of ellipsis in discourse.
  - Elliptical NPs:
    - My own *camera* is Japanese. However, Peter's ----- is German.
  - Ellipsis of the predication in finite clauses:
    - I do not plan to *visit the manager tomorrow*. If I must ----, I can change my idea.
  - Ellipsis of a clause:
    - *Some workers are not willing to sign the new contract.* Someone should talk to them to understand why ----.
- Conjunctions work in one of five ways: adding information (additive), contradicting information (adversative), showing cause and effect (causal), illustrating time relationships (temporal), and displaying continuation of thought (continuative).
  - Additive—No one wants to be criticized. *And* to prevent criticism, people often try to do things perfectly.
  - Adversative—Some people eat to live. Mary, *however*, lives to eat.
  - Causal—There are rules in the schools. The students often follow them. *Consequently*, there exists an environment where students are kept secure.
  - Temporal—I started my career working at a state high school. *Then*, I found a position at a university.
  - Continuative—Each language has different mechanisms to express the same meaning. We *of course* need to draw the attention of the learners to these constraints.

Linguistic context is important for ELLs because both anaphoric and cataphoric reference work in ways that they may not in other languages. For example, the phrase "I brush my teeth" might seem simple, but it contains an anaphoric reference that would not be used in French. A speaker of French would state "Je me brosse les dents," or "I me brush the teeth." Other languages have similar constructions.

Linguistic context is one of many "instinctual" aspects of language that go unquestioned by those who were raised in a language, yet can prove quite challenging to those who were not.

Situational context

Situational context differs from linguistic context in that it is dependent on the nonlinguistic issues beyond the text itself. Some utterances may be interpreted correctly only when viewed in relation to the situation in which they are uttered. The situation includes the place, the people talking, the topic of conversation, and the purpose.

Situational context requires a degree of cultural awareness since concepts related to gender, age, formality, and even technical concerns like speech volume and speed differ between linguistic communities. ELLs are sometimes surprised to find that they encounter teachers who prefer to be referred to by their first names. Even seemingly simple statements like "Can you help me? I'm lost" take on different meanings depending on whether they are stated in the classroom, or when walking down a busy street. As with linguistic context, the situation in which language is used bears heavily on its implications.

In communication, we craft the messages we want to express based on sweeping assumptions of listeners'/readers' background knowledge (Yule, 2020). These are called *presuppositions*. Often presuppositions are culturally based or communally based, which can lead to some miscommunication in the L2 classroom. It is a consideration when planning and delivering English language lessons.

Yule (2020) describes the study of pragmatics as the investigation of "invisible meaning" or "how we recognize what is meant even when it is not actually said or written" (p. 150). The context allows us to depend on shared understandings and knowledge of the world to make inferences about meanings that are not explicitly said or written. *Inference* is a process of deriving meanings based on spoken or written information and one's background knowledge. It is an important part of understanding texts that is often overlooked in the classroom.

Maxims of conversation

The first of the topics that relates to situational context is cooperative principles, also known as Grice's maxims of conversation. Paul Grice claims that any conversation between people is governed by these maxims (1989). More specifically, for a meaningful information exchange, people cooperate and understand what is said though it may not be said directly. What follow are Grice's conversation maxims:

Maxim of quantity	*Say neither more nor less than the discourse requires*
Maxim of relevance	*Be relevant*
Maxim of manner	*Be brief and orderly; avoid ambiguity and obscurity*
Maxim of quality	*Do not lie; do not make unsupported claims*

These maxims are difficult enough for those who grew up with a language and it is likely that each of us knows someone who frequently ignores these maxims despite communicating in their L1. While they are applicable to all cultures and languages, each culture applies them differently. Understanding these maxims and keeping them in mind when giving feedback to learners can go a long way toward giving them a concrete means of conceptualizing the importance of context.

Speech act theory

Another area in pragmatics that is related to situational context is *speech act theory*, developed by John Austin (1962). This theory claims that an utterance can be used to perform an action. In other words, we can do things by saying. Before Austin, it was thought that we use language only for saying things, but now it is known that we can ask others to perform actions with our utterances. Most languages have a simple, one- or two-word exclamation that is intended to silence another speaker. In French, it is "Tais-toi." In Russian, it is "Tisha." In English, it is "Shhhh!" or "Shut up." These are not requests. They are intended to have a direct effect on another person, and they exist in most, if not all languages. They are truncated sentences, developed to convey very rapidly a complex concept: "I need quiet right now." Austin's point is that the intention of these statements is generally not to interact with an interlocutor, but to create a state of quiet. However, because they are truncated, they defy "compositionality" since certain parts of the "sentence" are only implied.

As with metaphor and idiom, speech acts are deeply rooted in cultural values and practices, and they are complicated. In some places, simply saying, "I bet..." means a wager has taken place. In others, the two parties must "shake hands on it." Some people take *"I swear..."* as a complete speech act, while others require swearing on a Bible, or on the memory of a relative who died: "I swear on my mother's grave." It's important to remember that these speech acts are understood by speakers not because they are logical or rhetorically clear, but because they are customary.

The study of pragmatics is also concerned with pragmatic markers. Pragmatic markers help the speaker express how an utterance is intended or what the speaker's attitude is (Yule, 2020). For example, pragmatic markers include forms, such as *you know, well, so, unfortunately, however, frankly, I admit, please, perhaps, didn't you, could you, no way,* and *clearly*. One type of pragmatic marker that is discussed in L2 classes is discourse markers. Discourse markers indicate how the utterance, sentence, or paragraph relates to the ongoing discourse (Fraser, 1996). They signal changes in topic, contrasts of ideas in two sentences or paragraphs, elaborations on the message, or conclusion of a message.

Finally, pragmatics is concerned with how people convey politeness and face. Of course, politeness encompasses words and expressions employed in discourse to show respect and to be socially acceptable (i.e., not rude), but scholars of pragmatics define it beyond language usage to comply with social conventions. According to Yule (2020), *politeness* is "...showing an awareness and consideration of another person's face" (p. 156). *Face* is the self-image you present in public. We attempt to maintain a positive self-image when communicating with others and attempt to allow others to maintain a positive self-image as well. The most direct bearing that face has on L2 classrooms is limiting face-threatening acts, such as causing embarrassment. TESOL educators are aware of how threatening learning another language can be, because of all the possible errors and mistakes; therefore, we make choices in our language and actions to reduce learners' embarrassment and potential for public criticism.

Pragmatics is a favorite subject among our students, because the area explores the relationships between language, context, and people. It is one of the more invisible areas in language, because the pragmatic information is between sentences and requires knowledge of people in general and culture.

Questions for reflection

- What did you find intriguing about pragmatics? What would you like to further explore?
- In what ways do you think information about pragmatics will have an impact on your teaching and ELLs' learning?
- How will you explain some of the patterns within language related to pragmatics to ELLs?

Sociolinguistics

Sociolinguistics is the study of how language is used in society. More specifically, it investigates how we speak differently in differing social contexts, and how we may also use specific functions of language to convey social meaning or aspects of our identity. Moving through the different contexts of our lives, we see that we use language differently depending on the context, the relationships between ourselves and others, what we are trying to accomplish, etc. These differences result in variations of language use.

Furthermore, different individuals, based on their socioeconomic class, gender, race, or home dialect, vary their language use. Language variation studies systematic differences among different language users of the same language. Specific areas that have an impact on teaching language are: linguistic varieties; social, ethnic, and gender-related varieties; and stylistic varieties.

Linguistic varieties

Linguistic varieties include semantic, syntactical, morphological, and phonological differences spoken within a language. *Dialect* and *lingua franca* are two of the major domains that clearly illustrate these differences.

Dialect

A *dialect* is a form of language used by a particular social group or within a specific region. Dialects have systematic differences from other varieties of the same language. For instance, British, Australian, Canadian, and American Englishes. Even within these dialects there are regional variations. A language is known to be a collection of different dialects that can be used to communicate in the same society, but when these dialects can no longer be understood, they become separate languages. Therefore, dialects are group difference in the way people of the same society and same language speak the language.

Dialects are affected by a number of factors, including region, heritage, and social class. They are important to ELLs because in their interactions within their L2 they will undoubtedly encounter nonstandard uses of English, and will need to determine where/when/with whom a particular expression is to be used. Something as simple as ordering a soft drink can be frustrating when the generic term used ranges from "soda" to "pop" and even "coke" as a generic term for all soft drinks. Some areas might use "pidgins," which are simplified versions of a language used between people who do not have a language in common. An ELL in Hawaii might hear a phrase like "Dat ono" and not realize that it means "This food is delicious." Adding dialect to lessons can help learners understand that the English they encounter will not always be formally correct, and that they will need to maintain flexibility.

Lingua franca

A *lingua franca* is a shared language used in a region where there are people who speak diverse languages. It is used particularly to communicate for commercial purposes. For example, English is a lingua franca globally in that people whose native languages are not English use English to communicate. On the other hand, French used to be the lingua franca of diplomacy because people of different languages used French for diplomatic purposes.

While the lingua franca in a particular region may have its own unique characteristics, one need not understand all of them to be able to communicate. A lingua franca is based on the formal conventions of the language. Learners who are aware of formal conventions within the L2 will be able to use it as a lingua franca regardless of whether regional dialects are being used.

Sociolinguistics is a field of study that has had a significant impact on the field of TESOL. We have discussed only the tip of the iceberg of information in the field of sociolinguistics. We recommend that you explore it more to identify other areas of influence on ELT.

Questions for reflection

- Based on your observations, how do speakers modify their language for different audiences? Think of some examples of how you have modified your language use for different groups of people (e.g., informal/casual—friends, family; formal—work colleagues, bosses, religious leaders, or professors)?
- In what ways do you think information about sociolinguistics will have an impact on your teaching and ELLs' learning?

Functional linguistics

Structural linguistics attempts to understand language and its rules through analysis of its patterns of syntax, semantics, phonology, morphology, and pragmatics. Functional linguistics, on the other hand, strives to understand language based on how speakers of the language use it for communication. Researchers in functional linguistics investigate meanings shared in communication from the speaker's and hearer's perspectives. They analyze authentic samples of "language in use" according to the functions, or purposes, the language achieves and other linguistic elements, not an idealized form of the language. For example, they may analyze the following set of sentences from old or given information and new information.

> My great-aunt Beverly was always very kind to me. A couple of years ago, **she** sent me pictures from when I was little.

Kate is pretty sure this is a sentence she has actually uttered, so it is an authentic sample. The new information in each sentence is underlined. The old or given information is in bold. The given information allows the speaker to connect the two ideas.

Michael Halliday, a functional linguist, has been extremely influential in applied linguistics due to his research on "functions of language." Based on the analysis of the grammar of children, he was able to outline seven functions of language:

1. the instrumental function serves to manipulate the environment, to cause certain events to happen;
2. the regulatory function of language is the control of events;
3. the representational function is the use of language to make statements, convey facts and knowledge, explain, or report to represent reality as the speaker/writer sees it;
4. the interactional function of language serves to ensure social maintenance;
5. the personal function is to express emotions, personality, and "gut-level" reactions;
6. the heuristic function used to acquire knowledge, to learn about the environment; and
7. the imaginative function serves to create imaginary systems or ideas (Halliday & Webster, 2009, pp. 113–144).

In this list, which serves as categories of functions, the functions common in schooling, such making a statement, conveying facts, and explaining can be seen in #3. Asking questions and problem solving are present in #6. All of these functions are present in one form or another within a school day. In spite of the environment, we are preparing students for successful use of language, so we would need to teach the function of greetings (part of #4), describing a feeling (part of #5), and imagining/wondering (part of #7).

Functional linguistics has had a significant influence within language education today. Examples of Halliday's influence are present in the Functional/Notional Syllabus, WIDA's (2020) English Language Development Standards, ELT textbooks, and in this book's Chapters 6–8. This brief foray into functional linguistics is only the tip of the iceberg, we strongly recommend you to read more on the topic (see Van Valin, 2003; Halliday & Webster, 2009; Bartlett & O'Grady, 2017).

Chapter Conclusions

Linguistics studies language in a general sense. For the purposes of TESOL, linguistics is most useful as a theoretical underpinning for classroom practices including curriculum design and interaction with students. We do not necessarily teach this information explicitly to English language learners. Understanding that all languages have particular characteristics can help educators to activate learners' schemas based on their L1, and to transfer them to the L2. An overall understanding of linguistics also helps to diagnose misunderstandings within the classroom, and to give learners a stronger sense of agency. Sociolinguistics has had a big influence on TESOL, particularly in the investigation of different variations of English.

Discussion questions

1 Which area of linguistics (i.e., phonology, morphology, semantics, syntax, and pragmatics) do you think are the most important in your day-to-day ELT? Why?
2 How will knowledge of phonology, morphology, semantics, syntax, and pragmatics guide your teaching? How does knowing this information about language change how you plan to teach English?
3 Which dialect of English do you speak? How would you handle it if your students wanted to learn a different accent?

Tasks

1 Transcribe these quotations using the IPA. Answer the questions that follow.
  a. Quotations:
    i. "Tell me and I forget. Teach me and I remember. Involve me and I learn."— Benjamin Franklin
    ii. "Great minds discuss ideas; average minds discuss events; small minds discuss people."—Eleanor Roosevelt
    iii. "Love yourself first and everything else falls into line. You really have to love yourself to get anything done in this world."—Lucille Ball
  b. Questions:
    i. What did you discover about the sound system of English in this process? How did you discover this?
    ii. What was easy and challenging about it? Why?

Further reading/read and discuss

Read about linguistics in:

Bartlett, T., & O'Grady, G. (Eds.). (2017). *The Routledge handbook of systemic functional linguistics*. Routledge.

Freeman, D. E., & Freeman, Y. S. (2014). *Essential linguistics: What teachers need to know to teach ESL, reading, spelling and grammar* (2nd ed.). Heinemann.

Fromkin, V., Rodman, R., & Hyams, N. (2017). *An introduction to language* (11th ed.). Cengage.

Gordon, T. (2012). *The educator's guide to linguistics: A textbook*. Information Age Publishing.

Halliday, M., & Webster, J. J. (Eds.). (2009). *The essential Halliday*. Continuum International Publishing Group.

References

Austin, J. (1962). *How to do things with words.* Harvard University Press.

Bartlett, T., & O'Grady, G. (Eds.). (2017). *The Routledge handbook of systemic functional linguistics* (Routledge Handbooks in Linguistics) (1st ed.). Routledge

Chomsky, N. (1976). *Reflections on language.* Temple Smith.

Chomsky, N. (1980). *Rules and representations.* Basil Blackwell.

Chomsky, N. (1981). *Lectures on government and binding.* Foris.

Fraser, B. (1996). Pragmatic markers. *Pragmatics, 6*(2), 167–190. https://doi.org/10.1075/prag.6.2.03fra

Grice, H. P. (1989). *Studies in the way of words.* Harvard University Press.

Halliday, M., & Webster, J. J. (Eds.). (2009). *The essential Halliday.* Continuum International Publishing Group.

Liontas, J. I. (2018). Idiomaticity: A riddle wrapped in a mystery inside an enigma. In J. I. Liontas (Ed.), *The TESOL encyclopedia of English language teaching,* Vocabulary volume 5. Wiley. https://doi.org/10.1002/9781118784235.eelt0947

Sapir, E. (1921). *Language: An introduction to the study of speech.* Harcourt Brace.

Shakespeare, W., & Furness, H. H. (1963). *As you like it.* Dover Publications.

Twain, M. (1963). How to tell a story. In C. Neider (Ed.), *The complete essays of Mark Twain now collected for the first time* (p. 188). Doubleday & Company, Inc.

Van Valin, R. D., Jr. (2003). Functional linguistics. In M. Aronoff & J. Ress-Miller (Eds.), *The handbook of linguistics* (pp. 319–336). Wiley.

World Class Instructional Design and Assessment (WIDA). (2020). *WIDA English language development standards framework, 2020 edition kindergarten—Grade 12.* Board of Regents of the University of Wisconsin System.

Yule, G. (2020). *The study of language* (7th ed.). Cambridge.

5

What Are the Various Areas of Second Language Acquisition Theory and How Do They Guide Instruction?

This chapter introduces various areas of second language acquisition (SLA) theory and how these areas guide instruction. The chapter also discusses why TESOL educators need a working understanding of SLA. The relevant concepts are introduced, defined, and exemplified in relation to the teaching and learning practices that can be applicable in the classroom. This chapter offers a brief overview of theories and includes reflective questions intended to help with synthesizing the points made and developing praxis.

Learning Outcomes

At the conclusion of this chapter, you will be able to:

- identify concepts in SLA that are relevant to teaching
- interpret the SLA theories in line with teaching practices
- question the existing teaching context depending on the theoretical arguments in SLA

How would you describe your initial years of second language learning and/or acquisition? What would have helped you to learn better? In this vignette, one TESOL educator shares his initial language learning process and how he came to understand there was a better way to learn another language.

TESOL Voices

My Second Language Learning Journey

I started learning English when I was 12 years old in 1984. In the secondary school I attended in Turkey, the English as a foreign language (ELF) courses were based on learning basic vocabulary and grammar by drills and repetition. There were no authentic listening and speaking activities in which we could attempt to practice the newly learned language to communicate with others outside of the classroom. The teachers only expected us to repeat what they said, and they thought we

---

Introduction to TESOL: Becoming a language teaching professional, First Edition. Kate Mastruserio Reynolds, Kenan Dikilitaş, and Steve Close.
© 2022 John Wiley & Sons, Inc. Published 2022 by John Wiley & Sons, Inc.

would learn enough of the pronunciation by speaking and participating in conversational interaction.

It was much like explicit learning of language structures and patterns with full consciousness of what I was learning. The point was only to memorize structures and forms for future remembering in the exams. Back then I did not have any opportunity to practice English apart from filling in the blanks and repeating the words I needed to learn. I was also not able to process basic sentence structures, but was replacing individual words in a given sentence with another word to create new meanings. This lasted for about 6 years, including my high school education.

English was a subject just like other courses, math, history, or geography. As a student I was not even helped to become aware of the role of English in my future career. Now when I look back, I can see that grammatical repetition and word learning dominated my whole initial learning experience. I had a hard time adapting myself to speaking and writing to promote fluency and automaticity, which made me avoid using language as part of my communication.

I suppose I was undeterred, because I continued on to become a professor of TESOL. I learned about second language acquisition and learning, and discovered that the ways I was taught were not congruent with effective language learning practices as informed by second language theory and research. The theories and principles that come from second language acquisition and learning guide my instructional practices now, so I am an effective second language and teacher educator.

Kenan Dikilitaş
Professor of TESOL

SLA

In TESOL, we distinguish between an individual's first language, the one they begin learning in infancy, and their second or additional languages. In some cases, children learn two or more languages from birth in their homes. In other cases, they only speak their first language until they encounter another/others in school or society. When we say "second language" in TESOL, we understand that it could be any additional language learned at any stage. In this book, we refer to a language other than the first as their second language, unless otherwise noted.

SLA refers to the process of acquiring and/or learning another language simultaneous to or after the first language. Acquisition is often used to mean "picking up" the language through natural exposure; it is akin to the process of a child acquiring their first language without explicit teaching. For example, when adults or teenagers move to other countries whose language they cannot speak, they learn the language through exposure and interaction with others. Acquisition is a slow process of learning largely through incidental discovery and meaning-making to communicate for authentic purposes. Learning, on the other hand, implies the presence of a teacher and of a classroom context where a certain curriculum is followed with particular books designed to teach the new language.

You will see TESOL educators use both of the terms, acquisition and learning, generally or specifically. You may also see the term instructed second language acquisition to refer to the teaching of second languages in ways that are conducive to language acquisition.

L1 and L2 Acquisition Compared

What is the relationship between L1 and L2 language learning? How are the processes the same and different? L1 acquisition is a process that begins early in childhood with pure exposure to meaningful contextualized interaction through discovery of the language sound system, linguistic rules, and language use. This is also a process that automatically begins and evolves through living in a social community unless one has a biological deficit that blocks the processing of language. L1 acquisition experiences form the basis for the learning or acquisition of other languages that might follow. Second or third languages will not be learned without such a basis since the human mind needs to commence language acquisition early while the neurological mental evolution is in progress.

L1 acquisition is not a process that involves learning to read and write but rather is learning to speak and comprehend what is being spoken in communication. Verbal interaction is key to acquiring complex linguistic features of specific languages, so babies need to be actively exposed to a social environment where they first comprehend meaning. However, in very early years, babies produce sounds to which they attach meanings and use to express what they need to say. Sound–meaning matchings are based on a quest for discovering a language system and producing forms. Although it is sometimes believed that babies imitate their parents' talk, this is readily undermined by the fact that the way babies use language is never modeled by parents. This implies that babies follow a particular path to developing language skills although they might be imitating some of the fixed language structures and ways of producing sounds used around them. However, the complex language structures cannot be discovered and acquired fully by imitation, rather they need to be processed and produced by learners in appropriate contexts of communication.

L2 learning or acquisition on the other hand is a different process with some similarities. Some learners begin acquiring or learning another language very early subsequent to the commencement of L1 acquisition. An early involvement might help in acquiring L2 much like L1 since learners can still discover L2 in a similar way, while late exposure might make it relatively harder and slower to acquire. Language acquisition takes place with a great deal of natural exposure to authentic communication, while the degree of exposure might influence the rate and amount of acquisition.

Cook (2008) compares and contrasts L1 and L2 foreign language acquisition process in terms of the following features:

- *Mastery*: while L1 refers to the full acquisition and perfect mastery by children, for adults L2 is not likely to be achieved at the same level of perfect mastery.
- *General failure*: in L1 context learners are guaranteed to achieve perfect mastery while in L2 foreign language acquisition full success might be rare.
- *Variation*: children show very little variation in the level of success and route, whereas L2 learners differ in ultimate degree of success and route of acquisition.

- *Goals*: a full acquisition of target language competence is expected in L1 while in L2 varying degrees of fluency and accuracy are the goals for learners.
- *Fossilization*: it is not known whether L1 speakers have fossilized mistakes, but L2 learners often have fossilized inaccurate and inappropriate use of language depending on the context in which they learn L2.
- *Intuitions*: L1 speakers normally have natural intuitions regarding what is grammatical and what is not, which they may not be able to account for, whereas L2 learners might not have intuitions since they have not acquired but learned the language, so they often make judgments about grammaticality, which might always not be clear.
- *Instruction*: children learning L1 do not need instruction while acquiring language although parents might sometimes recast their mistakes, which may not even be helpful since children construct their own language system by going through a predetermined route of acquisition. On the other hand, for L2 learners, implicit or explicit correction is often needed and useful for their rate of acquisition. L2 learners who are not offered corrective feedback might develop more fossilization than others who are.
- *Affective factors*: the social and personal factors that might impede L2 acquisition and determine the level of proficiency in L2 learners may not be involved in L1 acquisition since L1 acquisition is a natural process of exposure to language and communication that begins with the activation of predisposition in the human brain.

Cook (2008), however, notes that success for L2 learners is considered to be the level of mastery of native speakers because L1 is a necessary process for human language and cognitive development (Tomasello, 2000), which commences with the setting of the parameters that are unique to the language acquired (Chomsky, 1982). A second language, on the other hand, may be acquired/learned at any stage of life from very early in childhood into late adulthood. It might offer similar advantages with early exposure and acquisition. All children go through particular stages of development, although their rates of progression might differ. L1 speakers acquire the language following almost the same route.

Questions for reflection

- How do you think your L1 has influenced your L2 acquisition process?
- What were the specific areas of your L1 that facilitated the acquisition of specific features of the L2?

How Fast Can ELLs Acquire/Learn Another Language?

The rate of L2 acquisition is not fixed since each individual might acquire L2 at different rates depending on the amount of exposure to L2 and the compatibility of the input with the level of the learner. If an L2 learner is exposed to a higher level of input that he may not be comprehending clearly it might not lead to acquisition or may slow down the rate of the acquisition compared with a learner who is provided with a more appropriate level of input. The speed with which a learner can acquire L2 also depends on the individual efforts invested such as reading for pleasure and authentic communication with others as well as the support they are provided with by others who can speak L2.

Cummins' (1979) research on the rate of acquisition of social language (1 to 3 years) and academic language (5 to 7, and up to 10 years depending on whether schooling was interrupted) is informative though. Many educators refer to Cummins' research, so colleagues and administrators comprehend the length of study an ELL may have to acquire both social and academic language. For more on social and academic language, see Chapter 1.

What Sets of Knowledge and Abilities Make an ELL Proficient?

Savignon (1976, 1983), who was influenced by Dell Hymes' ideas of communicative competence (1966), expressed the idea of a learner developing a competence or ability to communicate in the L2, which moved away from the idea of "fluency." She defined *communicative competence* as the knowledge native speakers have that allows them to interact effectively with each other.

From this initial definition of communicative competence, Canale and Swain (1980) developed a model of communicative competencies. Their model, which informs many theoretical and practical discussions today, comprises four categories of knowledge that inform performance (Brown, 2007).

1. Grammatical/linguistic competence is knowledge of sentence-level syntax, grammar, lexicon, semantics, morphology, and phonology.
2. Discourse competence refers to the learner's knowledge of discourse patterns above the sentence level (e.g., in paragraphs, essays, monologues, and conversations). In other words, discourse competence is knowledge of topic shifts and changes, transitions in discourse as shown by discourse markers (i.e., however, yet, because, first, then, next) and cohesion.
3. Sociolinguistic or pragmatic competence describes the learner's knowledge of the sociocultural conventions of language and culture, meaning that the learner is aware of the social context and conventions (e.g., participants' roles and relationships to each other; the information they share; and the purpose of the interaction), and can modify his or her language accordingly.
4. Strategic competence refers to the ability to employ communication strategies employed during breakdowns in communication or to redirect misdirected talk in an appropriate manner.

Various TESOL scholars have further explored this model and it is still influential today. This model reminds TESOL educators that to be able to communicate effectively in a second language, we need to go beyond teaching sentence-level grammar and create diverse learning opportunities to ensure learners develop each of these competencies.

Models of SLA

Within the study of SLA, schools of thought based on the most important aspects of SLA have been developed. The main schools of thought are cognitivist, innatist, interactionist, and sociocultural. We will attempt to provide a basic description of each of these schools of thought and highlight the major theories that have emerged from them. For an extensive look at SLA theories, please see Ortega's *Understanding Second Language Acquisition* or Mitchell, Myles, and Marsden's *Second Language Learning Theories*. Lightbown and Spada have an informative classroom-centered SLA theories text, *How Languages Are Learned*.

James W. Carey, in his work in communications, described his beliefs that we develop metaphors for communications that coincide with the current technology of the time (1992). In some ways, theories of SLA have developed in this manner as you will see in the text that follows.

Cognitive Theories

Many second language researchers and theorists are interested in how second languages are processed in the brain. These research theorists are not specifically concerned with the physical parts of the brain while processing language as neurolinguistics researchers/theorists are; rather, they are interested in cognition (i.e., thinking). They would like to know how second language learners think about, use, and retain information in their long-term memories.

The focus of cognitive theorists began in the 1950s as a reaction to the behaviorist model of learning (Ortega, 2009). In behaviorism, researchers and theorists, such as Watson (1930) and Skinner (1957) believed that individuals learn through a conditioning or training process during interaction with their environment. Skinner claimed that individuals learn behaviors, which are responses, to certain stimuli from their environment. From this theoretical perspective, behaviors apply to verbal behaviors. The application of behaviorist theory to language learning and acquisition was derailed by Chomsky in his famous review of Skinner's *Verbal Behavior* text.

Cognitive theorists were simultaneously discussing thinking and retention of knowledge. From this era of research, we employ the principles of long-term and short-term memory as well as declarative (i.e., knowing about something) and procedural knowledge (i.e., knowing how to do something).

Information processing model (cognitive)

One model developed in the 1970s to explain how humans think is the information processing model. This model employs the metaphor of a computer processing incoming data (i.e., information) and relaying it in the form of output. According to Ortega (2009), the information processing perspective makes three assumptions. First, these theorists believed there is a difference between knowledge and processing. The second assumption is that there are automatic, unconscious processes and voluntary, or controlled, conscious processes. The third assumption is that attention and memory are limited.

From this school of thought emerged the principle of automaticity (Anderson, 1992; Bialystok, 1994), which describes the automatic and unconscious processing of language. Bialystok theorized that through prolonged and repeated practice knowledge stored in long-term memory becomes changed, becoming more elaborate and specific (2001, as cited in Ortega, 2009, p. 85). Many educators continue to be guided by this principle.

Interlanguage (cognitive)

Interlanguage, coined by Selinker (1972), describes the system of learner language that approximates that of the L2, which learners develop during a particular period of acquisition (Van Patten & Benati, 2010). Interlanguage is a dynamic cognitive process whereby L2 learners develop a linguistic system that is similar to that of the target language by constructing it with influences from both the L1 and the L2. Most L2 learners have an interlanguage since they do not normally attain native-like competence.

Within a learner's interlanguage system, there can be a great deal of variation in grammatical, lexical, syntactic, and phonological systems. They may have some grammatical forms mastered and can use them with ease most of the time, but they still may make errors. According to Selinker (1972), they will move through four stages of variation:

1. Initial stage—The learner may use *the* for all articles.
2. Free variation—The learner may use *the*, *a*, and *an* interchangeably.
3. Systematic variation—The learner may use *an* for words starting with a vowel, and *the* and *a* for all others.
4. Categorical use—The learner may use *the* before a specific singular or plural noun, *a* before a nonspecific singular noun beginning with a consonant, and *an* before a nonspecific singular noun beginning with a vowel sound.

Within the interlanguage we use four processes between the L1 and L2: transfer, overgeneralization, interference, and fossilization. *Transfer* refers to both positive and negative linguistic influences from the L1 to the L2. *Positive transfer* describes helpful linguistic tools, such as cognates. Cognates are words that are the same or similar in form and meaning between two languages. For example, the word *debate* in English is similar to *débat* in French, *debate* in Spanish, dibēto in Japanese, and dezbate in Romanian. When we see this word from our L1, and learn it is the same in the L2, we transfer our schema for that word. And we can use it quickly and easily.

Negative transfer, on the other hand, is the unproductive transferring of linguistic tools between languages. The transfer may cause learners to be confused or express themselves incorrectly. Negative transfer involves *overgeneralizations* of rules within the L2. For example, a student may learn that will is a word used in the future tense, but the gerund form is also used, so they may combine them into, "I will going tomorrow." The other kind of negative transfer is interference.

Interference is when one language muddles the other. For example, "He is my professor. She taught me well." This error is common with L1 speakers of Mandarin, because they do not distinguish between *he* and *she* in Mandarin. When they need to use a pronoun in English, they often use them variably.

Finally, *fossilization* is a phenomenon in which language learners permanently use incorrect forms from overgeneralization or interference in their interlanguage. If we were to use the example of the L1 Mandarin speaker who varies in their use of he and she, this variability would become a permanent feature of their interlanguage.

Interlanguage is a highly idiosyncratic form, and is closely related to the amount and quality of the exposure to input that is provided through authentic interaction and formal language instruction. This theory has developed into a principle of SLA that steers many educators today.

Questions for reflection

- In which areas do you agree and disagree with the cognitive theorists on SLA. Why?
- How would describe your own initial L2 acquisition process? What were the types of transfer you were going through and why?
- How can you help your L2 learners overcome their L1-influenced errors and become fluent and automatic in recalling the functional features of the L2?

Innatist Theories

The monitor model (innatist)

Stephen Krashen's monitor model is similar to Chomsky's notions about the innate abilities of humans to acquire language using their language acquisition device (LAD) (see Chapter 4 regarding Chomsky's universal grammar, UG). Innate simply means that we are born with an ability of a mental resource set, or LAD, to acquire our first and second or additional languages. Krashen believe that if we are exposed to enough comprehensible language we will acquire it.

Krashen, who developed his theory of SLA in the 1980s, primarily argued for inductive learning by learners with only minimal language knowledge that might enable understanding of comprehensible input (1985). He suggests that acquisition occurs as a result of exposure to input that makes sense to learners and whose meaning can be determined through intuitive processing. He believes this cannot be achieved through drills and explicit memorization of rules and vocabulary, but in fact needs to be learned over time by interpreting meaning in context. Another key facet of SLA that Krashen emphasizes is that L2 learners need to engage in meaningful interaction. Meaningful interactions allow learners to focus on expressing and receiving authentic and meaningful messages, without being concerned about the form of what they are trying to say. He suggests that this is possible when the input (i.e., incoming information) learners are exposed to is comprehensible to them and when learners are focused on comprehension rather than production. An instructional implication of this theory is that acquisition can be achieved through reading for pleasure, which he believes could lower the anxiety of learners when they are exposed to the language.

In addition to these overall arguments he put forth, Krashen formulated five hypotheses concerning how languages are acquired as a second language (1985).

The acquisition-learning hypothesis

The first focuses on the distinction between the "acquired and learned" language systems known as the acquisition-learning hypothesis. The former is constructed subconsciously, while the latter takes place through formal instruction. He also describes the pedagogically appropriate ways of fostering acquisition and learning. A teacher-driven deductive approach in a classroom environment often leads to learning, while a learner-centered inductive approach facilitates acquisition of language knowledge.

Although educators are offered courses on how to teach based on how languages are learned, they are not adequately equipped with courses on how to enable acquisition with innovative approaches. Fostering acquisition requires educators to shift their inherently assigned roles from knowledge provider and transmitter to interlocutor, to facilitate interaction that proceeds in natural ways. Few educators can achieve this shift while supporting learners' SLA process, because methodological models of acquisition do not have a particular structure and order. This makes it hard for educators to design their lessons, and inevitably assigns learners more roles and responsibilities, introducing a level of "risk" in teaching. Such practical instructional models might challenge both educators and learners as they disturb the inherent roles they naturally possess in the pedagogical sense.

The monitor hypothesis

The monitor hypothesis shows more clearly how learning differs from and how it influences the process of acquisition. It argues that speakers of learned languages rather than acquired ones monitor what they say constantly and tend to correct and recorrect their mistakes as they speak or write, which often defies fluency. While learning inherently leads learners to produce accurate or correct sentences, acquisition helps them produce fluent speech. Krashen implies automaticity in speaking is curbed by constant planning, editing, and correction.

For example, it is clear that second language speakers usually want to speak accurately, often at the expense of fluent speech. They monitor their use of key language features such as using -s, the third-person singular marker, and the past tense marker (e.g. confusion in regular and irregular forms, or even pronunciation of words). These kinds of behaviors in a speaker or writer demonstrate that that person must have learned the language rather than acquired it.

Questions for reflection

- How can you help learners to avoid monitoring their speech?
- What are the factors that lead to speech monitoring?

The input hypothesis

The third hypothesis Krashen puts forward refers to the *input hypothesis*, concerning the nature of the input to which learners are exposed. Krashen argues that input should be challenging and in turn comprehensible, which means that it has to enable the learner to deduce the meaning without too much effort. It has to be a bit beyond the linguistic level of the learner so that they can be constantly challenged to discover forms, meanings, and functions. Krashen describes comprehensible input as i + 1. He argues that with challenging second language input (i + 1), learners follow a natural order of acquisition. However, he also argues that the existing linguistic levels of learners might differ, so it is often hard to implement these theoretical arguments in pedagogical domains. His suggestion is based on providing learners with natural communicative input which might guarantee that each learner will access the challenging level of exposure to input. Although the definition of i + 1 input is blurry and hard to gauge, it involves working with input that encourages learners to construct the meaning of the message with some difficulty just as children discover meaning from utterances in early stages of L1 acquisition. So, comprehensive input is not only a linguistic issue but a pragmatic one. Learners need to be provided with input within a natural context, which will help them discover meaning and continue to understand and/or communicate.

Questions for reflection

- Do you feel that you have learned your second language with an input such as that described above?
- What kinds of materials can help you teach in accordance with the input hypothesis?
- How would you overcome the challenges caused by language learners' linguistic differences in providing i + 1 input?

The affective filter hypothesis

The fourth hypothesis Krashen proposed refers to the "affective filter" hypothesis based on the existence of affective variables that facilitate the acquisition process. Krashen argues that learners will learn little when encountering messages that they find to be below their developmental level, perhaps finding them insulting or condescending. At the same time, they will have a similarly negative reaction to messages that they find to be above their developmental level, which they will perceive as frustrating. Krashen argues that the acquisition process should be supported and facilitated by making learners feel motivated and self-confident, but not anxious. If learners are experiencing strong, negative emotions, like anxiety, their affective filter will be high, and acquisition will not occur.

Questions for reflection

- Think about your affective filter when you were learning a second language? What influenced it positively or negatively back then?
- How can you guarantee that affective variables are addressed, and learners are supported to learn without mental blocking?
- How can you relate language assessment to the affective filter hypothesis?

The natural order hypothesis

Krashen's final hypothesis is the "natural order" hypothesis, which describes the existence of a predictable natural order of acquisition of grammatical structures. Krashen argues that this order is not directly caused by teaching grammar in a sequential order, but through exposure to linguistic forms in natural communication that is comprehensible (i + 1). The acquisition process, as he argues, is largely free from a linguistically defined order of forms in the input. When one acquires language, this happens in a social environment, where the type and degree of input are based on the needs of communication rather than grammar. So, when learners are exposed to conversational or written input that includes a range of simple to difficult words and structures, they acquire certain grammatical structures that they are able to acquire and need to acquire first, while others will be acquired later.

The richness of the content of the linguistic input offers flexibility in the way and rate of acquisition for learners, who also might differ from one another. Such an input is also naturally differentiated so that each learner learns what they need to learn depending on their needs and interests. For example, when you listen to a song as input in the classroom, while some focus on the accent and pronunciation, others might focus on learning certain vocabulary that they want to learn. This suggests that it is hard to check what each learner learns, but maybe this is not necessary.

Educators have key instructional and interactional roles in adjusting their teaching practices to enable learning. We can argue that there are educators who focus on facilitating and enabling acquisition, while others focus on controlling and assessing learning/teaching in the context of the classroom. This suggests that particular formal features of language can be discovered and acquired over time through systematic exposure to input and following a certain order and stages. This also shows the role of Krashen's hypothesis of comprehensible input, which argues for the key role of reading for pleasure in acquiring such formal features.

Route and processes of language acquisition

The route of acquisition refers to acquisition order and developmental sequences (Van Patten & Benati, 2010). Order of acquisition means the order in which certain morphemes are acquired over time, while developmental sequence refers to the stages that learners go through in the acquisition process of particular features of language. However, there are arguments against the positive role of instruction in the acquisition sequence of formal features of language (e.g., Cook, 1998). It is argued that linguistic features can only be acquired in an order and developmental sequences need to be followed, which seems to be unalterable. Cook also supports this argument with reference to principles of UG, positing that learners need no instruction and L2 acquisition occurs when they are exposed to input and process it with the inherently possessed universal principles of language structure.

Questions for reflection

- It is hard as a teacher to monitor a natural order of SLA, but sometimes it is possible to do so. Do you remember a time when you acquired different forms or different linguistic aspects from the same input your teachers provided?
- How can you as a teacher make sure your students learns what you want them to when they are exposed to rich authentic input not designed specifically for teaching particular linguistic features?

Interactionist Theories

Interaction hypothesis (interactionist)

Interactional studies argue that the amount of interaction is one of the key factors that determine how much one can acquire. Krashen argues that the comprehensibility of the input by the learners is key to successful acquisition. To complement this argument, Swain (1985, 2005) suggests the use of comprehensible output that involves learners' engagement in producing oral and written language where input is activated to use the language. This suggestion has become known as *pushed output*. L2 learners need to be provided with opportunities to use that language with systematic pushed output activities that encourage them to move beyond their comfort level of proficiency (Nation, 2011). The pushed output offers L2 learners the chance to use language in context and generate meanings whereby they test the knowledge they have gained through receptive activities such as reading and listening. Swain (1985) highlights several cognitive benefits of pushed output activities that lead L2 learners to form and test hypotheses about the knowledge they have internalized, notice various aspects of language usage and use (Wang & Castro, 2010), develop automaticity and fluency (DeKeyser, 1997), process input relatively more automatically (Gass, 1997; Swain, 1985), and promote metalinguistic knowledge by re-elaborating on the internalized input (Izumi, 2002). In addition, Skehan (1998) argues that engagement in pushed output activities helps learners generate better input as an active interlocutor.

The interaction hypothesis (Long, 1996) argues that SLA is promoted through active engagement in interacting with others and communicating ideas in social environment. Being in interaction and communication helps learners negotiate their meanings by asking clarification questions to comprehend the message, checking comprehension to make sure they comprehend the incoming message, and asking confirmation questions to ensure they have correctly comprehended. During the interaction, it is also likely that learners:

- receive negative evidence and learn correct use and usage of language (Ellis, 2007);
- are exposed to more input to understand, process, and respond to (Richards & Schmidt, 2002); and
- link knowledge acquired to the ways it is used in interaction (Gass & Selinker, 2008).

However, Ellis (1997) notes that the input that interaction provides might be more complicated and overwhelm learners when learners are pushed to engage in interaction with insufficient knowledge.

Sociocultural model (interactionist/sociocultural)

The sociocultural model (Vygotsky, 1978) suggests that interacting with others including family members and peers is key not only to cognitive development but also to human learning. The model also characterizes learning as a social process that requires others' help for learning to occur. Vygotsky argues that potential cognitive development occurs at the *zone of proximal development* (ZPD). He proposes that learners (i.e., novices) start at their actual level of development. Think of their actual level as where they can perform independent of instructional support. Vygotsky says that novices learn through social interaction with a more knowledgeable individual (i.e., an expert). The social interaction is known as instructional conversation, in which the expert provides linguistic, conceptual, and physical supports for the learning. These supports are called scaffolds, and educators today commonly discuss them. When they learn, they move from their actual level of development to their potential, or proximal, level of development. The proximal level represents the individual learner's potential in terms of the most the individual can learn at that time with the assistance of the expert.

The ZPD offers learners a space for exploring relevant knowledge that might be challenging to achieve without social interaction with others. In the classroom context, such help is mainly modeled by the concept of scaffolding, which involves supporting learners while they are in the process of exploring knowledge and developing complex skills. In the ZPD, there are some pedagogical strategies to follow, which include collaborative learning, modeling, and providing temporary supports to aid the learner to learn new information.

Questions for reflection

- In what ways do you agree and disagree with the interactionist theoretical perspective? Why?
- In what ways do you think that Vygotsky's sociocultural model accounts for SLA? Are there ways that it does not account for SLA?
- In what ways does this perspective inform your teaching?

Social- and Culturally Based Perspectives on SLA

The final school of thought to be discussed in this chapter centers on the acquisition process in the social and cultural domains. The theories presented in this section are mentioned in chronological order, and those described toward the end of the section continue to influence much of educators' practices today.

The acquisition of a second language is invariably influenced by the home and target cultures and learners' cultural competence. Social and cultural similarities and differences affect how a learner acquires/learns the L2. Learners are concerned, and rightly so, with the social and cultural perceptions of the language, the target language communities, and the target language communities' attitudes and behaviors toward language learners. Graham and Brown (1996) found that ELLs' favorable attitudes toward the English-speaking community and their close friendships with peers facilitated their language acquisition.

Some language learners may want to integrate into the target language community through immigration or marriage, for example. This is known as *integrative motivation*. Other learners do not have an interest in integrating into the target language community; rather, they see the language as a tool (i.e., *instrumental motivation*) for work or living. This is the theory or integrative or instrumental motivation (Gardner, 2001). Today, many English as a lingua franca (ELF) users do not interact with the target language community at all. As we consider the social and cultural factors involved with SLA, we will want to keep these distinctions in mind.

Culture shock

1. Culture shock is a term to describe the process of adjusting to a new culture. There are five phases of culture shock that our learners may experience if they are newcomers.
2. The honeymoon phase describes the initial excitement or euphoria a learner experiences in the new culture. They may enjoy the new sights and sounds or feel they are on a vacation.
3. The culture shock phase depicts the period when a learner may become overwhelmed, angry, or aggressive. They may feel frustrated with everyday experiences, such as the food or language. In some cases, they react strongly to or deride the new culture's patterns.
4. The initial adjustment or recovery phase is when the learner gradually feels more comfortable and at home in the new culture. They are more familiar with the patterns of daily life, customs, and language, and they may begin to enjoy their surroundings.
5. The depression or rejection phase is when some students, but not all, experience sadness and unwillingness to participate in the new culture. They may reject the customs, language, or other aspects of the culture.
6. The acceptance and integration phase is when the learners become at home with the customs, language, and other cultural features, and establish a comfortable routine.
7. In some cases, the learners will return to their home cultures and experience, The reverse culture shock phase. In this phase, they may be unfamiliar and uncomfortable with their home culture.

Culture shock can be observed in the classroom through the behaviors learners may exhibit. For example, ELLs may be confused, disconnected, and/or easily frustrated or angry. They may complain of being exhausted or disliking their new culture.

The process of cultural adjustment takes time. As TESOL educators, we are mindful of how learners may be feeling when they first arrive in a new culture. We attempt to alleviate any additional pressures upon them at the most critical phases and help them work through their feelings by being supportive and kind.

Researchers have theories to describe the different types of approaches to integration into a new culture. Some individuals feel that they need to assimilate into the target language and give up their home language and culture, so they resemble the target language culture. The target culture absorbs them in the *cultural assimilation* process. This can be a challenging for individuals and families and may threaten individuals' identities (Bosher, 1997).

Acculturation is a process of cultural interaction in which both cultures are changed. The minority culture continues to retain features of their home culture, such as language, food, and traditions. In 1986, John Schumann presented an early model of SLA in which he defines acculturation as a process of social and psychological integration of the learner into the target community (p. 379). Unlike assimilation, the degree of acculturation into a new culture is thought to be positively and strongly linked to attainments of higher levels of L2 proficiency (Schumann, 1986; Waniek-Klimczak, 2011; Hammer & Dewaele, 2015); however, in a study on acculturation and SLA of Chinese learners in the United States by Jiang et al. (2009), the findings conflicted with the two other studies mentioned here.

Schumann's acculturation model asserts that psychological factors of language shock, culture shock, motivation, and ego permeability (i.e., a well-defined sense of self) and social factors of social dominance, integration pattern, enclosure, cohesiveness, size, cultural congruence, attitude, and intended length of residence influence SLA attainment (see Table 5.1 for the definitions of each). These became known as social distance variables (see Table 5.1). Schumann (1986) stated, "I also propose that any learner can be placed on a continuum that ranges from social and psychological distance to social psychological proximity with speakers of the target language, and that the learner will acquire the second language only to the degree that he acculturates" (p. 379). In other words, the degree that the learner feels socially distant from the target language culture will influence L2 acquisition.

Table 5.1 Social distance variables.

- Social dominance
  - Which group (NL or L2) is politically, culturally, technically, economically dominant, nondominant, or subordinate?
- Integration pattern
  - Is the L2 group interested in assimilating, acculturating, or preserving their home cultural patterns?
  - What is the L2 group's degree of "enclosure" or separate identity?
- Size and cohesiveness
  - How big are the groups of different cultures?
  - What is the L2 group's size and cohesiveness?
- Congruence
  - Are the NL and L2 groups' values and belief systems similar and congruent?
- Attitudes
  - What are the attitudes of each group toward the other?
- Permanence
  - What is the L2 group's intended length of stay in the target culture?

Second language socialization (sociocultural)

Second language socialization theory (Duff, 2007) refers to developing communicative competence in a new authentic context or in a language classroom. Both are based on the socially driven acquisition of language through interactions with speakers of the community (Duff, 2012) by engaging in authentic activities facilitated through both language learning and use (Duff, 2010). Such an engagement in the target language and its culture is barely provided in the classroom setting, which makes study abroad a unique experience for enacting the second language socialization process of students. Study abroad experiences provide students with fully contextualized linguistic input and authentic interactions (Köylü, 2016) for rich and continuous meaning-making in real time. During study abroad, in addition to acquiring micro level linguistic features such as idiomatic vocabulary, comprehensible pronunciation, and relevant discourses, learners also nurture macro features by negotiating their ideologies and values rooted in their own L1 whereby they construct a new identity (Anderson, 2017) to earn membership and affiliation in the target community. Students are also argued to experience personality changes through social investment in the study abroad process (Tracy-Ventura et al., 2016). Advanced language development also depends on other factors including the quality of exposure to and immersion in the social activities, students' high degree of socialization (Alfred & Byram, 2002), propensity for acculturation to the new community, and social networking (Lybeck, 2002).

Second language socialization typically commences in the classroom where students use language among their peers and with their teachers. As TESOL teachers, we might need to create an environment conducive to acquiring English to allow for language socialization through immersing learners in authentic language learning and use and providing them opportunities to make meanings in classroom interaction.

Questions for reflection

- Do you agree with the social and cultural perspectives on SLA? Why or why not?
- How might these theories influence your classroom instruction?

Personal/Individual Differences in SLA

Each L2 learner might be influenced by their different personal characteristics and preferences, which in turn influence their learning process. These factors determine how fast they will learn and in what ways they will engage in learning. Some of these include:

- *Aptitude*—Individuals' inherent cognitive ability to learn including their aptitude for learning.
- *Motivation*—Individuals' personal willingness to learn and the locus of that interest.
- *Learning style*—Individuals' preference for the idiosyncratic ways in which they can learn, such as when knowledge is presented in written form, when concretely presented or in abstraction, and/or when interacting with others.

- *Learning strategies*—Individuals' own ways of regulating their learning, mainly categorized as direct strategies, which include memorizing, engaging cognitively, and compensating, or indirect strategies, which include metacognitive, affective, and social activities that support learning.

Age of acquisition

Age of onset is key to the nature of L2 acquisition and the competence that will be developed later in the higher proficiency levels. *The critical period hypothesis* argues that beyond a certain age the L1 is not likely to be acquired since biological mechanisms function up to a certain period. Therefore, children must be exposed to sufficient interactional input in social contexts. This has been interpreted for the L2 acquisition and it is hypothesized that learners who have successfully acquired the L1 will not be able to acquire L2 with the same mechanism that functioned for the acquisition of the L1 though L2 learners might attain a high level of proficiency through formal instruction.

Applied to the L2 acquisition context, the critical period hypothesis positions L2 acquisition in different ways as is discussed by Van Patten and Benati (2010):

1. L2 acquisition is influenced by a critical period and L2 learners cannot attain a language ability akin to that of native speakers of the L1.
2. L2 acquisition is *not* influenced by a critical period since L1 and L2 acquisition have fundamental similarities and can be acquired by using the same linguistic mechanisms, with difference in outcomes depending on nonlinguistic personal factors.
3. There are various critical periods, or perhaps critical periods for certain dimensions of language but not others.

Aptitude

Aptitude refers to cognitive abilities that learners rely on when they engage in acquisition, namely L2 here. Some of these abilities might include how to encode sounds or ability to recognize patterns in the input, which makes L2 acquisition easy for them. L2 learners with aptitude often demonstrate higher inductive learning ability and select relevant information that might help them acquire better. For example, DeKeyser (2000) reported a strong positive correlation between the scores of linguistic tests and those of aptitude tests, which Skehan (1989) also found. However, as Dörnyei reported, there is still need for further empirical findings that show such correlation.

Affective factors in SLA

Affective factors are seen to influence SLA. These include *attitude, motivation, self-esteem*, and *anxiety*.

Learners, for example, might have attitudes toward the learning of SLA that lower or increase their interest in L2. These attitudes might originate from the differences between L1 and L2 that might make it hard to learn, or the complexity of the L2 linguistic system, which might demand more cognitive resources to process. Therefore, the L2 learners might develop negative or positive attitudes toward the L2 for a variety of reasons.

Motivation

Motivation has been characterized as one of the key constructs in explaining the success and failure in SLA. It is categorized as a cognitive-oriented construct that involves the mental self of learners and their desire to learn (Van Patten & Benati, 2010). There are a number of studies that relate motivation to success of the learner and suggest that motivation is a key indicator of successful acquisition of second language.

Motivation as a construct has been categorized according to the locus of motivation (intrinsic or extrinsic) and purpose of learning (integrative vs. instrumental) (Gardner, 1985; Ryan & Deci, 2000). Intrinsic motivation refers to a natural predisposition to learn and internalize knowledge and skills. Such learners often find value and benefit in learning and do not need to be pushed by others to engage in learning or studying. Such students are said to achieve and acquire more. Extrinsic motivation, on the other hand, is related to external control creating desire to acquire or engage. Such students often develop resistance and can barely overcome dissatisfaction and disengagement. The control of others on engagement demonstrates a short-lived effect since they may not be activated without external push. These learners are usually motivated by rewards such as candy. The other binary categorization is integrative and instrumental constructs. Integrative motivation refers to the desire to acquire the L2 since they aim to become part of the community that speaks that language, develop a network with an international community, and participate in cultural occasions and engage in reading literature in that particular language. Such learners are said to develop an intrinsic motivation as well and engage in acquiring the L2 as a lifelong learning pursuit. However, instrumental motivation is related to the materialistic gains in educational and economic benefits that the L2 acquisition will bring, such as higher scores in the lessons, promotion in their career, or passing a test, rather than self-regulating their internal motivation and truly engaging in acquiring L2 on a long-term basis.

In addition to this binary and dichotomous categorization, Dörnyei (2014) argued the L2 motivational self-system is based on possible selves, which represent individuals' ideas of what they *might* become, what they *would like to* become, and what they *are afraid of* becoming. Dörnyei introduces SLA as a process of experiences that include the following dimensions. Self-guides includes the *ideal self*, which involves the characteristics that learners would ideally like to possess, whereas *ought-to self* involves the attributes that learners believes they ought to possess.

Possible selves present a broad overarching constellation interrelating motivational, cognitive, and affective areas. Accordingly, emotion and thought influence action and motivation toward a vision of the future or future self. Once an L2 learner develops and transforms emotions actuated by the thought of learning, this can help create a future vision of learning, thereby shaping future self. Self-guides, on the other hand, function effectively depending on L2 learners' appraisal of their own capabilities and the personal circumstances that could anchor their vision in realistic expectations that they can attain. Self-guides also involves learners' repertoire of task-related strategies that can be activated.

In the L2 context, for example, in a small-group discussion the educators might ask the following questions so students can articulate and activate their motivational L2 systems:

- How will the information about self-guides (ideal and ought-to selves) and the learning environment's roles in motivation influence your:
  - lessons/courses designs;
  - group work;
  - activities/tasks used in class; and
  - feedback to learners.

Self-esteem

Self-esteem refers to confidence and satisfaction in one's self. Branden (1969) defines it as one's self-perception of being praiseworthy and competent in overcoming challenges, whereas Coopersmith (1967) describes it as one's beliefs about how capable one is and how significant, successful, and worthy one perceives oneself.

Brown (2007) classifies self-esteem into global, specific/situational, and task self-esteem:

- Global self-esteem: How one aligns interpersonal and intrapersonal experiences with the external world.
- Situational or specific self-esteem: How one judges oneself on a particular life occasion.
- Task self-esteem: The assessments one would make of a specific situation.

In the context of SLA, development of self-esteem can be supported by educators' scaffolding when students are observed to have low self-confidence and low motivation by understanding them or by amending the task types and calibrating task complexity to provide achievable challenges.

Anxiety

According to Krashen's (1985) affective filter hypothesis, anxiety might negatively influence the process of SLA, which is also echoed by Liu (2006), who specifically highlights the impact on achievement in the L2. The level of anxiety is also considered to be one of the predictors of achievement (MacIntyre & Gardner, 1991). An excessive amount of anxiety might lead to low achievement, while a necessary amount of it may engender higher motivation and ambition to acquire. In supporting this, Mizruchi (1991) argues that low levels of anxiety help performance while high levels hurt.

Facilitative and debilitative anxiety

Anxiety is commonly considered as a reaction motivated by a variety of negative emotions that might pose a debilitative influence on SLA. According to Krashen (1985), anxiety is part of the affective filter that may prevent learners from processing and learning the language. In contrast, it is also suggested that anxiety can function as a facilitative factor in the process and can be correlated with motivation in learners (Pekrun et al., 2002). It is important for TESOL educators to be aware of the degree of learners' anxiety, so they may help reduce it if it is too high; however, facilitative anxiety may cause learners to be more aware and work harder.

There are a number of ways of overcoming debilitative effects of anxiety. For example, Lazarus and Folkman (1984) introduce three coping strategies: problem-focused strategy, which involves activities such as information-seeking, increasing investment, planning, and revisiting priorities for learners; emotion-focused strategy, which involves activities such as seeking emotional support, positive reframing, expressing (voicing), approval, and aspiring thinking; and behavioral efforts such as reducing required effort (removing self from situation) and psychological efforts such as denial, blocking, or mental distancing that might help learners avoid stressful circumstances.

Language anxiety

Language anxiety refers to the fear or apprehension experienced when L2 learners perform in a second language (Gardner & MacIntyre, 1993), which might debilitate the L2 acquisition process. Language anxiety might also lead to communication apprehension and fear of negative social evaluation as well as test anxiety. The anxiety arising from the language use can often cause the L2 learner to avoid communicating, which could be a great opportunity to develop language skills and acquire the L2. The avoidance is due partly to the fear that they are to be judged when they use the L2 in unsuccessful ways. Many students also develop anxiety about being tested and may not demonstrate their full potential of knowledge and language skills.

To overcome language anxiety, what TESOL educators should do is not to force L2 learners to speak before they feel ready to do so (Krashen, 1982) since levels of anxiety can be accelerated when learners' competence is not sufficient to perform speaking and basic communication. Forcing L2 learners to speak might also lead to negative emotions, thereby constraining L2 acquisition in general.

Inhibition and risk-taking behavior

Personality-related factors also affect L2 acquisition such as *inhibition* and *risk-taking behavior*. The former refers to how individuals protect themselves. When learners have language ego, which might be hindering the smooth acquisition of the L2, they often do not risk making mistakes. The avoidance can stabilize the developmental process of acquisition. TESOL educators need to help learners to adapt themselves to the idea that making mistakes is a natural part of acquisition and give up being overly critical about their performance. Learners should be provided time and space in which they can freely use language without being judged and inhibited by their teachers. In relation to this, students need to be supported to take risks when they use language. Risk-taking is also categorized as part of personality-related factors, which specifically refer to the ability to make informed and intellectual guesses (Rubin & Thompson, 1994) to comprehend meaning and construct one's own language knowledge by making use of the contextual clues. Taking risks and producing oral and written language pave the way to testing one's own knowledge and strengthening it as it is responded to by the listeners including educators and peers.

Extroversion and introversion

Another factor in the same category is whether individuals are extrovert or introvert. The former often tend to take risks in using the language and behave sociably in the community (i.e., the whole class group), whereas the latter tend to be reserved and seem active in small groups. Being sociable and active in groups like classroom settings might contribute positively to the process of L2 acquisition and these individuals will also create more opportunity to expose themselves to meaningful input and to practice and review language through more participation in communication. However, there are inconclusive research results regarding whether being extrovert leads to higher scores or more successful language acquisition. The suggestion would still be to help L2 learners to become more linguistically active and sociable by taking advantage of producing language in meaningful contexts. Such students brainstorm more and build confidence and show willingness to take risks with language practice.

Cognitive styles

Cognitive styles are the characteristic way in which an individual processes information and experience they are exposed to when they need to. More specifically, it is related to an individual's own consistent and unique ways of organizing and processing information (Messick, 1984). Cognitive styles are seen to be stable characteristics and function in line with fundamental information processing mechanisms (Peterson et al., 2009). These styles reflect one's typical or habitual mode of problem solving, thinking, perceiving, and remembering (Cassidy, 2004). The specific cognitive styles include holistic–sequential (Pask, 1976), holistic–analytical (Riding & Cheema, 1991), verbalizer–imager (Betts, 1909), and field-dependence/field-independence (Witkin et al., 1977).

Learning styles

Learning styles, on the other hand, refer to the ways in which individuals process materials. These styles are considered to be individual skills and preferences for how learners perceive, gather, and process learning materials (Jonassen & Grabowski, 1993). They also refer to preferred strategies with which to achieve the learning objectives (Soflano et al., 2015). Dörnyei (2014) describes it as the individual's habitual and preferred approach to learning while perceiving, interacting with, and responding to the learning environment.

Both cognitive and learning styles help and/or inhibit L2 acquisition in various ways depending on the material to be studied and knowledge to be acquired as well as the context of acquisition.

Auditory, visual, and kinesthetic learners

According to Dunn (2003), visual students prefer the visual presentation of material, such as flowcharts, graphics, and diagrams; auditory students prefer to listen to the material, while kinesthetic/tactile students prefer to undertake physical activity and actively apply the material.

Analytic/global thinkers and reflectivity/impulsivity

Dunn and Griggs (2003) categorize these learners as psychological variables. The former involves individual preferences for looking at the whole picture (analytic) while acquiring L2 rather than at the details (global thinker), while the latter refers to learners who need more time to decide on an issue (reflective learners) or who might reach conclusions very quickly (impulsive learners).

Questions for reflection

- Which of the personal/individual differences most resonated with you? Why did it?
- What can we do to support ELLs in the SLA process if they have traits that make the process more challenging?

Chapter Conclusions

Researchers and theorists have long analyzed the relationship between L1 and L2 acquisition/learning. They have studied the factors affecting the rate and the route of processes of SLA. SLA theories and relevant theoretical arguments have been developed over time by many schools of thought, which situate the learning of a L2 in cognitive, innate abilities, interaction, or sociocultural domains. Likewise, SLA research has identified personal variables in the SLA process. These arguments are known to second language teachers, who often rely on them to guide the instruction in their classrooms.

Discussion Questions

1 How do you envision an English lesson that could be informed by some of the theoretical discussions in the chapter?
2 What are the arguments in SLA that are relevant and interesting for your current students?
3 How can you make your lessons theory-informed for your current or future learners to increase learning and/or to boost motivation?

Tasks

1 Reflection:
  a. Can you reflect with your students on how they feel about the process of English language learning/acquisition? Explore whether they are in the process of learning or acquiring the language?
  b. Can you reflect with your colleagues on how they teach and identify the practices that seem to be informed by SLA theory?

2 Research/investigation:
   a. Investigate your students' learning strategies by asking them to write down the way they study English themselves and see how you can categorize them according to the given categorization of language learning strategies?
   b. Ask your students to tell you about their language anxiety and see if their anxiety is facilitating and debilitating?
3 Projects:
   a. Create a group work where students reflect on and discuss the differences among themselves while learning English. Ask them to prepare a presentation focusing on the differences and similarities that group members have in the SLA process.
   b. Design a template document for your students asking them to note the mistakes they often make and thinking about where these mistakes originate from. Ask them to trace it to their L1 and think about how they can overcome these.

Further Reading/Read and Discuss

Read about theories of language development and reflect on how you teach and can implement new arguments in your classroom:
   Whong, M. (2011). *Language teaching: Linguistic theory in practice*. Edinburgh University Press.
   Read about language learning and teaching motivation:
   Dörnyei, Z. (2018). Motivating students and teachers. In *The TESOL encyclopedia of English language teaching* (pp. 1–6). TESOL.

References

Alred, G., & Byram, M. (2002). Becoming an intercultural mediator: A longitudinal study of residence abroad. *Journal of Multilingual and Multicultural Development*, 23(5), 339–352. https://doi.org/10.1080/01434630208666473

Anderson, J. R. (1992). Automaticity and the ACT* theory. *American Journal of Psychology*, 105(2), 165–180. https://doi.org/10.2307/1423026

Anderson, T. (2017). The doctoral gaze: Foreign PhD students' internal and external academic discourse socialization. *Linguistics and Education*, 37, 1–10. 10.1016/j.linged.2016.12.001

Betts, G. H. (1909). *The distribution and functions of mental imagery*. Contributions to *Education Series*, No. 26, Teachers College, Columbia University.

Bialystok, E. (2001). *Bilingualism in development: Language, literacy, and cognition*. Cambridge University Press.

Bialystok, E. (1994). Analysis and control in the development of second language proficiency. *Studies in Second Language Acquisition*, 16(2), 157–168. 10.1017/S0272263100012857.

Bosher, S. (1997). Language and cultural identity: A study of Hmong students at postsecondary level. *TESOL Quarterly*, 31(3), 593–603. https://doi.org/10.2307/3587843

Branden, N. (1969). *The psychology of self-esteem.* Bantam Books.

Brown, H. D. (2007). *Principles of language learning and teaching* (5th ed.). Pearson.

Canale, M., & Swain, M. (1980). Theoretical bases of communicative approaches to second language teaching and testing. *Applied Linguistics,* 1(1), 1–47. http://dx.doi.org/10.1093/applin/I.1.1

Carey, J. W. (1992). *Communication as culture: Essays on media and society.* Routledge.

Cassidy, S. (2004). Learning styles: An overview of theories, models, and measures. *Educational Psychology,* 24(4), 419–444. https://doi.org/10.1080/0144341042000228834

Chomsky, N. (1982). *Some concepts and consequences of the theory of government and binding.* MIT Press.

Cook, V. J. (1998). Relating SLA research to language teaching materials. *Canadian Journal of Applied Linguistics,* 1(1–2), 9–27. https://journals.lib.unb.ca/index.php/CJAL/article/view/19807

Cook, V. (2008). Multi-competence: Black hole or wormhole for second language acquisition research. In Z. Han (Ed.), *Understanding second language process* (pp. 16–26). Multilingual Matters.

Cook, V. J. (1998). Relating SLA research to language teaching materials. *Canadian Journal of Applied Linguistics,* 1(1–2), 9–27.

Coopersmith, S. (1967). *The antecedents of self-esteem.* W.H. Freeman.

Cummins, J. (1979). Cognitive/academic language proficiency, linguistic interdependence, the optimum age question and some other matters. Working Papers on Bilingualism Toronto, (19), 197–202.

DeKeyser, R. (1997). Beyond explicit rule learning: Automatizing second language morphosyntax. *Studies in Second Language Acquisition,* 19(2), 195–221. https://www.jstor.org/stable/44488683 (accessed March 22, 2021).

DeKeyser, R. M. (2000). The robustness of critical period effects in second language acquisition. *Studies in Second Language Acquisition,* 22(4), 499–533. https://doi.org/10.1017/S0272263100004022

Dörnyei, Z. (2014). *The psychology of the language learner: Individual differences in second language acquisition.* Routledge.

Duff, P. (2007). Second language socialization as sociocultural theory: Insights and issues. *Language Teaching,* 40(4), 309–319. https://doi.org/10.1017/S0261444807004508

Duff, P. (2010). Language socialization. In N. Hornberger & S. McKay (Eds.), *Sociolinguistics and language education* (pp. 427–452). Multilingual Matters.

Duff, P. (2012). Second language socialization. In A. Duranti, E. Ochs, & B. B. Schieffelin (Eds.), *Handbook of language socialization* (pp. 564–586). Wiley-Blackwell.

Dunn, R. (2003). The Dunn and Dunn learning-style model and its theoretical cornerstone. In R. Dunn & S. A. Griggs (Eds.), *Synthesis of the Dunn and Dunn learning-style model research* (pp. 1–6). St. John's University's Center for the Study of Learning and Teaching Styles.

Ellis, R. 1997. *Second language acquisition* Oxford Introductions to Language Study. Oxford University Press.

Ellis, R. (2007). The differential effects of corrective feedback on two grammatical structures. In A. Mackey (Ed.), *Conversational interaction in second language acquisition* (pp. 339–361). Oxford University Press.

Gardner, R. C. (1985). *Social psychology and second language learning: The role of attitudes and motivation.* Edward Arnold.

Gardner, R. C. (2001). Integrative motivation and second language acquisition. In Z. Dörnyei & R. Schmidt (Eds.), *Motivation and second language acquisition* (pp. 1–19). The University of Hawai'i, Second Language Teaching and Curriculum Center.

Gardner, R. C., & MacIntyre, P. D. (1993). On the measurement of affective variables in second language learning. *Language Learning*, 43(2), 157–194. https://doi.org/10.1111/j.1467-1770.1992.tb00714.x

Gass, S. M. (1997). *Input, interaction, and the second language learner*. Lawrence Erlbaum Associates.

Gass, S., & Selinker, L. (2008). *Second language acquisition: An introductory course*. Routledge.

Graham, C. R., & Brown, C. (1996). The effects of acculturation on second language proficiency in a community with a two-way bilingual program. *The Bilingual Research Journal*, 20(2), 235–260. https://doi.org/10.1080/15235882.1996.10668629

Hammer, K., & Dewaele, J. M. (2015). Acculturation as the key to the ultimate attainment? The case of Polish-English bilinguals in the UK. In F. Forsberg Lundell & I. Bartning (Eds.), *Cultural migrants and optimal language acquisition* (pp. 178–202). Multilingual Matters.

Hymes, D. (1966). Two types of linguistic relativity. In W. Bright (Ed.), *Sociolinguistics* (pp. 114–158). Mouton.

Izumi, S. (2002). Output, input enhancement, and the noticing hypothesis: An experimental study on ESL relativization. *Studies in Second Language Acquisition*, 24(4), 541–577. https://doi.org/10.1017/S0272263102004023

Jiang, M., Green, R. J., Henley, T. B., & Masten, W. G. (2009). Acculturation in relation to the acquisition of a second language. *Journal of Multilingual and Multicultural Development*, 30(6), 481–492. http://doi.org/10.1080/01434630903147898

Jonassen, D. H., & Grabowski, B. L. (1993). *Handbook of individual differences, learning & instruction*. Lawrence Erlbaum Associates.

Köylü, Z. (2016). *The influence of context on L2 development: The case of Turkish undergraduates at home and abroad* (Unpublished dissertation). University of South Florida.

Krashen, S. (1982). *Principles and practices of second language acquisition*. Pergamon.

Krashen, S. (1985). *The input hypothesis: Issues and implications*. Longman.

Lazarus, R. S., & Folkman, S. (1984). *Stress, appraisal, and coping*. Springer.

Liu, D. (2006). Anxiety in Chinese EFL students at different proficiency levels. *System*, 34(3), 301–316. http://doi.org/10.1016/j.system.2006.04.004

Long, M. (1996). The role of the linguistic environment in second language acquisition. In W. Ritchie & T. Bhatia (Eds.), *Handbook of second language acquisition* (pp. 413–468). Academic Press.

Lybeck, K. (2002). Cultural identification and second language pronunciation of Americans in Norway. *The Modern Language Journal*, 86(2), 174–191. http://doi.org/10.1111/1540-4781.00143

MacIntyre, P. D., & Gardner, R. C. (1991). Language anxiety: Its relationship to other anxieties and to processing in native and second languages. *Language Learning*, 41(4), 513–534. http://petermacintyre.weebly.com/uploads/1/0/1/8/10187707/language_anxiety1991.pdf (accessed March 22, 2021).

Messick, S. (1984). The psychology of educational measurement. *ETS Research Report Series*, 1984(1), i–55. https://doi.org/10.1002/j.2330-8516.1984.tb00046.x

Mizruchi, M. S. (1991). Urgency, motivation, and group performance: The effect of prior success on current success among professional basketball teams. *Social Psychology Quarterly*, 52(2), 181–189.

Nation, I. S. P. (2011). Second language speaking. In E. Hinkel (Ed.), *Handbook of research in second language teaching and learning* (pp. 445–454). Routledge.

Ortega, L. (2009). *Understanding second language acquisition*. Routledge.

Pask, G. (1976). Styles and strategies of learning. *British Journal of Educational Psychology*, 46(2), 128–148. https://doi.org/10.1111/j.2044-8279.1976.tb02305.x

Pekrun, R., Goetz, T., Titz, W., & Perry, R. P. (2002). Academic emotions in students' self-regulated learning and achievement: A program of qualitative and quantitative research. *Educational Psychologist*, 37(2), 91–105. https://doi.org/10.1207/S15326985EP3702_4

Peterson, E. R., Rayner, S. G., & Armstrong, S. J. (2009). Researching the psychology of cognitive style and learning style: Is there really a future? *Learning and Individual Differences*, 19(4), 518–523. https://www.researchgate.net/publication/287990468 (accessed March 22, 2021).

Peterson, E., Rayner, S., & Armstrong, S. (2009). Researching the psychology of cognitive style and learning style: Is there really a future? *Learning and Individual Differences*, 19(4), 518–523.

Richards, J., & Schmidt, R. (Eds.) (2002). Interaction hypothesis. In J. C. Richards & R. Schmidt (Eds.), *Longman dictionary of language teaching and applied linguistics* (4th ed., p. 290). Longman.

Riding, R., & Cheema, I. (1991). Cognitive styles—An overview and integration. *Educational Psychology*, 11(3–4), 193–215. https://doi.org/10.1080/0144341910110301

Rubin, J., & Thompson, I. (1994). *How to become a more successful language learner*. Heinle & Heinle.

Ryan, R. M., & Deci, D. L. (2000). Self-determination theory and the facilitation of intrinsic motivation, social development, and well-being. *American Psychologist*, 55(1), 68–78. https://doi.org/10.1037110003-066X.55.1.68

Savignon, S. J. (1976). *Communicative competence: Theory and classroom practice*. Addison-Wesley.

Savignon, S. J. (1983). *Communicative competence: Theory and classroom practice: Texts and contexts in second language teaching*. Addison-Wesley.

Schumann, J. H. (1986). Research on the acculturation model for second language acquisition. *Journal of Multilingual and Multicultural Development*, 7(5), 379–392. doi:10.1080/01434632.1986.9994254

Selinker, L. (1972) Interlanguage. *International Review of Applied Linguistics*, 10(3), 219–231. https://doi.org/10.1515/iral.1972.10.1-4.209

Skehan, P. (1989). *Individual differences in second language learning*. Edward Arnold.

Skehan, P. (1998). *A cognitive approach to language learning*. Oxford University Press.

Skinner, B. F. (1957). *Verbal behavior*. Copley Publishing Group.

Soflano, M., Connolly, T. M., & Hainey, T. (2015). An application of adaptive games-based learning based on learning style to teach SQL. *Computers & Education*, 86(C), 192–211. https://doi.org/10.1016/j.compedu.2015.03.015

Swain, M. (1985). Communicative competence: Some roles of comprehensible input and comprehensible output in its development. In S. Gass & C. Madden (Eds.), *Input in second language acquisition* (pp. 235–253). Newbury House.

Swain, M. (2005). The output hypothesis: Theory and research. In E. Hinkel (Ed.), *Handbook of research in second language teaching and learning* (pp. 471–484). Routledge.

Tomasello, M. (2000). Culture and cognitive development. *Current Directions in Psychological Science, 9*(2), 37–40. https://doi.org/10.1111/1467-8721.00056

Tracy-Ventura, N., Dewaele, J. M., Köylü, Z., & McManus, K. (2016). Personality changes after the 'year abroad'?: A mixed-methods study. *Study Abroad Research in Second Language Acquisition and International Education, 1*(1), 107–127. https://doi.org/10.1075/sar.1.1.05tra

Van Patten, B., & Benati, J. (2010). *Key terms in second language acquisition*. Continuum.

Vygotsky, L. S. (1978). *Mind in society: Development of higher psychological processes*. Harvard University Press.

Wang, Q., & Castro, C. D. (2010). Classroom interaction and language output. *English Language Teaching, 3*(2), 175–186. doi:10.5539/elt.v3n2p175

Waniek-Klimczak, E. (2011). Acculturation strategy and language experience in expert ESL speakers: An exploratory study. *Studies in Second Language Learning and Teaching, 1*(2), 227–245. doi:10.14746/ssllt.2011.1.2.4

Watson, J. B. (1930). *Behaviorism* (revised ed.). University of Chicago Press.

Witkin, H. A., Moore, C. A., Goodenough, D. R., & Cox, P. W. (1977). Field-dependent and field- independent cognitive styles and their educational implications. *Review of Educational Research, 47*(1), 1–64. https://doi.org/10.3102/00346543047001001

Part Three

TESOL Professionals' Knowledge of Instruction, Planning, and Assessment

6

How Does Theory Inform and Guide Instructional Practice?

This chapter will investigate links between SLA theories and instructional practices. Macrostrategies to guide instruction are included to highlight the links between SLA theory and instructional practice. Background on how TESOL has developed its research-informed practices will be discussed along with some of the key methodologies.

Learning Outcomes

At the conclusion of this chapter, you will be able to:

- compare and contrast various approaches and methods of teaching English
- implement the communicative language teaching approach and integrated skills instruction
- design lessons for differing proficiency levels that align with the 10 macrostrategies in the post-methods condition
- describe professional and methodological debates with regard to English teaching over the past decades

Have you considered the ways educators make instructional choices? What guides their choices? In this vignette, see how one educator makes choices about her teaching that connects educational and SLA theories and instructional practices.

TESOL Voices

Practitioner's Perspective

How is it that after decades of teaching, instructional choices almost become second nature? When I began my career, I struggled to find a balance between teaching content and fostering my students' well-being. While content is, of course, fundamental, students remember classroom atmosphere—the extent to which they felt part of a community. As such, I strived for students to feel welcomed, accepted, and appreciated in the classroom, and I continue to acknowledge that

---

Introduction to TESOL: Becoming a language teaching professional, First Edition. Kate Mastruserio Reynolds, Kenan Dikilitaş, and Steve Close.
© 2022 John Wiley & Sons, Inc. Published 2022 by John Wiley & Sons, Inc.

I have as much to learn from them as they do from me. This work is hard and ongoing, yet it influences my instructional choices each day. So much so that I tend to not even second guess my choices, including the SLA theories, as they support instructional choices engrained in my approach to teaching.

There are a few SLA theories and practices that take me back to my earlier career and continue to guide my day-to-day instructional choices, including how I make students feel welcome. The theories and methods that most influence me are: communicative language teaching (CLT), Krashen's input hypothesis, content-based instruction, sheltered content instruction, and social constructivism. These theories have been embedded into my pedagogical practices and have shaped me as an educator and guided my teaching practices. For instance, no one can effectively learn when their affective filter is high. Theoretically, the affective filter hypothesis was developed by SLA theorist, Stephen Krashen, who describes how a student's attitudes, motivations, and anxieties can impact the success of language learning. If students are experiencing high anxiety in the classroom, their learning is hindered. Therefore, I continually ask myself how to best support learning through a lower affective filter. But I'm not always thinking about it in those theoretical terms. I'm just continually applying best practices for my students.

Here is a very specific example of a theoretical practice that has become almost second nature to me. In line with the affective filter hypothesis, working toward increased motivation, lowered language anxiety, and positive learning attitudes takes time to develop. Successfully fostering relationships among learners creates a sense of purpose and belonging in the classroom resulting in greater student participation and rapport. From the first day of class to the very end of the semester, I work toward creating a strong classroom community. I develop a rapport not only between teacher and student, but also between students. In the classroom, I make sure to say every student's name, every class period. By the end of the first week of my course, every student knows every classmate's name—lowering the affective filter and allowing for more engaging and authentic learning to happen. Building a strong classroom community allows students to lower the affective filter and real learning can begin.

Continuous lifelong learning and demonstrating that practice to my students is essential throughout any course. In any classroom I teach in, I strive to create an effective learning atmosphere for all learners based on theory and research, whether young students or adult learners, by using authentic and communicative practices in the classroom and, with time, this practice will begin to feel second nature to any instructor.

Mari Bodensteiner, Instructor
University ofvWisconsin-Eau Claire

Methodological Overview

Formal language teaching has been occurring for centuries (Howatt, 2004). How educators were prepared to teach second languages related to beliefs of the time about second language learning and practical goals and needs of learners. As these beliefs and goals/needs shifted and changed with increased physical mobility of peoples in the later part of the second millennium, so did the methods of instruction. In the 20th century, educational researchers became increasingly interested in understanding how languages are learned and how we should teach them. This chapter will focus on instructional practices, emphasizing the methods that are most common and effective for second language learning, whereas the next chapter will focus on key SLA research and how it informs our instructional choices.

Teacher preparation traditionally involved preparing future educators to follow the method: the single "popular" way of instruction at a given time. This approach has been labeled *prescriptivism*, or following the one prescribed method. This type of teacher preparation produced educators who could teach in the one way very well, but could not effectively modify that way of instruction to incorporate new research findings or innovative ideas. These educators tended toward stagnation in their instructional practice, and rejection of new methods and ideas.

The field of TESOL experienced the same pattern as general education. We developed and utilized a wide variety of "methods" that could be employed as an instructional package: one set of procedures to be followed explicitly. Some of our more recognized examples are: The Silent Way, Suggestopedia, grammar translation, the natural approach, community language learning, and CLT. What we learned from these methods is that one method alone cannot accomplish the task of SL/FL instruction that suits all kinds of learners and contexts (Prabhu, 1990) (see Figure 6.1).

Questions for reflection

- How would you characterize the changes in instructional models over time?
- Do you think it is better for educators to have flexibility to make instructional choices based upon their learner population, learners' goals and needs, and context, or is it better to have a single model to follow? What are the pros and cons of each approach?
- Why is it important to TESOL educators' careers that they are informed in a wide array of approaches and methods?

Brown (1994, 2000) outlined principles of an *Informed Eclectic Approach* to language teaching. Brown's approach sees effective educators as those who are knowledgeable about SLA, methodologies, learners, and learning context, and who vary methods and techniques based upon this knowledge for the specific population of learners. An informed eclectic approach draws upon activities and techniques from methodologies

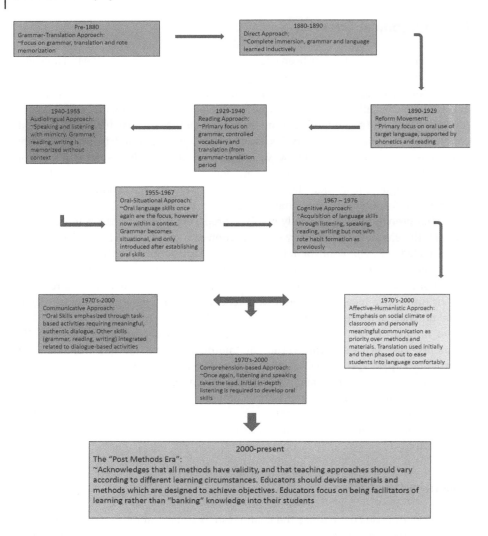

Figure 6.1 Instructional methods over time. Used with permission of Kathryn Metzger.
*Note that this flowchart represents a Western vantage point. Time frames and methodological influences would differ in the east and other locations.

of the past and innovates instruction without the constraints of a particular method. For more on this topic, see Mellow's summary of principled eclecticism (2002). Brown's principles align well with those of Kumaravadivelu, whose work we will discuss in the text that follows.

In 1994, Kumaravadivelu outlined 10 research-based practices he labeled macrostrategies to guide second language teaching. These strategies provide us with identifying overarching principles of language teaching, which educators can draw on and enact in their teaching. Kumaravadivelu also highlights with these principles how educators can nurture learner identity that is characterized by a critical and autonomous learning process.

Questions for reflection

- Once you have reviewed these macrostrategies, can you think about how you might use them to guide your instructional choices as a TESOL educator?
- Try to think of these not just in the context of TESOL, but in the context of teaching in general. Have you attended classes that used similar strategies?

1. Macrostrategy one: Maximizing learning opportunities.

Macrostrategy one is a suggestion to create and use learning experiences for the maximum benefit of the learners. Educators can construct lessons that cause learners to engage with the language, whether it is analyzing grammatical points in a piece of writing or learning to introduce themselves orally in the target language, which will also provide abundant opportunities for learners to practice the language. Furthermore, educators should engage in reflective teaching and modifying lessons toward improvement. During and after lessons educators should note aspects of the lesson that facilitated language learning, and those that could be improved to enhance the language learning.

Next, Kumaravadivelu encourages us to change our view of "educators simply as teachers and learners simply as only learners" (1994, p. 33). In other words, we should change our role relationships and view the verbal interaction and the knowledge in the classroom as co-constructed between teacher and learners. When we alter our perceptions of roles, learners are empowered to take the lead at times. They can tell us what they need, assist each other, and challenge assumptions about language and language learning, which will be more memorable and meaningful to them. Through this alteration, learners are placed at the center of learning. How we are teaching is not the focus, but a key facilitating factor in students' learning experiences.

2 Macrostrategy two: Facilitate negotiated interaction.

Building on macrostrategy one, macrostrategy two suggests creating in-class opportunities for learners to have meaningful peer-to-peer linguistic interaction. Interaction, whether it is oral or written/in person or online, is considered a crucial principle of SLA. These two macrostrategies can be combined: when we have ample opportunities for learning and the interaction is meaningful, ELLs are more likely to acquire the language.

One additional component of macrostrategy two is "negotiated interaction." Negotiated interaction means that students have opportunities to interact and ask each other questions to clarify, confirm, and negotiate their understandings. During interaction when learners express their ideas and negotiate meanings in order to flesh out what they mean, they also arrive at new understandings of words, expressions, and ideas. TESOL educators are encouraged to teach the tools for negotiated interaction explicitly (i.e., clarify, confirm, request, modify their linguistic contribution, etc.) while providing ample, meaningful interaction.

Questions for reflection

- How do you envision macrostrategies one and two working together?
- How might you achieve these goals in your current or future classes?

3 Macrostrategy three: Minimize perceptual mismatches.

Macrostrategy three guides TESOL educators to reduce misunderstandings that may hinder or obstruct learners based on differences in ways of thinking communicating, using linguistics, teaching, learning, and evaluating as well as attitudes/beliefs, strategies, cultures, and procedures. Some of these areas are evident. For example, it's important to avoid a mismatch between the learners' culture(s) and the target language culture(s) or to reduce the differences in the instruction or evaluation procedures that learners anticipate and those to be employed. These differences can be accommodated or new procedures, along with a rationale for employing them, can be taught. Other areas where mismatches and misunderstandings can occur are less obvious. For example, educators sometimes encounter attitudes and beliefs that can present a significant roadblock if the teacher is not aware that they are presenting a concept/topic from a contradictory angle. Beliefs and attitudes about religion, roles of men and women, race, LGBTQ status, wealth and poverty, politics, and war can unexpectedly derail a lesson because the beliefs of the learners differ from those of the teacher or materials used. In some cases, educators may not be aware that a mismatch has occurred. They may only observe the outcome, which may be a range of emotions, tuning out, or an inability to learn the concept. Such mismatches might need to be dealt with; otherwise, learners will feel disengaged, even though although they might really want to learn English. Some modification in the teaching materials' reference to these sensitive issues can be considered and carried out accordingly.

4 Macrostrategy four: Activate intuitive heuristics.

A heuristic is a replicable method or approach for directing one's attention in learning, discovery, or problem solving. Since we cannot possibly teach all aspects of another language, we should help language learners to develop their linguistic intuition (i.e., to think and problem solve using their knowledge of the language). For example, we can teach language learners to identify patterns through analysis so as to give them a tool for understanding incoming linguistic data. This also refers to inductive learning, which positions learners as processors of linguistic structures that enable them to generalize language rules. In such a way, they develop skills to acquire language indirectly, without explicit instruction. Learning takes place through a mode of learning that requires no goal-oriented "lesson." This also applies to learning the meaning of words and acquiring discourse or conversation structures. Once learners are taught to interpret forms to induce functions and meanings, they can become students who know how to learn.

5 Macrostrategy five: Foster language awareness.

Macrostrategy five guides TESOL educators to create instructional opportunities for learners to develop their understandings of linguistic forms, functions, and meanings through consciousness-raising and monitoring activities. Educators can direct learners' attention to a specific form in context and discuss the meanings and uses of the form to increase their language awareness. This metalinguistic awareness does not mean that learners need to learn a grammatical form in a traditional manner; rather, it may mean that a nuance of language use is highlighted to illustrate a sociocultural pattern.

Once learners have an awareness of a particular form, they can monitor their own language use to see if they are employing the form correctly. This is known as *self-monitoring*. While, in Krashen's terms, self-monitoring is a factor that might defy the process of attaining fluency, it has the potential to contribute to learners' awareness of their own linguistic development (Krashen, 1982). Self-correction and self-regulation of use of language are useful in the sense that learners process and reprocess their own language production, which strengthens their metacognition, by facilitating the monitoring and evaluation of their own learning process.

Questions for reflection

- How might you reduce perceptual mismatches in your lesson planning and delivery? What do you need to learn about your learner population to help you reduce perceptual mismatches?
- How might you engage your learners' abilities to problem solve while raising their awareness of language patterns and forms in use?

---

6 Macrostrategy six: Contextualize linguistic input.

Macrostrategy six directs educators to provide authentic and meaningful contexts for real language use. This involves using readings, dialogues, situations, and tasks that learners may encounter in their lives, thus providing them with meaning and applicability for the learners.

Aside from teaching through contextualized language use, macrostrategy six encourages educators to provide grammar, phonology, and vocabulary examples that are actually employed in real communication. In doing so, macrostrategy six avoids the issue of isolated, individual sentences that are removed from an authentic context: a style of learning that takes away vital linguistic information that can make it more difficult to comprehend or make meanings (Kumaravadivelu, 1994, p. 38). Contextualized input helps learners notice where they can use the newly learned linguistic forms. It also avoids the application of these concepts as seemingly arbitrary "rules," since it offers opportunities to incidentally learn words and functions that are encountered through natural discourse. It also includes information about the context, which makes the input enriched and vivid. For example, using a dialogue that comes from the perspective of authentic speakers will provide more contextualized input than a single sentence that exemplifies merely the form.

7 Macrostrategy seven: Integrate language skills.

Language skills (i.e., speaking, listening, reading, and writing) are "essentially interrelated and mutually reinforcing" (Kumaravadivelu, 1994, p. 39). This means that they should not be taught separately because skills help learners make meanings with other skills (see section on "Skills-based and Integrated Skills Instruction"). When we integrate the four language skills into classes, language learners who are stronger in some areas can rely on those areas to help them build the ones in which they are not particularly strong. Macrostrategy seven guides educators to integrate speaking, listening, reading, and writing into classes in meaningful and authentic ways.

The integration of skills needs to be designed in ways that allow the skills to complement each other. One way to do this effectively is by assigning a certain function to each skill that is integrated. It is also possible to design lessons that integrate several language skills rather than only integrating two skills. For example, learners might start by watching a video or listening to a recording, followed by a relevant reading that offers the essential information about the topic. They then continue to discuss the topic (speaking) with others using the background knowledge that was introduced to them through two modalities (watching/listening and reading). In language courses, educators usually take it for granted that learners can talk about specific topics that they have been exposed to at length in classroom activities. However, the number one reason for not speaking in discussions is, in fact, the learner's feeling that they lack sufficient understanding of the topic. A well-understood topic can activate learners' minds and provide them with necessary words and phrases that they use. The purpose in offering such knowledge multimodally is that each modality can address diverse input processors (i.e., seeing the action, hearing the voice, and decoding the text). In this way, the ultimate goal of helping learners to speak will be more efficiently conducted.

Questions for reflection

- How do you plan to contextualize linguistic input and integrate language skills simultaneously in your current or future classes? Is this difficult or relatively easy to achieve?

---

8 Macrostrategy eight: Promote learner autonomy.

Kumaravadivelu argues that it is best when learners are able be comfortable working independently whether in our classes, in interaction outside of class, or in classes later in their education. When we teach learners how to use language learning strategies to improve their second/foreign language process, they are building their confidence and ability to learn more language independently. According to Oxford (1990), there are six groups of language strategies, which include memorization, cognitive, compensation, metacognitive, affective, and social strategies. A learner's range of language learning strategies has a direct impact on their success. Learner autonomy can also be promoted by providing learners with freedom to choose, alternatives to try, and agency to control their own learning process. Since all learners learn differently, the concept of autonomy is an important element in helping them learn. Rather than referring only refer to learning independently or individually, learner autonomy refers to the ability to work interdependently within collaborative learning communities.

9 Macrostrategy nine: Raise cultural consciousness.

Kumaravadivelu acknowledges the interrelated nature of language and culture, arguing that when learning another language, one may need to understand some of the culture(s) where the language is used. He explains that educators should, "establish a common ground for integrating the target language and culture" (1994, p. 41). TESOL educators are encouraged to create opportunities for learners to share their cultural understandings and misunderstandings.

There are, however, some issues that arise when trying to combine language and culture. First, we want to teach about the culture of the target language when appropriate, but we must avoid cultural imperialism, meaning promoting one culture's values and patterns over another. So, we should approach the relationship between language and culture from a multicultural perspective and analyze the various cultures' usage of language. Second, more people all over the world are using English than ever before. Many have no interest in learning about the cultures that originated a language. There are many places in which different language speakers interact and have nothing to do with the cultures that originated the language. Therefore, we would need to balance the interests and goals of the learners with choices made about teaching culture. In some situations, it is best to discuss cultural perceptions and understandings as they relate to language and be sure to avoid any perception of promoting a culture.

10 Macrostrategy ten: Ensure social relevance.

Educators need to be mindful of the context of learning—"societal, political, economic, and educational environment" (Kumaravadivelu, 1994, p. 42)—to ensure that the learning is in tune with learners' goals, needs, etc. While it may seem that a topic like language would simply be perceived by learners as "content-based" (much as one might see a chemistry or algebra class), a successful language learner must be introspective and flexible in their thinking. In this way, a language class is more like courses in literature or art, which require a degree of personal investment in the topic. The context for language learning is inevitably personal and individualized to each student.

While the social context of a classroom may seem obvious, a language class is as much about the learners as it is about the language itself. Included within the characteristics that have the potential to impede learning are the individual schema that each student brings to the learning environment. We can make predictions about potential reactions of classes as a whole, subcommunities within the classroom, and even individual students. Anticipating and accommodating those reactions can make the difference between an engaged learner and an alienated learner.

TESOL educators strive to make informed choices about their instructional choices and employ the 10 macrostrategies and SLA theories to guide their choices. For the remainder of this chapter, we will discuss the three contemporary and noteworthy methods and the tools that emerged from the method, so you can call upon these tools in your own teaching. You might start by reflecting on which macrostrategies are present in the methods while you read.

Questions for reflection

- What is the relationship between macrostrategies four and eight? How do they address different, but related, skills?
- What is the relationship between macrostrategies three and nine? How do these macrostrategies guide us to treat culture(s) in our classes?
- How do the macrostrategies guide instructional planning, delivery, and assessment? How do they help us?
- Is there anything missing from the macrostrategies? Would you add another important principle or theory to this list?

Ellis' 12 Principles of Instructed SLA

In 2014, Rod Ellis, a world-renowned expert on SLA theory, shared a summary of guiding principles of second language instruction. These guiding principles are derived from hundreds of research studies, so you may recognize them from Chapters 4 and 5.

Some of these principles align with the macrostrategies; others are unique. As you read, compare the two lists to observe their similarities and differences as well as their priorities.

- Principle 1: Instruction needs to ensure that learners develop both a rich repertoire of formulaic expressions and a rule-based competence.
- Principle 2: Instruction needs to ensure that learners focus predominantly on meaning.
- Principle 3: Instruction needs to ensure that learners also focus on form.
- Principle 4: Instruction needs to be predominantly directed at developing implicit knowledge of the L2 while not neglecting explicit knowledge.
- Principle 5: Instruction needs to take into account the learners' "built-in syllabus." Learners follow a natural order and sequence of mastering new forms, which are fixed and universal in order.
- Principle 6: Successful instructed language learning requires extensive L2 input.
- Principle 7: Successful instructed language learning also requires opportunities for output.
- Principle 8: The opportunity to interact in the L2 is central to developing L2 proficiency.
- Principle 9: Instruction needs to take into account individual differences in learners.
- Principle 10: In assessing learners' L2 proficiency, it is important to examine free as well as controlled production.
- Principle 11: Learners need to engage collaboratively in talk about linguistic problems and try to agree on solutions to them.
- Principle 12: Instruction needs to take into account the subjective aspect to learning a new language (Ellis, 2014).

In this list, you will notice the emphases on meaningful communication (Principle 2), and language exposure and use (i.e., input, output, and interaction in Principles 6, 7, and 8, respectively). Principles 2, 6, 7, and 8 all interact, too. Input should be meaningful and comprehensible to the learner. Output and interaction should be meaningful too. Principles 1 and 3 are about patterns of language and learners' knowledge of the language patterns. Principle 5 is also about patterns of language, yet it reminds educators that there is sequence of stages in L2 acquisition/learning. Principles 9 and 12 remind educators of the differences of individual learners and their unique perspective on the learning of a new language. Principle 10 helps educators to include controlled and open-ended activities. Principle 11, which Ellis sees as an extension of Principle 7, emphasizes the need for learners to engage in collaborative analysis of language, and linguistic ambiguities and problems, and problem solving.

Ellis and Kumaravadivelu both include meaningful communication and input, output, and interaction in their lists. In the next section, you will read about one methodology that includes these concepts as essential components.

Communicative Language Teaching

Although form-focused approaches continue to impact language teaching and learning in many ways, the implications of communicative approaches are more profound and widespread worldwide in current instruction. These approaches emerged as a shift from and reaction to the structural approaches. The most influential of the communication-focus paradigms is *communicative language teaching* (CLT). Hallmarks of CLT include integrating speaking, listening, reading, and writing into lessons, interacting in oral and written forms in authentic contexts, discovering linguistic patterns implicitly, and developing ability to communicate meaningful messages rather than only learning about the structures and words (see "Sample communicative language teaching activities" box). The notable distinction from other methodologies of the time was that in CLT learners interacted with each other often. Grammar and vocabulary were not the focal point of lessons. Although many CLT classes also include explicit instruction in grammar and vocabulary today, originally CLT classes did not include instruction on the structures of English.

In most communicative classrooms learners learn social language: the language needed to establish and maintain social relationships as well as participate in daily activities, such as conducting a bank transaction, finding the right library book, or returning a purchase at a shop. The subject of these language classes is learning the grammar patterns, vocabulary, and ways to express oneself in real-life or authentic situations.

Sample communicative language teaching activities

Discussion Activities

As the name indicates, discussion activities are about engaging learners with compelling topics, so they want to share their ideas and opinions. The topics must be relevant to the age, location, and culture of the learners. Some topics just do not work in some settings.

1. Should homework be banned? If so, why? If not, why not?
2. What do you think about having an international space force?
3. Is it a good idea for the cafeteria to serve junk food? If so, why? If not, why not?
4. Should communities be able to ban a book from a school or library? If so, why? If not, why not?
5. What is gained by a university education? Is a university education worth the money?
6. Should governments have a mandatory national service? If so, why? If not, why not?
7. Should uniforms be required in schools? Why or why not?

These discussion topics would allow learners to share their insights and perspectives and listen to those of their peers. Often, TESOLers will ask pairs or small groups to summarize their discussion when the class reunites as a whole group.

Through this process learners interact meaningfully, have opportunities to clarify and ask questions, elaborate their thinking, and repeat/rephrase their contributions. Learners may be asked to take notes, write a summary, or read more on the topic too.

Role-plays and Dialogues

These activities mirror the interaction and sequencing of lessons you see in "Discussion Activities." They differ from "Discussion Activities" in that learners assume a new or alternative persona and act the part in the activity. Kate met her long-time friend, Kevin, in French class in college during a role-play in which she was the interviewer and he was Madonna!

1. Interview a classmate. One student plays the role of a celebrity or historical person and the other the interviewer.
2. Going to the doctor. One student is the patient with a specific ailment, while the other is the doctor who will treat them.
3. Going on a first or blind date. Each student would choose a persona and characteristics (good or bad) they wish to exhibit through their words and actions. They can choose what type of date and then enact it.
4. TV talk show. Learners can present a product and get feedback like on *Shark Tank*. They can be panelists like on *The View*.
5. A detective and client. The client would bring their case to the detective and the detective would need to ask questions to be sure they understand the case and all the important players.

Role-plays and skits can focus on speaking and listening without time to prepare but may also include writing and reading of the skit in advance.

Songs

The songs in a CLT classroom can be anything from traditional to contemporary songs. Multicultural music or various genres are good for representing diversity and heightening the chances of learners finding some music they like. With songs, just as other communicative activities, the choice of songs would need to be culturally, topically, and age/grade appropriate. With contemporary songs, educators need to be mindful too of potentially vulgar themes or language. The speed of the music would also impact learners' abilities to comprehend the lyrics, so choosing appropriate songs for the proficiency level is important too. Songs with which ELLs might already be familiar, and that provide easily understood, but thought-provoking lyrics are:

1. "I Am a Rock" by Simon and Garfunkel.
2. "Imagine" by John Lennon.
3. "If I Were a Boy" by Beyoncé.
4. "Count on Me" by Bruno Mars.
5. "Our House" by Madness.
6. "Friday, I'm in Love" by The Cure.
7. "Happy Birthday."
8. "My Favorite Things" by Rodgers and Hammerstein.

Chants are another variation on songs, which have distinct, repetitive rhythms. Carolyn Graham was the originator of using chants for language learning in the 1980s and based her chants on jazz rhythms. Many jazz chant resources are available.

Using songs or chants allow for the integration of listening, reading, and speaking. Learners can listen to, read along with, and sing along with the lyrics.

Games

1. Hypothetical games/What if...
   a. If you were an alien anthropologist and you encountered the following items, how would you describe them? What are they used for? (List items)
   b. If your ship was going down and you could only grab X things, what would they be and why? If you could save only X people (from the list) who would it be and why?
   c. If you knew a close friend had committed a crime, what are your options? What would you do?
2. Guessing games:
   a. Twenty questions—Learners attempt to guess the key word or phrase within 20 yes/no questions. The student who knows the key word or phrase can only answer yes or no.
   b. Charades—Using only nonverbal language, a student would attempt to demonstrate the key word or phrase.
   c. Pyramid game—One student gives clues about a key word or phrase either orally or nonverbally but cannot say the key word of phrase. The other student attempts to guess the key word.

Each of the above exercises is based on the idea that we learn language through communication, rather than by studying isolated aspects of the language. With the communicative paradigm, which prioritized the sociopragmatic aspect of language as opposed to linguistic structures alone, the following fundamental changes and/or developments came to the fore with specific emphasis on language learning and teaching (see Chapter 5). The basic tenets of CLT include:

- Language needs to be learned and appropriately used in social environments to learn to communicate.
- Language is learned through meaningful practice when interacting with others on various topics and for diverse purposes in assorted settings.
- Language use is a contextualized process where meanings can vary depending on who utters it to whom, as well as how, where, and when it is used.
- Learners can be actively using language while learning rather than offered/taught language knowledge by the teacher.
- Learning is a process rather than a product that can be tested and evaluated in a particular time and place.
- Intensive and extensive use of language during the learning process is key to the development of fluency and automaticity (for more on automaticity, see Chapter 5), which are key to learning and acquisition of other languages.

Learners in communicative classrooms use language for the kinds of social and personal activities they are likely to encounter in life. Most activities in life typically have language associated with them. We call the language associated with certain tasks "*speech acts*" (e.g., making requests, sharing preferences and opinions, or giving an apology) (see Chapters 4 and 8 for more on speech acts and functions of language). You may observe a communicative classroom of learners listening to a dialogue, in which the speaker is requesting a book in the library and then making their own request for a book.

Controversy in the field—CLT

In the past, educators presented information to learners. Learners were expected to listen, take notes, memorize/learn the material, and demonstrate their knowledge on tests. Educators did not discuss the nuances of the learners' backgrounds or what they would bring to the classroom in terms of expectations. Education began changing based upon research and developing more participatory and interactive models.

In the 1980s and 1990s, TESOL educators were sharing their experiences using the CLT method with Japanese students learning English, for example. CLT changes the role relationships between educators and learners. In CLT, educators facilitate learning by creating interactive activities for the learners to exchange ideas while practicing oral and written English. Learners do not memorize grammatical rules or long vocabulary lists. Educators provide feedback to learners by gently and subtly rephrasing learners' contributions in the corrected form, but not highlighting that the student made an error. This methodology did not suit the culture of the Japanese learners. It was misaligned and incongruent. With L2 learning, often learners would perceive a teacher as being a poor teacher if they did not correct learners' errors explicitly.

Other educational research in the 1980s and 1990s, notably work by Au and Jordan, Mohatt and Erickson, Cazden and Leggett, and Gay (Aronson, 2016), highlighted educational challenges for learners who experienced a cultural mismatch in the format, expectations, or roles for participation in schools. Studies found repeatedly that mismatches between culturally based expectations of the classroom caused learners to be more challenged in the learning process. These researchers championed culturally congruent pedagogy, meaning instruction that is aligned with the cultural patterns of the learners.

CLT caused a cultural mismatch in L2 teaching in Japan and elsewhere during the 1990s, but what should be done? Comply with more traditional teaching of English, even though it does not help learners to develop their language proficiency? Or continue to employ CLT methodology even if it is a mismatch for learners, can cause problems, and possibly cause educators to lose learners' respect? This is a false dichotomy. It is really not an either/or situation. Actually, many TESOL educators have determined ways to compromise and accommodate learners' needs and expectations, while ensuring learners could interact in and develop their L2.

Fast forwarding to today, culturally relevant education (Dover, 2013) is a standard for teaching in many countries. Schools expect educators to be able to accommodate both culture and learning expectations in the classroom through a thoughtful and subtle dance between expectation sets or utilizing methods and techniques that accommodate learners and are aligned with current educational research.

Since communicative language courses are not focused on the explicit teaching of structures and vocabulary separately or isolated from other areas, but aim to foster the ability to use language appropriately, they have two areas of emphasis: (a) meaning focused, and (b) allowing for the acquisition of grammatical and vocabulary implicitly through authentic language practice. Educators should be intentional about whether to include form-focused instruction in lessons depending on the learner population and the expectations of the learners (and possibly their caregivers), and instructional patterns of their home culture.

Questions for reflection

- Have you ever learned language in a classroom with such pedagogical practices? Reflect on your experiences.
- How do you think you can develop your language skills in such a classroom?
- How would you feel and interact with such pedagogies of learning?
- Are all interactive strategies appropriate for all learners? What classes might benefit most from each of these strategies?

Task-based Instruction

Task-based instruction is one of two other methods that share much of their philosophy and research base with CLT. Think of them as methodological siblings. The task-based instruction/language teaching (TBLT) approach includes meaningful tasks, which involves physical, mental, and linguistic engagement in the process of learning. For example, learners may be asked to solve a real-life problem. In addition to offering learners a meaning and purpose for the given tasks, the authenticity of the content of tasks is key to developing genuine interaction among the learners who work on and practice language skills through the collaborative tasks (see the "Sample tasks" box for examples). Tasks often have these features:

- A task involves a primary focus on exchanging ideas and meanings.
- A task has a clearly defined outcome and may have a product.
- A task has a series of steps language learners must take to complete it.
- A task has some kind of "gap" in knowledge between participants.
- The participants choose the linguistic resources needed to complete the task.

Tasks that educators can use in the classroom might include real-life scenarios or have an explicitly visible pedagogical purpose (Willis & Willis, 2007), which might be practicing newly learned vocabulary and structures by communicating through them during the task engagement. The task is designed and instructed in a way to engender learners to use the new linguistic forms. The already-learned structures through instruction are thought to be made automatic (see automaticity in Chapter 5) by actively using them in the group, which shifts learners' linguistic focus and attention from forms to meanings. Learners then have the opportunity to develop communication strategies, which in turn contributes to their interactional skills. The tasks offered should therefore have a purpose clearly communicated with the learners, an outcome that is produced through the tasks, which might include a solution to an identified problem, a physically constructed artefact, or an argument that is developed through group discussion. Most importantly, the task should include relevance to the real work activities and problems.

Sample tasks

Information-gap Tasks

Information-gap activities give two learners a mutual task for which they need to share information to complete the task. Information can be shared either in one direction (one-way) or in both directions (two-way). In one-way gap activities, one learner has information the other needs (e.g., one learner gives directions to a place on a map to the other, who would trace the route on the map). In two-way gap activities, both learners have different sets of information and must share it with each other to complete the task.

Surveys and Questionnaires

Surveys and questionnaires work with any topic. Learners are given short surveys with three to five questions. Sometimes, choices between a couple items are possible; other times it is open-ended, and learners need to write down the responses. Learners circulate in the classroom to ask others for their opinions on the topic.
   Topics for surveys include:

1. What they had for lunch.
2. What color they prefer to wear.
3. What their birth month is.
4. What music they prefer.
5. If they agree/disagree with a statement.
6. Whether they are more outgoing, reserved, energetic, or playful?
7. Their opinions on solutions to a problem.
8. Whether they have ever … driven a car, ridden a rollercoaster, ridden a horse.
9. Whether they think it will rain tomorrow?

Surveys and questionnaires create opportunities for speaking and listening using yes/no, either/or, and wh- questions. Answers or surveys/questionnaires can be one word or much longer. Responses can be recorded by the questioner using hash marks, circling an answer, or taking notes. The amount of interaction, therefore, can be managed in the design of the survey/questionnaire for the proficiency level of the ELLs.

Ranking Tasks

Ranking tasks can be employed with any numbered list. Textbooks often have lists for learners to read and remember. Look at a L2 textbook for lists with which to use this task.
   The essential idea is to choose an adjective for comparison/superlative and ordering. For example, if you have a list of 10 qualities of the ideal roommate, you can ask your learners to read them, and rank the items from most to least important to them individually. Then, they can work with a partner to discuss their rankings and rationale for their decisions. See Table 6.1 for examples of comparatives, superlatives, and topics that can serve to prompt your brainstorming.

Table 6.1 Examples of comparatives, superlatives, and topics for ranking tasks.

Comparatives:	Bigger/smaller, taller/shorter, heavier/lighter
	Kinder/meaner, sweeter/more sour, gentler/rougher, smoother/rougher, happier/sadder/angrier, bolder/shyer
	Important/less important, influential/less influential, more interesting/less interesting, more surprising/less surprising
	Familiar/unfamiliar, newer/older, safe/risky
Superlatives:	Best/worst, biggest/smallest, hardest/easiest, greatest/least great, coolest/least cool, most/least popular, most/least important, most/least memorable, etc.
Topics:	• Characters in a story
	• Attributes of an occupation
	• Animals in a climate zone
	• Reasons for a historical event
	• Pieces of music
	• Chemicals in the element chart
	• Qualifications for a job

Problem-solving tasks

Problem-solving tasks stimulate discussion. It is important to pose a problem that is complex enough that small groups of learners need to work through it, but not so complex that there is no solution. Learners may be asked to furnish their shared apartment on a budget, determine changes they can make to their lifestyle to reduce their carbon footprint, or brainstorm ways to obtain more bilingual books for the school library. Learners can be challenged to think creatively, research solutions, and possibly to enact the solutions.

Project-based Instruction

Another methodological sibling of CLT and TBLT is project-based instruction (PBI). PBI is a way of engaging learners in an active process of language learning through shared projects. Small groups of ELLs design projects on either an assigned topic or one of their own choosing within a range. When they are designing, researching, and constructing their projects, they are involved in the active and meaningful use of language, sometimes without even realizing it. Similar to TBLT, PBI could involve the real-world issues to be addressed by the learners as a project that promotes communication and collaboration. In PBL, there is also focus on developing relevant content knowledge (such as pollution, human body, protection of animals). Learners are expected to investigate, analyze, and address an authentic issue, which might be challenging and complex, through critical thinking. PBI is also characterized by the principles of learning by doing (i.e., *experiential learning*) through which learners engage in projects that simultaneously offer an implicit and incidental learning of the course content. The experiences in the projects help learners develop knowledge that they need to learn and strengthen over time. The approach also implies that learners can self-regulate their learning and exercise autonomy over the active process of learning.

PBI centers around the following characteristics: (a) driven by a question, challenge, or problem; (b) engagement in inquiry; (c) focus on critical thinking, communication, collaboration, and creativity; (d) choice and autonomy granted to learners; (e) ongoing exchange of feedback though multiple revisions; and (f) ability to problematize and address authentic and real-time problems.

Digital engagement in tasks and projects

Although task-based instruction and PBI are originally thought of as manual and face-to-face engagement in the classroom, recent digital developments in technology have created opportunities to engage learners in tasks and projects in online communities and platforms in ways that would not be possible in traditional classroom settings. Collaborative online work enables projects to be developed and conducted more efficiently without requiring physical presence, which gives learners opportunities for flexible time management. For example, there are online documents that could be used to promote collaborative or guided writing beyond the classroom time through asynchronous sustained support and feedback. There are also tools and resources that enable simultaneous interaction on the tasks where the joint work could be improved with the digital integration. The online collaboration, for example, can be even deeper when all the learners can express their ideas typed or recorded to be monitored later and improve the arguments compared with the classroom environment where learners need to speak one after the other in limited class periods.

Questions for reflection

- Have you learned another language in any of these methodologies? What were your experiences? What were the benefits and drawbacks of using the method?
- How do you think such digital experiences influence the way you work collaboratively and the learning that takes place?
- In what ways do you think you can promote learners' engagement in learning in the online projects?

Skills-based and Integrated Skills Instruction

In language teaching approaches focused on building knowledge of grammatical structures, the language skills of reading and writing took precedence over speaking and listening, since most learners had no need for oral interaction. The tools of grammar and vocabulary, which form part of the skills, were emphasized as well.

Throughout time, educators have designed classes for learners who wished to develop one particular skill. Learners might have had an "academic writing" class or an "intensive listening" class. These classes became known as *"isolated skill"* classes. One challenge in teaching these classes is that, technically, the educator was not supposed to focus strongly on any other skill. In practice, it is extremely difficult, if not impossible, to teach only one skill in the classroom. Can you imagine a speaking class in which learners would not listen?

The recognition of natural interdependency of the language skills coincided with the advent of CLT. Furthermore, educators realized that the language skills mutually reinforce each other. This means that if a student listens to a dialogue one time and then reads the dialogue during the second listening, the student can use both skills together to arrive at understandings of the words and make meanings. Having all four language skills (i.e., speaking, listening, reading, and writing) integrated into language classes became the standard that continues to this day. *Integrated skills* classes mean that during lessons all four skills will be included for some period of time in ways that complement one another. It is often the case that input being exposed to learners receptively provides a thematic or topical basis for learners to build on to be able to discuss the topic. These could include watching followed by speaking; listening followed by writing; or reading followed by speaking and then writing. One should purposefully select the relevant materials that support each other in terms of offering relevant ideas, structures, and words that are characteristic of the specific topic. The purpose of integration is not just to offer variety in the mode of language use, but to help learners to be able to communicate by developing potential interlocutor roles such being a listener or being a speaker.

When using the communicative approach, educators integrate the language skills of speaking, listening, reading, and writing throughout the lesson sequence of activities. A class may start with learning new vocabulary words by listening and practicing them in meaningful situations. For example, if learning the names for fruit, the teacher may have real fruit as well as a visual of the fruit with the name of the fruit listed. Learners would listen to the teacher present the word strawberry and see the written form of the word and the real strawberries with the image. After all the new words were presented, the learners would practice the new vocabulary words orally in brief activities. They may share with a partner which fruit they like and those they do not. Alternatively, they may survey the class to find out which fruit the learners like the best and the least. Next, they may read a dialogue or description of grocery shopping and choosing the right fruit. Afterward they might write a recipe for the ultimate fruit salad using the fruit they like best and share their ultimate fruit salad by presenting to the class. The rationale for integrating the four language skills into every lesson is that each language skill helps learn the other language skills and the grammatical and vocabulary forms. Interaction in real life involves integrated language skills. Furthermore, learners get practice with each skill so they can use them later in authentic ways. In conversations, for example, we take turns speaking and sharing our thoughts and experiences and listening to others' thoughts and experiences. In communicative classes, we engage in conversations on topics as we would with others in differing settings. The SLA principle is that interaction in the language is what leads to language acquisition.

The instructional sequence an educator may design for an integrated skills class may resemble the sample integrated skill instructional sequence in the box "A sample integrated skill instructional sequence." Note the words in bold, which represent a language skill.

A sample integrated skill instructional sequence

1. The teacher introduces the topic by **asking** ELLs what they see in a photo. As new vocabulary words on the topic are needed, the teacher or peers **explains** them and **writes** them on the board.
2. The teacher **presents** any additional new vocabulary with visuals, realia, and other supports prior to the reading. The learners create (**write**) a visual vocabulary reference for each word that includes a visual, the word, an informal definition, a synonym, and any collocations. The teacher leads the class in a brief choral chant (**speaking**) of the new vocabulary words. The teacher reinforces the new vocabulary concepts with a fun vocabulary game.
3. The teacher previews the reading passage by guiding learners to review the titles, subtitles, and images and to predict what the reading will be about (**read** and **discuss**).
4. The learners **read** the passage by doing a jigsaw/popcorn reading.
5. The learners complete a graphic organizer (**write**) on the reading when **listening** to other groups share their parts. The learners who are listening **ask** questions of the learners **sharing** their portion of the reading.
6. The teacher leads a summary of the reading by facilitating a **discussion** of the main ideas and supporting details in small groups first then with the whole class.
7. The learners **write** opinions of the passage using stem sentences/sentence frames.
8. In small groups, the learners analyze the passage (**read** and **discuss**) for a specific grammar form in use and guess how they think it works and what context(s) it is used in.
9. The class **discusses** how they think grammar form works (i.e., what the rule is).
10. The teacher **presents** the rule for the new grammar form (**listening**).
11. The learners practice the grammar form in brief **written** and **spoken** exercises and then in communicative **speaking** and **listening** activities.

There are many ways to focus on the skills needed to communicate in a second language. One could focus on the oral or writing skills or receptive and productive skills. These are different ways to approach our work, and you will hear TESOL educators referring to these different skill sets.

Language teaching has often focused on enabling language learners to develop language skills including receptive skills such as listening and reading, and productive skills such as speaking and writing. The next three chapters elaborate on first oral and writing skills and then receptive skills followed by productive skills.

Questions for reflection

- What metaphor can you think of to describe integrated language skills?
- How would you justify integrating language skills in a program that treats language skills in isolation?

Chapter Conclusions

In this chapter, we considered how methods have developed and changed over time leading deliberation to a belief that there is no one right way; rather, the instructional practices we choose as TESOL educators are based on our learners and contexts. We have analyzed the theory to practice links by deliberating how SLA theories provided guidelines for instruction in the 10 macrostrategies. Moreover, we started delving into instructional practices of CLT, TBLT, and PBL. Some examination of integrated language skills was included, which will be further explored in the next chapter.

Discussion Questions/Activities

1 Design an illustration of the macrostrategies that unites them together. Share your illustration with your peers.

2 Which macrostrategies did you see evidence for in CLT, TBLT, and PBL? Which were not evident? Do you think these macrostrategies were part of the methodology in practice? If so, how and why? If not, why not?

3 Which method(s) do you see yourself using while teaching at this point? Why?

4 How might you integrate language skills in your future classes? What choices might you make about the sequencing of lesson activities so that students have what they need to be successful in the upcoming activity? What could happen in a classroom if you did not anticipate the sequencing of lesson activities?

Tasks

1 Reflection
   a. How will the macrostrategies guide your teaching? How will you make them memorable while you are planning and teaching?

2 Research/investigation
   a. Investigate a location that you would like to teach in. Try to find out which methods they utilize the most or promote for their school? You may look at school and school district websites, ministries or offices of education, or ask questions of educators in the community either online or in person. Prepare to share your findings in class.

Further Reading/Read and Discuss

Read about the history of second/foreign language methods in:
Richards, J. C., & Rodgers, T. S. (2001). *Approaches and methods in language teaching*, 2nd ed. Cambridge University Press.
Why did various methods become the primary means of teaching in different time periods? Were methods employed universally or were different methods employed in different places for different periods of time?

Read the brief by Jack Richards on CLT:

Richards, J. C. (2006). *Communicative language teaching today*. Cambridge University Press.

How is Richards' contemporary description of CLT different from the original version presented here? Why do you think these changes occurred? Would you employ a more contemporary or traditional version of the method? Why or why not?

References

Aronson, B. (2016). The theory and practice of culturally relevant education: A synthesis of research across content areas. *Review of Educational Research*, *86*(1), 163–206. https://doi.org/10.3102/0034654315582066

Brown, H. D. (1994). *Principles of language learning and teaching*. Prentice Hall.

Brown, H. D. (2000). *Principles of language learning and teaching* (2nd ed.). Longman.

Dover, A. G. (2013). Teaching for social justice: From conceptual frameworks to classroom practices. *Multicultural Perspectives*, *15*(1), 3–11. https://doi.org/10.1080/15210960.2013.754285

Ellis, R. (2014). Principles of instructed second language acquisition. In M. Celce-Murcia, D. M. Brinton, & M. A. Snow (Eds.), *Teaching English as a second or foreign language* (pp. 31–45). National Geographic Learning/Heinle Cengage.

Howatt, A. P. R. (2004). *A history of English language teaching* (2nd ed.). Oxford University Press.

Krashen, S. (1982). *Principles and practice in second language acquisition*. Pergamon.

Kumaravadivelu, B. (1994). The postmethod condition: (E)merging strategies for second/foreign language teaching. *TESOL Quarterly*, *28*(1), 27–48. https://doi.org/10.2307/3587197

Mellow, J. D. (2002, March). Toward principled eclecticism in language teaching: The two-dimensional model of the centering principle. *TESL-EJ*, *5*(4). http://tesl-ej.org/ej20/a1.html

Oxford, R. (1990). *Language learning strategies: What every teacher should know*. Newbury House.

Prabhu, N. S. (1990). There is no best method—Why? *TESOL Quarterly*, *24*(2), 161–176. http://links.jstor.org/sici?sici=0039-8322%28199022%2924%3A2%3C161%3ATINBM%3E2.0.CO%3B2-M (accessed March 25, 2021).

Willis, D., & Willis, J. (2007). *Doing task-based teaching*. Oxford University Press.

7

What Do Educators Need to Know About Teaching the Language Skills of Listening and Reading When Using Integrated Language Skills?

You will learn about the relationships between language skills and structural "tools" (e.g., grammar). This chapter will also focus on specifics of individual language skills (i.e., listening and reading). Finally, you will read about the tools developed by several methods from the past that were used in the design of listening and reading lessons, so some notable "designer methods" will be introduced.

Learning Outcomes

At the conclusion of this chapter, you will be able to:

- outline the relationship of the four language skills (i.e., speaking, listening, reading, and writing) with grammar, vocabulary, pronunciation, and spelling
- describe characteristics and considerations of teaching listening and reading in integrated language instruction
- develop interactive classes that integrate listening and reading skills

Depending on many factors, you may have taken coursework in a second language that integrated the four language skills or treated them separately. In this vignette, an educator describes her context for teaching and how she treats listening and reading in an integrated skills course design.

TESOL Voices

Knowing Your Students is the First Step

I am a bilingual teacher of a transitional bilingual education program in an elementary school just outside of Chinatown, Chicago. My students are in fourth, fifth, and sixth grade, a transitional period in their early schooling years. They are able to speak Mandarin Chinese, and it is my job to help improve their English proficiency to prepare them for their academic and personal lives in the United States. A few students in my classes grew up in the United States, but barely use English outside of school; some may have lived in the United States for a year or two; while others may have joined the class halfway during the school year migrated

---

Introduction to TESOL: Becoming a language teaching professional, First Edition. Kate Mastruserio Reynolds, Kenan Dikilitaş, and Steve Close.
© 2022 John Wiley & Sons, Inc. Published 2022 by John Wiley & Sons, Inc.

freshly from mainland China with other family members. In this school, it is very common to get newcomers any month of the school year.

Owing to the varying backgrounds of my students, they have different strengths and weaknesses when it comes to different language skills. I find that, in general, newcomers may have better grammar and spelling overall; however, pronunciation and authentic use of vocabularies are easier for students who are accustomed to living in the United States. Knowing my students is critical in the planning process, because it helps me bring engaging and meaningful activities to them. Making contents comprehensible for students is another aspect of lessons that will lend itself to learning and construction of knowledge. In addition, I find it helpful to provide contents that are relatable to students, whether this is a connection with current topics in another subject or something that would spark thoughts about their own life.

Listening and reading skills are the essential input for the output that students are expected to produce at one point or another. To maximize the language input I provide, activating background knowledge is the first step in any listening and reading activity. It can be as simple as having a brief discussion on the general topic of the material or as complicated as building common background knowledge with a frontloading preactivity. Second, giving students a purpose during the listening and reading will guide their attention to the selected parts of the material that I intend to focus on in the lesson. Students should be informed of the learning outcome and see a connection between the activity and the learning outcome. This further prepares the students' minds for the learning. An effective closure to any listening and reading activity may include providing an oral or written summary of the material, making a connection between the learning and students' lives, reflecting on the key learning outcome and finding other applications in other occasions. As you can see from the description above, completely separating receptive skills from productive skills is quite impossible. In fact, it benefits students to have them integrated because that is how communication is practiced in real life.

J. Jiao
Bilingual educator
Chicago, IL

Relationships Between Language Skills and Tools

In Chapter 6, you read about integrated language skills. In order to be able to integrate language skills effectively, we must analyze the characteristics of each language skill. Additionally, we must envision how grammar, vocabulary, pronunciation, and spelling support each language skill. As a simple reference, we will call them tools. It is important to note though that we are not advocating compartmentalizing the various language skills; they are all intertwined and work in concert together.

Reading and writing rely on written grammar and vocabulary. Writers gear their word choices and grammatical forms based on factors such as audience, tonal concerns (e.g., formality, power, idiom), and authorial voice. Writers use their knowledge of spelling, even in the world of spell check. Like writers, readers utilize their knowledge of formal rules like spelling, grammar, and even style to make sense of what they are reading. For example, if a reader is reading a fantasy story, there would be many adjectives to bring the story to life. We rely on our understandings of the role and placement of adjectives to describe nouns. We also depend on our knowledge of the meanings of the myriad adjectives (vocabulary). Readers sometimes even utilize their knowledge of pronunciation to sound out a new word. Therefore, we can see that literacy skills incorporate the tools of grammar, vocabulary, spelling, and pronunciation.

Speaking and listening also rely on some of these tools. For example, speaking utilizes oral grammar. Speakers need to know the grammatical forms to choose within the situation and be able to use them with fluidity/fluency (i.e., with ease and without hesitations). They also consider audience, tone, and presentation of themselves. These considerations influence grammar usage and word choice. For example, a speaker may decide to use a modal (e.g., would, could, should, might, may) instead of a command (i.e., get this, do that), so they appear less controlling or rude. Speaking leans heavily on pronunciation, but entails far more than this one aspect. Speakers must consider the expectations and needs of listeners. Listening, like speaking, depends on understandings of oral grammar, vocabulary, and pronunciation. Listeners will hear incoming messages, so their understanding of how words are pronounced will influence their comprehension. For example, if a learner thinks a word is pronounced in a different way than they hear, they may think the word they hear is a completely new or different word. Again, we see that the tools of oral grammar, vocabulary, and pronunciation are part of speaking and listening. As an illustration of this concept, see Figure 7.1.

Figure 7.1 represents the different emphases within TESOL, rather than how much time TESOL educators spend on the different language skills, or how we sequence lessons. How much time we spend on each skill depends on the goals of the learners, while how lessons are sequenced is based on evidence of effectiveness in language learning and learners' comprehension.

Now that we have a sense of how the four language skills are related to the tools of grammar, pronunciation, vocabulary, and spelling, we can examine each of the language skills individually. This chapter focuses on listening and reading, Chapter 8 looks at speaking and writing, while Chapter 9 investigates grammar, vocabulary, pronunciation, and spelling. As we discuss different skills, we will integrate methods and activities for teaching these skills.

TESOL is a complex and extensively developed field. However, an important caveat must be noted before proceeding. Some TESOL scholars and educators will spend their entire careers delving into the details of specific subfields, for example, teaching second language writing. The goal of this text is to provide an overview and resources for further exploration, but it cannot provide an exhaustive account of each topic. We will provide you the basics. As you read this chapter, try to identify areas of interest to you, so you may continue your professional journey through the readings provided.

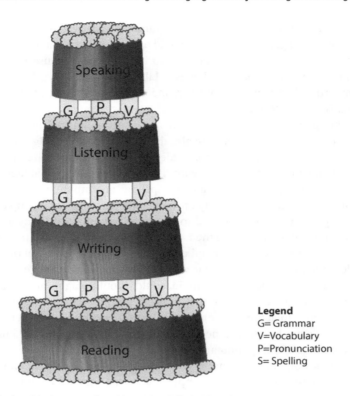

Figure 7.1   Relationship between four language skills and tools.

Oral Skills

Orals skills refers to the use of language during communicative experience, with the speaker choosing proper words, initiating a rational argument, and expressing ideas to represent perspective and messages clearly. Therefore, it not only encompasses speaking with someone else in an informal conversation, but also includes the ability to create a meaningful speech in front of an audience. Developing oral skills then requires the teachers to have these skills themselves and set a good model when they talk in the classroom. Chen and Goh (2011), for example, found that teachers' self-efficacy in their own oral skills is one of the challenges in developing those of the students. In countries like China, for example, oral skills development presents challenges owing partly to the varying levels of oral competence among teachers.

Writing Skills

Reading and writing are considered writing skills. They may also be described as literacy skills. Literacy, though, is defined to include reading and writing, and other related skills (e.g., oral language skills used to talk about and support reading and writing development; critical thinking for real-life and academic purposes; critical reading/understanding that reading and writing are closed connected to power, social identity, and ideologies) (Ediger, 2014). ELLs may also develop skills and functions needed to find, identify, evaluate, use, and communicate using a wide variety of resources (e.g., text, visual, audio, and video), which is called new literacy (Ediger, 2014).

Questions for reflection

- How do you envision integrating language skills and tools into your future classes?
- How would you evaluate your own oral skills as a teacher?
- Are you a strong reader and writer? How would your abilities in these skills influence your teaching and your students' learning?
- What do you think you could do to help your students to develop these skills?

Receptive and Productive Skills

Another way of viewing the language skills, aside from oral or writing skills, is according to whether learners receive incoming input or produce output. We call receiving incoming input "receptive skills," and these are listening and reading. Learners can receive input from different sources both in person or digital. When learners produce output, we call that "productive skills." Productive skills are speaking and writing.

Receptive Language Skills: Listening and Reading

People sometimes believe, erroneously, that receptive skills are intuitive, and that students perform and develop these skills reflexively simply by listening to someone, reading a text, or having a conversation. However, comprehension is a complex cognitive activity that requires an active thinking process to infer the message from the *input* (i.e., any incoming information the learner receives aurally or visually). The messages in the *input* are highly unlikely to be absorbed without any individual, intentional investment into understanding. In addition, we communicate through indirect implicit messages that need to be inferred through the use of contextual clues, whereby we guess at the most likely meanings of the words used. A sentence can have many interpretations depending on the context and a message can be conveyed in several ways.

Listening and reading are similar in some respects, but also differ from each other. Both skills rely on linguistic information that we receive—for this reason they are referred to as receptive skills. Listening and reading can be described as a process of constructing meanings based upon making connections to background and world knowledge, deciphering the oral or written forms and linguistic clues, visualizing, predicting, or anticipating what will come next, and monitoring one's own thinking process (i.e., metacognition). Reading and listening are therefore cognitively demanding activities, which require attention, thinking, and practice. WIDA (2020) refer to listening and reading as interpretive skills, which they are too since learners need to interpret, but not translate, the incoming information.

The only differences between listening and reading are in the format of incoming information—oral or written. Listening is oral, so accent, pronunciation, and speed of speech are factors. With reading, pronunciation matters less and the incoming information is paced much more slowly than that of listening. Reading does have some pronunciation when words are sounded out, read aloud, and silently "pronounced" within the mind of the reader. The process of comprehending reading material might prove challenging if a learner has less exposure to oral language, because individuals rely on their ability to recognize and pronounce the written words. When listening to someone talking, the speaker might offer clues or references within the setting that could ease comprehension (e.g., "please hand me that black coat on the chair over there" (accompanied by a pointing gesture)).

Reading can often be a slow process that can be self-regulated by the reader. It is also a "recursive" form of interaction, meaning the reader can go back and reread sections that do not make sense at first. Listening, by contrast can hardly be so. With the exception of listening to recorded material, it is not possible for a listener to rehear sections that were unclear. Listeners can ask for clarification, but often do not for various reasons.

Beginner language learners often need more contextual clues to understand a message conveyed through linguistic input (both spoken and written) owing partly to insufficient vocabulary knowledge. Situational dialogues, in which students participate in hypothetical language situations, or role-plays (e.g., a role-play to make a request for a library book) are used in classes because they are thought to facilitate the development of comprehension and interaction skills (such as asking and answering questions, clarifying, explaining a word). When reading, individuals do not have access to the same interactional opportunities and support, so comprehension can be relatively more challenging. Readers lack visual, gestural, and tonal clues, which necessitates guessing based on what is present in the textual clues. On the other hand, listening to and interacting with a person may be more difficult for language learners than for those who grew up in the culture that developed the language being used, since it requires guessing based on a potentially overwhelming number of observable features of the conversation such as intonation and stress, gestures, facial expressions, body movements, and the physical situation in which the talk happens. Constructing a message from interaction-based listening could be less stressful and less demanding for language learners or it could be more so if the speed of the interaction is too fast or there is no opportunity to clarify meanings.

Questions for reflection

- Which kind of input do you think you need to expose learners to—linguistic input through reading or through listening? Why?
- What are the advantages and disadvantages of exposing beginners to reading-based input or listening-based input?
- How can you enhance the linguistic input learners are exposed to through technology?

Details of Teaching Listening

To communicate, people use listening more than any other skill. We began acquiring our first languages through listening to the incoming information we were exposed to. Many TESOL educators believe that the skill of listening precedes the development of other language skills, but listening is often neglected in classrooms. It is assumed that listening occurs automatically. Listening, though, is like any other skill that can and should be developed in the L2 classroom.

Listening comprises the ability to hear incoming sounds, render the incoming sounds comprehensible in terms of language through our cognitive processing, and attach meanings to the sounds by drawing upon our knowledge in long-term memory. We do not decode linearly sound by sound to make a word and then move along to the next word. The listening process is nonlinear, so we are doing all of these activities in random order without a great deal of conscious thought in milliseconds. It is pretty impressive!

How do we teach ELLs to develop their listening skills, if it is so complex? Much in the same way as teaching other skills—through meaningful and engaging instruction and practice. We want to provide a good number of opportunities to listen to various models of English language speech in receptive and interactive situations. As the teacher, our language use will provide an important model of English language in an immersion classroom. When we are speaking, we want to increase our wait time after a spoken phrase to 5–7 seconds, so students have time to process the incoming message. We can also make our speech more accessible by pausing more often between thought groups and employing slower speech. Furthermore, we want to include voices of diverse speakers of English with a variety of accents and rates of speech in order to hone learners' abilities to comprehend various speakers.

Organizations of listening lessons

When focusing on teaching L2 listening in lessons, we want to include opportunities for students to listen to different topics for diverse purposes. Helping students to acknowledge the purpose of listening to a particular lesson is considerably helpful for them to understand what they are listening for and why. For example, do we want them to listen selectively or for a general message? Telling them prior to the listening experience what they need to focus on will make them better prepared for the activities after listening. We also want to include opportunities for listening to passages of different lengths and formats (e.g., monologue/lecture, dialogue/discussion). These listening experiences can be receptive only or interactive (for more on this, see the section on "Subskills of Listening and Reading"). We also want to consider including listening and speaking early in a lesson, prior to reading and writing activities.

Sequencing lessons emphasizing listening

Sequencing listening-focused lessons typically involves three phases: before listening, during listening, and postlistening. At each of these phases, educators will enact a couple of assorted types of activities. During the prelistening phase, educators will connect to learners' background knowledge on the topic in order to access their schemas on a topic. *Schemas* are in theory how the brain stores information in interconnect concepts. For example, a schema for a whale may include that they are large in size, live in the ocean, breathe oxygen so they need to swim to the surface, eat krill, and give birth to live young (i.e., a mammal). When we access and consciously acknowledge learners' schemas on a topic before listening to the passage, learners are more likely to comprehend what they hear because they can connect the concepts presented to those they already have stored in their schema. If the learners do not have prior knowledge about the topic, educators will build their background knowledge on the topic, so that they are successful in comprehending the listening passage. The second priority for educators in prelistening is to preteach key vocabulary words necessary for comprehension of the listening passage. Other priorities are to give a purpose for listening and provide a task that learners will carry out during the listening experience.

At the *prelistening* phase, we can teach learners to utilize conscious strategies when listening to increase their comprehension and help them build their listening skills independently. There are three categories of listening strategies that we can teach learners: metacognitive, cognitive, and socio-affective strategies. Metacognitive strategies are about the learners' abilities to think about and analyze their own thinking. This category includes monitoring their understanding, predicting what may be coming next, focusing their attention, and planning. Cognitive strategies are about the learners' thinking, how they process and make meanings from the input. Cognitive strategies include questioning, connecting to known information, elaborating, translating, repeating, summarizing, inferencing, and making educated guesses. Lastly, socio-affective strategies describe the ways learners manage their emotions and anxiety, encourage themselves, and seek help (e.g., ask clarification questions, confirm their understandings with others). We teach these strategies by breaking them down into easy steps and allowing students to practice them. A good rule of thumb before teaching any new item though is to find out what strategies the student is already using.

The second phase of a listening-focused lesson takes place *during* listening. This focus helps build learners' comprehension, and can be seen when the teacher allows learners to listen to the passage more than once. It is considered a best practice for students to listen to a passage first for the general ideas, second for specific information, and lastly to confirm their understandings (see more in the section on "Subskills of Listening and Reading"). Depending on the focus of the listening activity and whether it was the second or third listening experience, students may be given a written transcript to follow along with the speaker. This simultaneous listening and reading allows students to make meanings between language skills. Also, during listening, students are often asked to practice the new listening strategy and perform a task, such as taking notes or completing a graphic organizer. They are encouraged to monitor their own comprehension.

After the listening experiences is the *postlistening* phase. Postlistening is important for confirming comprehension on the parts of the learner and the teacher. The learner needs to be sure they understood correctly, so they can revise understandings, if necessary. The teacher needs to determine what the learners comprehended from the listening passage. The teacher also wants to make sure that the students could identify specific information in the passage and make inferences. Therefore, the teacher designs discussions, activities, or exercises to check learners' comprehension, selective listening, and inferencing. Often, postlistening activities serve as a springboard to integrating other language skills into lessons. Students may follow up a postlistening comprehension discussion with a reading on the topic or a written response to the topic of the listening passage.

Questions for reflection

- How will you make sure that listening is not an overlooked skill in your classes?
- What sorts of activities will you employ at the different stages of a listening-focused lesson? Why would you use these particular activities?

Total Physical Response and Total Physical Response Storytelling

Total physical response (TPR) is one method developed in the 1970s to address the challenges of verbal comprehension in ELLs. Considered a "designer method," TPR supported learners in the meaning-making process by linking the oral language with a gesture, object, or expression. It altered the teacher's role in direct teaching to guiding instruction. Learners are actively, physically engaged in TPR lessons, because they listen to the teacher's commands, observe the teacher doing the action, and physically do the action themselves. For example, in lessons about clothing, teachers may direct students repetitively to put on the jacket, take off the jacket, put on a sock, take off a sock, etc. Students would learn the vocabulary words for the clothing as well as the commands and phrasal verbs for "put on" and "take off" through the repetitions.

Typical TPR lessons began with teacher-directed activities, with repetitions of actions in a sequence and students following along by orally repeating and doing the action. Once students were able to do the sequence of actions without much confusion, teachers would alter the sequence of the commands giving them in random order. After a period of time with students demonstrating their understanding of the commands in a random order, the teacher would give the command orally without the action to confirm if students could do the action independently. Finally, students would be asked to volunteer to give the commands.

TPR is also a systematic practice of a psychological theory that involves the simultaneous coordination of speech and action. The implication for language learning is that second language learning occurs like first language acquisition, which takes place through a prolonged engagement in listening and meaning-making without producing a word or giving a verbal response. After interpreting the meaning of the prompt, children respond by carrying out what the utterance says. In this way, the processes used by babies in their first months—calculated guesses as to meaning and ensuing responsive acts—are adapted to language learning, particularly to the context of young learners. The meaning conveyed in these daily utterances offers a comprehensible input for children, which is also predicted using contextual clues in the environment. The comprehensibility of the communicative language also reduces the potential affective factors (i.e., anxiety, inhibition, fear of risk taking) in language learning since it does not force children to give a verbal response, but, rather, to make the corresponding physical response. TPR teachers also felt that this process reduced the stress that learners might experience when they need to learn another language. The method turns the learning process into a game where they can respond to English prompts properly, thereby fostering self-confidence and giving a sense of success. While this method seems to help learners to comprehend particular instructions accurately, it also actively prepares them to be able to speak, even if they do not yet feel ready to do so.

TPR worked well with regard to teaching comprehension, but had drawbacks as a comprehensive instructional method. The format made it challenging to employ with some topics or beyond a certain proficiency level. First, it emphasized oral language and included no written language. Second, it focused on a set of concrete items in the vocabulary and thus was not very useful for abstract vocabulary that did not lend itself well to physical examples. Nor was the vocabulary presented in a meaningful context. Third, actions and action verbs in the command form were the focus. If a verb was not an action verb, for example, a stative verb such as believe, prefer, imagine, or suspect, it was difficult to teach using TPR. Verbs also presented problems in that they were mostly in the present tense only, so other verb tenses and aspect were not taught. Since commands were the most repeated grammatical form, they were learned; other grammatical forms were not easily included. Students would not receive enough input, interaction, and output opportunities using other grammatical forms to learn them.

Total physical response storytelling

To address some of the concerns with TPR, Blaine Ray modified TPR to total physical response storytelling (TPRS). In TPRS, teachers use all of the TPR techniques to teach vocabulary, and they situate the words within a story. The educator develops a short, engaging storyboard with several visuals and a sentence written in the target language. The teacher first presents the character(s) and the story orally with gestures and actions to represent the characters and events while students participate by mimicking the gestures and words. This part would follow the same sequence as a TPR lesson as described in the preceding paragraph. Once the students had mastered the initial concepts they would move to the reading of the story. They would read individually, aloud to a peer, and would be encouraged to do the actions/gestures along with the reading.

TPR and TPRS were based upon Krashen's (1982) comprehensible input model, in which he argued that comprehensible input, or input + 1 (i + 1) for short is when incoming information to learners, input, needs to be accessible to them, comprehensible. Learners need to be able to understand what they are exposed to—either verbal or written—to be able to acquire the language. Although his main argument is based on reading as a pleasure activity in normal life rather than as part of school assignments in the formal setting, we can extend his proposal to listening for pleasure. This could include listening to songs, podcasts, etc.

Questions for reflection

- How do you think you might use TPR or TPRS in your classes? How often will you employ these methods?
- What is the downside of using these methods? How might you remedy the drawbacks?
- What would you need to do to prepare a lesson or part of a lesson that employs TPR or TPRS?

Students and teachers find TPR and TPRS to be fun, engaging, and conducive to learning. Today, educators use these methods for a single lesson or two or as an activity within more communicative methods.

Subskills of Listening and Reading

When teaching listening and reading, educators need to be specific regarding the part of the skill being developed. It is not enough to write on a lesson plan that students will listen, because it presumes that students know how to do it and what to focus on. The subskills that follow could be the focus of a lesson to strengthen students' receptive skills.

Listening for the gist/reading for the main idea

Students may be requested to listen/read for the messages or main ideas being conveyed in a listening or reading passage. They will arrive at a general or rough approximation of the message, which is referred to as the gist. This is also referred to as top-down listening. TESOL educators will often ask students to listen/read for the main ideas the first time they listen/read to a passage, so students can a rough understanding upon which they can build the next time listening/reading to the same passage. Students may be asked to listen/read to a dialogue, radio broadcast, podcast, or video recording on nonfiction or fictional topics.

Listening/reading for key information

Students may be asked to listen/read for the setting, characters, and/or events in a story, dialogue, or audiobook. The setting is typically described as a location for learners, the characters would have names and personal characteristics/attributes, and the events are presented to create a plot. All of these items are present in the story, so students can listen/read for a specific word or phrase. This is an example of a selective listening/reading activity. Students are often asked to answer questions or complete a graphic organizer with the information located in the story. For example, where did the story happen? Who was the story about? What did they do? How did it end? Students can also listen/read to nonfiction texts, podcasts, or lectures to identify specific information present in the passage. TESOL educators often ask learners to narrow their attention and listen/read selectively during the second time listening/reading to a passage. This is also referred to as bottom-up listening.

Listening/reading to make inferences

The final area that ELLs need to practice in listening/reading is focused on information that is technically not present in the text but is understood based upon the information provided and their background knowledge. Inferencing is the process of reasoning in which a conclusion or judgment is made based on information or evidence. For example, if in a listening/reading passage an individual were to steal a classmate's backpack, one could infer any number of things: that the individual is mean, that they are poor, that they are a trickster, or that they are a troublemaker. When listening/reading we take into account all of the facts presented to us, draw upon our background knowledge of similar situations, and determine the most likely implication. We often call this "reading between the lines" of a passage. Sometimes, though, our logical inferences are manipulated by an author or culturally dissimilar. ELLs who struggle with getting the gist or identifying information that is present in the passage/text will be unable to make inferences. For this reason, inferencing is often tested to determine the learners' level of comprehension.

Listening Activities

Listening activities can take two formats—one-way input only and two-way interaction. One-way input activities are activities in which the ELLs listen to a passage, but do not need to respond orally to the input. They may demonstrate their comprehension by drawing what they hear or circling a true/false or multiple choice item. Two-way interaction activities require learners to listen and respond meaningfully to what their partner said.

Communicative activities and tasks often have meaningful interaction through two-way listening and speaking activities (see Chapter 6). Other ideas for one-way and two-way listening activities are included in Table 7.1.

Table 7.1 Ideas for listening activities.

One-way listening	Two-way listening and speaking
TV, movies, videos, monologues	Communicative activities (e.g., games, role-plays/skits, dialogues)
Radio, podcasts	Tasks (e.g., information gap)
Guest speakers	Projects
Tours and tour guides	Interactive simulation games
Virtual field trips	Interactive video games
Listening apps	Virtual reality
Audiobooks	Phone conversations

Questions for reflection

- How would you evaluate your listening skills as a language learner?
- What was easy about L2 listening and what was more challenging to you?
- Where there any listening strategies you attained to enhance your listening abilities?
- What do you think you could do to help your students to develop listening skills?

Details of Teaching Reading

Second language reading is a complex topic, because L2 reading is dependent upon several variables. For example, whether a student has a certain degree of oral proficiency in the L2, reads in their first language (and how well), how old the learner is, what the L1 is, and the quality of their schooling background. If a learner begins to read in their L2 in high school, for example, and they are already literate in their L1, they will transfer their reading skills from the first to new language (Carson et al., 1990; Royer & Carlo, 1991; Cummins, 2017). However, if the learner is learning to read in the new language, but has not learned to read in the first (a language they are orally fluent in), they may struggle. Thonis (1980) describes the challenge of L2 reading:

> The written symbols stand for a sound system which they have not been accustomed to hearing. The word order, the structures, and the arrangements of sound patterns are different from those with which the pupils are familiar. The meanings which may be attached to such sounds and structures may not necessarily be equivalent to the meanings stored as a result of experiences mediated by the native language. (Thonis, 1980, p. 103)

For ELLs learning to read in English or learning to read for the first time, educators need to be mindful of the challenges in order to be able to break the process down into manageable chunks. Our goals for ELLs' reading are to help them process, interpret, and evaluate written language with understanding and fluency (WIDA, 2007).

With the exception of sign language, languages are oral. But not all languages are written. Some languages, for whatever reason, did not develop a written system. Ethnologue estimates that 3,135 languages are unwritten (Eberhard et al., 2020). Other languages developed their written system within the recent past. For example, the Hmong language did not have a written form until the 1950s. The fact that not all languages are written impacts teaching language in interesting ways. If an ELL comes from a tradition that does not include literacy in the home language, the learner may struggle with emerging literacy abilities, such as understanding that print conveys meanings, that books are read in a particular direction (e.g., in Arabic right to left and English left to right), or that written symbols (i.e., letters) represent sounds.

What do L2 readers need to learn?

Educators can focus lessons in reading on these different subskills or areas.

- Decoding/encoding symbols and words:
  - Phonemic awareness: Segmenting phonemes in a word; sound blending; rhyming.
  - Phonics: Alphabetic and letter knowledge (letter naming; sound/symbol connections).
- Vocabulary, vocabulary, vocabulary (e.g., teach word attack strategies).
- Drawing meanings from phrase- and clause-level grammatical/syntactic formations.
- Making meanings and associations; connect words/icons with meaning.
- Using reading strategies (e.g., previewing the text, predicting, identifying main idea, self-questioning, monitoring understanding, clarifying understandings, summarizing, inferring, visualizing and evaluating, making connections, integrating, and synthesizing information for critical reading, etc.).
- Practicing to work toward fluency/automaticity of processing.
  - Recognizing and understanding:
  - format;
  - transitions;
  - relationships;
  - main ideas, supporting details (e.g., anecdotes, statistics, examples, comparisons);
  - different genres; and
  - different discourse patterns/structures in text.

Young learners in elementary school

Many language learners in second language settings will enter school with their native-speaking peers and begin to learn oral English. Both groups, native and nonnative speakers, will learn to read and write in English together. Native English-speaking children use their oral language as a springboard for their literacy development, connecting oral sounds to the written symbols. Nonnative English-speaking students do not have the oral language (orality) upon which to build their new literacy skills. For this reason, the cleverest way to teach L2 reading and writing is to start with L1 reading and writing and transfer the skills. Some locations, however, do not allow the teaching of L1 literacy. In this situation, TESOL educators simultaneously build both oral and written language abilities by interweaving speaking, listening, reading, and writing.

Phonemic awareness and phonics

For young learners learning to read in their L2, we want to teach *phonemic awareness*. Phonemic awareness is the ability to identify and manipulate sounds in words. Partly, too, phonemic awareness is knowledge that words comprise individual sounds. Teachers instruct ELLs to decode the sounds of the words. There are many different activities to focus learners' attention on the phonemes (i.e., individual sounds that have a corresponding letter) present in a word; for example, phoneme identification, phoneme isolation, phoneme blending, phoneme segmentation, phoneme addition, phoneme deletion, and phoneme substitution.

We also focus on developing ELLs' knowledge of the relationship between the sounds and the symbols (i.e., letters), known as *phonics*. In English, there are often multiple ways to represent sounds in written form through a detailed and complex system that assigns a character to each possible sound in isolation. For example, a /f/ sound can be written as an *f* or a *ph* sound. A /k/ sound may be written as a *c*, *k*, or *q* sound. The letter *e* may sound like /i:/ or /ɛ/. The written combinations of *ee, ea, ie, ei* all may sound like /i:/. These different ways of representing sounds evolved over hundreds of years into a system that is a bit challenging when learning to read. Phonics for ELLs is important, though, because they may not have the oral language background to help them with the sounds. A dual focus on the sound/letter correspondence will aid ELLs to acquire both. Teachers of ELLs build learners knowledge of the sound/letter relationships through letter tracing and identification of letters based on the sounds. They may also use rhyming as a means to highlight similarities of sounds and letters combinations. For example, they may use a poem, limerick, or chant with the word ending *-ing*.

Phonemic awareness, decoding, and phonics are considered *bottom-up instructional strategies*, since they start at the smallest unit and build. Phonemic awareness and phonics are often paired with learning to read new vocabulary words. Research has shown the ELLs' vocabulary size has a direct impact on their reading ability (Coady, 1997; Grabe & Stoller, 2002). Moreover, ELLs must recognize at least 95% of words for adequate comprehension of a text; however, they need 98% word recognition for fluent reading and comprehension the passage (Nation, 2008; Pulido & Hambrick, 2008; Laufer & Ravenhorst-Kalovski, 2010).

Word recognition and vocabulary

Educators at lower elementary school teach vocabulary words for *word recognition*, so learners can understand the meaning on sight without needing to sound it out; however, word recognition implies that the learner is already familiar with the word orally, which some ELLs may not be. Some teachers use vocabulary lists for lower grades named Dolch or Fry words, and these words are very common in English (more on vocabulary later in Chapter 9). One difference in teaching ELLs and native English speakers word recognition is that with native speakers, if they can sound out the word, they will be able to connect it to its meaning. With an ELL, though, if they sound it out, but they do not have a certain degree of oral proficiency in English, they may not understand the meanings of the vocabulary words. ELLs need to have the meanings specifically taught with word recognition.

As teachers gradually develop students' phonemic awareness, phonics knowledge, and vocabulary, they read aloud and conduct read-along activities for the students to see that texts carry meanings. One recommendation that is often given to ELLs' parents is to read to them in their L1 (if the language is written and the parent literate). These instructional strategies help learners understand the bigger picture, so they are called *top-down instructional strategies*.

Reading comprehension and fluency

Teachers will also ensure that students comprehend texts and build reading fluency as they progress in their literacy development. Reading comprehension is the ability to understand what was read. Reading fluency is the ability to read quickly with relative ease and comprehend what was read. These two subskills combine at times. One can read quickly, but without meaning. Or one can read for comprehension, but lose track of the meaning by reading too slowly.

Effective reading balances both subskills of comprehension and fluency. To build reading comprehension, teachers direct the focus of students on both understanding and recalling the main ideas and details of a text. They do this by creating opportunities before, during, and after reading to discuss what learners understood from the text. For example, before reading a teacher may ask the students to predict what the reading may be about. It helps connect with their background knowledge (schema) and helps the learners to comprehend what they are about to read since they need to call upon background knowledge in the process of making meanings. During the reading, the teacher may ask critical thinking questions to help students make connections between ideas. Or they may ask them to discuss with a partner, for example, *think–pair–share*, the meaning of a key word or phrase. After the reading, teachers engage learners with multiple discursive and kinesthetic activities to help them discuss their understandings, make connections, and reinforce the learning. Often, teachers will ask comprehension questions that encourage learners to revisit the text to find evidence for something they think about the text. They also ask inference questions, so students learn to understand implications intended by the author that are not physically present in the text.

When the teacher's goal is to build ELLs' reading fluency, instead of introducing many different texts as they would in building comprehension, they focus on reading the same text a couple of times. Other times, they will encourage ELLs to read texts that are below their level of readability or grade level. Readability is an indicator of how easy it is to read a text based upon the complexity of the grammar, vocabulary, and writing of a text. There are several online tools for readability. The Flesch–Kincaid readability test, for instance, assigns a score that is based on the average number of words per sentence and average number of syllables per word (for more on readability see https://readable.com/blog/the-flesch-reading-ease-and-flesch-kincaid-grade-level). For example, many newspapers have a readability at the tenth-grade level. Publishers like Scholastic and Fountas & Pinnell have many-leveled readers to help teachers provide readers for fluency development. In some situations, educators will ask students to speedread the same passage several times and try to increase their reading speed each time while maintaining their comprehension of the text.

Teens or adults learners

For older learners who are literate in their L1, educators start with connecting L1 and L2 sounds and symbols (i.e., phonics), if there is a large difference between the languages. Teen and adult ELLs need to know which letters have the same sounds as their native language has, but this does not need to be taught as thoroughly as it does with children.

Earlier in this chapter we mentioned that the L1 is an important aspect in L2 reading. If ELLs come from a L1 that is not in the same language family as English or that has a different written system, the learners cannot draw upon the L1 for sound/letter correspondences, or for shared root words. Therefore, connections to the letters in the learners' L1 only work with some ELL populations and in some contexts. The same is true of using root words.

Vocabulary instruction and practice reading simplified texts are a good next step for teens and adults who are at the beginning level of proficiency.

Educators often engage in intensive and extensive reading with ELLs who are teens and adults. *Intensive reading*, also known as close reading, emphasizes comprehending a text on a deep level while grappling with new vocabulary, with grammar that is new or just above their current level, or with complex sentence structures. Linguistically, students practice decoding, comprehending increasingly complex sentence structures while increasing their vocabulary knowledge. Educators engage upper elementary, high school and adult ELLs with texts through comprehension activities and discussions to explore a text in depth. *Extensive reading*, on the other hand, is reading many different passages or texts on the same subject. The working idea with extensive reading is that learners will develop their comprehension and fluency while reading widely on one topic. Extensive reading has some clear advantages, because when learners read extensively on one topic, it is explored from various angles using the same vocabulary set, which leads to better comprehension of the topic.

Language experience approach

One method to support learners in their literacy development is the language experience approach (LEA). It was first described in the 1960s as a way to bridge oral to written language. TESOL educators guide groups of learners through a process of orally articulating their narrative of a shared experience. The educator writes the students' oral contributions on the board to connect the written word to the spoken. Then, the learners are guided through steps to read the groups' narrative. The underlying theory (Freire, 1972) is that learners are empowered in their learning if they own the story and share information that is meaningful to them.

Steps in a LEA lesson:

1. Start with common experience or prompt (e.g., field trip, video, experiment, photo etc.).
2. Teacher elicits the students' ideas about the experience.
3. Teacher writes down the students' ideas exactly as they are shared, errors and all.
   - Grammar issues (at advanced level) are discussed. The teacher prompts the students to consider another way of saying the same idea with correct grammar.
4. The teacher reads aloud the story/text while pointing out the words as they read.
5. The students and teacher read it again in a choral reading.
6. Reread a couple more times.
7. Individual students take turns reading with assistance from the teacher.
8. Students write down the text.

If the teen or adult is not literate in their L1 or comes from an unwritten language background (so members of the community are not literate), the same processes and choices would apply as for children. The materials, speed of instruction, and methodology may vary considerably though. For more on this subject, the Center for Applied Linguistics (CAL) has a brief article authored by Burt et al. (2008) with instructional suggestions and resources.

Questions for reflection

- Why is teaching reading to young learners so different from teaching for older learners?
- How would you design a lesson for reading with young learners as opposed to older learners?

Teaching Reading Strategies

You may have noticed that the word strategy/ies is written frequently in this book, and that the use of strategy/ies is accompanied by an adjective. We try to modify our use of the word strategies to differentiate between the strategies employed by the teacher and those used by learners. For example, instructional strategies are tools, techniques, activities, etc. that the educator employs. Strategies used by learners to further their abilities and allow them to become more independent in their learning process are called *learning strategies* or *language learning strategies*.

Reading has its own set of strategies, which are used by learners to comprehend what they read. Initially, educators teach students how to use the strategy and provide practice opportunities. The most commonly taught reading strategies are previewing the text, predicting, identifying the main idea, self-questioning, monitoring understanding, clarifying understandings, summarizing, inferring, visualizing, evaluating, making connections, integrating, and synthesizing information for critical reading. These reading strategies are how strong readers will approach and engage with a text. You will notice that these reading strategies are interwoven throughout the next section on reading lessons.

Language-rich classrooms

An instructional support that builds literacy is creating a language-rich classroom. Language-rich classrooms have written language present throughout the room on the walls, boards, and shelves. What is added to create a language-rich classroom would depend heavily on the learners' proficiency level and age. Learners look to these resources when they need to refresh their memory or to learn new words or concepts.

- Label classroom objects in the languages of the students and English.
- Provide reading materials in English and students' native languages.
- Decorate the bulletin boards or reading areas with:

- alphabet;
- word walls of vocabulary being studied or high-frequency vocabulary;
- spelling words;
- illustrated vocabulary words;
- grammar concepts being studied;
- reading strategies; and
- songs or poems.
- Give students access to dictionaries, picture dictionaries and thesauruses.
  - Offer readable texts for learners that are bilingual or in English only.

Organization of Reading Lessons

Reading lessons, like listening lessons, often take a pre/during/postreading structure (see "Organization of Listening Lessons"). What educators choose to do at each phase is connected to whether they are reading fiction or nonfiction texts. Different types of passages will lend themselves to different instructional choices.

Prereading

The prereading phase of a lesson includes identification of the purpose of reading, connection to learners' schema/background building, discussion of new vocabulary necessary to comprehend the reading, and reading strategy instruction (Figure 7.2). Before the reading, educators can support ELLs' reading comprehension by:

- Identifying a purpose for reading (e.g., K-W-H-L).
- Accessing or building background knowledge; making personally meaningful connections (e.g., going on field trips; using videos/film, visuals, experiments).
- Connecting to or developing background information on the topic; brainstorming about the topic in general (e.g., anticipation guides).
- Preteaching important concepts and vocabulary (creating word banks); using visuals.
- Previewing the text through picture walks, scanning, and discussing headings/subheadings, setting the stage for the reading/piquing interest.
- Teaching reading strategies (e.g., skimming, scanning, predicting, questioning).
- Using directed reading–thinking activity (DR-TA) questions, which involves a series of guiding questions to guide students' thinking and predictions. For example, what do you predict/think will happen? What are your reasons for this prediction?

Figure 7.2 Pre-, during, Postreading sequence, part one.

While reading

During the reading phase of a lesson (Figure 7.3), we want to use a balanced literacy approach. Balanced literacy brings together top-down (i.e., whole-language) and bottom-up (i.e., phonics, word recognition) approaches and activities in lessons. We also want to revisit (reread) the text several times, but in new ways.

In the past, educators often asked students to take turns reading aloud in what is called *round robin* or popcorn reading. Research shows that round robin reading is not a highly effective instructional strategy to help learners to learn to read in the during-reading portion of a lesson (Hoffman & Rasinski, 2003; Ash & Kuhn, 2006; Optiz & Rasinsky, 2008). Many other instructional strategies can be employed that are more conducive to helping and supporting learners in their reading development. Some instructional strategies for revisiting the text in different ways are: teacher read-alouds (and acting out meanings), silent reading, guided reading (i.e., readings supported and guided by the teacher, usually in small groups), choral readings, jigsaw readings, oral paired reading, individual whisper readings, readings along with audio, and teacher think-alouds (i.e., think-aloud modeling). How might you employ and in what order would you use two or three of these instructional strategies for reading?

During the reading, educators can support ELLs' reading comprehension by:

- Encouraging students to:
  - assign a main-idea label to a paragraph;
  - use reading strategies (e.g., take notes, summarize, evaluate, monitor their comprehension and clarify when necessary, use context clues, mark confusing passages, reread, visualize, infer meaning);
  - revise prior knowledge and predict by asking themselves:
    - How am I adding to what I already know?
    - What will happen next?
  - self-question:
    - Do I understand what I am reading?
    - Can I summarize what I'm reading?
- Encouraging the use of the ELLs' native language(s) (i.e., meaning-making; clarification in L1).
- Increasing interaction with the text by questioning the author.

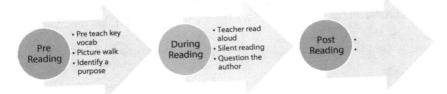

Figure 7.3 Pre-, during, postreading sequence, part two.

- Raising ELLs' awareness of discourse structure (i.e., outlines, graphic organizers, underline lexical clues (e.g., cause–effect; problem–solution) by highlight conjunctions and transition words).
- Identifying for ELLs challenging parts of the text (e.g., lack of concrete examples, abstract imagery/theorizing, assumed background knowledge, conceptual complexity, confusing formatting, density of text, grammatical complexity, lack of clarity in writing, length of sentences/text, new conceptual knowledge, poorly signaled organization, unfamiliar content, unfamiliar vocab/new meanings) and providing tips for understanding the passage.

All of these strategies for thinking and processing information about the ideas and patterns in the text will help learners to affirm their understandings or clarify misunderstandings. For this reason, it is important to revisit the text from various angles.

Postreading

After the reading phase of a lesson (Figure 7.4), educators want to confirm learners' comprehension of the passage as well as their understandings of the inferences alluded to in the text. TESOL educators check comprehension of concrete items/understanding concepts by asking students to summarize, paraphrase, or retell a passage by drawing, talking, or (re)enacting it. There are many engaging ways to ask learners to share their understandings of the text. For example, writing a new title or headline, creating a bumper sticker, or outlining with a storyboard or sequencing pictures of events. Older students are often asked to summarize, paraphrase, or compare/contrast their understandings and possible interpretations.

TESOL educators also wish to engage the learners' other language skills to support their language learning and understandings of the text. They may employ communicative activities, tasks, or projects during the postreading phrase for this purpose. For example, integration of other language skills can be accomplished through extension activities, such as jigsaw readings, cooperative group discussions, role-play, games, K-W-H-L charts, illustrations of the text or creation of alternate endings, character and/or plot maps and analysis, student-created versions of texts, research theme of text, free write, organize note-taking, reflect and respond to writing or discussion prompts, write in journal, literature circles, or writing workshops.

Figure 7.4   Pre-, during, postreading sequence, part three.

After the reading, educators can support ELLs' reading comprehension by:

- Outlining the main ideas and details or events in the story.
- Analyzing the discourse structures and difficult parts of the text.
- Relating text to academic reading, current events, or the students' lives.
- Increasing interaction interpersonally and with the text after the reading. For example, by finding evidence to answer the *why* questions.
- Discussing the text from different angles:
  - confirm the main idea;
  - locate details;
  - determine author stance, bias, or position; and
  - compare and contrast with another information source.
- Reflecting on their predictions and understandings and adding new knowledge.
- Utilizing supplementary materials. For example, you may read topically related texts and at reading level.
- Labeling maps and diagrams with necessary information.

Questions for reflection

- What are the similarities and differences in the three phases of a reading lesson?
- Which of the three phases is the most crucial for reading comprehension? Why?

Receptive skills and digital technology

Listening and reading have also changed from traditional communication patterns owing to developments in digital technologies. Nowadays we not only listen, but also watch. Materials for listening only are often enhanced by the contextual sounds in the background for listeners to name the context of conversation. For example, if it is in a restaurant, the background noise reflects relevant incomprehensible human sounds or other environmental sounds. These materials have been replaced by listen-and-watch materials, which offer a great number of contextual clues for comprehension in much the same way as listening in conversation. In most language-teaching materials—printed or digital—there are video elements, which not only draw attention and prolong concentration time, but also facilitate comprehension if they are appropriate for the proficiency level.

Students also have access to authentic international radio, vlogs, news, and podcasts, which allow them to learn about culture and the ways people communicate using less formal language. Similarly, reading has been enhanced in digital formats to include pop-up hyperlinks, more relevant pictures and videos, immediate access to unknown word meaning though online links to dictionaries, and use of various fonts and typing features to create salience in the linguistic input. These are called hypertexts, and are now commonplace. Also, there is relatively more access to reading materials supported by audio recordings, so that a reader can follow the text as it is read aloud. These developments offer more opportunities to help listeners and readers develop their skills. See Table 7.2 for examples of digital technologies for listening and reading.

Table 7.2 Sample digital technologies for listening and reading.

Audiobooks	Videos	Sing-along songs
• StoryNory: This site offers free audio downloads of classic fairy tales, world fairy tales, fables, 1001 Nights... • Lit2Go: Hundreds of free audiobooks, but many of the books and poems have free PDFs to download and print so that children can read along, highlight, and mark up the passage being read. Historical. • Project Gutenberg: More than 50,000 free ebooks, but not all of them are audiobooks. Copyrights have expired. • International Children's Digital Library: Thousands of books in many different languages.	• Alison: Standards-based education material covering a wide range of academic topics. • CosmoLearning: Free, online video lessons and documentaries. • Coursera: Lectures taught by world-class professors and reinforced through interactive exercises. • EdX: Courses designed specifically for interactive study via the web. • FutureLearn: Offers a diverse selection of courses from leading European universities. • iTunes U: Free lectures, language lessons, audiobooks, and more accessible via Apple iTunes. • PBS Video: Free videos from your favorite PBS programs, including NOVA and Frontline.	• ESLAuthority: Has 45 free songs for teaching English. • BusyTeacher: Nearly 1,800 free songs. Includes both the song lyrics and exercises for teaching listening at different levels of proficiency. • Games4ESL: Offers 10 pop songs with video for ESL students. Some songs have closed captioning. • YouTube has a channel called Songs for ESL Students, with 80 pop videos.

Questions for reflection

- How is L2 developed when learners are exposed to it through technology?
- What other digital technologies can you brainstorm to teach listening or reading?

Chapter Conclusions

Integrated language skills include speaking, listening, reading, and writing in each lesson, so the skills mutually reinforce each other. The tools of grammar, vocabulary pronunciation, and spelling are subskills that work within some or all of the language skills.

Listening and reading provide much-needed linguistic input for language learners. Effective listening and reading instruction support learners in the process of making meanings and comprehending new words and concepts. In both skills, we build from prior knowledge and add new information to our existing schemas. In both language skills, we also focus first on comprehension, and then on fluency (i.e., automaticity of processing) and inference. The age of learners heavily influences the reading process but has little influence on the listening process. Both listening and reading skills can be explicitly taught through specific strategies that, when modeled and practiced, will assist the learners in developing these skills and being more independent in their learning. Both language skills involve a pre-, during and postlistening/viewing/reading sequence in order to engage and motivate learners, support them in the meaning-making process, and clarify and reinforce their comprehension and understandings of the experience.

Discussion Questions

1 How do you envision an integrated skills lesson that focuses on either listening or reading? Why would you want to create this type of lesson?
2 Why is listening a skill that is often overlooked for explicit instruction? How will you ensure that you teach listening in your future lessons?
3 Reading is a complex skill with many moving parts, among them relationships between sounds and symbols, making meanings, fluency, and vocabulary. For your current or future learners, which of these areas do you think will be most important? How might you balance all of the competing parts?

Tasks

1 How did you learn to improve your second language listening? What instruction or strategies helped you and what did not?
2 Did you first learn to read in a new language, bilingually, or in your native language? What do you recall of the process?
3 Investigate how schemas are formed, developed, and eliminated. How does this impact second language learning?
4 Neurolinguistics: Investigate how the brain processes incoming linguistic information. How does the brain convert these incoming sounds into meanings?
5 Create a multicultural set of texts, both fiction and nonfiction, on a theme that you could use in your current or future classroom. Try to include two or three bilingual texts on the theme.
6 Design a language-rich classroom diorama. Include how you would organize desks, reading areas, text, and audio/visual resources. Why did you make the choices you did?

Further Reading/Read and Discuss

Read about working with adults who have limited L1 literacy:

Burt, M., Peyton, J. K., & Schaetzel, K. (2008, July). *Working with adult English language learners with limited literacy: Research, practice, and professional development.* Center for Applied Linguistics. https://cal.org/adultesl/resources/briefs/working-with-adult-english-language-learners-with-limited-literacy.php (accessed March 25, 2021).

Read about language learning strategies:

Oxford, R. (1990). *Language learning strategies: What every teacher should know.* Newbury House.

References

Ash, G. E., & Kuhn, M. R. (2006). Meaningful oral and silent reading in the elementary and middle school classroom: Breaking the round robin reading addiction. In T. Rasinski, C. Blachowicz, & K. Lems (Eds.), *Fluency instruction: Research-based best practices* (pp. 155–172). The Guilford Press.

Burt, M., Peyton, J. K., & Schaetzel, K. (2008, July). *Working with adult English language learners with limited literacy: Research, practice, and professional development.* Center for Applied Linguistics. https://cal.org/adultesl/resources/briefs/working-with-adult-english-language-learners-with-limited-literacy.php

Carson, J. E., Carrell, P. L., Silberstein, S., Kroll, B., & Kuehn, P. A. (1990). Reading-writing relationships in first and second language. *TESOL Quarterly, 24*(2), 245–266. https://doi.org/10.2307/3586901

Chen, Z., & Goh, C. (2011). Teaching oral English in higher education: Challenges to EFL teachers. *Teaching in Higher Education, 16*(3), 333–345. https://doi.org/10.1080/13562517.2010.546527

Coady, J. (1997). L2 vocabulary acquisition through extensive reading. In J. Coady & T. Huckins (Eds.), *Second language vocabulary acquisition* (pp. 217–228). Ablex.

Cummins, J. (2017). Teaching for transfer in multilingual school contexts. In O. García, A. M. Y. Lin, & S. May (Eds.), *Bilingual and multilingual education* (3rd ed., pp. 104–113). Springer.

Eberhard, D. M., Simons, G. F., & Fennig, C. D. (Eds.). (2020). *Ethnologue: Languages of the world* (23rd ed.). SIL International. http://www.ethnologue.com

Ediger, A. M. (2014). Teaching second/foreign language literacy to school-age learners. In M. Celcia-Murcia, D. M. Brinton, & M. A. Snow (Eds.), *Teaching English as a second or foreign language* (4th ed.) (pp. 154–169). National Geographic Learning & Heinle Cengage Learning.

Freire, P. (1972). *Pedagogy of the oppressed.* Penguin.

Grabe, W., & Stoller, F. L. (2002). *Teaching and researching reading.* Pearson Education.

Rasinski, T., & Hoffman, J. V. (2003). Oral reading in the school literacy curriculum. *Reading Research Quarterly, 38*(4), 510–522. https://doi.org/10.1598/RRQ.38.4.5

Krashen, S. (1982). *Principles and practices of second language acquisition.* Pergamon.

Laufer, B., & Ravenhorst-Kalovski, G. C. (2010). Lexical threshold revisited: Lexical text coverage, learners' vocabulary size and reading comprehension. *Reading in a Foreign Language, 22*(1), 15–30. https://citeseerx.ist.psu.edu/viewdoc/download?doi=10.1.1.1001.2472&rep=rep1&type=pdf (accessed March 25, 2021).

Nation, I. S. P. (2008). *Teaching vocabulary: Strategies and techniques.* Heinle Cengage.

Optiz, M. F., & Rasinsky, T. (2008). *Good-bye round robin: 25 effective oral reading strategies, updated edition.* Heinemann.

Pulido, D., & Hambrick, D. Z. (2008). The virtuous circle: Modeling individual differences in L2 reading and vocabulary development. *Reading in a Foreign Language, 20*(2), 164–190. doi:10.7916/D89C7900

Royer, J. M., & Carlo, M. S. (1991). Transfer of comprehension skills from native to second language. *Journal of Reading, 34*(6), 450–455. https://doi.org/10.1016/S0166-4115(08)61662-3

Thonis, E. W. (1980). *Teaching reading to non-English speakers*. Collier Macmillan Teacher's Library.

World-class Instructional Design and Assessment (WIDA). (2007). *English language proficiency standards and resource guides* (7th ed.). University of Wisconsin System and WIDA Consortium.

World-class Instructional Design and Assessment (WIDA). (2020). *WIDA English language development standards framework, 2020 Edition Kindergarten—Grade 12*. Board of Regents of the University of Wisconsin System.

8

How Do TESOL Educators Teach Speaking and Writing in Integrated Language Instruction?

This chapter will focus on specifics of individual language skills (i.e., speaking and writing). TESOL educators employ instructional strategies from various methods from the past that align with speaking and writing lessons, so some notable "designer methods" will be introduced.

Learning Outcomes

At the conclusion of this chapter, you will be able to:

- describe shared and unique characteristics and considerations of speaking and writing
- develop interactive classes that integrate speaking and writing instruction

Teaching both speaking and writing necessitates finding one's voice, literally and figuratively. There are many facets to speaking and writing, one of which, culture, has an impact on both format and voice. Observe, in this vignette, how one educator discovered this intersection and modified accordingly.

TESOL Voices

Cultural Influences on Writing

I've always loved writing. When I was an awkward teen, prone to saying things that I understood, but that others didn't quite get, writing gave me a fighting chance. Especially with girls. Instead of saying "Uh, well, uh, I was wondering, the concert tonight, if you wanted, you know..." I could spend an hour or so writing a brilliant note that would actually get results. I eventually became a writing teacher, helping other people learn how to express their thoughts in writing. One year, I was assigned a "Bridge" course consisting of a group of Japanese college students who had just arrived in the United States. The course was intended to teach them writing styles that would help them succeed in American college courses. I gave them my usual description of college-level writing: using words like "authoritative," "argumentative," "predictable," and "convincing," I explained the need to lead readers through every

---

Introduction to TESOL: Becoming a language teaching professional, First Edition. Kate Mastruserio Reynolds, Kenan Dikilitaş, and Steve Close.

step of an argument without leaving loose ends, unanswered questions, or unresolved issues. I noticed one student who hesitantly raised his hand. When I called on him, he asked a simple question, in flawless English: "Is my reader stupid?"

Writing expresses thoughts and technical skill, but it also expresses cultural understandings, beliefs, and assumptions. If the student in the Bridge class hadn't spoken up, I might have been frustrated throughout the entire class, thinking that the Japanese school system simply doesn't teach effective writing. Why? Because my students would have lacked the "voice" that I've grown to expect in American college writers. Because one student spoke up, at a time when many students simply wouldn't have, I was able to reframe the class around a cultural concept: American college writing starts with an idea, then gathers evidence to prove it (deductive), while Japanese college writing starts with evidence, then poses problems for the reader to think about (inductive). For those Japanese students, no amount of skill in the rules of the English language could have overcome that barrier, because it was cultural rather than linguistic.

For me, writing illustrates one of the major ideas that comes up again and again in TESOL: fluency—the effective meeting of the expectations of your conversation partner—comes from a combination of factors, both technical and cognitive. I try to remember that every time I teach a class.

Steve Close
Professor of English and Communications Instructor

Productive Skills of Speaking and Writing

Much like the receptive skills of listening and reading, speaking and writing play a crucial role in second language development. The teaching of receptive language skills emphasizes comprehension of incoming messages and automaticity in processing in the incoming input, whereas learners extend their automatic processing when they practice productive skills of speaking and writing. Speaking and writing are called productive, because learners produce oral or written language. World-class Instructional Design and Assessment (WIDA, 2020) has renamed productive skills as expressive skills, which emphasizes how these skills allow ELLs to share their ideas. Using productive/expressive skills allows ELLs to frame their own thoughts using the grammatical forms/patterns, vocabulary, and oral or written format expectations, while gearing this message and the language choices they make to the audience. In this way, learners extend their language abilities. In this chapter, we will explore details of each of these skills and discuss relevant instructional practices, in order to clarify further how productive skills can be taught.

Teaching Speaking

What is speaking? Is it oral grammar, vocabulary, or pronunciation? Is it a combination of these areas or a skill unto itself? What are TESOL educators' goals in teaching speaking? In the past in many world language classes, educators focused on the oral grammar, vocabulary use, and "authentic" pronunciation of the target language. Speaking relies heavily on these tools, but focusing only on these characteristics is not enough.

Speaking involves framing a message that the learner wants to convey. The learner considers what they need to say and to whom, leading them to think about whether they would need more formal or informal language and what vocabulary and grammar they might need to form the message. It should be understood that this connects to the communicative competencies discussed in previous chapters. The speaker may identify a speech act or formulaic expression to use, so the process is faster and easier. They may identify a colloquial expression, slang phrase, or an idiom to help them. Or they may organize their message into a statement or question, which includes knowledge of word order (i.e., syntax). They must consider the subject (i.e., noun or pronoun), subject/verb agreement, verb tense, direct or indirect objects, adjectives, adverbs, conjunctions, prepositions, and articles. If they need to speak more than one sentence, they may need to consider connections between ideas in different sentences. All of this occurs in their brains in a couple of milliseconds. Then, they need to deliver their message orally. The message delivery involves voice volume, pronunciation, hesitations, pauses, floor-holding devices (e.g., um, erm), contractions/reductions, breathing, message clarity, and reception. Other intriguing aspects of spoken English that distinguish it from written English are that spoken English has many repetitions/rephrasing, interruptions (both of oneself and others), misstarts (i.e., when a speaker starts a sentence and does not like it, so begins again), turn-taking, clarifications, comprehension checks, and confirmation checks.

Speech acts in the second language classroom

Acquisition begins by interpreting the spoken language to identify what is meant by what has been said. Children can easily comprehend what is indirectly said and behave accordingly. So indirect speech acts are inherent in human communication. For example, in the following dialogue, the child interprets what their mother has said as the rejection of the permission request though the mother does not directly do so.

CHILD: Can I play some more games in my room?
MOTHER: We are about to leave home.
CHILD: I don't want to come with you...

Having learners interpret speech acts might help them avoid memorizing fixed response structures and express their responses indirectly because a good portion of communication is indirect and implied.

In spoken English, there are many patterns that make it cognitively less taxing to engage in the rapid exchanges of information we have daily. One type of pattern is called "speech acts," a concept that was originated by J. L. Austin in his book, *How to Do Things with Words* (1962). There are six categories of speech acts, which can be connected to verbs.

Types of speech acts:

- Representatives: assertions, statements, claims, hypotheses, descriptions, suggestions.
- Commissives: promises, oaths, pledges, threats, vows.

- Directives: commands, requests, challenges, invitations, orders, summons, entreaties, dares.
- Declarations: blessings, firings, baptisms, arrests, marrying, judicial speech acts such as sentencings, declaring a mistrial, declaring something of order.
- Expressives: speech acts that make assessments of psychological states or attitudes—greetings, apologies, congratulations, condolences, thanksgivings.
- Verdictives: rankings, assessments, appraisals, condoning (combinations such as representational declarations: You're out!) (Schiffman, 1997).

The influence of speech acts in second language teaching/learning causes textbook authors to include dialogues and practice on common speech acts. TESOL educators tend to teach the typical ways English speakers conduct the speech acts. In some instances, educators may teach variations on these speech acts as well.

Greetings

Setting: Two acquaintances seeing each other in the hallway.

SPEAKER 1:   Hi! How are you?
SPEAKER 2:   I'm fine. How are you?
SPEAKER 1:   Good. Thanks.

Conversational Closings

Setting: Two close friends who had not seen each other in a long time after a conversation.

SPEAKER 1:   It's been nice chatting. I have to go.
SPEAKER 2:   Yeah, it's been great catching up.
SPEAKER 1:   Keep in touch, okay?
SPEAKER 2:   Yeah, sounds great. Bye.

Agreeing/Disagreeing

Setting: Two colleagues trying to solve a problem on a work project.

SPEAKER 1:   I think we should try to fix the issue by talking to our partners and seeing if we can get an extension.
SPEAKER 2:   I don't think that is a good idea. That will make us look bad. I think we should pay more to get the items shipped to our partners faster.

Making Requests

Setting: In a library, requesting help with a book.

SPEAKER 1:   Excuse me. Do you have the book, *The Book Thief*? I looked on the shelf, but couldn't find it. Could you please help me?
SPEAKER 2:   Good morning. Hm. Let's look at the computer to see if it is available. [types] Yes, I see that it is available. It came back in this morning. It might need to be reshelved. Let me see if I can find it.
SPEAKER 1:   Thank you so much.

All speech acts occur in a setting that helps speakers to know what degree of formality, politeness, familiarity, and brevity they should use. Often settings are provided to guide learners to gear their linguistic choices to the participants, situation, and topic. This approach also helps make speaking practice more authentic to the types of situations language learners may encounter in their lives.

Many of the speech acts are now commonly taught in the classroom through the use of sentence starters, stem sentences, or conversational moves.

How might you teach speech acts to develop learners' oral language proficiency? Are there different speech acts for different levels of proficiency?

Speech usually involves interaction, so participants in an interaction think about the setting, the other participants (i.e., interlocutors), roles, and goals of the interaction. The speaker guesses what the listener may know and what they may not, and thinks about and frames their own contribution to the interaction. Finally, speakers monitor what they are saying and correct themselves as they are going, as well as monitoring the understanding of the listener(s) (see the textbox, "Tool for analyzing settings for teaching L2 speaking").

Tool for analyzing settings for teaching L2 speaking

Dell Hymes (1962, 1974) developed a research tool to analyze the setting of an interaction, which is helpful to TESOL educators when teaching speaking.

S for **Situation**, which includes both the scene and the setting. This is where the activities are taking place and the overall scene of which they are a part.

P for **Participants**, includes the people present and the roles they play, or the relationships they have with other participants.

E for **Ends** or goals of communication can be studied.

A for **Acts**, or speech acts, which include both form and content. That is, any action can be considered a communicative action if it conveys meaning to the participants.

K for **Key**, mood, manner, and/or tone of speech. How the speech sounds or was delivered. This may include casual or formal language and register.

I, **Instrumentality** or the channel through which communication flows can be examined.

N, the **Norms** of communication or the rules guiding talk and its interpretation can reveal meaning—reaction and interaction.

G for cultural or traditional speech **Genres**, such as proverbs, apologies, prayers, and small talk, problem talk, etc. (Ethnography of Communication, n.d.).

Differences between spoken and written language

Spoken and written English have some similarities, but not as many as people may think. They are similar in that they both use statements and questions with corresponding syntax patterns, different types of sentences, sentence-level grammar, discourse patterns, sociocultural/sociolinguistic awareness (i.e., awareness of audience, cultural expectations, degrees of formality/informality, etc.), and inferencing. Speaking and writing have different characteristics as well. Some of the differences are shown in Table 8.1.

Table 8.1 Differences between spoken and written language.

Spoken language	Written language
Faster rate	Slower rate
Little thinking time	More opportunity to think, analyze, and reflect
Opportunities to correct yourself or restart	Opportunities to revise and edit
Opportunities to ask questions to better understand the message and/or to check the listener understands. The speaker and listener share information within the setting that they do not have to make explicit	Written language includes only opportunities to question yourself and the author without opportunity to receive an answer (unless you tweet the author or attend a book reading). It also tends to be explicit, clear
Opportunities to read nonverbal behavior	No contact with the author or characters
Generally, more slang and colloquial expressions are employed	Limited use of slang (except in some fictional works). Nonfiction writing tends to include exact vocabulary usage in order to be accurate and succinct
Less concern about the message in some settings	Care taken with the message
Rules tend not to be taught with spoken language with few exceptions. An exception is the use of *ain't*. Many native English speakers are taught explicitly not to use it	Formal rules for writing are taught and expected
Spoken language evolves and changes constantly	Written language tends not to evolve or change much
Spoken English has many dialects and regional variations	Written language tends not to have dialects or regional variation unless an author chooses to use them in a fictional work, such as *The Adventures of Huckleberry Finn*
Spoken language is more diluted, because speakers repeat/rephrase, pause, hesitate, etc.	Written language tends to be dense. In writing, being concise and to the point are valued. So, fewer words are used
Spoken language typically is gone within seconds unless it is digitally recorded	Longer lasting. Written texts can exist for millennia
Spoken language comprises sounds and prosodic features (see more in pronunciation). Connected speech and delivery	Written English comprises letters, words, sentences, paragraphs. Cohesion and clarity

---

Questions for reflection

- What have you observed about speaking?
- What are the differences between informal conversations and more formal speech?

Details of teaching second language speaking

Four concepts are important to keep as a major focus when planning lessons, teaching and assessing L2 speaking: appropriacy, authenticity, fluency, and accuracy. When educators consider these concepts, they can orient lessons for learners to emphasize those needed by the learners.

Appropriacy of language use while speaking

First, we want to teach learners to be aware of appropriate language usage for the setting. *Appropriacy* includes awareness of the listener(s). To be appropriate, the speaker will evaluate what they know of the listener: who the listener is, what they do/want, what they value, and what the relationship to the speaker is. The speaker will evaluate what they know of the setting (i.e., office, classroom, store, bank, gas station), and the roles of relationships and language use in the setting (see the box "Tool for analyzing settings for teaching L2 speaking"). TESOL educators teach learners which phrases and expressions are spoken in which types of settings. For example, the teacher may provide two dialogues on giving advice, one informal and the other formal. After listening, reading, and orally practicing the dialogues, students would be asked to analyze the differences in the language used in both. The teacher would facilitate a discussion with learners to share their insights as to what grammatical and lexical items were used in each setting and their thoughts on why. This sort of activity helps learners make connections between language forms and setting. In their home language and culture, they would have different degrees of formality and rules for participation in these settings, so it is incumbent upon the teacher to illustrate how English is used in similar settings. Without explicit instruction on appropriate language use, the learner may make subtle mistakes that would have serious ramifications.

Authenticity of language

Second, TESOL educators need to teach authentic speaking, so that our learners are prepared for the real situations in which they will need to interact orally with others. *Authenticity* refers to language that is true to life, typical, or real. As was discussed earlier in this text, communicative language teaching (CLT) was a method developed in reaction to the Audiolingual Method (ALM). In the ALM, students were instructed to repeat sentences and questions that did not necessarily have an application in their real-life communication. The comedian Eddie Izzard provided a hilarious example of this lack of applicability in her experience learning French (https://www.youtube.com/watch?v=x1sQkEfAdfY). Some of the points TESOL educators may stress to ELLs about speaking authentically are: repeating/rephrasing, pausing, floor-holding, asking for clarification, etc. We can help ELLs become comfortable using these common techniques in speaking, so they are more successful and confident.

Speech acts, whether they are for social or academic interaction, are another way that educators can ensure that the speaking activities we employ are authentic and applicable. We can analyze a situation, for example, a classroom discussion on different economic systems, for the speech acts/patterns of oral interaction we hope the learners can use. Then, we can preteach those patterns, so ELLs are successful in that discussion.

Activities focused on fluency or accuracy

The third set of critical concepts for teaching speaking is fluency and accuracy. *Fluency* is better understood as the fluidity of language in use. It is important to maintain the distinction between fluency and proficiency/language ability. A good working definition of fluency is when words are spoken with ease, coming at a reasonable pace without awkward pauses or hesitations. *Accuracy*, on the other hand, is when the speaker avoids any grammatical, syntactic, pronunciation, or vocabulary errors. What is fascinating about these two concepts is that when it comes to speaking, they often have an inverse relationship. If a learner is too concerned about being accurate in their language use, the words may not be spoken fluently. If a learner focuses more on expressing a message and does not worry about being accurate, they may make more errors.

When it comes to fluency/accuracy, there are individual, cultural, and proficiency-level differences. Individual learners may be more or less inhibited, so they may not focus on the message delivery, and may make more errors. Kate was so worried about looking foolish when studying French that she often did not sound as fluent. Interestingly, when learning Spanish later, she was less concerned about embarrassment, so would speak Spanish fluidly while making loads of errors. In some cultures, making an error may result in a loss of face or embarrassment, which is not acceptable. For that reason, some learners may be less likely to take risks when speaking English and may focus on accuracy over fluency. Lastly, learners at different proficiency levels may focus on either fluency or accuracy. Often, at lower levels of proficiency, it is important to encourage learners to use the language and develop automaticity in speaking. Learners may want to focus on accuracy at lower proficiency levels, but it may hinder their automaticity and learning since they would not have as many opportunities to use their emerging oral English skills. At the lower levels of proficiency, if a learner is focusing on conveying the message but has errors, educators can provide some feedback to help them along without focusing too much on it and risking inhibiting the learner. Feedback on accuracy of oral language becomes more important as learners move up the levels of proficiency. As learners are more comfortable with speaking and they are more able to convey messages with ease, providing increased feedback on forms and accuracy is important. See Figure 8.1.

What is emphasized in the skill of speaking when planning and delivering lessons has a significant influence on ELLs' oral proficiency. Educators make critical decisions about including activities/tasks that are meaningful speaking opportunities, allowing students to focus on appropriacy of their message, and emphasizing both fluency and accuracy, which will impact both learners' experience and abilities.

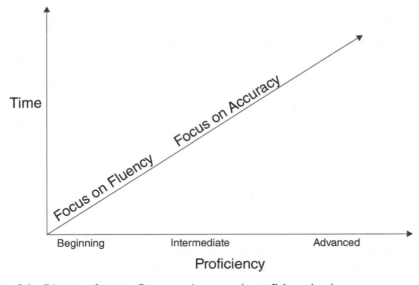

Figure 8.1 Educators focus on fluency and accuracy by proficiency level.

Questions for reflection

- When learning a new language, did you focus more on fluency or accuracy?
- How did your teacher ensure that speaking activities were authentic?
- How did you learn about appropriacy of language use?
- How would you explicitly teach conversation management strategies (i.e., turn-taking, interrupting, clarification, repetition, slow down, explain, change topic, how to gain time to think)?

Proficiency levels and speaking abilities

In the 1980s, the American Council of Teachers of Foreign Languages (ACTFL) was the first organization to attempt to describe learners' abilities in L2 speaking at different levels of proficiency (ACTFL, n.d.). The development of these guidelines was a notable advance for the field of L2 teaching and learning, because it helped educators and learners gauge and assess speaking abilities. The guidelines also provided a window through which educators could determine what they needed to teach to help learners advance to the next proficiency level.

Chapter 1 discussed the four proficiency levels: novice, intermediate, advanced, and superior. Novice, intermediate, and advanced each have three tiers: low, mid, and high. The levels are distinguished by the complexity of the grammar, the frequency of vocabulary (i.e., common or uncommon), the topics (i.e., personal and familiar or social and unfamiliar), the conversational partner's familiarity with L2 speakers, and the length and complexity of the discourse. For example, at lower levels of proficiency, speakers are at the "word-use" level. They can use words or lists of words and formulaic expressions. They can convey personal information and ask simple questions. Moving upward, they can discuss a wider range of topics with increasingly complex language forms. At higher levels, speakers can engage in longer exchanges of information or monologues and shift time frames (i.e., tenses) on topics that become increasingly more impersonal and abstract. At the advanced and superior levels, speakers have greater linguistic control and accuracy. They can handle unexpected complications. At the superior level, they can converse using different discourse/rhetorical formats (i.e., narratives, arguments, explanations, descriptions, opinions) (for more information, see https://www.actfl.org/resources/actfl-proficiency-guidelines-2012/english/speaking).

The differentiation of proficiency levels aided educators in determining where a learner was initially and what knowledge and practice they needed to provide the learners in terms of topics, length of discourse, grammatical forms, vocabulary, and discourse formats (see Figure 8.2). Educators also perform a mediating function in communication. Figure 8.2 demonstrates that student-to-teacher interaction (S–T) is easier than student-to-student (S–S) interaction, because teachers are better able to comprehend and cooperatively support the ELL when they are attempting to express a new or difficult linguistic form.

Knowing other information about the ELLs in a class also helps guide instruction. The previous chapter on listening and reading explained that the L1 influences those skills. So too does the L1 influence speaking (and writing). The learner's prosody (i.e.,

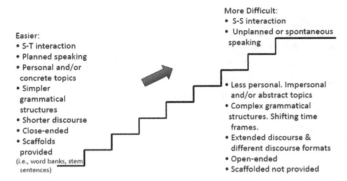

Figure 8.2 Continuum of speaking activity difficulty.

rhythm, intonation, pitch, word stress, and prominence) and L1 pronunciation of pho-nemes (i.e., sounds) influence their speaking in English—if the learner's L1 is a tonal language and the meaning of a word is based on the tone or pitch used when speaking, for example. If the learner does not have a particular pattern for word stress or a sound, such as /th/, they may struggle with being comprehensible. The topic of pronunciation will be discussed more in the next chapter.

Instructional practices for teaching second language speaking

One of the first considerations when teaching speaking is creating a learning environ-ment that is conducive to speaking freely without inhibition or fear. Without this foun-dation, learners will not be comfortable taking the personal and social risks associated with speaking in the second language. Many students may feel anxious, fearful, or embarrassed when using languages that they are learning. Many may worry about neg-ative judgments from their peers or the teacher. For these reasons, TESOL educators strive to establish a good rapport with their classes. Rapport in this sense is a harmoni-ous relationship with open communication between the educator and their students, so the students are comfortable sharing their feelings and thoughts. Educators also try to set up low-stress interactions by avoiding singling students out in a negative manner. The principle of a low-stress environment that is safe for risk-taking in the learned lan-guage aligns with Krashen's hypothesis, the affective filter (Krashen, 1982, p. 30) (see Chapter 5). When we treat errors as a normal and expected part of the learning process, students feel more comfortable taking risks. Errors are merely a means to show where instruction and feedback are needed. Additionally, TESOL educators strive to help learners in their classes develop interpersonal relationships with their classmates, so they can learn together without fear of judgment or embarrassment. These relation-ships do not have to become close friendships, but familiarity with their peers through classroom activities helps to break the ice and allow them to learn collaboratively.

Another consideration is the method(s) that are to be employed. It should be clear at this point that the method(s) chosen are directly related to an educator's philosophy and beliefs regarding how second languages are learned. This text has focused on instruc-tional practices informed by SLA research and principles. As the field continues to evolve through research, principles of L2 teaching and learning will evolve accordingly.

In the past as part of teaching speaking, learners were invited to repeat what was said by the educator (see the section on "The Audiolingual Method (ALM)"), and/or answer a short question or give one-word responses (see the section on "Direct Method"). Today they participate in second language classes in communicative activities, completing tasks and projects that allow them to develop their language skills through interaction with peers. See Chapter 6 on CLT, task-based language teaching, and project-based learning. These methods allow learners to interact in authentic and meaningful ways on topics ranging from personal and concrete to abstract and global. They also tend to require learners to use vocabulary in contexts that are meaningful to achieve their goals. These activities/tasks may be structured in a way that allows them planning time, so they can prethink what they want to say, or that is impromptu and spontaneous. Different activities/tasks provide opportunities for using different discourse formats and lengths of discourse. These methods tend not to have explicit/direct instruction of grammatical forms, but they may if the teacher considers the situation calls for it. At other times, the teacher will provide a stem sentence or sentence starter to give learners ways of expressing a particular idea without the need for grammatical explanations. Ultimately, educators want to be careful to monitor whether students have the linguistic resources (i.e., grammar form, sentence type, vocabulary, expressions) they need for success in the activity/task.

Organization of speaking lessons

TESOL educators plan speaking lessons for students' success by organizing lessons at first to provide stimulus materials (i.e., visuals, listening passages, or texts on the topic), so learners have something to contribute to conversations. These materials precede speaking activities/tasks by using sequenced instruction that equips learners with the language forms or skills the teacher has anticipated students will need during the activity (i.e., enabling skills/language).

To prepare ELLs in this manner, TESOL educators also preteach vocabulary words and phrases learners may need to use. In addition to discussing stem sentences, they thoroughly prepare for any upcoming discussion through brainstorming and exchange of ideas with the whole class. They also preteach the grammar forms and provide exercises for practice (i.e., close-ended exercises or structured-output activities) (see more about exercises in grammar translation in the next chapter). Closed-ended exercises are for situations in which there is only one right answer. Structured-output activities exercises do not provide many linguistic options for learners, but are communicative in nature. With fewer linguistic options, the activity is less challenging. Some examples of close-ended exercises and structured-output activities include fill in the blank, sentence completion, matching, indicating agreement/disagreement, completing a questionnaire, and comparing a ranked list with a partner. Educators follow close-ended exercises and structured-output activities with more open-ended activities, such as ranking tasks, role-plays, or values clarification discussions.

Being mindful of these preparation stages helps TESOL educators avoid the dread moment when learners do not have the language or information they need to participate in a speaking activity. They also help avoid hearing from the learners, "I don't know" or "I don't have an opinion."

Stem sentences/sentence starters

Stem sentences, sentence starters, or sentence frames are sentence beginnings that provide ELLs with alternative, formulaic ways of expressing an idea while providing a structure they can use and learn for future interactions. They provide support for language learners by allowing learners to use a "chunk" of language without having to construct each part of the sentence individually. Analyze these examples and try to determine how they may be used to support ELLs in speaking.

Giving opinions:

- I think/feel/believe that...
- In my opinion, it is/isn't...
- I prefer...
- I would rather...
- The best/worst is...
- My favorite/least favorite is...
- Everyone should...
- From my point of view...
- I am convinced that...

Agreeing/disagreeing:

- I agree/disagree with you on...
- I agree/disagree that...
- I would argue the same thing, because...
- I like/dislike what you are saying about...
- I concur with you, because...
- I don't think that is right, because...
- My view is different, because...

Apologizing:

- I'm sorry that I...
- My bad for...
- I feel really bad about...
- Please allow me to apologize for...
- Please forgive me for...
- It was wrong that I...
- My apologies for...
- Please accept my apologies for...

Educators use them in language and academic content classes to provide ELLs a means for engaging more easily in conversation. Their meanings are often discussed in class prior to using them. They are also written on posters and anchor charts so students can refer to them. Stem sentences are available in textbooks and on the internet or can be brainstormed by the teacher. You only need to imagine a typical way to participate in the speech act or ways people express these ideas.

Cooperative learning/group work

Group work is a common feature of ESL/EFL/ELT classes. TESOL educators are thoughtful about groupings. They rotate members of pairs, triads, or small groups regularly for specific purposes. At times, they will group learners at the same proficiency level, so that learners can work on the same linguistic forms or with more support. Other times, they will group learners across proficiency levels, so they have access to differing levels of linguistic input or they need to explain their thoughts in negotiated interactions. There are other ways that groupings may occur that are not random, for example, same gender, introverted/extroverted, or by the same/different L1.

Activities for teaching second language speaking

TESOL educators want learners to interact actively in the classroom to develop their speaking; therefore, they plan for a variety of activities/tasks that are appropriate for the learners' proficiency levels and ages and geared toward learners' specific goals and needs. Learners at lower proficiency levels may need more close-ended exercises than open-ended, but that does not mean we should not include them. We also need to match the type of activity and topic with learners' cognitive and development stage by age. Keeping in mind the learners' goals and needs will ensure that we use exercises/activities/tasks that mirror their daily communicative activities.

There are numerous speaking activities for use in the L2 classroom. Below are some suggestions for teaching speaking in your L2 classes:

- exercises (true/false, matching, fill in the blank, sentence competition);
- ALM drills;
- story telling;
- games:
  - Charades;
  - Pictionary;
  - Catch phrase;
  - Would you rather...
- communicative activities/tasks:
  - information gap;
  - jigsaw;
  - ranking activities;
  - values clarification;
- problem solving;
- discussions;
- role-plays;
- plays/readers' theater;
- reporting information, summarizing, synthesizing;
- debates (structured);
- peer tutoring;
- simulations; and
- analysis of a video of native speakers involved in heated discussion, asking learners to pay attention to the speed and pitch of speech, body movements, and gestures.

Sometimes educators provide learners with opportunities to interact with more proficient peers and native speakers. Other ways to increase interaction include inviting visitors/guest speakers for question/answer sessions, allowing for team teaching, interacting in Snapchat/chatrooms with former students, or holding English-speaking events and discussion groups.

Today, students are more actively involved in using language to communicate with others, usually real people, at the other end of a digital communication tool such as Skype, WhatsApp, FaceTime, etc. Use of these tools can greatly extend the ELL's L2 speaking skills, if a degree of caution is exercised. Digital tools have changed the way productive skills can be taught, since students can use English free of their teachers anywhere and anytime beyond the classroom. Self-regulation and the opportunity to exercise freedom in developing productive language skills in their own context with personal purposes (e.g., games, chatting, sharing, etc.) have led to new learner profiles, enabling ELLs to interact with teachers in the classroom while learning more through this interaction. These mutually comprehensible interactions have become accepted as a learning tool that offers comprehension and language practice opportunities. In Chapter 11, we will discuss further digital tools for the language classroom.

Questions for reflection

- What activities did your teachers use to help you develop your L2 speaking skills?
- How will you encourage your learners to practice speech outside of your classes?

Historic Methods Employed to Teach Speaking

Over time, as you read in Chapter 6, different methods were designed to teach speaking. Some of these methods will appear effective immediately, while others may seem peculiar. It is important to consider what we can learn from each of these methods.

The Audiolingual Method (ALM)

The ALM was developed out of a need to communicate in war time (World War I and World War II) when soldiers needed to decipher the exchanged communication of their enemies and communicate with residents of the countries they were in. The target language needed to be learned quickly, so short-term intensive courses were developed.

The ALM was the first method to be developed based on learning theories. The linguistic theory underlying the method was structuralism, which claims language is composed of small linguistic units such as words and phrases, which then form whole sentences. Richards and Rodgers (2001) emphasize the systematicity and structural aspects of language (from minimal forms such as phonemes, morphemes, words, and phrases to relatively longer forms such as sentences and discourse), which are used to encode meaning. Therefore, the learners were assigned to dismantle sentences and then reframe them or vice versa in order to learn sentence structure from minimal forms to more complex ones. To achieve this, the techniques include dialogue drills, transformation drills, and backward build-up drills, among others. Here are some examples:

1. Dialogue drills—The ALM presents grammar and vocabulary through dialogues. Each dialogue also has a cultural context, such as shopping for clothing.
   a. The teacher first reads each line of the dialogue or presents it through a recording.
   b. In chorus, students repeat each line of the dialogue after it is presented, eventually memorizing it through many repetitions.
   c. The teacher then takes one role and the class takes the other, and they later change parts.
   d. As additional activities, a small group or an individual student may role-play the dialogue with the teacher. As a finale, pairs of students practice the dialogue together and present it to the class.

2. Substitution drills—In substitution drills, the teacher gives a sentence and the students substitute one or more items in the sentence.
   a. I have a _____ (e.g., pen, pencil, paper, thumb drive, paperclip, or marker).
   b. On break, I like to _____ and _____. (e.g., read, sleep, relax, hike, ski, draw, etc.).

3. Transformation drills—In transformation drills, teachers give a sentence and the students transform a specific, previously identified part of speech.
   a. Make the following sentences past tense (irregular verbs):
      i. I eat apples in the fall. ≫ I ate apples in the fall.
      ii. She rides her bike to school. ≫ She rode her bike to school.
      iii. They go to the library to find good books. ≫ They went to the library to find good books.
      iv. We fly to Peru on break. ≫ We flew to Peru on break.

4. Question and answer drills—In question and answer drills, the teacher makes a statement and asks a question. The student then responds to the question and asks another person a question.
   a. Respond to the question with your own thoughts and ideas.
      i. My favorite food is sushi. What is your favorite food?
      ii. My favorite book is *The Alchemist*. What is your favorite book?
      iii. Favorite movie is *Stardust*.
      iv. Favorite TV is *Good Omens* and *The Marvelous Mrs. Mazel*.
      v. Favorite place is Kyoto, Japan.
      vi. Favorite season is spring.

5. Expansion drills—In an expansion drill, the teacher asks students to add a part of speech to the sentence. For example, adverbs. The teacher gives the beginning statement and students add the adverb and say the whole statement.
   a. Add an adverb to the sentences I give you.
   b. Willy Wonka is zany.
   c. Willy Wonka is always, never, often, rarely zany.

    i. People: the president, Michael Jackson, Donald Duck, Kim Kardashian, Superman, Lady Gaga.

    ii. Adjectives: lucky, vivacious, happy, jolly, grumpy, enchanting, fair, old, hip, quirky.

6. Backward build-up—The teacher breaks down a troublesome sentence into smaller parts. The teacher starts with the end of the sentence and has the class repeat just the last two words. When they can do this, the teacher adds another word or two, and the class repeats this expanded phrase. Little by little the teacher builds up the phrases until the entire sentence is being repeated.

    a. Example:

      i. for sledding

      ii. warm clothes for sledding

      iii. all of our warm clothes for sledding

      iv. so we put on all of our warm clothes for sledding

      v. mean fun, so we put on all of our warm clothes for sledding

      vi. and snow days mean fun, so we put on all of our warm clothes for sledding

      vii. a snow day, and snow days mean fun, so we put on all of our warm clothes for sledding

      viii. It was a snow day, and snow days mean fun, so we put on all of our warm clothes for sledding.

The other underlying theory behind using these drills was behaviorism, which involves conditioning and habit formation as the major learning strands. The learners were expected to memorize chunks through repetition in the drills. The belief was that by repeating the same verbal activity several times under a particular condition, learners would develop the linguistic behavior as theorized by Ivan Pavlov, a Russian physiologist.

Similarly, in language teaching through ALM, learners read aloud using particular dialogues, which are the main tool for presenting forms and meaning. Learners are expected to learn the language structure inductively and guess meaning from the conversational context through repeated exposure and practice.

Although this method brings together the four language skills, this still happens discretely and disproportionally. Speech is given the priority in the implementation of the method. Speaking is practiced in the form of repeating the dialogues rather than creating personal new meanings or expressing ideas in authentic contexts.

The language production is seen to be akin to the stimulus–response model as in behaviorism. However, in linguistic human communication there is never a one-to-one correspondence between question and answer. A sentence can have multiple meanings depending on the context of use, just as a piece of meaning can be expressed in multiple ways using various linguistic structures. Considering these linguistic constraints, ALM addressed a need of the time it as originated and developed as a pedagogical tool in second language teaching.

Questions for reflection

- Do you think that drills would be effective for teaching L2 speaking?
- When would you employ these kinds of drills?
- What modifications would you make to improve their use?

The Silent Way

Although the teaching practices with the above-mentioned methods were dominated by a teacher, TESOL experienced a shift to learner-centered teaching with the Silent Way in the 1970s. *Learner-centered teaching* is the idea of concentrating efforts on learning and learning processes, not teaching. Caleb Gattegno developed the method based on the assumption that second language learning is different from first language acquisition in that learners had already acquired some prior linguistic knowledge. Gattegno believed that the existence of such knowledge could only make L2 learning an unnatural and well-ordered process. Gattegno also emphasized the role of silence of the teacher to encourage learners to be actively, wholly engaged in the learning tasks. Later, the idea this became the notion of "learning to learn."

The Silent Way method offers an experiential process of learning during which teachers intervene only when needed. The method serves as a counterpoint to ALM in that it does not corroborate pedagogically the use of repetition as a teaching practice, but encourages students to self-regulate their own learning and engage in an interactive and collaborative learning process. The method can be seen as one of the first to develop autonomy in language learning by prioritizing the role of learners in their own learning process. Learners are encouraged and guided to discover meanings and forms as well as solve relevant problems using some physical objects.

In the first Silent Way lesson of a course, the teacher would explain in the learners' L1 how the class was going to be organized. First, the teacher would express to the students that the teacher would remain silent during the lesson and point out letters on color-coded Fidel charts. Pronunciation is seen as foundational, so beginning students would start their study with pronunciation. Much time in each lesson is spent practicing letter/sound relationships in words. The students would watch and say the sounds the teacher is pointing out on the charts and verify that learners' pronunciation is close to the target pronunciation. Students would also collaborate to figure out the sounds. Learning is designed to be facilitated by students' problem solving in order to understand the material to be learned. At times, too, teachers use gestures and facial expressions to give feedback or convey meanings.

After the learners had acquired some basic words, the teacher would silently guide students to put letters/sounds together into word combinations and sentences. Learning is facilitated through using Cuisenaire rods to represent words (i.e., little rods for articles, prepositions, pronouns, and auxiliary verbs, and longer rods for nouns, verbs, adjectives, and adverbs).

The Silent Way is not commonly employed today owing to many drawbacks and criticisms. Some of the drawbacks are listed here. Students must be literate in their L1 and share the same L1. Learners need to be motivated, engaged, and participatory, so classroom management was a potential problem. This method also would not be effective for young learners. A great deal of time is spent on concepts that could be acquired more quickly using other methods. Form is more important than meanings, at least initially.

Although this method is sparsely used in language teaching, its underlying principles constituted strong pedagogical arguments in language teaching education including autonomy, learner-centered teaching, discovery-based learning, and reduction of teacher talk. The Silent Way also gave rise to the emergence of other humanistic pedagogical methods for language teaching, which reidentify the role of learners in learning and position them as part of or the key agents of learning.

Direct Method

The Direct Method was established in Germany and France around 1900. It was a reaction against the grammar translation method (see Chapter 9), which focused on translation of grammar and vocabulary and rote memorization. The basic idea of the Direct Method was that L2 learning should be more like L1 learning, meaning immersion in the target language, oral interaction, spontaneous practice of the speaking and listening, no translation between L1 and L2, and little or no analysis of grammatical rules.

Educators using the Direct Method had to be highly proficient in both the language of the students and the target language, but the teacher only spoke the target language to ask and answer questions. Even instructions were in the target language. The teacher was the center of the learning, so the teacher asked questions and students responded individually. Students could ask the teacher questions, too. But there was no student-to-student interaction, so there was not a great deal of opportunity for speaking practice. Furthermore, since the interaction between teacher and students was in the question/answer format, there was little opportunity for extended discourse or instruction of discourse formats.

The teacher explained new vocabulary in the target language using real objects (i.e., realia), visual aids, and/or demonstrations. The vocabulary taught was mainly practical vocabulary and phrases for daily use. Grammar rules were taught inductively, meaning that learners would be exposed to authentic language samples of the rule for them to identify the pattern and figure out. Accuracy of grammar and pronunciation were high priorities in the Direct Method classroom.

The format of Direct Method lessons comprised several techniques all led by the teacher. Teachers might plan a lesson around a new word, sentence, conversation, or cultural point. In the L2, the teacher would show the concept of study to students using a real object or visual, so the learners understood the lesson goal. Second, the teacher would introduce the item with clear enunciation and precise grammar. Third, the students would try to say the item. Fourth, the teacher would correct the students' errors and demonstrate how to properly say/pronounce the item. Students would be led through a series of repetitions of the item. These techniques could be reordered in various ways to further illuminate the concept. Teachers might also ask the students to answer questions, participate in dialogues, fill in the blank exercises, or read from a work of literature.

While there are elements of the Direct Method that can inform our current instruction, this method has drawbacks that make it less effective. Clearly, it is teacher-centered with no student-to-student interaction, so learners have minimal practice opportunities. The method includes little reading and writing instruction; learners need to be able to read and write in order to participate in the class. Therefore, many learners could be excluded, depending on context. Grammar explanations would not be taught in a Direct Method lesson, which would not help older students who can benefit from explicit grammar instruction. The Direct Method also is not suitable for large classes, because the teacher needs to be able to interact with all learners many times in each class. Lastly, but importantly, many students may not understand some of the language, so they could become frustrated, overwhelmed, and/or fall behind.

Aspects of the Direct Method are still evident in many ESL classrooms, specifically the use of the target language for all class instructions and the use of visuals and realia to illustrate meaning. Immersion in the target language, with support, is a standard of current L2 teaching.

Questions for reflection

- Do you think you have learned a second or additional language with one of the methods above? If yes, explain. If not, which of the specific practices might you have been involved?
- Which method seems most and least likely to be effective? Why?

Teaching Second Language Writing

Most of us encountered writing instruction in our L1 in K–12 schooling through learning the orthographic system of our L1. Three main types of orthographic systems are alphabetic (i.e., alphabet representing sounds), logographic (i.e., symbols representing words or concepts), or syllabic (i.e., symbols representing syllables). ELLs may come from any of these orthographic traditions or from a nonliterate tradition (as you read in Chapter 7).

Once we learned our orthographic system, we built upward to expressing combinations of concepts. In English, we would have learned to write words and sentences. Next, we would have been expected to write as a way of either sharing our understandings of our learning on a topic or independent research we conducted for a class. We were steered to follow a set of formalized writing practices of which we were not fully aware and for which we did not fully understand the rationale. Weigle defines writing as a "socially and culturally situated set of literacy practices shared by a particular community" (2014, p. 223). Essentially, groups of people agree on how we share ideas in written form.

Writing involves many skill sets: word order (i.e., syntax), grammar (e.g., verb conjugation, article use, preposition use, pluralization), vocabulary, spelling, punctuation, capitalization, organization, and analysis. Treating all of these areas in depth is beyond the scope of this text, but we will outline key concepts.

In second language writing, it may have been assumed that an ELL could write the language once they had been introduced to a set of vocabulary and grammar forms. Educators may have relied on a transfer of knowledge of writing from the ELL's first language. However, this assumption can be problematic, because second language writers can only transfer their writing abilities after they have acquired a sufficient proficiency. They may also translate directly from their L1 or follow patterns learned about L1 writing. TESOL educators are mindful though that the process of L2 writing uses knowledge from the L1 and L2 of genre, process, syntax, and grammar to convey messages. At times, we may encourage ELL writers to use both languages to convey their message (i.e., translanguaging).

The reciprocal relationship between reading and writing

TESOL educators recognize the mutually supportive and informative relationship between reading and writing. For example, learners with more exposure to reading in general and reading in various fiction/nonfiction genres and discourse/rhetorical formats (e.g., narrative, expository, argumentative, process) will be more familiar with how certain concepts and patterns could be written. They also understand that the knowledge of oral language informs writing as well. Finally, TESOL educators realize that L2 writers make choices based on their knowledge of the possible readership of their writing (i.e., audience) and may approximate the message they wish to convey if they lack the L2 skills to express it more fully. How do we ensure that L2 writing does not overly rely on L1 writing conventions? How do we ensure ELLs are supported in their L2 writing?

Questions for reflection

- How might you teach L2 writing to ELLs coming from a different orthographic tradition?
- How would you include other areas L2 writers need, such as syntax, grammar, discourse formats, vocabulary, and spelling, into your classes?
- How might you integrate writing and the other skills into writing-focused units?

Young writers

As with teaching L2 reading, L2 writing is affected by the age of the learners. With young second language learners who enter kindergarten and begin to learn to read and write with the native-speaking peers, their orality in the L2 is a significant consideration. If they have oral language abilities in English, they will have the same linguistic abilities upon which to build to learn L2 reading and writing. If they do not have the L2 orality, it is important to simultaneously build the oral and written language abilities by interweaving speaking, listening, reading, and writing.

For a kindergartener or lower elementary ELL, TESOL educators may build oral language skills on a topic and access background knowledge. They may introduce new vocabulary words through visuals and physical actions. When learners were adequately prepared in these ways, the educator would transition to prereading and reading activities. Perhaps the educator would link the spoken and written word through using the language experience approach (LEA) (see Chapter 7). At some point, the educator would explicitly teach how to write the alphabet and vocabulary words. Later, students would learn to write sentences. Some educators, not just TESOL educators, would stop at this stage and would not expect more than sentence-level writing. This is now considered unfair to the learners, because they do not have the opportunity to learn how to write paragraphs, essays, or reports, all of which are written formats needed for academics and professions.

The process writing approach

Moving up in the grades (starting in middle elementary and continuing through university), the learners might learn to write longer texts through the process approach to writing or the *writing process*. This aptly named approach walks learners through a series of steps they can employ with any writing task (Figure 8.3). The steps are presented in a sequential manner, but strong writers commonly use them in a nonsequential way.

At each stage in the writing process, learners might perform certain tasks that help them move to the next stage. Prior to beginning, it is important to give an overview of the plan (or process) for organizing and writing, including due dates and rubrics, so learners see the goal and understand that each stage is contingent upon the prior stage.

The first stage in the writing process is prewriting. TESOL educators guide ELLs to identify and discuss the audience. Learners brainstorm possible topics through talking with others or making lists. Other ways to identify a good writing topic are to use word or visual association, mind mapping, freewriting, journaling, cubing, strategic questioning, quick writing, or conducting interviews/dialogues.

Writers would then expand the topic through researching and reading, writing pros and cons, using the SCAMPER technique (SCAMPER = substitute, combine, adapt, modify/magnify, put to another use, eliminate, reverse), analyzing the strengths/weakness/opportunities/threats, or storyboarding depending on the writing assignment.

At this stage, educators are encouraged to model the writing task for learners and provide focused lessons to help learners improve some aspect of their writing. They may teach learners about a using transition words, combining sentence, connecting ideas logically from one sentence to another, a syntactic pattern, or a grammar point. They may also help learners analyze the discourse/rhetorical format or genre. A wonderful tool for illustrating different formats and genres that can be use from kindergarten to university is the Write Source by Houghton Mifflin (http://thewritesource.com), which provides models of formats and genres with key features highlighted.

The second stage is organizing ideas. Students are encouraged to arrange their ideas by outlining or clustering concepts. They can arrange their thoughts chronologically, emphatically (emphasizing the point by putting it first or last), generally to specifically, by importance or discourse format (e.g., cause/effect, comparison). At this stage, it is important that the learner puts their thoughts on paper (or in at the computer).

The third stage is drafting. Drafting is the most challenging stage for most people. If the prewriting and organizing is well done, this stage can be less difficult. Some ways to approach the task of drafting include writing from beginning to end in one or more

Figure 8.3 The writing process.

sittings or writing components one at a time. For example, Kate enjoys writing one component at a time, but will vary her writing to proceed from beginning to end. This chapter was written in three components (speaking, other methods for speaking, and writing) and proceeded in the order they appeared in the chapter. In each section, though, she jumped around to write parts she most wanted to write at the time or that occurred to her in other places.

At this stage, learners will think through how to express their thoughts with appropriate grammatical correctness. We want learners to express their thoughts, and keep in mind how the L2 expresses ideas. Accuracy in spelling, word order, grammar, and word choice is a consideration as well. TESOL educators would weigh the learners' abilities and guide them at this stage to focus on the areas that would most improve their writing skills.

The fourth stage is editing one's own work. Editing is an ongoing activity while writing, involving looking at the words that have been written, rearranging and changing them, then addressing issues in grammar or spelling. Beyond technical aspects, editing involves thinking about whether the thoughts/ideas intended are conveyed in a manner that readers will understand. Thoughts that are not conveyed effectively are reconsidered and rephrased. Yet, at the end of drafting, all of the work is again read through and revised from beginning to end.

We can teach ELLs to edit their own work by using checklists to guide what they look for. An awareness of syntax, grammar, and word choice is very important for writers at this stage. Some learners may need explicit instruction in these areas if they are old enough to be able to use them. One learning strategy for editing that can be taught to relatively young learners is the CUPS strategy.

- Capitalize—names, places, titles, months.
- Usage—nouns and adjectives agree; verbs tenses are correct.
- Punctuation—periods, quotes, commas, semicolons, apostrophes are correct.
- Spelling—check words in the dictionary if unsure.

TESOL educators raise learners' awareness of syntax, grammar, word choice, and format through activities such as:

- rewriting exercises;
- slash sentences (e.g., He/go/school/day/ time);
- dehydrated sentences (e.g., He go park); and
- sentence/paragraph scrambles (e.g., not careful slip slowly backed cliff the he to from).

The fifth stage is obtaining feedback and revising. Educators utilize the peer feedback strategy, so learners have another voice and insight into their writing prior to the teacher receiving it. This is a common strategy that needs to be guided by a TESOL educator. Many ELLs do not feel they are knowledgeable enough about the language to provide any feedback on the forms or format. Therefore, the use of a checklist or guidelines for what to check on will help ELLs to provide feedback. Another strategy is to ask peer reviewers simply to highlight an area they are unsure about or do not understand. They writer can then check to make sure the part makes sense and is accurate. You can also arrange to have more advanced writers provide feedback.

Writing conferences and providing feedback on writing

Writing conferences can be a useful tool. The educator can sit down with the ELL writer to read their work aloud and provide feedback, or arrange for a peer to do so, thus helping improve the initial quality of the draft. The educator can also record feedback, to save time.

TESOL educators prioritize giving feedback on the meanings shared as well as the ways in which they were shared. We tend to have discussions about the concepts as much as the forms and formats in the writing. We ask questions about the writing or make statements about what the writer shared. For example, "Oh! How interesting. I didn't know you were into ping pong." Or "Have you ever seen this band in concert?"

One crucial point is to avoid correcting every error. The practice of correcting every error is overwhelming for the learner, so the feedback is likely to be ignored or internalized as a personal judgment, which can be discouraging. A good rule of thumb is to identify a couple of features of their writing that can bring about a significant improvement. Sometimes, the features identified will be directly connected to areas that were taught in the prewriting or drafting stages. Other times, the areas will be unique to the individual learner. When we do provide feedback on errors, we try to give examples of ways to express the idea or use the form.

The final stage is sharing the written work. Not all educators ask students to share their work, but when educators do, it provides learners an authentic audience and serves a source of pride. TESOL educators may have learners share their writing with their families, with their class or other classes, with a penpal, or on a private classroom blog.

Implementing process writing in the classroom

Process writing is not an approach that you teach in one lesson or one time. Rather, it is necessary to plan ahead within units the different parts of the process, so that there is enough time for learners to learn about and practice each stage. Ideally, it would be a good choice to begin teaching ELLs about the writing process early in an academic year or course, and repeat the process each unit, so that learners are well versed in it.

Process writing is a critical academic skill for ELL writers from elementary to adult. We modify the length and topics of focus depending on the ages of the learners. Next, we will look at some unique considerations of teen and adult L2 writers.

Questions for reflection
• Did you learn to write using the process approach to writing? What do you like about the process and what is challenging for you? If you did not learn process writing, do you think you will try it in your own writing? How do you think it will help you? • How might you plan a unit with the writing process sequenced over time? How much time do you think each stage will need? Is there a critical deadline that cannot be missed? As an educator, how would you accommodate a missed deadline?

Teen and adult writers

Teens and adults who are literate in their L1 are also taught to write using the "process" approach to writing. If their goal is academically oriented, they would use the writing process to write research papers or literature responses. If their goal is professional, they could use the writing process for developing a PowerPoint presentation to market a product or an annual report for their team. Ideally, TESOL educators align the types of writing with learners' goals, needs, and interests.

Young learners' writing may benefit from some syntax and grammar instruction, but they also may acquire grammatical forms implicitly. Teen and adult L2 writers, on the other hand, will definitely benefit from form-focused instruction. Typically, the structures taught align with the type of writing, but educators may also identify a general need for a particular form from their students' writing. More on grammar instruction can be read in Chapter 9.

If teen or adult learners do not read or write in their L1, they would learn to copy the alphabet and write words. At this stage, they may be asked to write lists of words, such as a grocery or "to do" list. Note, what they are asked to write is appropriate for their ages. They would learn about and practice sentence and paragraph formation. They may write about themselves and their families or a story from the past. In the next sections, we will discuss copying to essay writing.

Questions for reflection

- What are the reasons for the similarities in teaching L2 writing to children, teens, and adult writers?
- Can you think of any other differences between these populations of L2 writers?
- What L2 writing challenges can you foresee if teens enter high school without a literacy background? How will you ensure you provide them the practice and skills they need without making them feel like children?

Plagiarism

All writers need to understand what plagiarism is and how to avoid it in writing. Diverse cultures view ownership of ideas differently from one another. In some countries, ideas, creative products, or innovations are owned by someone. In other countries, one cannot own ideas, etc. Some countries consider copying of a text or product without citing the source to be fair use. In China, many students are encouraged to copy/use quotes from the works of Confucius. They do not cite Confucius as the source of the idea, because all students learn these works. They do not need to cite him. As a result, TESOL educators need to teach about fair use and plagiarism, but they need to do so mindful that this is not an ethical failing on the part of the student. They simply might not know.

To support ELLs in effective writing and avoiding academic problems in the West, we need to teach our ELL writers to summarize, paraphrase, and directly quote. Learning to develop summarization and paraphrasing skills is a complex cognitive undertaking. Learners need to be able to read, simplify the text, and put it into their own words. Learning to quote directly seems easier, but requires some sort of citation system or style guide to be taught.

Proficiency levels

The ages or grade levels of the ELLs and their proficiency levels have direct bearing on L2 writing. Earlier, we discussed the fact that a direct relationship between age/grade and proficiency does not necessarily exist. For example, a fourth-grade student may be able to write multiple paragraphs, while a tenth-grade student may still be copying letters. It all depends on the learner's prior exposure to English writing.

The main differences between proficiency levels for L2 writing pertain to length and complexity of ideas and grammatical and/or syntax forms. The lowest proficiency levels are characterized by shorter length and may start at the letter or word level of writing. There is not any real complexity at this level, because words are simply listed. Moving to intermediate levels, learners can write phrases, sentences, and then elaborate sentences (e.g., compound, complex). Complexity of ideas and structures will begin to develop at these levels. At the highest levels of proficiency, learners are able to write longer passages of different types, organize their writing, and clearly express involved ideas while tailoring the more sophisticated grammar and syntax to the purpose.

Copying letters and words

At lower levels of proficiency, learners may start with tracing letters or copying upper and lower case letters in print. Techniques for tracing and copying can be quite creative. For example, students can trace letters in the air, in sand, or in shaving cream. At some point, though, young learners will have to learn how to hold a pen/pencil and trace it on paper.

Gradually, with practice they can make the transition to copying sight words or high-frequency vocabulary words. When teaching the meanings of new vocabulary words, we can focus on spelling and ask students to copy or write the words. We always want to keep in mind that copying of words should be meaningful.

Note: If the learners are from an orthographic tradition that does not follow left-to-right reading/writing patterns, you may need to teach learners this concept explicitly.

Writing words

Writing words is a process of encoding the sounds into their written counterpart. ELLs need to know how the sounds are represented in written form (see the section on "Phonics" in Chapter 7). We can guide them to sound out words and recall how those sounds are represented in English. A strategy that teachers use with younger learners for word writing practice is "look, cover, write, check," in which they look at a word, cover it over, and write the word from memory. Next, they uncover it and check if they have got it right. We will discuss spelling more in the next chapter.

Labeling and listing are ways that TESOL educators encourage learners to write words they are learning. They could label parts of a diagram or drawing. They could write their family tree. They could make lists of their favorite possessions or foods.

Sentence-level writing

At the sentence level, students need to understand word order. In English, as we explained in Chapter 4, the most basic syntax pattern for statements is subject, verb, object (SVO). In English, too, we have other basic forms:

- Subject + verb: I ate.
- Subject + verb + object: I ate the pizza.
- Subject + verb + adjective: The bird was colorful.
- Subject + verb + adverb: The dog ran quickly.
- Subject + verb + noun: She is the conductor.

We elaborate sentences with the addition of adjectives, adverbs, and direct and indirect objects. For example:

- Subject + verb + adjective + noun: I ate the cold pizza.
- Adjective + subject + verb + adverb + prep + noun: The colorful bird flew quickly to the tree.

We also have stative sentences, meaning something exists, in which we use the forms this is/there are.

We use commands in English as well. A command is also called an imperative. The subject of the command is always the person you are talking to, so "you," but we do not always say the word you. For example, "Open the window" or "Turn on the light." We might write commands in dialogues, but they are not common in other types of academic writing.

For questions, four syntax patterns are common:

- Yes/no questions: Do you like to go to the movies? (Do + S + V + O)
- Wh- questions: What do you like to see at the movies? (Wh- word + do + S + V + O)
- Inversion: Are you going to the movies? (V + S + O)
- Tag questions: You are going to the movies, aren't you? (S + V + O + Negative V + PN)

We can teach learners the different syntax patterns that are common, explicitly for older students and implicitly through models for younger learners.

TESOL educators employ diverse activities so learners can practice these various forms of sentences that go beyond asking students to write sentences of their own. Some stimulating activities include picture-description tasks, writing slogans or bumper stickers, writing texts to friends, stretching sentences (by adding addition words, such as conjunctions), good or bad sentence game (students identify if the sentence is a good/bad one), and jigsaw/sentence scramble (rearranging word cards to form a coherent sentence). Other techniques include dictation, editing, sentence matching, combining sentences, and rewriting/transforming sentences.

When teaching about sentence writing, TESOL educators also teach rules of capitalization and punctuation. A good reference for capitalization and grammar rules is Grammarly.com.

Paragraph-level writing

When teaching paragraph writing, educators are concerned with the connections between sentences, transitions between ideas, main ideas expressed as topic sentences/controlling idea, supporting details, and coherence (i.e., the ideas in the paragraph connect clearly and flow easily from one sentence to the other).

Formal rules within English dictate that topic sentences are usually at the beginning of the paragraph, but may appear anywhere in the paragraph. When they come elsewhere in the paragraph, they designate a change in direction. They may be a hook used to gain the reader's attention. Or they may help transition from the previous paragraph and can be longer than just one sentence. Basically, they are a representation of what the paragraph will contain, which would be about one main or controlling idea.

In the paragraph, the controlling idea will be further illustrated or described in other sentences. Writers give supporting facts, examples, details, or anecdotes that help elaborate the controlling idea.

Paragraph structure (i.e., topic sentences and support details) is typically taught to ELLs with examples and practice. They deliver direct instruction (i.e., when the teacher explains) on topic sentence construction. Educators will provide example paragraphs for analysis to illustrate the various ways of formatting a paragraph. Following the direct instruction on the aspects of paragraph writing, learners would be given many practice opportunities (see the sample activities that follow).

Cohesion is the linking of ideas, so they flow easily from one to the next. Writers may make their paragraphs cohesive by presenting familiar information before new information. They might utilize transition words and phrases that demonstrate agreement or addition of information, such as "in addition," "also," "as well as," "furthermore," "likewise," and "of course." Transition words and phrases that express disagreement or show alternatives include "even though," "however," "although," "in spite of," "on the contrary," "despite," and "whereas." ELLs often need to have the meanings and usage of transition words or phrases taught explicitly.

Paragraph writing activities

Depending on the age of the learner, assorted paragraph writing activities can be employed to provide ELLs the practice and feedback they need. In our daily lives, we write stand-alone paragraphs to accomplish certain tasks. Since these are writing tasks we normally encounter, they are authentic and can be made meaningful to the students; therefore, they align with the goals of CLT. TESOL educators will ask ELLs to write postcards, thank you notes, a personal ad, or give advice or instructions.

There are four types of paragraphs: narrative, descriptive, expository, and persuasive. To provide practice on these types of paragraphs and work on social language, TESOL educators would give writing prompts (i.e., topics or directions) on:

- Narrative:
  - Tell of a time you had an adventure.
  - Tell a story about your winter vacation.
- Descriptive:
  - Describe a family tradition you love.
  - Describe your favorite pet.
- Expository:
  - Explain how to make your favorite food.
  - Explain how to play your favorite video game.
- Persuasive:
  - What is the best season of the year? Why?
  - What is the best type of music? Why?

What are other authentic paragraph writing activities you can imagine?

Of course, TESOL educators will also teach paragraph writing for academic purposes. So, educators give writing prompts for ELLs to practice these types with academic materials they are learning or researching. For example:

- Narrative:
  - Narrate the key events in Nelson Mandela's life.
  - Tell of a situation that taught you that someone's appearance can be misleading.
- Descriptive:
  - Describe a character from a story.
  - Describe the setting of a story.
- Expository:
  - Explain how mitosis occurs.
  - Explain the process of a volcanic eruption.
- Persuasive:
  - What is your opinion about helping refugees? Should governments be obligated to help refugees or should they be allowed to close their borders to them?
  - What is your opinion of the most important cause of World War I?

Longer written passages

Educators employ some similar techniques to those used when teaching at the paragraph level for the instruction of longer written passages (longer written passages may be referred to as discourse and discourse competency is one of the communicative competencies). Longer written passages can use either social language, such as emails, letters, and stories (i.e., narratives), or academic language, such as essays (e.g., expository, process, persuasive, description), memos, and reports. The most significant differences between paragraph and essay-length writing are the discourse formats and use of introductions, thesis statements, and conclusions, each of which may need explicit instruction and practice.

Lou and Marilynn Spaventa have a valuable textbook series, *Writing to Learn*, that teaches details about sentence, paragraph, and essay writing. Keith Folse has a helpful series on writing text that focuses on sentences, paragraphs, and essays, *Great Sentences for Great Paragraphs*, *Great Paragraphs for Great Essays*, and *Great Essays*.

Questions for reflection
• What activities can you think of to teach word-level, sentence-level, paragraph-level, and longer writings at the grade you wish to teach? • What resources do you think you need to explore to learn more about teaching syntax? How might you make syntax fun and approachable for different ages of learners.

Current Trends in Developing and Supporting Productive Skills

Despite the long-standing use of the above-mentioned methods in English language teaching, in recent years the growing numbers of digital resources on the internet have allowed various other ways of teaching speaking. Exposure to spoken English as spoken across the world has also increased the chances of free communication with others, whether written or verbal. Although these are not formally structured pedagogical resources, a number of teachers have started to use them as teaching materials in their own classrooms.

While teachers strive to develop activities that might include genuine interaction close to real-life communication, this has often remained superficial to some extent since the people involved in such conversations are also role-playing and topics are often disengaging and far from real-life issues.

In this sense, speaking has evolved from in-class communication activity to an authentic activity that students normally do as part of their lives. With the introduction of tools such as SnapChat and Marco Polo, and verbal conversation opportunities through digital tools, interaction among people in diverse countries has become accessible and feasible. Teachers and students are not the sole interlocutors for language learners any more.

Building an international community of learners online is one of the key strategies to help learners practice their productive language skills with multiple people. The social media sites offer space for this purpose. Being part of such a communicating community, learners might use English as the language of communication rather than as a subject to learn.

Blogging and instant messaging or asynchronous written or verbal communication have also been very common authentic activities that ELLs can engage in. Such activities not only help students feel confident in initiating and sustaining communication, but also to acquire language by using it in real settings. Students who are exposed to such communication and participate actively in responding might develop their productive language skills much more than they could only drawing on classroom activities. For example, learners can co-write using Google Docs or engage in a dialogue journal using Penzu.

More and more authentic digital resources are being used either as a resource or as a means to produce verbal or written language. For example, the podcast has been a great digital tool to support students in speaking and recording their talk, whereas personal blog pages and discussion groups offer digital space for written communication. Such opportunities can be provided beyond class activities so students can start using what they have learned in their lessons.

Chapter Conclusions

Speaking and writing are both productive skills, which are directly related to their oral or written language counterpart, listening and reading. Both skills rely on other skills and abilities, such as pronunciation, vocabulary, grammar, and spelling. It is important to integrate language skills and tools to allow for the development of these intertwined areas. We need to be mindful that each of these areas requires thoughtful planning and support of learners in the process and may call for explicit teaching.

Discussion Questions

1   What would your priorities be when teaching speaking? How will you organize lessons to support these priorities?
2   What methods and techniques would you employ in your speaking lessons? Why?
3   How would you teach process writing to ELLs? How would you teach copying to adults?
4   What topics would be most appropriate for speaking and writing at the different grade and proficiency levels?

Tasks

1   What would a profile of a classroom of L2 writers look like for you? What are their ages and grade levels? What are their backgrounds with reading and writing? At which proficiency levels would they be? Based on these considerations, how would you teach L2 writing?
2   Interview an ESL/EFL/ELT teacher or a tutor in a university writing center (with ELLs, of course). Ask them about the writing abilities and needs of the ELLs they work with. Which areas do they spend the most time one? What areas do they not have to worry about? What kinds of writing tasks are most common? What do they teach about syntax and grammar for writing? How do they do it?

Further Reading/Read and Discuss

Read about discourse analysis of spoken English:
Carter, R., & McCarthy, M. (1997). *Exploring spoken English*. New York: Cambridge University Press.
Read about activities for speaking:
Klippel, F. (2013). *Keep talking: Communicative fluency activities for language teaching.* Cambridge University Press.

Ur, P. (2012). *Discussions that work: Task-centred fluency practice.* Cambridge University Press.

Read about activities for beginner writers:

Palmer, G. (2004). *Writing extra: A resource book of multi-level skills activities.* Cambridge University Press.

Brookes, A., & Grundy, P. (2005). *Beginning to write: Writing activities for elementary and intermediate learners.* Cambridge University Press.

References

ACTFL. (n.d.). *ACTFL proficiency guidelines, 2012.* https://www.actfl.org/resources/actfl-proficiency-guidelines-2012

Austin, J. L. (1962). *How to do things with words* (2nd ed.). Harvard University Press.

(n.d.). Ethnography of communication. http://www.cios.org/encyclopedia/ethnography/index.htm (accessed March 25, 2021).

Hymes, D. (1962). The ethnography of speaking. In T. Gladwin & W. C. Sturtevant (Eds.), *Anthropology and human behavior* (pp. 13–53). Anthropology Society of Washington.

Hymes, D.H. (1974). Ways of speaking. In R. Bauman & J. Sherzer (Eds.), *Explorations in the ethnography of speaking* (pp. 433–452). Cambridge University Press. https://edisciplinas.usp.br/pluginfile.php/4093974/mod_resource/content/1/Bauman-Sherzer-1974-Toward_an_ethnology_of_speaking.pdf accessed March 25, 2021).

Krashen, S. (1982). *Principles and practices of second language acquisition.* Pergamon.

Richards, J. C., & Rodgers, T. S. (2001). *Approaches and methods in language teaching* (2nd ed.). Cambridge University Press.

Schiffman, H. F. (1997, November 27). *Speech acts and conversation. Language Use: Functional approaches to syntax.* Retrieved August 7, 2020, from https://www.sas.upenn.edu/~haroldfs/edling/handouts/speechacts/spchax2.html

Weigle, S. C. (2014). Considerations for teaching second language writing. In M. Celcia-Murcia, D. M. Brinton, & M. A. Snow (Eds.), *Teaching English as a second or foreign language* (4th ed., pp. 222–238). National Geographic Learning & Heinle Cengage Learning.

World-class Instructional Design and Assessment (WIDA). (2020). WIDA English language development standards framework, 2020 edition kindergarten—Grade 12. Board of Regents of the University of Wisconsin System.

9

Tools: Grammar, Vocabulary, Pronunciation, and Spelling

This chapter will provide a basic overview of teaching grammar, pronunciation, vocabulary, and spelling. TESOL educators utilize the techniques from various methods from the past to design lessons, so notable "designer methods" that align with these tools will be introduced.

Learning Outcomes

At the conclusion of this chapter, you will be able to:

- describe characteristics and considerations of each of the four tools: grammar, vocabulary, pronunciation, and spelling
- develop interactive classes that integrate the four language skills with the enabling tools of grammar, vocabulary, pronunciation, and spelling
- justify institutional course delivery choices related to these tools with pros and cons

Often learners studying a second language are provided a list of vocabulary words to memorize. These words may or may not be used in the classroom. Have you thought about this instructional practice? In this vignette, a TESOL educator discusses how she has come to think about teaching vocabulary to ELLs.

TESOL Voices

Building Community and Vocabulary

Introducing new vocabulary to build comprehension and support language acquisition for English language learners within lessons felt like an overwhelming task. Once I started writing the lesson plans, I realized I was separating vocabulary from other lesson parts and that I should incorporate vocabulary seamlessly into existing lesson plans with a little extra thought and preparation. Using visuals alongside the key terms, giving simple definitions, acting out the word while saying it in various vocal tones, as well as providing sample sentences helped introduce my lessons, while providing connections to upcoming material. I used to be overwhelmed at the thought of fitting more into my lessons, but found it helped to

---

Introduction to TESOL: Becoming a language teaching professional, First Edition. Kate Mastruserio Reynolds, Kenan Dikilitaş, and Steve Close.
© 2022 John Wiley & Sons, Inc. Published 2022 by John Wiley & Sons, Inc.

structure my days better and make them flow more smoothly. I now make it a point to stack learning vocabulary with other activities, and each lesson only lasts about 15 min, followed by a silly song, chant, role-playing, or activity to make learning as fun and stress-free as possible. My students love a "silly teacher," as they would say, and I love to see them smile and laugh while learning.

Teaching early learners includes a lot of repetition, teacher- and student-led activities, and building on student schemas and prior knowledge. To support the language acquisition process, I provide as much vocabulary exposure as possible though word walls, a book corner, toys based on their interests for informal vocabulary practice, and various role-playing opportunities. I plan art around what vocabulary words we are learning to allow for more practice of word meanings, spoken meanings, and to practice grammatical forms and behaviors, as well as read stories to them daily to spark their imagination and growth.

Using vocabulary that my students can use on a regular basis has helped connect meaning within their own lives and interests, helping them to become more proficient. I have seen the most growth with my ELLs when I teach to what topics interest them the most. I encourage student interaction through group activities, helping my ELLs feel more connected to their peers, which encourages them to approach and play with them during lunch and recess. I start each year by teaching vocabulary needed to be successful in a school environment, and gradually move to more topic-based, or academic, vocabulary while also reinforcing previously taught vocabulary. If I have a particularly shy student I have them start off teaching me new vocabulary in their native language; they get excited when they can teach the teacher, and it helps to build trust and compassion. To encourage the biggest growth from my ELLs I am cognizant of their English proficiency levels and plan which vocabulary words should be taught prior to each lesson. I keep vocabulary simple and fun to help create a positive environment where they are successful and feel safe to make errors. Most importantly I celebrate each new vocabulary word my students master; it is a proud moment for both of us!

I thoroughly enjoy learning about my students and their families, and it is such a humbling privilege to have the opportunity to work with such a diverse population of students and make lifelong connections. Their backgrounds, culture, and stories inspire me to continuously improve as a person, as well as an educator, to provide the most inspiring and well-rounded education possible.

Katie Lembra
Early childhood educator

Relationships Between Language Skills and Tools

As you have read previous chapters, you have learned that language skills and tools are intricately connected and tailored for the type of interactional event (i.e., specific situation and social or academic language). Each language skill—speaking, listening, reading, and writing—relies on combinations of grammar, vocabulary, pronunciation, and spelling, depending on the modality (oral or written). Grammar functions in different ways in different communication modes and delivery. While it can strengthen structural aspects of the language produced, it can also affect the meaning of utterances with subtle differences in the word order. Knowledge of how to teach these tools and how they are used in spoken and written discourse is vital for TESOL educators.

These tools directly connect to and form the basis of educators' knowledge of linguistics, which needs to be possessed or acquired over time. These tools also function as the source of knowledge of teaching by informing the content of teaching practice. A TESOL educator can generate practices that are informed by the principles of various linguistic domains.

In Chapter 4, you learned about semantics, syntax, phonology, morphology, pragmatics, and discourse. In Chapter 8, you saw how knowledge of syntax relates to teaching sentence-level writing, but it also relates to sentence-level speaking. Syntax also helps listeners and readers made sense of incoming information. Semantics (i.e., meanings of words, phrases, sentences, or longer discourse) connects directly to vocabulary and sentence meanings in the four skills. Morphology (i.e., the smallest unit of meaning, such as final -s or -ed) is linked to vocabulary as well. Phonology, the sounds and sound system, informs the teaching of pronunciation, which connects to the four skills. Pragmatics relates to word choice, discourse patterns, knowledge of context, and participants' roles in the four skills. For example, it is easy to see how word choice and pragmatic knowledge work in speaking situations when we choose to use a form that is more polite to show respect. But pragmatic knowledge also plays a role in making meaning from listening passages or readings, because word choices help us to understand the relationships between characters, for example. All of these areas connect to the goal of teaching learners the knowledge and skills they need to build their communicative competencies. You can look at any facet of linguistics, the communicative competencies, the four skills, and the four tools to observe how they intersect. While most of this information is at the back of TESOL educators' minds when planning, delivering lessons, or assessing, it plays a substantial, if invisible, part in the learning experience. We also argue that basic linguistic knowledge might help TESOL educators provide language courses based on specific evidence from the science of language. Explaining to students how words are formed in relation to morphological knowledge would make it easier for students to discover word formation and strengthen their ability to guess the meaning of the words they may not know.

What Is Grammar?

Throughout this text, you have seen a general reference to grammar. When we could be more specific, we have identified syntax, or other areas. Grammar can be employed as a catch-all term for how language behaves at the word, sentence, and discourse levels. It can also refer to specific grammatical forms and functions taught in the second language classroom. It generally involves syntax, semantics, and morphology, but we will not delve into that deeply here. In this section about teaching L2 grammar, we will mainly refer to grammar generally, but may specify when necessary. For a stimulating look at different approaches to answering the question "What is grammar?", see Anne Burns' article, "Grammar and Communicative Language Teaching: Why, When, and How to Teach It?" (2011). The book this comes from offers a great deal of pedagogical grammar that teachers can rely on when connecting knowledge about language including metalanguage with actual teaching of grammar in the classroom. It is often argued that TESOL teachers and students who are able to articulate metalanguage of grammar can better process and learn language structure.

In second language teaching, grammar often includes nouns, pronouns, possessives, prepositions, adverbs, adjectives, direct objects, indirect objects, and verbs and verb tenses. It may also include referential pronouns and filler subjects (i.e., it/there). Since these areas are the basics, TESOL educators minimally need to know the parts of speech (see Table 9.1) and verb tenses and aspects (see Figure 9.1) and be able to explain this information to students. The intricacies of English grammar are innumerable, but we cannot explore them here. Two exhaustive resources on the subject are Marianne Celce-Murcia and Diane Larsen-Freeman's *The Grammar Book: An ESL/ EFL Teacher's Course* and the *TESOL Encyclopedia of English Language Teaching*, Grammar volume by Wiley.

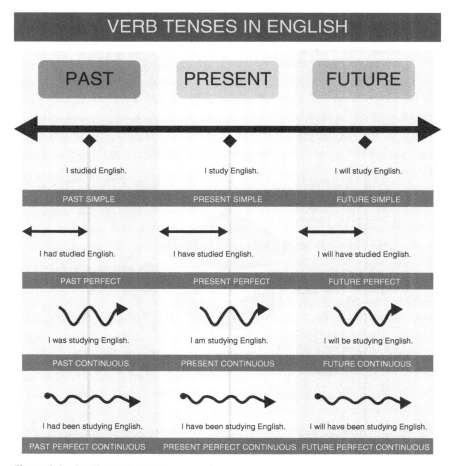

Figure 9.1 English verb tenses.

Table 9.1 English parts of speech.

Part of Speech	Definition	Examples
Noun	The name of a person, a place, a thing, or idea	Maddy, Amsterdam, tulips, wish *Maddy wished to visit Amsterdam to see the tulips*
Pronoun	A pronoun replaces a noun or noun phrase to reduce repetition	I, you, he/she/it/they (singular), we, you (plural), they (plural) *I wanted to go, too*
Adjective	They tell more about a noun or pronoun There are different kinds of adjectives, such as descriptive, quantitative, proper, demonstrative, possessive, interrogative, and indefinite They can be used in a series: (1) quantity, (2) opinion, (3) size, (4) physical quality, (5) age, (6) shape, (7) color, (8) origin, (9) material, (10) type, and (11) purpose	1) quantity—five, some, a couple 2) opinion—lovely, common, weird, luxurious 3) size—small, medium, large 4) physical quality—smooth, warm, abrasive 5) age—young, old, middle aged, new 6) shape—round, triangular, circular, wavy 7) color—red, orange, gold, teal 8) origin—Thai, Arabic, Kenyan 9) material—cotton, metal, plastic, silk, wood 10) type—socket (wrench), stop (sign), evergreen (tree) 11) purpose—shopping, swimming, washing, towing *The Dutch tulips were lovely, young, and multicolored*
Verb	They show an action or state of being Some verbs require a preposition and are called phrasal verbs. In many cases, phrasal verbs require a direct or indirect object Infinitives are verbs in their unconjugated form	Is (to be), have, sleep, eat, hear, talk, walk, swim Ask around, add up, break up, call off, calm down, check out, look after *My daughter is 15 years old, so she sleeps a lot* *To have, to sleep, to think*
Adverb	They describe a verb, an adjective, or another adverb. They indicate how often, when and where There are seven types of adverbs: adverbs of manner, frequency, time and place, relative time, degree, quantity, focus, and those that function as attitude markers	Very, always, never, too, quickly, harmoniously *She is so sleepy, she never gets up until 11 a.m. I rarely see her*

(Continued)

Table 9.1 *(Continued)*

Part of Speech	Definition	Examples
Direct objects (D.O.)	A person or thing who receives an action/is the recipient of the action. Only transitive verbs require direct objects. Formed: subject + verb + who or what	Any noun *Mireya was so angry, she kicked the mailbox*
Indirect objects (In.D.O.)	A person or thing who is affected by the action, but is not the primary object. Often preceded by "to" or "for"	Any noun *She gave me the plate* S V D.O. In.D.O. *I showed my test result to Jamie* S V D.O In.D.O.
Preposition	They show relationships between nouns, noun phrases, or pronouns and another word	Up, down, on, in, into, above, beneath, below, next to, beside, at, from, with, about *The children jumped up and down the steps*
Conjunction	They connect two words, phrases, or ideas together The conjunction used shows how items are connected	And, but, or, if, because, yet, so *The tulips are beautiful, but they don't have a strong fragrance*
Interjection	They are used to show a strong emotion in a word or phrase	Ouch! Oh my! Oh! Hey! Yipes! *Yipes! There's a spider*

Teen and adult learners will ask questions about grammar, even if we are not teaching grammar explicitly. TESOL educators may need to explain a grammatical point to learners, such as why to use one verb tense/aspect or another; therefore, this knowledge becomes essential. The grammatical forms that are taught are specific to the goals of the learners, their needs (i.e., usually indicated by needs assessments, diagnostics, and errors), and their proficiency levels (i.e., what they can do and what they need to be able to do at the next level). Most importantly, we want to teach grammatical concepts that are useful to students and that they can comprehend and utilize.

Grammar instruction today

Whether or not we teach grammar depends on several factors. The demands of the context are an important factor as well as the learners' ages, goals, and needs. Yet we do know that grammar affects the process (i.e., route) and the rate of SLA.

The route of SLA depends upon where the learners begin (e.g., their L1 or multiple languages), how they are exposed to the language, and which linguistics features they are exposed to. In Chapter 5, you read about *interlanguage*, the theoretical concept that L2 learners proceed from their L1 into their L2 via exposure to the L2 (Selinker, 1972; Tarone, 1979). You may recall that the interlanguage is the form between L1 and L2, which has linguistic characteristics of each and some unique features all its own. ELLs will rely on their L1 when starting out. Eventually, they will move to relying on L2 patterns. Grammar is one set of the characteristics of interlanguage. Learners may be exposed to a grammatical form early in the process, but may not master it until much later. An example of this is prepositions. They are often taught early, but owing to the complexity of English preposition use, they are not mastered until learners are at an advanced level of proficiency. Furthermore, language learners are typically exposed to more than one linguistic form at a time (think about the interconnected nature of language) even from the first day someone speaks to them. While it may be convenient to think we teach one form at a time when we present grammar sequentially, learners do not learn one grammar form at a time.

The rate of SLA varies according to the amount and quality of exposure to the target language, age, and other factors, too. Mastery of grammatical forms takes time. Learners will continue to make grammatical mistakes even after it seems like they have learned it. Learners may have knowledge about the grammatical form (i.e., competence), and not yet be able to use the form correctly all the time (i.e., performance).

Although grammar is key to developing language skills, its pedagogical value has recently been diminished in language teaching since most of the structural rules can be discovered and generalized over time as a result of iterative exposure to meaningful comprehensible input. More and more children and/or students can improve their language skills with a minimum level of grammatical and lexical knowledge. Imagine children playing interactional, online computer games as part of their socialization and leisure time where they are incidentally exposed to words, phrases, and utterances they need to understand to be able to function in the game. The iteration of such compelling exposure urges them to interpret the meaning even though they may not be able to guess the exact meaning. They ascribe functional meanings to the words and utterances rather than literal or linguistic meaning. For example, the imperative phrase "click" in the game design has the functional meaning "start," as interpreted by players. Unless players are explicitly given the meaning initially, they will rely on the function of the button and derive the meaning from this. Players develop top-down guessing skills as part of the games and interaction with the games and other players who speak English.

Implicit and explicit grammar

Second language learners will acquire or learn English grammar implicitly and explicitly. *Explicit grammar instruction* is when learners are taught forms in classes and it can provide learners with valuable information to develop their L2. The concepts are explained to learners and some amount of practice is provided. Implicit learning is picking up patterns of grammar in use that learners are exposed to without needing instruction on it. An example of *implicit grammar instruction* is when teachers present input to learners and engage them with the language, but do not explain the grammatical form overtly. Learners would be exposed to the grammatical form through classroom interaction without discussions of conjugations or word form. Implicit grammar instruction may have a "secretly structural" form present in the input, but learners' attention is not drawn to the form.

Implicit grammar instruction is thought to be most effective with children. Some TESOL educators believe that children can "pick up" grammar more implicitly than adults through exposure, because their language acquisition device (LAD) is still functioning (Chomsky, 1965; Krashen, 1982). Children also have the time they need to acquire it implicitly, because they do not have the day-to-day pressures of adults. Additionally, children will not "attend" to grammatical forms like adults will—they would be turned off and bored by too much explicit grammar instruction. Finally, children do not have the cognitive and meta-analytical skills (i.e., the ability to think about the patterns of language and think about their own thinking) of adults to understand the systems of grammar and to see them as a tool.

Explicit grammar instruction is when educators teach grammatical forms in class by describing and explaining the forms. Many of you learned your second language in this manner, particularly if you started learning in high school. Teens and adults are thought to be able to "pick up" grammar more implicitly, like children do. They may not have the same amount of time to learn and practice the language without pressure as children though. Teens and adults can attend to grammatical forms and use them as a tool to extend their proficiency. They may or may not be turned off and bored by explicit grammar instruction some of the time; it depends on the individual learner, context, and learning expectations. Finally, teens and adults have the cognitive and meta-analytical abilities to understand and analyze grammar forms and patterns and put them to use.

Implicit grammar instruction can be employed with less complex and more frequently used forms of language since students can discover meaning and generalize formal rules easily. However, explicit grammar instruction is also needed when the grammatical forms are more complex and less frequent, which makes it hard for students to discover the rule. In that case, teachers need to explain the relevant rule with multiple examples in context and assist them in building knowledge of grammar.

Secretly structural lessons are lessons designed to implicitly highlight a particular grammatical or linguistic feature. The input of listening and reading would present the form repeatedly in context. For example, if you wanted fourth-grade learners to acquire implicitly the modal forms "would, could, should," you might create lessons around giving advice, since these forms are exceedingly common in advice-giving. Perhaps the lesson would start with what advice is and who gives learners advice in their lives. Then, maybe you would ask students to tell you what sorts of advice they have received. Next, you might have the learners listen three times to a passage of someone giving their friend advice on what they should do over the summer. After that, you would check comprehension, of course, and ask students what advice they would give in a similar situation. You could focus their attention on how the advice was given. Next, you might do prereading activities and readings on the topic of giving advice. Lastly, you could have students give each other advice in spoken form on a new topic using stem sentences. At the end of the lesson, you could ask your students to write to their international penpal with advice about studying. All throughout this lesson, modals would be infused into the lesson. Learners may think that they are learning to give advice, but they are also learning to use the modal form. The modals would not be acquired in one lesson though, so there would need to be other secretly structural lessons that would build upon this foundation.

Grammar can be explicitly taught and included at a couple places in a lesson. The teacher can present new material, in this case, the explicit grammatical form. Teachers can ask learners to analyze a listening or reading passage for a particular form and how it is used. Teachers can create opportunities for close-ended and open-ended practice of the grammatical form. Finally, teachers can provide feedback on grammar in use in writing or speaking.

Grammar lessons sequences

Two approaches to presenting new information about grammar are deductive and inductive presentation formats (see Figure 9.2). When teachers present a grammatical rule followed by close-ended and open-ended practice, this is called the *Presentation-Practice-Production* (PPP) format (Maftoon & Sarem, 2015). It is a deductive approach to teaching the grammar form (see Figure 9.3), meaning that learners learn a rule and then apply it to various linguistic formats. For adult learners, some research indicates that deductive approaches to teaching grammar are more effective (Şik, 2014; Tzampazi, 2019); these effects, however, may have been related to the educational contexts in which learners expect to learn and memorize rules in this manner.

When teachers ask learners to analyze a listening or reading passage for a form and guide the learners to identify the rule in use, this lesson is an inductive approach (see Figure 9.4). The inductive approach is about discovery learning, in which learners skim for/attend to the form, analyze it in a meaningful context, identify patterns, compare and contrast, problem solve, and match to prior knowledge. Some course books in language classrooms introduce functional, meaning-based, and use-driven activities where grammar and vocabulary are implicitly infused for students to learn through discovery. Students discover the pattern, which is thought to be more meaningful and longer-lasting learning (Silver et al., 2012). Al-Kharrat (2000) reviewed both deductive and inductive approaches to presentation of grammar rules in his study of their effectiveness. He concluded that both techniques were worthwhile to use in the L2 classroom. However, Shaffer (2013) investigated young learners of English and determined that guided inductive grammatical lessons were effective in providing them the patterns necessary for communication.

TESOL educators vary their approach to presenting new grammatical forms between these two approaches, depending on the form. Some forms are easier comprehended and presented in a deductive manner; others in inductive.

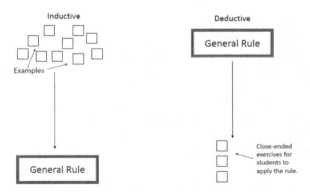

Figure 9.2 Deductive and inductive approaches to grammar instruction.

Whether the approach you employ is deductive or inductive to begin with, you will need to present/review the rule (see the next section) and provide multiple close-ended and open-ended practice opportunities (see Figures 9.3 and 9.4). Think of these practice opportunities as a means to try/retry, review, revisit, and recycle the grammatical concept from different angles. Some guidelines for practice opportunities are:

- Use multiple exposures to the grammatical point in a variety of contexts.
- Move from controlled input/output work to open-ended communicative activities.
- Create authentic and contextualized communicative activities.
- Use multiple language skills (i.e., speaking, listening, reading, and writing).
- Utilize differing groupings: pair work, small-group, and group work.
- Use a *variety* of activities:
  - Close-ended—drills, fill in the blank, matching, sentence completion, error analysis, editing activities, dehydrated sentences, and multiple choice.
  - Open-ended—games, communicative activities and tasks.

For a collection of communicative activities on grammar, see Penny Ur's *Grammar Practice Activities* and Hinkel and Fotos' *New Perspectives on Grammar Teaching in Second Language Classrooms*.

Presentation of new grammatical forms

For any presentation of new grammatical form, TESOL educators study the form and prethink how they will explain it. Sometimes, they will script what they are going to say in advance, meaning write out what they are going to say so it is memorable and clear. Or they create videos or PowerPoint presentations of the grammatical point. They may find videos or songs online to help illustrate the concept. No matter what tools they use to illustrate the concept, they provide clear grammatical explanations in learner-friendly language geared toward the learners' level of comprehension. They

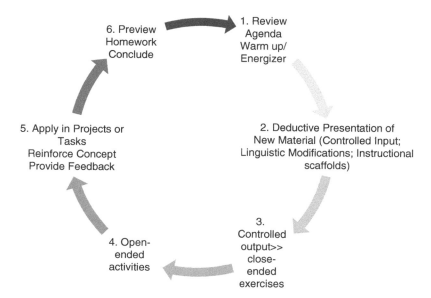

Figure 9.3   Sequence of a deductive grammar lesson.

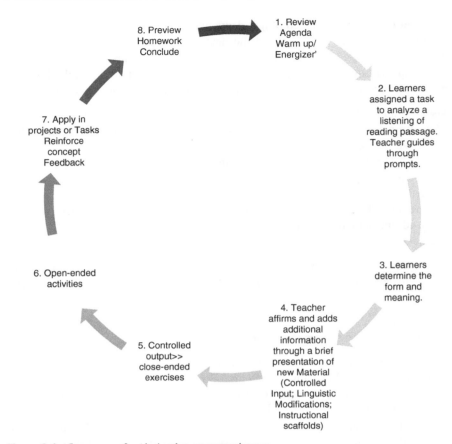

Figure 9.4 Sequence of an inductive grammar lesson.

generate authentic example sentences for their presentation. When they do present they speak slowly and provide several models and examples.

It may seem that less is more when it comes to grammar explanations. That can be true some of the time as too much explanation can be confusing at times. TESOL educators strive for the sweet spot of providing just the right amount of information, so learners can understand the concept in context, while avoiding overdoing it.

Grammaring: What you teach about a grammar form

Diane Larsen-Freeman spearheaded an approach to teaching grammatical forms called grammaring (Larsen-Freeman, 2003). In grammaring, L2 teachers need to be able to explain grammatical forms, their meanings, and how they are used in authentic contexts. Grammaring = form, meaning, and use.

The *form* is the grammatical pattern, whether it is how to conjugate a verb tense or what an adverb is. For example:

- Simple past—They are constructed by adding an -ed to the end of the infinitive. When the verb ends consonant + vowel + consonant, the final letter is doubled.
- Definition of an adverb—They describe a verb, an adjective, or another adverb.

The *meaning* refers to what the form means. For example:

- Simple past refers to an action that began and ended in the past. The specific action is indicated by the verb: to walk/walked, to learn/learned, to shop/shopped/.
- Adverbs indicate how often, when, and where: walked quickly, learned in elementary school, shopped at the market.

The *use* refers to how the form is used in the context of the sentence/paragraph and appropriately in differing contexts:

- Simple past—It is placed after a noun in a statement.
  - The dog walked to the car (subject verb object format).
- Adverbs—Placement does not impact the meaning. Adverbs can be placed at the:
  - beginning of a sentence;
  - before most verbs;
  - after the verbs to be, can, may, must, will, have, shall, and auxiliary verbs; or
  - end of a sentence:
    - Quickly, the dog walked to the car.
    - The dog quickly walked to the car.
    - The dog walked quickly to the car.
    - The dog walked to the car quickly.

Grammar is nuanced and can be used in many different ways. Grammar can also be murky, because areas of overlap exist between grammatical form/meaning and use. Sometimes, too, grammatical forms can be overlapped with lexical form (i.e., vocabulary). The word "he," for example, means male entity and plays the grammatical role of pronoun, someone previously named.

An educator can design a lesson that includes the three grammaring areas of form, meaning, and use to teach these areas explicitly in a deductive format followed by controlled exercises and open-ended, communicative activities or tasks.

If an educator chooses to teach the form, meaning, and use of the grammatical concept inductively and implicitly, they may read a passage with the learners and conduct comprehension check discussions or activities. Next, the educator may ask learners to discuss the timeframes present in a reading of a story and request they provide evidence from the story that led them to these conclusions. The learners may point to clues about the setting and verbs that are written in the past tense. In this instance, because the reading passage is a story, there would be shifting past tense verbs, so the educator would need to be aware of this and channel learners' attention to a particular past tense verb form. Through guiding questions, the educator may ask them to explore these verbs further and discuss the patterns in form(s) and meaning(s). For example, "what does the form of this word tell you? How does it differ from the other verbs? How do you know this action is happening over time? Is there anything in the way the word is written that causes you to think this?" The use of the form(s) would be in context in the reading, but the educator could extend and reinforce the students' understanding of the use by providing other instances in which the learners might find this form. For example, "Here is a secret clue about reading, you will find this verb form every time you read about events in the past that are being described in progress or in action over time" (i.e., past progressive). Learners would probably see this approach as a means to better understanding the story.

Educators, therefore, have myriad options for combining explicit/implicit approaches, deductive/inductive approaches, controlled and open-ended activities, and analysis of grammatical forms, meanings, and uses. All these options would be dependent upon the age and cultures of the learners, but maintaining some variation in approaches would ensure you reach all learning styles, build linguistic analysis skills, and keep classes interesting and meaningful.

Grammar translation method

Long before Saussure's definition of language as a structured system of arbitrary signs in the 1920s (Joseph, 2017) and Chomsky's structural generative grammar theory in the 1950s, education paradigms envisioned language teaching in line with these theories and developed models that cohered with them. To Chomsky, the structures of language systems are a finite set of linguistic rules than can potentially be employed to generate an infinite number of sentences. The language teaching practices resulting from *transformational grammar* theory (Chomsky, 1951; Cook, 1998; Collins, 2008) prioritized the application of linguistic rules to the construction and generation of sentences that stood alone in isolation.

Language teaching and learning used to be regarded as a process of learning about the structure of language, memorizing vocabulary, and producing accurate grammatical sentences independent of the cohesion of spoken or written forms. TESOL professionals describe longer spoken or written passages as *discourse.* Many methods that dominated the language teaching and learning field in the past focused more on the minute grammar forms and vocabulary choices (i.e., discrete language items) instead of on the discourse, which is an essential component of real communication and interaction. Although linguistic structure is key to learning another language, it is not the only need when learning another language.

Grammar translation methodology, which has been in use since the late middle ages/early Enlightenment, was primarily structural, meaning the focus in the teaching and learning process was deconstructing the meaning of grammatical or vocabulary structures with reference to L1. The origins of the field of TESOL were rooted in the teaching of language structures, rather than a system designed to communicate, which influenced the way other languages were taught. The grammar translation approach, which has also pervaded the educational materials since the 16th century, was used to help students to learn how to think critically and analytically about Classic Latin and Greek texts, which were dead languages at that time. The purpose was not to use the language for communication with real people in the community, so there was no oral language included.

Grammar translation and other structural approaches viewed the language learning process as memorizing and analysis of grammatical rules and patterns and vocabulary words in isolation and then practicing them in sample sentences in order to build incrementally language knowledge toward eventual use in written translation. Learners were expected to memorize vocabulary and write grammatically accurate statements and questions. Knowing grammatical rules, making well-formed grammatical sentences, and producing accurate, but context-free language, were quite common in language teaching since they were translating and not expressing their own ideas. Translation was the main pedagogical activity in the classroom and the target performance of success was the ability to translate a text accurately, finding out the equivalent forms in each language and generating linguistically equal texts.

Grammar translation is characterized by translation and close-ended exercises. Close-ended exercises are activities for which there is only one right answer. Think of it as the exercises narrowing the options. Many people have experienced these exercises: sentence completion, fill in the blank, matching, cloze exercises (i.e., a paragraph or longer with blanks starting in the second sentence and occurring every fifth or seventh word), word/sentence translation, verb conjugations, dictation, scrambled sentences, and "dehydrated sentences" (see box for examples of common grammar translation exercises).

Grammar translation exercises

Fill in the Blank with Word Bank

Directions: Write the correct word from the word bank on the blank in the sentences.

Word Bank
macaroni and cheese   peanut butter   toast grocery   coffee

1. Sally drove her car to the _____ store to buy milk.
2. For breakfast, I usually eat _____ and drink _____.
3. My mother makes _____ and jelly for my school lunches.

Matching

Directions: Draw a line from the meal to the food you eat for that meal.

1. Breakfast   a. Celery and peanut butter
2. Lunch   b. Cereal
3. Snack   c. Ham sandwich
4. Dinner   d. Udon noodles with chicken

Cloze Exercise

Directions: Read the passage below. Write the correct word from the word bank in the blank.

Word Bank
will the ethnic for loves curry eat she only to over family

Constance loves food. She loves to _____ all kinds of food from all _____ the world. She likes to visit _____ restaurants to try new foods. Lately, _____ has been eating a lot of _____ and noodles. She tries to make _____ new foods at home for her _____. She had made sushi and shashlik _____ them. They loved the shashlik, but _____ her mother liked the sushi. She _____ not give up though, because she _____ ethnic food! One day, she hopes _____ become a chef.

Scrambled Sentences

Directions: Move the order of the words so they form a correct sentence.

1. going taking ball I and home am my
2. cheese you eat are pizza going to plain
3. car I my for looking am keys

Dehydrated Sentences

Directions: Add all the missing words, change the numbers to words, and modify the verbs and plurals to make the sentence grammatically correct.

1. We/to plant/4 tree/3 bush/and/6 flower.
2. Car lot/to have/3 kind/truck/and/2 sedan.
3. Class/to include/18 girl/and 17 boy/with/2 girl name Ashley/4 name Madeline.

What was missing in grammar translation, among other areas, was the pragmatic aspects of language, which is concerned with how languages are used appropriately to create the meaning of our messages. Note that we can communicate even with ungrammatical sentences like "they has not come yet" or "I coffee want." Although these sentences violate subject–verb agreement and word order rules, respectively, they might still sound interpretable to the individuals. Individuals may be able to communicate/exchange their ideas despite the ungrammatical forms. Generating meaningful sentences to get the message across was often neglected in the way additional languages were taught. This made learners focus first on the forms rather than meaning and communication. Once learners were observed to be unable to speak adequately when instructed through structural paradigms, communicative aspects of language teaching and learning became the focus (see Table 9.2 for a comparison of the characteristics of the structural and communicative paradigms).

Table 9.2 Summary of structural and communicative paradigms.

Structural-based paradigms	Communication-based paradigms
Prioritized language aspects and skills	Missing language aspects and skills
Literary language	Spoken language
L1 use while teaching	Lack of opportunity for L2 practice
Reading and writing skills	Speaking and listening skills
Grammar rules	Language use
Deductive teaching	Inductive learning
Sentence-based instruction	Conversation exchange
Teaching vocabulary in isolation	Learning vocabulary in context
Spelling and writing words	Pronouncing words
Grammar rules as content	Daily language for communication

The grammar translation method also had some pedagogical concerns, including the positioning of the learners as passive recipients of knowledge from the teachers, which authorized teachers as the sole source of information. For all the weaknesses discussed above, it functioned well in its time and led to the growth of other subsequent methods, which addressed the aspects and skills that were not prioritized in the grammar translation method. With the rise of the need to communicate in the international context, the method fell short of fulfilling the demands that expect people to speak rather than understand and translate literary texts. The grammar translation method was therefore argued to be insufficient to allow for developing ability for communicative language use.

Errors, mistakes, and feedback

Errors and mistakes may look the same on the surface. The learner's knowledge of the form is the difference between them. A mistake is when the learner knows the correct form, but does not employ it accurately in the speaking or writing moment. When their attention is drawn to it, the learner can correct the mistake. In this situation, the educator only needs to draw the learner's attention to the form through hints. An error, on the other hand, is when the learner does not understand the proper use of the form. In this situation, the educator would need to explain the accurate and appropriate contexts of the form and provide examples. So, errors require teaching, while mistakes require reminding.

It is also important to note how teachers can know whether the student has made a mistake or an error. They can pay attention to the consistency of incorrect usage during the lesson and arrive at a decision. They can also first try providing hints and if they think the incorrect form is not self-corrected they can explain and teach it. Unattended errors caused by lack of knowledge cannot easily be self-corrected and need to be dealt with by teachers.

There are two sources of errors. The first type is an *interference error* in which the patterns from the L1 are generalized to L2. The second type is a *developmental error* meaning that the learner is relying on L2 patterns, but they are not yet fully acquired. For interference errors, the educator would want to highlight the differences between patterns and possibly explain the rules of the pattern. For developmental errors, it is good to acknowledge the attempt being made and emphasize the correct pattern.

Errors are inevitable and signal where the students are developing in their English. Creating a learning environment in which errors and mistakes are not negatively judged by the teacher or peers is a key concern. When learners are comfortable using their language without anxiety, educators can guide instruction toward these grammatical, lexical, or phonological patterns for practice.

Two additional ways of categorizing errors influence how we give feedback to learners. Local errors are when there is a grammatical, lexical, or phonological error, but the message is understandable. For example, the dog to the park she walked. In this case, the meanings are understandable and we only need to provide feedback on the word order. Global errors are when you cannot understand the meanings being conveyed. In this situation, it is important to try to learn what the learner is seeking to convey and help them formulate it into a L2 pattern. Global errors are generally more important than local errors, depending on how marked or problematic the local error is.

Proficiency level and age influence the choices we make about handling errors. We want to be sure to help learners convey their meanings no matter what the proficiency level or age. You may recall from Chapter 8 in the section on speaking we discussed focusing on fluency more at lower proficiency levels and, increasingly, accuracy as the learners move up the proficiency scale. This does not mean we do not attend to accuracy at all with lower proficiency levels, but it is not the primary focus. The same is true of the advanced levels with accuracy.

We will choose whether the younger learner can use feedback on form/pattern or if we should rely on their implicit learning to acquire the form. For older learners who can utilize their metacognitive skills, we can provide feedback on form as well. How explicitly and in how much depth we teach the form/pattern is based upon contextual, individual, and instructional factors in a given moment. In some situations, it is best to wait on giving explicit and complex feedback until a proper time. For example, it is best to avoid individual embarrassment in front of the whole class during a discussion, so we remember the issue and discuss it with the learner one on one.

Best practices in giving feedback on form

Based on understandings of anxiety in SLA, TESOL educators have derived several guidelines for appropriately providing feedback on forms. First, we want learners to view errors in a positive light as a sign of progress. Second, students have fear of a negative social evaluation either by the teacher or their peers. If we embarrass or humiliate a student in front of their peers, they are less likely to take linguistic risks in the future.

Third, we want to highlight progress made by praising students for correct answers and even for partly correct ones. This will raise their self-esteem related to L2 learning and encourage them to take more linguistic risks. This does not mean always praising every contribution; rather, if a contribution is only partial correct, we would praise what is correct in an answer and guide the learner toward fixing the error. For example, "You said that perfectly in the past tense! Well done. And you might want to look at your pronunciation of the final -ed endings."

Fourth, when a learner does employ an incorrect form, TESOL educators use a technique to provide feedback called "recasting." Recasting is when the teacher repeats back to the learner what they said in the corrected form. We rephrase the error into a corrected form. For example:

> S: I go with sister to groceries last night.
> T: Oh, you *went** with your sister to get the groceries. That's nice.

*The corrected form is highlighted through the use of prominence (more on prominence in the section on "Pronunciation").

Fifth, an obvious way of shutting down the learning process is by correcting every error. We do not want to mark every error on a page or stop the learner every time they say something incorrectly. It can be stifling for learners and the learning process. We want to choose the most important form to provide feedback on. Look for patterns of global errors and work your way to smaller issues.

Sixth, learners are more likely to remember a form if they are prompted to recall how the form works. Through teacher-generated hints, we can guide students to self-correct. This is particularly important if it is a form that you have been working on.

Lastly, remember that giving feedback is not editing. We do not want to tell them what to write or reform their work through editing. We choose instead to highlight areas that are unclear or need some attention. We may provide examples of how people can express the idea in English.

You may have noticed in this section on giving feedback that we were not only discussing grammar errors. Instead, we mentioned forms, which can be grammatical, lexical, phonological, or spelling. All the tips provided apply to each of these areas.

Questions for reflection

- What practices do you consider to be the most effective for ELLs when teaching grammar and word order?
- For your learner population, which do you think are better matches: incidental acquisition or explicit grammar instruction? Why?
- How will you provide feedback on grammar and syntax? How will you avoid learners overlooking the feedback or being too direct? How will you help them learn without increasingly their anxiety?

Vocabulary

Vocabulary is like the linguistic muscles that carry the meaning of what we intend to communicate, just as the structural system would be the skeleton that connects all these muscles together. Communication then is based on the coordination between these grammatical and lexical systems.

Knowing vocabulary without structure would lead to a flawed use of language, which would not allow for comprehensible communication; rather it would make communication unintelligible and almost impossible with many misunderstandings. Because of the organic interconnection, the learning/acquisition of lexical and syntactic forms is inseparable and invariably occurs at the same time. Words gain meaning within sentence and context. We are always exposed to words in utterances when we first start to acquire or learn language. This combination is called *lexico-grammatical* system, which develops together.

Lexico-grammatical knowledge is learned and developed simultaneously since we need to learn the meaning of words to infer sentence meaning while also considering the syntactic structure. In teaching beginners, it is often the case that students have unpredictable challenges since they are bombarded with lexico-grammatical knowledge that might require them to memorize words and activate the corresponding grammatical structures.

Background basics about vocabulary teaching

Psychologists have long been concerned about how the brain stores information. Bartlett described the organization of culturally based knowledge in the memory as *schemas* (Bartlett, 1995; McVee et al., 2005). It is believed that learners construct schemas, or interconnected webs of related concepts, through exposure to new information from birth. The schemas become more complex and detailed with more learning and experience. Word webs or mind maps serve as a good illustration of how schemas are thought to work (Figure 9.5).

When a child is young, caregivers give names/labels to the things present in the environment by explicitly pointing them out or through implicit reference. For example, "Oh, look at that cat crossing the street." Cat is then assigned in the child's mind to this four-legged,

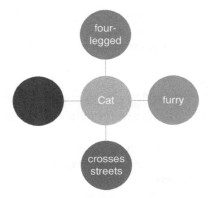

Figure 9.5 Mind map of a young learner's concept of cat.

furry creature when the parent points it out. The caregiver may or may not realize they are implicitly labeling the word "street" too. When children are young, they overgeneralize the concepts in their schema. For example, all four-legged, furry creatures might become "cat." So, the child points at a dog or a horse and says "Cat." Caregivers then differentiate cat from dog from horse. As children grow, they learn more about cats (Figure 9.6).

Schemas are thought to be experientially and culturally based, so they are somewhat shared and somewhat unique to the individual and the culture(s) of the person. Most people would share similar schemas for sleep, for instance, with minor differences. However, the concept of irrigation system may mean Roman aqueducts to some, to others it might mean pop-up sprinklers that are electronically controlled, and yet to others it could be a tiered landscape designed to collect and distribute rainwater. Kate's favorite example of the culturally based nature of schemas is "fire hydrant." Some cultures have them and others don't. If they do have them, they aren't necessarily red and dogs do not necessary go to the toilet on them. This later concept comes from observations in U.S. culture.

How do schemas relate to language learning? Schemas are thought to work also in organizing words of vocabulary concepts in the second language. When we learn that cat is "gato", "chat," or "聊天室" (i.e., liáotiān shì), we link the new word to the concept in our existing schema. We also connect to the relevant grammar patterns (e.g., part of speech, pluralization for cat, placement in sentences, what articles to use with it if any, etc.) the written form of the word/spelling as well as the oral form/pronunciation of the word to the schema. We may also assign the target language culture's attitudes and beliefs to the concept. For example, monkeys are considered highly dangerous in India but clever and playful in China.

Helping learners to develop their schemas for vocabulary in English may be as simple as connecting the word to their previous knowledge or building a new schema for a concept. However, TESOL teachers need to know that such connections involve teaching words with games and responsive activities that offer them meaningful lengthy exposure to the meaning of the word in contextualized information.

Intentional and incidental vocabulary learning

A distinction that TESOL educators have pondered is the difference between intentionally studying a new vocabulary word with the intention of learning it and

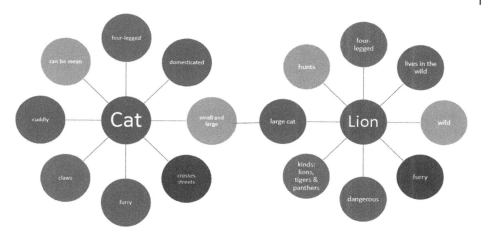

Figure 9.6 Concept of cat developing conceptually.

incidentally acquiring a new word when happening upon a word in context, but not trying to learn the new word intentionally. The concept of incidental vocabulary learning is that when the learner is exposed to the word it is meaningful and comprehensible, but they are not trying to specifically learn it; rather, they may be more focused on the meanings being conveyed in the moment. It is thought that learners can acquire new words incidentally with enough meaningful exposure. For a fascinating discussion of incidental and intentional vocabulary learning, see Susan Gass' (1999) article, "Incidental L1 Vocabulary Acquisition: Theory, Current Research and Instructional Implications.".

Intentional and incidental vocabulary learning are close to, but not fully equivalent to, explicit and implicit teaching of vocabulary. Explicit and implicit teaching of vocabulary is just like that of grammar. Explicit vocabulary instruction would involve direct instruction on the words with definitions, synonyms, descriptions, examples, visuals/realia, and/or collocations, for example. In contrast, implicit vocabulary instruction requires the teacher to expose the learner to the vocabulary repeatedly without any direct instruction.

These two sets of concepts are rooted in beliefs about second language learning and acquisition. Your beliefs will guide your choices of how to teach new vocabulary words. For example, if you are working with children, you may decide that input flooding with high-quality input and pushed output, but no explicit grammar or vocabulary, is most effective. On the other hand, you may decide that children can learn new vocabulary words alongside input flooding with high-quality input and pushed output (making them linguistically active and interactive), and choose to teach key vocabulary. Many K–12 educators today follow the second set of beliefs and choices.

How many and what types of words do ELLs need?

English has a rather large number of words and expressions. Nation and Waring (1997) cited two other research studies that indicated English has roughly 54,000 word families. A word family is all the related forms of the word (e.g., civil, civilize, civilized, civilization, civility). Native English speakers have an active vocabulary of up to 20,000 words depending on education and other variables. The overall goal for our learners, which could be achieved over time, is 6,000–9,000 word families, so that ELLs are able to understand an assortment of unsimplified spoken and written texts (Hirsch & Nation, 1992; Nation, 2006). Graves et al. (2013) noted that schoolchildren encounter over 180,000 words in their books and other reading materials. You may recall from Chapter 7, ELLs must recognize at least 98% of word for fluent reading and comprehension of a passage (Nation, 2008; Pulido & Hambrick, 2008; Laufer & Ravenhorst-Kalovski, 2010).

At the beginning, ELLs need a number of basic vocabulary words to participate in simple spoken and written interactions. Mastery of the 3,000 most common word families is typically the target, because they encompass 83% of general and academic words (Qureshi, 2018). TESOL educators categorize how common vocabulary words are by the frequency that they are used. Words, such as *a, is, he,* and *like* are *high-frequency vocabulary* words, meaning very common. *Low-frequency vocabulary* words are technical and subject specific. Lists of words, such as the Academic Word List, rank the frequency of words based on corpus linguistics research to help educators determine whether to teach a particular word or form. TESOL educators concentrate on ensuring ELLs know the meaning of basic words such as swing, truck, or imagine before presenting more challenging, low-frequency words (August et al., 2005).

How do we know what a word means?

What does it mean to know a word? We understand it when someone says it? We understand it when we read it? We can use it in spoken or written communication? How about if we can define it or give a synonym? Vocabulary can be oral or written and receptive or productive. The words we listen to or read are considered receptive vocabulary. The words we speak or write are productive. In a case study of a young ELL, Yoshida (1978) found that an ELL's receptive vocabulary was 2.2 times the size of his productive vocabulary. In other words, we understand a lot more vocabulary than we actively use in our speaking/writing. That is because recognition of words and inferring the meaning is enabled by the linguistic context. Even though we do not know the meaning of some words in an utterance or a sentence, we can either easily infer their meaning or do not need to know if the meaning or message is clear enough. An ELL then does not need to learn all the words to be able to understand an utterance; rather, he needs to develop an ability to guess the meanings from linguistic context or the physical context where the utterance was produced.

The features of a word that ELLs need to know to be able to use a word actively are tied to the form of the word, the grammatical or phonological form(s), and the meanings. Word knowledge sheds a bit of light on the lexico-grammatical overlaps. Nation (1990) and Zimmerman (2014) outlined what learners need to know about a word.

1. Meaning(s)—There are different facets of word meaning. A word has a definition and a literal and/or figurative usage. It has synonyms and antonyms. It has connotations, which are implied additional meanings, and associations, which may be historical or cultural. It has relationships to other similar words.
2. Written form—What the word looks like in context and how it is spelled.
3. Spoken form—What the word sounds like/pronounced by itself or in context.

4. Grammatical form—Words have a part or parts of speech (word class); word family; word category (e.g., body parts, people, food, clothes, or jobs). The word may have Greek or Latin root or affixes (i.e., prefixes or suffixes) shared by other languages.

5. Grammatical behavior–What patterns the word occurs in. It has a various possibilities for placement in a sentence (word order). It may have grammatical changes it undergoes in different linguistic contexts. It may have words that frequently occur with it in an exact word order, which are known as collocations (e.g., "stone cold" collocates, but "rock cold" does not; salt and pepper collocate).

6. Register and contexts—Whether the word is formal, informal, or neutral, which implies the settings where it may or may not be used appropriately.

7. Frequency—Whether the word is common (i.e., high-frequency) or rare (low-frequency).

TESOL educators do not teach all of these facets of word knowledge when introducing a vocabulary word. But they may choose the essentials to help learners understand the word at a basic level. For example, if a TESOL educator were teaching a group of first-grade ELLs the word "cow," she may present visuals and say something along the lines of:

> A cow is a noun. [Teacher writes the word on the board]. It is pronounced /kau/. Can you say it with me? [Students say cow]. Can you tell me what a cow is? [Students provide answers]. Right! A cow is a large animal that makes milk. Do you drink milk? We eat cow and call it beef. Have you had a hamburger? That's beef and it comes from a cow. [The teacher writes the following three sentences on the board]. A farmer lets the cows out into the field. The cow likes the farmer. The cows need to be milked two times a day. Sometimes, you may hear someone say, "Holy cow!" Have you heard that? [Students provide answers]. What do you think that means? [Students provide answers]. People use "Holy cow!" to show surprise and excitement, right? Holy cow! You are a smart class! ;-)

Notice how many of the features of word knowledge are present in this excerpt. Through this sort of presentation of a vocabulary word, the educator provides a great deal of knowledge about the word including words that collocate with it, such as farmer, field, milk, and holy. Having a discussion about words, their forms, meanings, uses, and learners' experiences with words is one technique for teaching new words.

When it comes to word knowledge, you may want to enliven and deepen your vocabulary instruction by adding some of these elements to your instruction, especially if they are not present in the texts or textbooks you are using.

Lesson sequences for vocabulary

Vocabulary research has yielded several informative practices for teaching vocabulary that are related to lesson sequencing. Overall, we want to teach toward meaning(s) of words, model appropriate use and repeated exposures, and provide interaction opportunities.

Number of exposures to a word

Nation's (2001) synthesis of several research studies identified the number of exposures ELLs need to learn a word so that it can be actively used. These studies found that learners need between 5 and 20 exposures to a word to learn it. Generally, though, the rule of thumb is between 7 and 12 exposures. The exposure may be the teacher's or peers' use of it in spoken interaction, listening, viewing, or reading a passage. The main idea is that the learner is exposed to the word often so they have to pay attention to it, retrieve it from long-term memory, manipulate it, and construct meanings with it.

Spaced repetitions

Another related principle about vocabulary learning is called *spaced repetition*. Spaced repetition, according to Sanaoui (1995), is when "the learners return to a lexical item sometime after they have encountered it and repeat it several times mentally or aloud." And these learners would recall the word a couple of times in a 2–3-day window. Teachers can provide lessons in which learners revisit the concept in several ways through interaction, communicative activities, tasks, exercises, extensive reading, and drills, for example. Vocabulary would be interwoven into integrated skills lessons through different activities over a couple times a day for 2–3 days to solidify the concept.

Combining number of exposures with spaced repetitions in lesson plans

If an educator were to focus on a reading or video, the educator would first want to discuss learners' background knowledge on the topic and observe which vocabulary words the learners were using to share their knowledge. Next, the educator would preteach the necessary vocabulary words including the different ways of knowing a word. To help learners feel comfortable saying the new vocabulary words, a quick choral repetition of them in a chant would be useful. Then, the class might do some total physical response (TPR), connecting the vocabulary words to a gesture and object with oral repetitions led by the instructor. The educator would move to a preview of the text through reading and discussing the title and subtitles, conducting a picture walk, and predicting what they will read. The educator could ask the students to skim the text for unfamiliar words, if necessary. Next, the educator would choose a format for conducting the reading, for example, silent reading or read aloud. Afterward, they would discuss the reading. Part of discussing the reading would include a discussion of the vocabulary words in context. Students could check their understandings of the vocabulary at this point. The teacher may follow up with vocabulary games, such as the fly swatter game, or a matching game. Afterward, the students might write about the reading from an angle that lets them investigate it or extend it. Check the number of times in this instructional sequence the students are thinking about and recalling the new vocabulary. Including the reading and writing portions, learners would have 9–11 passes at the new vocabulary. Depending on the length of class meetings, this sequence may take 2–3 days.

Teaching L2 vocabulary

Early practices prioritized the memorization of words in a list, which may have been topically or thematically linked. Some vocabulary instruction was organized by words that are pronounced similarly, have the same root, or have the same ending. Some other practices included teaching synonyms (i.e., words that have similar meanings) and antonyms (i.e., those that are opposite in meaning) of the target words to elaborate on the meaning and increase the vocabulary repertoire. For an interesting discussion of the different types of vocabulary sets, see Reynolds' (2018) "Teaching Notional Concepts: Time, Numbers, Distance, Size, Dimension, Shapes, Colors and Patterns" as well as Dikilitaş and Erten's (2018) "Homographs, Homonyms, Homophones, Synonyms, and Antonyms" in the *TESOL Encyclopedia of English Language Teaching*.

Learning a list of words that are unrelated has been shown to lead to confusion (I. S. P. Nation, 2000). However, in recent years, teaching words that are thematically linked within a meaningful context has become one of the key approaches. The context forms a theme that requires the use of meaningfully related words, which makes it memorable in the learning process. While thematically linked words allow for deeper processing of meaning by linking diverse lexical information, lists of words such as numbers, colors, and animals might require memorization without processing the meaning since they are not provided in a context. The human mind inherently processes meaning in context in childhood and knows how to derive appropriate meaning in communication. Therefore, we argue that ELLs need to be exposed to rich, comprehensible, and interesting input in order to help them with developing skills to guess rather than memorize word meanings.

Selecting the right words to teach

It is easy to become overwhelmed by the number of new words that may be present in a text or listening passage. TESOL educators must make choices about which words are the most appropriate to teach learners for different proficiency levels. One of the first considerations about which vocabulary to teach is related to the word frequency. Three tiers of vocabulary frequency have been identified.

1. *Tier one* words are the highest-frequency (daily or regularly used) words. Tier one words include common concrete nouns, verbs, etc. For example, words such as clothes, baby, clock, street, or happy. This tier may include words on the General Service List (http://jbauman.com/gsl.html), Dolch words (https://sightwords.com/sight-words/dolch/#lists), or Fry words (https://www.k12reader.com/subject/vocabulary/fry-words).
2. *Tier two* words include general academic or abstract words, such as describe, individual, justice, yield, categorize. Coxhead's Academic Word List is a good resource for tier two words (https://www.wgtn.ac.nz/lals/resources/academicwordlist). Marzano also has a list of tier two words by grade level (https://www.marzanoresources.com/reproducibles/vocab-common-core).
3. *Tier three* words are more sophisticated and subject-specific words. For example, words such as haplotype, isotope, phonological, lathe.

Depending on the learner's needs and goals, TESOL educators may consider the usefulness of teaching a specific word. Tier one words would be the most useful for daily interaction and social language. Tier two words are the most useful for general academics. Which tier two words would depend a bit on the grade level too. Tier three words would be most useful starting in high school and throughout university or vocational study.

The second consideration is whether the word is uniquely important or significant in the teaching context. For example, in the book *A Tale of Two Cities*, the word *solicitor* is used in place of the more modern *attorney* or *lawyer*. If the text is being taught, even though the word solicitor is not common, it may need to be explained. In this situation, the word solicitor has salience in the course content. Salience is a word that means special importance.

The final consideration is the role the word plays in the context. If the word is an extremely low-frequency adjective that learners are not likely to encounter again and it is not salient to the passage, there may be better uses of classroom time. Some extremely low-frequency adjectives include: contumacious, effulgent, rhadamanthine, uxorious.

One final note about which vocabulary words to teach: students may hear words in films, online, or on the street of which they want to understand the meaning. When learners wish to discuss and elaborate on the meanings of words, that is good; however, depending on the context you teach in, there may be words that you should avoid teaching. These words include taboo words, such as curse words, or they may be inappropriate for the culture and/or religion of your students. It is important to use your discretion and know your teaching context before you delve into a detailed description of a naughty word.

Materials for vocabulary teaching

You can avoid being on the spot or being the only source of vocabulary knowledge by having materials present in your classroom. Dictionaries, either monolingual or bilingual, are a standard. TESOL educators use ELL dictionaries for two reasons. First, they provide more information needed by the ELL (collocation, grammatical form, register, word parts, etc.). Second, they may employ only the first 3,000 words in the case of the Oxford ELL dictionaries, which makes them far easier for learners to understand. We also frequently use picture dictionaries, word cards with visuals, word walls, anchor charts, and bookmarks. These tools help provide learners with another source of rich exposure to words.

Effective techniques for presenting vocabulary words

When presenting new vocabulary words, there are several easy steps that will build the learners' comprehension. You will want to prepare in advance whenever possible. Plan to use everyday language that the learners are familiar with. Start with the basic meaning or general overview of the concept before providing details. You can use visuals, gestures, realia, demonstrations, or the L1 word. Try to categorize the word and/or provide a synonym before launching into a long, complex description or explanation.

For example, you might show a picture of a tuna fish and a can of tuna and explain, "A tuna is a type of fish. It is common in the Pacific Ocean. People eat it." Depending on the word, it may be useful to place it in a situation (e.g., Pacific Ocean) or context. Providing sample sentences with examples of the word both positive and negative can increase comprehension. For example, you could present an image of a ♥ and say, "Love is a feeling. In Spanish, love is 'amor,' right? We love our families and friends. People who do not feel loved are sad." Also, you might add to your presentation any of the aspects of word knowledge discussed above that are important for your learners to understand. Remember, though, that they need the basic understanding first before all the details.

Since learners may bring words to you or unanticipated events may occur, there will be times that you need to teach a word without any time to prepare. One time, Kate brought her students homemade cranberry and white chocolate cookies. One of the students asked what the cranberry was, which she answered. The student did not know about cranberries. It had slipped Kate's mind that cranberries are indigenous to North America, so they were not known commonly outside of North America. She did not have a phone or computer available to look up an image and drawing a small circle was not going to do it. The verbal description of a fruit that grows in bogs was dicey as well. In TESOL, we are constantly placed in situations where we need to explain new words quickly, succinctly, and without preparation time or support materials. It is a good idea to practice giving impromptu word explanations of various types of words (e.g., concrete, abstract) without any materials, and to anticipate these sorts of occurrences. When asked by students to explain the meaning of words, we can also draw on peer support and allow other students to explain if they want to. Students might find effective ways of describing words.

Effective techniques for practicing vocabulary words

The research on the number of exposures and spaced repetitions informs educators that we need to integrate vocabulary words into our lessons through speaking, listening, reading, and writing. Our goal is that they recall the word from memory and think about it in a meaningful context. In addition to close-ended exercises (e.g., true/false, fill in the blank, matching, sentence completion, and drills), we can engage learners to practice and acquire new vocabulary through interactive, communicative activities and tasks.

We can ask learners to alphabetize words by playing Scattergories, or the alphabet game, or keeping a vocabulary journal (alphabetized, of course). We can explore vocabulary words by categorizing them in various ways: part of speech, type, shape, positive/negative/neutral connotation, etc. We can place or rank them on a word strength continuum for learning word nuances (e.g., ecstatic, thrilled, happy, glad, content). We can label and describe items in a picture. We can sing songs or jazz chants. TPR is another interactive way to engage learners with new vocabulary. Games that are conducive to vocabulary practice are guessing games (e.g., 20 questions, I Spy), Pictionary, charades, or jeopardy.

Questions for reflection

- Why is having a large L2 vocabulary important for ELLs? How will you ensure learners have enough words, but that you teach them for memorability and use?
- How will you plan for vocabulary instruction and interweave it through lessons to achieve the number of exposures and spaced repetitions learners need so they can actively understand and utilize a word?
- How will you innovate your vocabulary instruction through materials and digital tools? Which ones?

Pronunciation

Pronunciation has been one of the controversial areas in second language teaching. Two main dilemmas have emerged regarding this: (a) should we teach pronunciation the way native speakers pronounce the words (one of the dominating views for many years); and (b) if this is the case, can it be achieved by teachers whose own pronunciation is different from native-speaker norms. Early methodology related to teaching pronunciation sought to prepare ELLs to speak like an idealized native speaker. The "ideal" native speaker was a problematic concept though. Was the ideal a British received pronunciation (RP) speaker (i.e., the Queen's English) or was it an American or Australian accent? And was there a better accent? The myth of a better accent has been dispelled in TESOL. It is recognized within the field that there are many accents even within the same country and no one is inherently better than another. Furthermore, there are many comprehensible nonnative (we would prefer not to use this term, but lack a replacement) accents that are commonly spoken and accepted. For example, there are Indian English and South African speakers of English who have clear, distinctive, and entirely acceptable accents. For a thoughtful discussion of accent in L2 pronunciation instruction, see Falkert (2016).

Historically, the field soon concluded that ELLs can communicate their messages without perfect pronunciation. TESOL professionals realized that words in sentences need to be pronounced clearly with comprehensible articulation, but learners do not need to speak with a perfect native-like accent. Moreover, it has become clear that the goal of native-like pronunciation may be an unrealistic goal for many, depending on the age the learner begins learning English (Marx, 2002).

Many factors influence acquisition of a second language phonology (i.e., sound system). Certainly, the first language of the learners matters. The learners will bring with them all of their pronunciation patterns and sounds from their first language and will base much of their new language pronunciation on it. They may not even be aware of these patterns. For example, Swedes frequently pronounce the /ae/ sound in the word *bad* like the sound /e/ as in *bed* (Swan & Smith, 2002). French speakers typically pronounce the *th* sound in *think* as the word *zinc* or *sink*. Swan and Smith provide an example of Greek intonation in comparison to English, "Some features of Greek intonation carried over into English (such as the use of a high fall where English would use a low rise) may make speakers sound abrupt and impolite. Special practice is needed in the intonation of polite requests..." (p. 132).

The age of acquisition plays a sizable role in L2 pronunciation. Almost all languages differ in terms of how they articulate sounds, so discrepancies make it difficult to adapt to the new language sound system. In our L1, phonemes (i.e., sounds) that are not in our native language are pruned from our brain's phonological system at around 1 year old (Werker & Tees, 1983; Vihman, 2009; Rosselli et al., 2014), which limits our ability to make the sounds. Phonological ability grows simultaneously with vocal organs, which are shaped to produce sounds peculiar to the L1. Around puberty, the muscles in learners' jaws and faces become more solidified, which makes it still more challenging to move the jaw in new and unaccustomed ways (Sharkey & Folkins, 1985; Smith & Zelaznik, 2004; Zharkova et al., 2011). For these reasons, early childhood exposure to English can have an effect on developing English pronunciation since the vocal organs are still growing. Young learners do not need an explicit focus on pronunciation for these reasons, too.

The amount and quality of input/exposure to English is another factor that influences pronunciation. It was hard for learners in the past to develop such ideal pronunciation skills owing partly to limited exposure to authentic speech and to sustained communicative practice. In the past, the primary concern in teaching pronunciation was addressed through receptive word exercises and drills as in the Audiolingual Method. Since learners were learning linguistic behaviors, it was important that they speak with proper phonemes, intonation, and word stress, for example. These drills did not provide enough linguistic input for learners to hear authentic language in use so they could approximate the sounds or patterns when they were speaking. They also did not have access to an extensive network of L2 language speakers outside of the classroom, unless they were in a second language context. Nor did drills allow for interactive practice or the extended discourse that is typical in real-life communication.

Finally, listening abilities are important, because learners derive their notion of target language pronunciation from the input received. Some learners may have strong auditory skills and be able to tune their ears to the sounds of the new language. Other learners may have auditory challenges that make the task highly challenging. When teaching pronunciation, whether in a class focused on the topic or in integrated skills classes, knowing about learners' listening abilities will guide you to set realistic expectations.

What makes learning L2 pronunciation difficult?

In Chapter 4, you read about phonology, the study of the sounds and patterns of English. You will recall that phonemes are the individual sounds, which are also called segmentals. Also, suprasegmentals were discussed (i.e., intonation, rhythm, word stress, prominence/sentence stress, thought groups, and connected speech). At this point, we will discuss what makes English pronunciation challenging while referring to these areas. If you do not recall them, you might want to refresh your memory on the topic.

Segmentals are perhaps the easiest facet of pronunciation to seize upon for pronunciation teaching, because of the clear differences between various languages' pronunciations of certain consonants and vowels. These differences make some segmentals very challenging for ELLs. English adds an additional curveball, because of the differences between the sounds and the written symbols. For example, an /s/ can be written as *c*, *s*, *z*, and it can be pronounced as /s/, /z/, /əz/, or /ɪz/. The ways that *s* is written and pronounced can be highlighted for learners who are learning to read orally. Educators need to be conscientious about which segments to spend time teaching and which can be acquired without explicit/direct teaching. For example, if a sound is the same in both languages, there may be very little reason to teach the sound. Telling the beginner learners that the sounds are the same may suffice. Depending on the age of the learner, time may be better employed highlighting the differences in phonemes between languages. With that said, it is critical to note that while segmentals may be attractive to teach, some learners will not be able to acquire the new segmentals no matter how hard they try. Additionally, segmentals do not have as much of an impact on overall comprehensibility as suprasegmentals do. We want to avoid discouraging learners through repetitive practice of an unattainable form. If the learner can approximate it—get close enough to it so that listeners understand—that is sufficient.

The speed of speech makes L2 pronunciation difficult. Learners do not have the time to think through every segment and suprasegmental as they are speaking to make sure they pronounce them correctly.

Finally, some of our learners' first languages do not have the same sounds as English. The reason for the French pronunciation of *think* as *sink* or *zinc* is that they do not have a /ð/ sound. This fact causes learners to experience frustration and challenges in replicating the sound. But educators and students are able to overcome these concerns. For these reasons, TESOL educators employ practices to support learners while reducing frustration and anxiety.

Effective practices for teaching L2 pronunciation

Research-informed guidelines exist to aid TESOL educators in teaching second language pronunciation appropriately. First, we want to raise learners' awareness of the segmental or suprasegmental patterns used in authentic and contextualized models. Focused listening activities, such as analyzing passages for sounds and patterns and audio recordings with focal questions, help learners hear the pronunciation pattern in longer passages. It is important that the learners have enough authentic input and focused listening so they can observe how the segment or suprasegmental acts in connected speech. You may also provide assorted contexts for use if the pronunciation point differs by context. Importantly, you will want to restrict the accent of the speaker to one kind so as to avoid confusing the learners.

You may have noticed that the approach to teaching the pronunciation form is inductive. You can start teaching about a sound or pattern deductively, but learners will still need focused listening to hear and identify how the sound or pattern acts in authentic interaction.

Second, we want to provide clear guidance on how to make the sound in terms of positioning of articulators and breathing. It can be awkward, unclear, or culturally inappropriate to point to your mouth or put your finger in your mouth to demonstrate a tongue movement. Thankfully, the educators at the University of Iowa have created a digital tool to help us called *Sounds of Speech*. For various segmentals, it shows how the jaw, tongue, and lips move as well as demonstrating the sound in the initial, medial, and final position in a word. Hand mirrors are a tool for learners to see how they are moving their tongues and lips, so many educators use them to illustrate a comparison between the target and the learners' production of the sound.

For suprasegmentals, we do not have a *Sounds of Speech* tool. TESOL educators use a variety of techniques to illustrate the particular pattern. The first type is visualization. We call on visuals to illustrate the pattern. For example, with prominence (i.e., the one major emphasis of the thought group—the word most stressed), which has a higher pitch, clearer vowel sound in the word, and slightly longer duration (i.e., a millisecond longer), we often draw lines above the sentence to show the prominent word and how the meaning shifts with different prominent words in the same sentence. For intonation (i.e., the musical rise and fall of the language), we draw lines over different types of sentences and questions to illustrate the falling or rising intonation.

We also employ kinesthetic movements to illustrate the suprasegmental pattern, which is the second type of technique. For example, for stressed syllables in words, educators give rubber bands to learners and ask them to stretch the rubber band when they hear the stressed syllable. We can ask learners to tap out the number of syllables in a word or make a hand motion for pauses between thought groups (e.g., a slashing motion), to illustrate the intonation of a statement or question (e.g., moving their hand up/down in a surfing motion), or to signify connected speech (e.g., a scooping motion). TPR is another means to link kinesthetic movements to the sounds and patterns.

The third technique is to provide rules. At times, for example, with word stress, we provide basic rules for pronunciation of nouns, verbs, adjectives, adverbs with two, three, or four or more syllables. Here is a selection of rules for word stress:

- Stress the primary and secondary syllable of a word.
- Nouns and other parts of speech tend to follow the same patterns.
- Verbs work differently.
- Words with the letter *e* in the first syllable also have different word stress patterns.
- Words that can be a noun or a verb will have different word stress, depending on the part it is playing in speech. For example, as-*so*-ci-ate (noun) (when pronounced the final syllable is reduced to sound like the word *it*) and as-so-ci-*ate* (verb) (the final syllable sounds like the past tense for *eat* >> *ate*).
- There are many, many exceptions.

Rules for rhythm center on the stress-timing rhythm of English. English does not have a regular rhythm on each syllable like some other languages do. Instead, certain words that carry meaning are stressed. This category of words is called *content words* in pronunciation discussions, because they carry meaningful content. This grouping includes nouns, verbs, adjectives, adverbs, interjections, wh- question words, and negatives. They tend to be the longer words in a sentence. These words are afforded regular, not prominent, stress. Function words are the destressed or underemphasized words that receive the least stress in pronunciation. These words include pronouns, prepositions, articles, conjunctions, and auxiliary verbs.

It goes without saying that we would want to present these rules to learners who are old enough to understand and use them. We want to present them succinctly in learner-friendly language while offering many examples to clarify the rule. One of Kate's favorite books for teaching pronunciation at the university level is *Well Said* by Linda Grant. The focus is on the suprasegmentals and each chapter is sequenced from listening to the pattern, rule discussions, controlled practice, and then communicative practice. It even has a needs assessment at the beginning of the text. If you would like to understand the rules of English pronunciation better, a great reference is Celce-Murcia, Brinton, and Goodwin's *Teaching Pronunciation: A Course Book and Reference Guide*.

The final technique TESOL educators employ is creating ample pronunciation practice opportunities that range from saying the word in isolation to contextualized, authentic speaking. Three categories of activities allow us to guide learners through pronunciation: controlled practice, guided practice, and communicative practice.

Types of pronunciation practice activities

Guided practice involves the educator providing a model and students mirroring that model. For example, Audiolingual Method drills and minimal pairs practice. Minimal pairs are sets of two words that are similar in all except one way. For example, sheep/ ship or dog/hog. Using minimal pairs highlights the differences in sounds and how these sounds influence the meanings of the words.

Controlled practice includes activities such as tongue twisters, jazz chants, and songs. They are controlled because they do not change in pronunciation each time you utter them. Often these are teacher-centered, but can be employed in pairs or small groups to allow more practice and feedback. Other close-ended activities can be employed too.

Communicative, open-end practice is important for the learners to be able to practice the sound or pattern in context and negotiate its meaningful use with peers. They may have to try to say it a few different times to convey the meaning they are striving to share. This practice will help them use the sound or pattern later in interaction outside of class. Some activities TESOL educators use are communicative activities and tasks that require learners to use the particular form. In this, they are also secretly structural. Students may be asked to tell stories, explain processes, or engage in roleplay or information gap activities/tasks. One teacher resource for teaching British pronunciation is *Pronunciation Games* by Cambridge University Press.

Feedback on pronunciation and monitoring one's own production

Giving every student ample feedback on pronunciation is a challenge. For this reason, TESOL educators frequently make use of digital technologies. Students are asked to audio or videotape themselves reading aloud, in a dialogue or an extended monologue that concentrates on the pronunciation form being studied. Learners are asked to listen to their recordings for the form and to analyze their own production. This strategy accomplishes two tasks: it raises the learner's awareness of their own pronunciation patterns, and helps the teachers identify whether the student can self-monitor. Teachers receive from the learners their recordings and written observations, and then provide feedback on the recording about the pronunciation point and the learner's awareness of the point.

Some practices that are ineffective need to be mentioned. First, overfocusing on pronunciation to the exclusion of other areas can be a problem, particularly with younger learners. There is so much to teach in a second language that we have to prioritize.

Moreover, as we noted earlier, the goal of pronunciation is clarity and intelligibility, so too much of a focus beyond that is unnecessary. We also need to bear in mind that pronunciation is also dependent on physiological evolution of vocal organs and muscles that might have established language-specific ways of pronouncing particular sounds and related words.

Second, ELLs may ask for a lot of pronunciation feedback and correction. Error correction that embarrasses the learner or makes them repeat a word or phrase when they clearly cannot say it is counterproductive. We want to provide focused and supportive feedback with examples whenever possible. In culturally sensitive classroom contexts, it is often recommended that TESOL educators need to recast the seemingly unintelligible pronunciation of a word by repeating it in the correct way in the subsequent moments so the student might be aware of it and self-correct. Systematic explicit correction might contribute to a negative reaction to speaking aloud in the classroom. Recasting might help reduce a judgmental stance toward student talk and offer positive environment conducive to talking without shame. Multiple exposures to pronunciation of words lead to it being displayed over time. Once again, this reveals the role of TESOL educators in the development of appropriate pronunciation learning by students.

However, learning the discrete pronunciation of a word (i.e., the word by itself) is not enough since words can be pronounced differently in sentence contexts. For example, without knowing which syntactic category a word is assigned in a sentence, we may not know how to pronounce it. The word *record* is pronounced differently when it is used as a noun or as a verb. Appropriate pronunciation in a contextualized sentence can make learning more meaningful for students. If students learn one way of pronouncing this word, they will do so regardless of its use in an utterance.

Third, we want to avoid focusing too much on segmentals and overlooking the suprasegmentals. We mentioned earlier that there will be some segmentals that are the same in both languages. Teaching learners which ones are similar can be accomplished quickly. Some emphasis on the dissimilar segments may yield results, although they may be limited by the learner's ability to make the sound. Teaching suprasegmentals, though, tends to yield stronger results, because the patterns can be taught and learned, unlike some of the suprasegmentals (depending on the age of the learner). And listeners rely on the accuracy of the suprasegments for their comprehension of a learners' speech; therefore, when we focus on teaching the suprasegmentals, learners' comprehensibility is increased. For example, the word *right* can be used with varying stress and intonation to convey different messages to the interlocutor. When articulated with a rising intonation, it could mean an agreement. When articulated with falling intonation, it could mean okay.

Questions for reflection

- What practices do you consider to be the most effective for ELLs when teaching pronunciation?
- How will you innovate your pronunciation instruction through materials and digital tools? Which ones?

Teaching L2 Spelling

Spelling is a significant part of word-level writing and reading (Willingham, 2015). It has been a overlooked field for many years, because of a philosophical belief that students would acquire correct spelling over time through literacy practice. Educators found that learners did not in fact acquire spelling knowledge through exposure, so spelling has made a recent comeback.

Spelling is the process of encoding sounds into letters, and letters into words. Phonological awareness that informs decoding processes during reading (discussed in Chapter 7) informs encoding processes in writing as well. Reading, writing, vocabulary, and spelling are interconnected. Spelling includes knowledge of how to apply phonics, patterns, and meaning. When learners have a sense of the ways that sounds can be represented as letters (letter knowledge), and the patterns in which letters are used in words, they are better able to spell words independently. Since writing needs to be comprehensible to the reader, correct spelling facilitates their comprehension and builds writing confidence.

What guidance does research provide for the teaching of spelling?

Spelling has been a somewhat neglected skill set in TESOL, so limited research has been conducted on teaching spelling to ELLs. Much of the research relies on teaching spelling to native English speakers, with some notable exceptions. Parlindungan (2018) summarized the research on spelling instruction with bilingual learners and described two key research findings. First, the L1 has a positive or negative influence on L2 spelling depending on how similar or different the two languages are. In other words, if the languages have similar patterns, for example, English and Spanish, positive transfer would occur (i.e., the knowledge of spelling in the L1 would support the spelling in the L2); whereas, with Chinese and English, two languages that are markedly dissimilar, learners may experience negative interference in their attempts at spelling (i.e., the knowledge of L1 sound/symbols would not assist in L2 spelling). Second, direct instruction in spelling with ELLs does lead to better spelling, but instruction in phonological awareness, letter knowledge, and orthographic knowledge is also important. Balancing and combining these areas should be a priority.

Often spelling instruction is coupled with reading (i.e., phonological and phonemic awareness, and phonics) and vocabulary word study (Marten, 2003). Word study is essentially analysis and is considered an effective instructional practice for teaching spelling (Johnston, 1999). When teaching spelling to ELLs it is important that our approach is "systematic, explicit and individualized" (Parlindungan, 2018, p. 320).

Guidelines for teaching spelling

Several guidelines help TESOL educators to determine when and how to teach ELLs spelling. These guidelines are a synthesis of research-supported instructional practices for teaching spelling to bilingual learners from the work of Bear et al. (2020), Giannotti (2009), Marten (2003), Shemesh and Waller (2006), and Stirling (2011).

Consider the specific learning population

Spelling instruction needs to be developmentally appropriate and aligned with learners' proficiency levels. Depending on the age and proficiency of the learner, we would teach words they are familiar with and common patterns in a progressive manner. For example, if the learners are in a second language context and started school with their native-speaking peers, they would learn letters and letter names first. This would be followed by short and long vowels. Then they would begin learning to spell short three-letter words with the consonant, vowel, consonant pattern (CVC) (e.g., sit, lit, pit, bit or pop, mop, top, cop). Next, they would learn four-letter patterns (e.g., CVVC = feet, meet, seat, meat, mean and CVCV = hope, rode, home, some, make, same) and consonant clusters as variations on the CVC pattern (e.g., stop, flop; sing, ring; song, long; rang, fang, bang; sting, fling, bling. Changes in words are addressed near this stage. For example, adding a final -s for pluralization, adding an -ed for simple past tense verbs, and adding -ing for progressive verbs and gerunds. Part of addressing changes in words is teaching about dropping the final -e. Other patterns can be included as well. After that, they would learn patterns within words and compound words (e.g., should, could, would, fought, ought, sought, brought; outline, input, football, stoplight). This would be followed by some focus on syllables in spelling, multisyllabic words, and common prefixes and suffixes. Mainly, as learners become older, we teach them increasingly longer words, more complex patterns, and more atypical patterns and exceptions. Remember to provide visuals for words and do activities, such as rhyming activities and categorization/sorting activities, so that the words are meaningful and recalled from memory numerous times (see the earlier vocabulary instruction regarding numerous exposures).

Educators can link the instruction of vocabulary words to the spelling patterns of the word. When teaching new vocabulary words, they can encourage sight-word recognition and highlight spelling patterns by systematically choosing sets of words that follow one spelling pattern at a time. When they choose vocabulary words from texts or listening passages that learners need for comprehension, they can look for common patterns that are shared by the words or discuss the spelling patterns learners see within the words, for example. Including in lessons opportunities to highlight spelling patterns within vocabulary instruction should be a natural and regular occurrence.

Invented spelling

Educators should use students' invented spelling as a tool to understand learners' developmental levels and build from there. As a beginning in writing, using invented spelling as a means to encourage student writers is a good approach. Educators need to be mindful though that learners benefit from learning patterns so they can be independent in their learning. Without some analysis and attention to the patterns, learners would be less likely to move to acceptable spelling on their own.

Inductive and deductive spelling instruction

Educators can teach spelling patterns either deductively (i.e., rule first) or inductively though learner analysis and discovery. Either way, learners need to be engaged with the spelling patterns through analysis and exploration. They can identify patterns, and

---

English spelling patterns

This sequence of spelling patterns starts at the smallest unit and moves to longer words, other patterns, and exceptions.

1. the alphabetic principle: sound = letter correspondences;
2. consonants at initial (beginning) and final (ending) positions in the word;
3. short vowel sounds in CVC word families;
4. digraphs (ch, sh, th, wh) (i.e., two letters representing one sound);
5. blends (s, r, l, others);
6. long vowel sounds in longer words (CVVC, CVCV, etc.);
7. r-controlled vowels;
8. diphthongs (oi, au, u in took);
9. single-syllable homophones;
10. plural endings;
11. compound words;
12. inflectional endings (ask*ed*, ask*ing*);
13. consonant doubling;
14. stress and accent of open and closed syllables;
15. prefixes and suffixes;
16. silent consonants;
17. consonant and vowel changes;
18. Greek and Latin word elements;
19. origins of words;
20. unusual plurals; and
21. often confused and mispronounced words.

---

generalize them to discover rules. Students can learn to develop their own hypotheses about patterns. These practices will make the instruction more stimulating and memorable for learners.

When we are teaching spelling, educators strive to increase learners' responsibility through a process of: I do, we do, you do with my help, you do independently. This process implies that teachers will explicitly teach spelling patterns or design inductive spelling tasks, the class will then practice together, which will be followed by guided practice opportunities, and then more open-ended spelling experiences. This sequence helps learners by supporting them in the process of making them independent users of the spelling pattern.

Careful about worksheet use

Importantly, while we want to teach spelling and spelling patterns and it is important to get students writing the words, we have to be thoughtful about the overuse of worksheets. They are controlled and relatively easy for learners, but they are also decontextualized, lacking in interaction, and somewhat boring and predictable. We need to be sure to be engaging in our choices of spelling activities by including hands-on and interactive experiences with spelling. We need to be sure to link spelling of words intentionally to meaningful writing experiences.

Engaging activities for teaching spelling

The types of activities educators use to provide practice with spelling are geared to the age and proficiency level. Elementary school educators teach rimes. Rimes in spelling refer to the onset and the following letters. For example, the word *pop* comprises the onset (p) + rime (op). They can teach rimes through word family spelling chants (word family = mop, cop, top, stop, lop, bop, fop). Learners can go on a plastic egg hunt with letters in eggs that the learners need to make into words. Learners can play spelling hopscotch (letters are written in squares and learners spell a word when they step), or spelling four-square (i.e., learners spell a word together when they hit the ball). Word walls are an effective support in lower grades as well. Older learners may practice spelling by making analogies, writing rhyming poetry, playing Boggle/Words with Friends, or participating in spelling races. For any age, effective instructional activities include: word analysis activities, word sorts, word building, word charts, playing with word parts to make words, word-study notebooks, and peer conferences.

There are many online games that can be found for teaching spelling and spelling patterns. Be mindful though that many are not interactive, meaningful, or contextualized. Here is a selection of websites. You can analyze them for their quality to determine if they align with SLA theory.

- https://topnotchteaching.com/lesson-ideas/35-spelling-games
- https://busyteacher.org/11555-10-fun-spelling-games-for-your-esl-class.html
- https://www.eslgamesplus.com/spelling-games
- https://howtospell.co.uk/spellingquiz.php

Questions for reflection

- How did you learn English spelling? Do you recall learning spelling patterns? Or did your teachers rely on other techniques? Which approaches were better in your opinion? Why?
- What is the most appropriate ratio of spelling activities to worksheets? How will you avoid only using worksheets?

Chapter Conclusions

Each of the tools described in this chapter (i.e., grammar, vocabulary, pronunciation, and spelling), represents countless structures and patterns, which can be incorporated into four-skill integrated learning of English. While there are different approaches to incorporating them, whether explicitly or implicitly, secretly structural, deductively, or inductively, educators consider their learner population and context while making these instructional choices. Learners' ages, proficiency levels, and goals will influence how educators choose to teach these tools. Educators must be informed about the ins and outs of each tool, so as to effectively communicate the patterns to learners and create authentic, engaging, and meaningful materials for learner practice.

Discussion Questions and Activities

1 From the list of grammar points (below), please choose one concept and script (or write everything you would say) to present this grammar point to a L2 class that has never seen it. List two close-ended and two open-ended activities you would use so learners can practice grammar points.
   a. copula (to be);
   b. subject–verb agreement;
   c. phrase structure;
   d. adjectives (physical, personality characteristics, etc.);
   e. demonstrative adjectives (i.e., this, that, these, those);
   f. comparatives and superlatives;
   g. negation;
   h. imperatives;
   i. wh- questions;
   j. articles;
   k. possessives;
   l. passive voice;
   m. prepositions;
   n. conjunctions;
   o. adverbs;
   p. conditional;
   q. one tense (choose from present, past, future, past perfect, simple past, future perfect, future perfect, simple future, progressive); and
   r. direct objects or indirect objects.

2 Make a visual vocabulary list for a topic you might study with your students. Topics/ themes can be friendship, honesty, justice, oceans, deserts, rainforests, grasslands, mysteries, dystopias, community, or art.
   a. Your list should address these areas:
       i. key words with an ELL-friendly definition;
       ii. visual of the word; and
       iii. examples of the word in sentences that can be read by the student.
   b. How would you present/teach the meanings of these words?
   c. Which activities would you use for ELLs to practice the vocabulary words? Provide two close-ended, controlled-output activities and two open-ended activities.

3 Find and share an activity for teaching L2 pronunciation. Note the grade level and proficiency level of the learners this activity would work best with. Answer the questions:
   a. What pronunciation form does this activity allow ELLs to practice? Why did you choose this form to focus on?
   b. What are the procedures to do this activity?
   c. Why would you do this activity?
   d. What do you anticipate could be problematic for ELLs?
   e. How would you approach feedback/assessment on this activity?

4   Identify two or three hands-on and two or three digital activities, so ELLs can practice spelling in a meaningful manner. Be sure that they are age and proficiency-level appropriate for your population. Answer the questions:

    a.   What spelling form does this activity allow ELLs to practice? Why did you choose this form to focus on?

    b.   How would you include this activity in instruction? What resources would you need to include it?

    c.   Why would you do this activity?

    d.   What do you anticipate could be problematic for ELLs?

    e.   How would you approach feedback/assessment on this activity?

Tasks

1   Outline your philosophy of teaching ESL/EFL/ELT to include your beliefs about teaching these tools and how you might teach them to your target ELL population. How has your philosophy changed as a result of reading about these tools?

2   How does the context of learning influence the instruction in these tools? How do the educational philosophy and belief system of the society and culture influence instruction in these areas? What would you do if your philosophy differed from that of the context in which you were working?

3   Interview two educators working in an ESL and an EFL context or two educators working at different grade levels to determine if or how they teach these tools in their ESL/EFL/ELT courses. Share your findings with the class.

Further Reading/Read and Discuss

Read about L2 grammar instruction:

Benati, A. (2017). The role of input and output tasks in grammar instruction: Theoretical, empirical and pedagogical considerations. *Studies in Second Language Learning and Teaching, 7*(3): 377–396.

Read about L2 vocabulary instruction:

Yousefi, M. H., & Biria, R. (2018). The effectiveness of L2 vocabulary instruction: A meta-analysis. *Asian-Pacific Journal of Second and Foreign Language Education, 3*(21). https://link.springer.com/article/10.1186/s40862-018-0062-2 (accessed March 25, 2021).

Read about L2 pronunciation instruction:

Gordon, J., & Darcy, I. (2016). The development of comprehensible speech in L2 learners: A classroom study on the effects of short-term pronunciation instruction. *Journal of Second Language Pronunciation, 2*, 56–92. https://doi.org/10.1075/jslp.2.1.03gor

Darcy, I. (2018). Powerful and effective pronunciation instruction: How can we achieve it? *The CATESOL Journal, 30*(1): 13–45.

Read about L2 spelling instruction:

Parlindungan, F. (2018). What research has to say about spelling instruction for English language learners? Proceedings from the *International Seminar on English language Teaching and Research (ELTAR)*, Malang, Indonesia.

References

Al-Kharrat, M. Y. (2000). Deductive and inductive lessons for Saudi EFL freshmen students. *Internet TESL Journal, 6*(10). http://iteslj.org/Techniques/Al-Kharrat-Deductive

August, D., Carlo, M., Dressler, C., & Snow, C. (2005). The critical role of vocabulary development for English language learners. *Learning Disabilities Research & Practice, 20*(1), 50–57. doi:10.1111/j.1540-5826.2005.00120.x

Bartlett, F. C. (1995). *Remembering.* Cambridge University Press.

Bear, D. R., Invernizzi, M., Templeton, S., & Johnston, F. (2020). *Words their way: Word study for phonics, vocabulary, and spelling instruction* (7th ed.). Pearson.

Burns, A. (2011). Grammar and communicative language teaching: Why, when, and how to teach it? In *English language teaching practice in Asia.* CamTESOL. http://dx.doi.org/10.5746/LEiA/ELTPA

Chomsky, N. (1951). *The logical structure of linguistic theory.* Chicago University Press.

Chomsky, N. (1965). *Aspects of the theory of syntax.* MIT Press.

Collins, J. (2008). *Chomsky: A guide for the perplexed.* Continuum International Publishing.

Cook, V. (1998). *Chomsky's universal grammar: An introduction.* Blackwell.

Dikilitaş, K., & Erten, İ. H. (2018). Teaching homographs, homonyms, homophones, synonyms, and antonyms. In K. M. Reynolds (Ed.), *The TESOL encyclopedia of English language teaching.* doi:10.1002/9781118784235.eelt0753

Falkert, A. (2016). The relevance of accent in L2 pronunciation instruction: A matter of teaching cultures or language ideologies? *International Journal of Pedagogies and Learning, 11*(3), 259–270. https://doi.org/10.1080/22040552.2016.1272533

Gass (1999). Incidental L1 vocabulary acquisition: Theory, current research and instructional implications. *Studies in Second Language Acquisition, 21*(2): 319–333.

Giannotti, J. (2009). *Spelling counts: Sounds and patterns for English language learners.* Michigan University Press.

Graves, M. F., August, D., & Mancilla-Martinez, J. (2013). *Teaching vocabulary to English language learners.* Teachers College Press.

Hirsch, D., & Nation, P. (1992). What vocabulary size is needed to read unsimplified texts for pleasure? *Reading in a Foreign Language, 8*(2), 689–696. https://www.scirp.org/(S(351jmbntvnsjt1aadkposzje))/reference/ReferencesPapers.aspx?ReferenceID=1581201 (accessed March 25, 2021).

Johnston, F. (1999). The timing and teaching of word families. *The Reading Teacher, 53*(1), 64–75. https://libres.uncg.edu/ir/uncg/f/F_Johnston_Timing_1999.pdf (accessed March 25, 2021).

Joseph, J. E. (2017, June). Ferdinand de Saussure. In Oxford Research Encyclopedias, Linguistics. https://oxfordre.com/linguistics/view/10.1093/acrefore/9780199384655.001.0001/acrefore-9780199384655-e-385

Krashen, S. (1982). *Principles and practice in second language acquisition.* Pergamon.

Larsen-Freeman, D. (2003). *Teaching language: From grammar to grammaring.* Heinle/Cengage.

Laufer, B., & Ravenhorst-Kalovski, G. C. (2010). Lexical threshold revisited: Lexical text coverage, learners' vocabulary size and reading comprehension. *Reading in a Foreign Language, 22*(1), 15–30. https://citeseerx.ist.psu.edu/viewdoc/download?doi=10.1.1.1001.2472&rep=rep1&type=pdf (accessed March 25, 2021).

Maftoon, P., & Sarem, S. N. (2015). A critical look at the presentation, practice, production (PPP) approach: Challenges and promises for ELT. *BRAIN: Broad Research in Artificial Intelligence and Neuroscience, 3*(4), 31–36. https://www.edusoft.ro/brain/index.php/brain/article/view/442 (accessed March 25, 2021).

Marten, C. (2003). *Word crafting: Teaching spelling grades K–6.* Heinemann.

Marx, N. (2002). Never quite a "native speaker": Accent and identity in the L2—and the L1. *Canadian Modern Language Review, 59*(2), 264–281. doi:10.3138/cmlr.59.2.264

McVee, M. B., Dunsmore, K., & Gavelek, J. R. (2005). Schema theory revisited. *Review of Educational Research, 75*(4), 531–566. https://doi.org/10.3102/00346543075004531

Nation, I. S. P. (1990). *Teaching and learning vocabulary.* Newbury House.

Nation, I. S. P. (2000). Learning vocabulary in lexical sets: Dangers and guidelines. *TESOL Journal, 9*(2), 6–10. https://doi.org/10.1007/978-0-387-30424-3_147

Nation, I. S. P. (2001). *Learning vocabulary in another language.* Cambridge.

Nation, I. S. P. (2006). How large a vocabulary is needed for reading and listening? *The Canadian Modern Language Review, 63*(1), 59–82. https://www.lextutor.ca/cover/papers/nation_2006.pdf (accessed March 25, 2021).

Nation, I. S. P. (2008). *Teaching vocabulary: Strategies and techniques.* Heinle Cengage.

Nation, I. S. P., & Waring, R. (1997). Vocabulary size, text coverage and word lists. In N. Schmitt & M. McCarthy (Eds.), *Vocabulary: Description, acquisition, and pedagogy* (pp. 6–19). Cambridge University Press.

Parlindungan, F. (2018). What research has to say about spelling instruction for English language learners. Proceedings from the *International Seminar on English language Teaching and Research (ELTAR)*, Malang, Indonesia.

Pulido, D., & Hambrick, D. Z. (2008). The virtuous circle: Modeling individual differences in L2 reading and vocabulary development. *Reading in a Foreign Language, 20*(2), 164–190. doi:10.7916/D89C7900

Qureshi, M. A. (2018). Teaching high-frequency vocabulary. In K.M. Reynolds (Ed.), *The TESOL encyclopedia of English language teaching.* Wiley. https://doi.org/10.1002/9781118784235.eelt0749

Reynolds, K. M. (2018). Teaching notional concepts: Time, numbers, distance, size, dimension, shapes, colors, and patterns. In K. M. Reynolds (Ed.), *The TESOL encyclopedia of English language teaching.* Wiley. https://doi.org/10.1002/9781118784235.eelt0792

Rosselli, M., Ardila, A., Matute, E., & Vélez-Uribe, I. (2014). Language development across the life span: A neuropsychological/neuroimaging perspective. *Neuroscience Journal.* https://doi.org/10.1155/2014/585237

Sanaoui, R. (1995). Adult learners' approaches to learning vocabulary in second languages. *The Modern Language Journal, 79*(1), 15–28. https://doi.org/10.1111/j.1540-4781.1995.tb05410.x

Selinker, L. (1972). Interlanguage. *International Review of Applied Linguistics, 10*(1–4), 209–231. https://doi.org/10.1515/iral.1972.10.1-4.209

Shaffer, D. E. (2013). An inductive approach to young learner grammar. *Korea Association of Primary English Education International Conference*, Seoul, South Korea.

Sharkey, S. G., & Folkins, J. W. (1985). Variability of lip and jaw movements in children and adults: Implications for development of speech motor control. *Journal of Speech, Language, and Hearing Research, 28*(1), 8–15. https://doi.org/10.1044/jshr.2801.08

Shemesh, R., & Waller, S. (2006). *Teaching English spelling: A practical guide.* Cambridge.

Şik, K. (2014). *Using inductive or deductive methods in teaching grammar to adult learners of English* [Unpublished Master's thesis]. Erzincan University.

Silver, H. F., Dewing, R. T., & Perini, M. J. (2012). *The core six: Essential strategies for achieving excellence with the common core*. Association for Supervision and Curriculum Development (ASCD).

Smith, A., & Zelaznik, H. N. (2004). Development of functional synergies for speech motor coordination in childhood and adolescence. *Developmental Psychobiology, 45*, 22–33. doi:10.1002/dev.20009

Stirling, J. (2011). *Teaching spelling to English language learners*. Lulu Publishing.

Swan, M., & Smith, B. (2002). *Learner English: A teacher's guide to interference and other problems* (2nd ed.). Cambridge University Press.

Tarone, E. (1979). Interlanguage as chameleon. *Language Learning, 29*(1), 181–191. https://doi.org/10.1111/j.1467-1770.1979.tb01058.x

Tzampazi, S. G. (2019). *The effects of deductive, inductive and a combination of both types of grammar instruction in pre-sessional classes in higher education (Publication No.)* Doctoral dissertation, University of Bedfordshire. University of Bedfordshire Open Repository.

Vihman, M. M. (2009). Word learning and the origins of phonological system. In S. Foster-Cohen (Ed.), *Language acquisition* (pp. 15–39). Palgrave Macmillan.

Werker, J. F., & Tees, R. C. (1983). Developmental changes across childhood in the perception of non-native speech sounds. *Canadian Journal of Psychology/Revue Canadienne de psychologie, 37*(2), 278–286. https://doi.org/10.1037/h0080725

Willingham, D. T. (2015). *Raising kids who read*. Jossey-Bass.

Yoshida, M. (1978). The acquisition of English vocabulary by a Japanese speaking child. In E. M. Hatch (Ed.), *Second language acquisition* (pp. 91–100). Newbury House.

Zharkova, N., Hewlett, N., & Hardcastle, W. J. (2011). Coarticulation as an indicator of speech motor control development in children: An ultrasound study. *Motor Control, 15*(1), 118–140. https://doi.org/10.1123/mcj.15.1.118

Zimmerman, C. B. (2014). Teaching and learning vocabulary for second language learners. In M. Celce-Murcia, D. M. Brinton, and M. A. Snow (Eds.), *Teaching English as a second/foreign language* (pp. 288–302). National Geographic Learning/Heinle/Cengage Learning.

10

What Themes, Topics, and Content Can I Employ?

How TESOL educators strive to meet students' personal and academic goals through choices about content in language, academic, and vocational programs will be discussed in this chapter. You will learn about topical or thematic instruction, content-based instruction (CBI), vocational English, and English for specific purposes (ESP).

Learning Outcomes

At the conclusion of this chapter, you will be able to:

- describe the complex balance between language and content instruction
- justify various approaches to content selection for differing learner populations
- apply different models of and instructional practices in CBI or ESP

Have you ever thought about how educators collaborate when one is an expert in science, math, history, health, art, or music and the other in TESOL? In this vignette, we observe how one TESOL educator collaborated with her colleague to create a meaningful learning experience in a push-in model of CBI.

TESOL Voices

As a doctoral student and then assistant professor, I spent about 6 years researching, presenting, and consulting on best practices for ESL teachers to collaborate with content teachers. Then, my husband's job transferred us to a different region of the world, and I excitedly accepted a position teaching ESL in a middle school. I was assigned to be a push-in teacher in a science class in addition to teaching ESL 1 and 2. Through past experience, as well as my own research, the push-in model was my least favorite model; I often saw the ESL teacher's expertise not being utilized as she usually sat watching the content teacher's lecture before walking around to support ELLs. I wanted to be an equal partner in the science teacher's classroom, but it was her space. I now had to rely on my own advice to propel our collaboration forward. I asked how she planned, and we discussed how we could work together to best support the learners' needs. She gave me a science text and

---

Introduction to TESOL: Becoming a language teaching professional, First Edition. Kate Mastruserio Reynolds, Kenan Dikilitaş, and Steve Close.

allowed me the opportunity to go through all of her teaching resources. We had a little time to plan together, but it was not enough to truly co-plan and co-teach. We did, however, email and have discussions during lunch. We got into a routine; I knew what she was going to focus on and how she was going to teach the material.

Because I attended science class with my ELLs, I knew what the expectations were. I could focus on their language needs while the science teacher focused on content. As a bonus, though, I was learning more about the content from her, while she learned more about language acquisition from me. When the students were in my class, I previewed the upcoming science lesson; I would pull out the key concepts to preteach. We would focus on building background, activating their prior knowledge so when they went to science class, they could more easily make connections. We had many different ways to do this. For example, students worked in groups with sticky tabbed chart paper with pictures or concepts on it. They would write what they knew, ask questions, and make predictions; they could add to the charts as we went through the week, adding words, phrases, sentences, or pictures. Students interacted and had opportunities to use their L1 to clarify and confirm understandings. Then, collaborating with our resourceful librarian, I would select a text, usually nonfiction, which connected to what their science lesson was going to be about. For a lesson on habitats and adaptations, we read a nonfiction story which was about arctic animals' survival that included many of the vocabulary words they were working on in science class, but was less complicated than their textbook. We also could work on reading and listening comprehension, and practice speaking and writing. There were some activities that the publishing company created for ELLs that were useful. For example, when learning about weather, we used a weather map activity where students had to identify the weather symbols to predict the weather. In science class, they were assessed by presenting a weather forecast to the class, so in ESL I made sure they knew the vocabulary, the symbols, and sentence structures to help them create their forecast, so they were prepared when they were in science.

The science teacher and I got into our groove, but what was really exciting was the interest of other teachers who wanted to co-teach. The principal supported this initiative, including making sure there was time for co-planning. I provided professional development for "how" to do this, and ultimately the teachers the following year would decide how they wished to carry it out.

Angela B. Bell, PhD
Visiting Assistant Professor, TESOL
Missouri State University

Topics, Themes, and Content, Oh My!

In the previous four chapters, you have learned about approaches to second language teaching that focus on language instruction. Topics and themes have been referenced in general since TESOL educators often employ them as a focal point of learning. Content has been treated as synonymous with material being studied or an academic subject. As this point, it is important to dive into and distinguish these areas as TESOL educators do.

With a topic or theme in mind, the educator can identify how to integrate the four skills, which aspects of the four skills connect, and what materials exist on the topic/ theme that would engage their learners. Of course, the topic/theme would be chosen according to the age, proficiency, and context of the language learners. We will first explore topical and thematic language instruction, then we will move onto other types of content.

Topics as unifying forces

In many contexts, students the world over learn English in authentic and meaningful ways through topics that are personal and social. These topics may include families, travel, school, daily living, occupations, holidays, entertainment, and sports. We may also teach topics such as the environment, technology, modern society, or social/polit-ical topics. For any of these topics, you can imagine what we say about them, listen to others talk about them, read, or write about them. Clear sets of vocabulary can be related to them. You can infuse into any of these topics many different activities and learning strategies.

Often educators will choose a topic, because it is compelling or fun for the learners. Deckert (2004) suggested that topic-focused lessons should be ethnically important. He writes:

> Lesson topics must help ESL students: (a) adjust to local surroundings, (b) appre-ciate unfamiliar learning strategies, (c) explore genuine interests, (d) embrace institutional standards of conduct, and (e) foster mutual acceptance in the face of conflicting perspectives. (p.73)

Deckert's perspective emphasizes contextual awareness and social responsibility in addition to learners' interests when choosing topics. When we focus on these things, learners will be more motivated in their learning. Often TESOL educators will conduct an interest inventory (i.e., a survey or questionnaire that gathers learners' favorite top-ics, subjects, hobbies, activities, etc.) at the beginning of a term or course to identify the areas of study that may be compelling for learners. This may be challenging when the textbook has long been ordered. A work-around is to provide learners an interest inventory and a list of topics from the text for them to rank.

Themes as unifying forces

Thematic instruction involves arranging learning around a unifying idea. For example, themes for lower grades may include exploration, mysteries, overcoming obstacles, hero-ism, and going green. For middle school, themes about equality and justice are good choices. Courage, adventure, power, change, and hope can be motivating for middle schoolers, because they are becoming increasingly aware of the world around them. High school and adult learners tend to do better with topics such as adulting (high school), individuality, tolerance, endurance, self-actualization, happiness, materialism/consump-tion, responsibility, compassion, humanity, spirituality, success, and peace and harmony.

Aren't topics and themes the same?

What distinguishes topical instruction from thematic instruction is that topics focus on a narrow subject, whereas themes are broad ideas that may be linked to other areas or perspectives. Students and educators can explore a theme from personal, social, economic, political, psychological, philosophical, spiritual, or environmental angles and identify resources from different genres, academic subjects, or voices. For example, when exploring the theme of happiness, educators can draw on literature or poetry about happiness, newspaper articles about the happiest country in the world (i.e., Denmark), or psychological measurements of happiness.

Thematic instruction is often made compelling for the learners through the use of an "essential question," which is open-ended and intellectually engaging. With the theme of happiness, essential questions could be: What is happiness? How do you know when you are happy? (For more on thematic instruction, see http://nhprojectliteracy. blogspot.com/p/thematic-instruction.html. For more on essential questions, see McTighe & Wiggins, 2013, http://www.ascd.org/publications/books/109004/chapters/ What-Makes-a-Question-Essential%A2.aspx)

Aside from topics (narrow subjects) and themes (ideas with interconnected areas/ perspectives), we must also address "content." Content is linked to the material being studied or an academic subject. As a term, "content" has a variety of definitions within TESOL. We use the context of the discussion to determine which definition of content is being utilized, and in this context, content refers to academic subjects. The instruction of academic subjects is called *content-based instruction* (CBI).

History of CBI

CBI originated in dual-language bilingual immersion programs in the 1970s. For example, learners may learn biology in French and geometry in English. But the relationship between language and academic subject learning was first outlined by Bernard Mohan in his book, *Language and Content* (1986). In it, he addressed ways in which English can be a medium of instruction for academic learning within countries where English is not the dominant language. This idea was contrasted to teaching "language," which, at that time, involved teaching topics via communicative language teaching, the Audiolingual Method, and other methodologies along with vocabulary sets, grammatical points, common expressions/phrases, and cultural patterns. CBI allows for teaching ELLs history/social studies, English literature, math, science, art, physical education, or music in either (a) general education classrooms with their native-speaking peers, or (b) "sheltered" classrooms with only other ELLs. Sheltered instruction may have both meanings though since the term has evolved to describe the instructional practices teachers can use to include and support ELLs in their classes (Echevarria et al., 2013).

What is general education and mainstreaming?

General education refers to the academic instruction that all students learn. For example, all students learn reading, writing, literature, math, history, and science. The concept of general education is distinguished by TESOL educators from

English language learning in ESL classes. Sometimes you may hear a TESOL educator referring to mainstream classes. They are referencing general education classes. Mainstreaming also refers to including ELLs in the general education class through content and language integrated instruction or sheltered-content instruction.

Controversy in the field: Which one has priority, content or language?

One controversial discussion about teaching CBI revolves around the question of which has most importance: language learning, academic information, or a balance of both. Imagine a continuum with language learning on one end and academic knowledge on the other (Figure 10.1). Moving the slider toward content allows the content learning to take on primary importance with language learning coming second. Moving the slider toward language renders language more important than the content.

This concept can be demonstrated with the example of learning French at an intensive language school, where the curriculum includes a course on the French Revolution. The instructor, a French teacher, would teach about the causes of the French Revolution, how the monarchy was overthrown, how many governmental changes occurred over the next 30 years as well as the key players (i.e., Louis XVI, Marie-Antoinette, and Robespierre), crucial moments (i.e., fleeing the Louvre Palace) and iconic concepts (i.e., Madame Guillotine). The instructor would teach the vocabulary related to the subject as well as any pronunciation or grammar concepts to support learners' acquisition of the language. The instructor would also provide opportunities for learners to interact on the different events and concepts. The details of the French Revolution would be less important than the exposure to and practice with the language. Learners would be assessed based on their listening comprehension, speaking, reading comprehension, and writing, not necessarily on the historical knowledge. This is a form of CBI that is more language focused, because language learning takes priority over the academic subject.

CBI that is more academic-information-focused occurs when learners study in K–12 or university and are held accountable for their grade-level academic knowledge on standardized tests. An example of this would be students who are learning the order of operations in math and the need to use this knowledge for all future learning. The teacher, a math educator, would explain the order of operations and why students need to follow this order to arrive at a result. The educator would make modifications in their instruction to support ELLs' comprehension (e.g., checking to be sure

Language   Content

Figure 10.1   Language and content continuum.

students know the vocabulary words for the different operations, slowing speech, giving examples and demonstrations), and possibly provide opportunities to interact on the subject. However, at the end of instruction it is critical that the students understand and can use the order of operations. If they learned the term "exponents" along the way, that is a bonus. So, the academic subject takes priority over the language learning.

Ideally, educators want to achieve a balance between both of these ends of the continuum, so that learners can learn the language to facilitate learning, but also develop their language abilities, while learning the content. This approach is now called content and language integrated learning (CLIL). The success of integrating and supporting both language and content learning may depend on the context and priorities of the school or program in which an educator works. In this volume, we often use the overarching term CBI to include all three of these approaches, but our philosophy and the suggestions we make come from the idea that both priorities can be fully integrated. Of course, depending on the context, educators may need to shift their priorities slightly in one direction or other on the slider.

Combining the teaching of language and academic subjects has evolved considerably since the 1980s. CBI has become a dominant instructional approach in second language contexts, and to a lesser degree employed in EFL contexts.

Questions for reflection

- Have you participated in a topical, thematic or CBI class? Was it motivating? Did it focus more on language, content, or balance them both?
- Which approach do you prefer for your own teaching? Why?

Controversy in the field

Educators are usually prepared to teach in one subject area. Science teachers learn to teach biology. Math teachers learn to teach algebra. History teachers learn about world history. ESL teachers learn to teach language. Right? These traditional field distinctions were blurred because of CBI. If learners are going to learn anatomy *and* acquire the language, who is the most qualified educator to teach them? Is it the science teacher or the ESL teacher? The ESL teacher does not know the science or inquiry learning and the science teacher does not know the English linguistics, SLA principles, or ESL instructional practices.

Many educators have sought to resolve this quandary. Four different approaches have been tried.

1. In a perfect world, it would be ideal to prepare educators equally in both areas. However, that approach could nearly double the time and money needed to obtain a teaching license, so it is not very realistic.
2. In some contexts, though, teams of academic subject and ESL teachers co-teach, so both areas of expertise can be called upon. A variant of that approach

is called push-in, in which the ESL specialist goes with the ELLs into the academic subject class for support purposes.

3. Another approach would be to only allow ESL teachers to become licensed to teach an academic subject and ESL. Many places do this.

4. Yet another approach is to require academic subject educators to become prepared to work with ELLs in their classes through their teacher preparation programs or professional development. In the United States, it is increasingly common for states to require general educators to have coursework about working with ELLs.

How schools and school districts resolve the issue of teaching expertise depends on many factors such as money, teacher preparation and receptivity, numbers of ESL specialists, and numbers of ELLs per grade in a given school, for example. Whatever approach schools and school districts decide upon, though, the decision should prioritize ELLs' learning in both the academic subject and the language.

Intersections of Content and Language Teaching/Learning

Models to combine the teaching of language and academic content have been developed since the mid-1990s. Educators, both general educators and ESL specialists, are prepared to teach ELLs the content and language they need to achieve in grade-level academics and language. We will provide an overview of some of the most prevalent models of CBI, all of which are represented by acronyms. The field, though, has a wealth of research, professional development material, and instructional practices on these models and others. For a detailed analysis of content-based ESL instructional models, you might want to explore *Approaches to Inclusive English Classrooms: A Teacher's Handbook for Content-Based Instruction* by Kate Mastruserio Reynolds (2015).

All models of CBI draw upon similar theories and instructional practices in language classes, with only minor variations. Comprehensible input (i + 1), pushed output, and interaction are theoretical principles common in CBI models. Some models are also built on cognitive learning theory. All CBI models will integrate the four language skills through interactive, communicative activities, games, songs, and tasks. Some emphasize literacy more than others. The four tools are implicitly acquired in some models through interaction, whereas other models are more explicit in their instruction of forms and linguistic patterns. All CBI models recognize the need for a supportive learning environment.

No matter which model is employed, the study of CBI is centered around several broad areas:

1. Lesson planning—content and language student learning outcomes,* learning strategy outcomes, and four skills integration.

2. Background knowledge.

3. Lesson delivery—comprehensible input in immersion/presentation of new material (e.g., making content input meaningful through teacher's linguistic modifications; clarity in direct teaching of concepts; explicit teaching of vocabulary; explicit and implicit teaching of language patterns such as discourse, syntax, and grammar patterns).
4. Pushed output through interaction, practice, and application.
5. Instructional strategies, tools, and techniques, which often come from ESL/EFL, teaching techniques, such as total physical response (TPR).
6. Materials support for ELLs.
7. Assessment accommodations and support.

*Student learning outcomes are similar to objectives mentioned in the studies described later in the chapter. You can read more about them in Chapter 12.

It is important to remember that all language teaching techniques discussed in the previous chapters should be infused at various places in lessons in CLIL in order to make content meaningful and memorable and interact in the four language skills.

Models of Content and Language Instruction

Sheltered instruction observation protocol

The sheltered instruction observation protocol (SIOP) model is a widely employed model that combines content and language into an eight-component instructional program. The model was the result of intensive observation of sheltered-content teaching in the United States to identify the practices that yield effective academic and language learning. The designers of the SIOP model have conducted research on the observation protocol and the model and have found that an intentional implementation of each of the components results in academic achievement and second language learning, particularly in areas of literacy (Short, 1993, 1994, 2002; Short & Echevarria, 1999; Echevarria, Short et al., 2006; Echevarria, Vogt et al., 2013; Kareva & Echevarria, 2013).

The SIOP model spans lesson planning, delivery, and assessment in these categories: preparation, building background, comprehensible input, strategies, interaction, practice/application, lesson delivery, and review/assessment (Echevarria et al., 2013). General educators and ESL specialists teaching sheltered-content courses prepare lessons that have a dual focus of academic content and language by creating objectives of each type for each lesson. They determine the learners' background knowledge of the academic topic and build it when necessary through direct instruction, discussion, or other input sources. SIOP educators are aware of comprehensible input and modify their speech to make it more understandable to learners. They pace their lessons, so allow for more thinking time. They also choose input sources that are accessible. They may preteach vocabulary to increase comprehensibility. SIOP educators may teach learning or language learning strategies and they do so by using a variety of ESL instructional strategies. SIOP lessons include time for students to interact in discussions to explore the academic topic, and practice and application activities and tasks. Finally, SIOP educators create opportunities for ongoing review and assessment of both content and language.

SIOP model

The SIOP model has 30 techniques organized within the 8 categories of the model. These are:

Lesson preparation:
1. Content objectives clearly defined, displayed, and reviewed with students.
2. Language objectives clearly defined, displayed, and reviewed with students.
3. Content concepts appropriate for age and educational background level of students.
4. Supplementary materials used to a high degree, making the lesson clear and meaningful (e.g., computer programs, graphs, models, visuals).
5. Adaptation of content (e.g., text, assignment) to all levels of student proficiency.
6. Meaningful activities that integrate lesson concepts (e.g., interviews, letter writing, simulations, models) with language practice opportunities for reading, writing, listening, and/or speaking.

Building background:
7. Concepts explicitly linked to students' background experiences.
8. Links explicitly made between past learning and new concepts.
9. Key vocabulary emphasized (e.g., introduced, written, repeated, and high-lighted for students to see).

Comprehensible input:
10. Speech appropriate for students' proficiency levels (e.g., slower rate, enunciation, and simple sentence structure for beginners).
11. Clear explanation of academic tasks.
12. A variety of techniques used to make content concepts clear (e.g., modeling, visuals, hands-on activities, demonstrations, gestures, body language).

Strategies:
13. Ample opportunities provided for students to use learning strategies.
14. Scaffolding techniques consistently used, assisting and supporting student understanding (e.g., think-alouds).
15. A variety of questions or tasks that promote higher-order thinking skills (e.g., literal, analytical, and interpretive questions).

Interaction:
16. Frequent opportunities for interaction and discussion between teacher/student and among students, which encourage elaborated responses about lesson concepts.
17. Grouping configurations support language and content objectives of the lesson.
18. Sufficient wait time for student responses consistently provided.
19. Ample opportunities for students to clarify key concepts in L1 as needed with aide, peer, or L1 text.

Practice and application:

20. Hands-on materials and/or manipulatives provided for students to practice using new content knowledge.
21. Activities provided for students to apply content and language knowledge in the classroom.
22. Activities integrate all language skills (i.e., reading, writing, listening, and speaking).

Lesson delivery:

1. Content objectives clearly supported by lesson delivery.
2. Language objectives clearly supported by lesson delivery.
3. Students engaged approximately 90–100% of the period.
4. Pacing of the lesson appropriate to students' ability levels.

Review and assessment:

1. Comprehensive review of key vocabulary.
2. Comprehensive review of key content concepts.
3. Regular feedback provided to students on their output (e.g., language, content, work).
4. Assessment of student comprehension and learning of all lesson objectives (e.g., spot checking, group response) throughout the lesson.

(Kareva & Echevarria, 2013, p. 248)

The SIOP approach has been criticized by some educators owing to the complexity of planning and implementation. One criticism from those preparing teachers to use the model is that it does not seem to be organized in a manner that makes sense. For example, SIOP places comprehensible input and background building as part of lesson delivery when it would seem more appropriate to view them as part of preparation. The model does highlight for general educators and ESL specialists critical considerations and effective practices for integration of content and language for ELLs. Despite these minor criticisms, SIOP continues to have positive effects within K–12 schools.

Specially designed academic instruction in English

Specially designed academic instruction in English (SDAIE) is a model of content and language integration that emerged from instructional practices used with ELLs by the Los Angeles Unified School District (LAUSD) and is widely employed in California (Reynolds, 2015). The model serves as a bridge between programs. It was initially geared toward high-intermediate ELLs to facilitate their transfer between bilingual classes to general education classes in only English. Since there are so many ELLs in Californian schools (i.e., high incidence context), learners who arrive are initially provided instruction in a newcomers' English language development (ELD) program. Once ELLs have achieved a level of social and academic language, they move to content and language instruction in the SDAIE model before they transition to general education courses.

The SDAIE model comprises four elements: content, connections, comprehensibility, and interaction (Reynolds, 2015). Content includes content, language, and learning strategy objectives and materials. Connections is about facilitating the links between learners' experiences and concepts, using examples they provide to enrich learners' understandings and linking old and new information in learners' schemas. The element of comprehensibility describes making the material comprehensible in presentations of new material, and checking students' comprehension during these presentations. Lastly, the element of interaction reminds educators to provide opportunities for the learners to use the language to talk about lesson content and represent their understandings in differing formats. One additional element was added by Díaz-Rico (2018). She included teacher attitude, which describes teachers' receptivity to learn from students. A good addition to teacher attitude is viewing ELLs positively for their bilingualism and funds of knowledge (i.e., background and experiential knowledge learners bring to the classroom) (Moll et al., 1992). Being willing to make language learning culturally congruent and relevant is also a factor that could be added in this element. While the SIOP model more or less follows an outline that flows from lesson planning and delivery to assessment, the SDAIE model is more fluid and dynamic in the ways the components interact (Cline & Nocochea, 2003).

The SDAIE model

The SDAIE model encompasses 18 planning and instructional practices that guide educators to make content learning comprehensible while building language abilities.

Content:
1. Content objective.
2. Language objective.
3. Learning strategy objective.
4. Materials and texts that are (a) clear and meaningful, and (b) support objectives.

Connections:
5. Bridging concepts and skills linked to student experiences.
6. Bridging examples students provide from their lives to content.
7. Schema building to link new and old learning through scaffolding strategies (i.e., webs, semantic maps, visual organizers, etc.).

Comprehensibility:
8. Contextualizing materials by using pictures, maps, graphs, charts, models, diagrams, gestures, labels, and dramatizations to illustrate concepts clearly.
9. Appealing to a variety of learning styles.
10. Modeling/demonstrating skills or concepts to be learned.
11. Speech adjustment: (a) slower rate of speech, (b) clear enunciation, and (c) controlled use of idioms.
12. Regular use of comprehension checks.

13. Appropriate questioning.
14. Recitation and paraphrasing.

Interaction:
15. Opportunities for students to talk/interact about lesson content (i.e., teacher to student, student to teacher, student to student, student to content, student to self).
16. Clarification of concepts in L1.
17. Use primary language material.
18. Re-presentation of understanding. Students transform knowledge through illustration, dramatization, song creation, dance, story rewriting, and critical thinking.

(Díaz-Rico, 2018)

Some criticisms of the model revolve around the lack of a formally structured format (i.e., operationalized definition in researcher talk) and lack of research validation. There are only three research studies into the effectiveness of the SDAIE model, which have conflicting findings (Reynolds, 2015). In research comparing the SDAIE model to the SIOP, Echevarría and Short (2010) noted these concerns, but also recognized the value of elements and techniques of the SDAIE model.

Cognitive Academic Language Learning Approach

The Cognitive Academic Language Learning Approach (CALLA) is the oldest approach to outline the practices that are effective for ELLs. It has been highly influential to other models of CBI.

Since it was articulated starting in the 1980s, the model has relied on theories and practices, but does not outline them like the SIOP or SDAIE models do. Based in cognitive theory, the CALLA approach emphasized three types of knowledge: declarative, procedural, and metacognitive. When we learn a concept and can discuss it, that is *declarative knowledge*. When we learn how to follow the steps to the scientific method, for example, that is *procedural knowledge*. When we can analyze our thinking about a concept or procedural, that is *metacognitive knowledge*. The CALLA approach encourages educators to build these three types of knowledge about the content and language. It also is concerned with learners' schemas and linking their content and language learning to existing knowledge structures in long-term memory.

Chamot and O'Malley, who developed the approach in 1986, were influenced by discourse analysis and studies of discourse patterns. They presented in their 1994 text discourse features of history, math, and science (Chamot & O'Malley, 1994). So, the patterns of language usage in these areas were explicitly taught to students in the CALLA approach.

They were also influenced by the language experience approach (see Chapter 7), which transforms students' oral descriptions of experiences into written form so as to build learners' knowledge of writing, reading, grammar, and vocabulary. They also spearheaded the notion of content and language objectives that connect, so learners can acquire the language using content material. They took this idea one step further by including learning strategy objectives too.

Within the CALLA approach, learning strategies and language learning strategies are "tricks" used by learners to remember, think about, and figure out new information, garner support in the language learning process, and compensate for areas of weakness. In the CALLA model, learning strategies are taught explicitly in a step-wise manner along with practice opportunities. Utilizing learning strategies is a means for learners to become more independent in their learning processes.

Prior to instruction, teachers using the CALLA approach assess learners' background knowledge through needs assessments. *Needs assessments* are pretests of content, language, or learning strategies. For more on the design and implementation of needs assessments, see Butler et al. (2015) and Reynolds (2015). For more information on the types of language learning strategies, see Oxford (1990).

Within the CALLA approach, instruction of content, language, and learning strategies follow five sequenced steps.

1. Preparation—The teacher develops students' awareness through activities that activate background knowledge.
2. Presentation—The teacher explains content, language, or learning strategies through direct instruction and modeling.
3. Practice—Students practice the concept or strategy through activities and tasks with guidance/coaching and detailed feedback from the teacher.
4. Evaluation—Students evaluate their own learning. The teachers assess learners' knowledge and skills.
5. Expansion—Teachers encourage the learners to transfer their knowledge and skills to other relevant areas. Students may do expansion activities to further elaborate their knowledge.

The model draws upon research in input, interaction, and output by Teresa Pica, Michael Long, and others, but only one research study has been conducted to validate the entire approach (Chamot, 2007). Most of the elements have been subsumed by other more widely known models, and this model has not been developed much in the past 10 years.

CLIL

The CLIL model was developed in the European Union (EU) for monolingual or bilingual language and content teaching of any of the 24 languages spoken in the EU. Educators who employ the CLIL model integrate two of the model's five elements into lessons. The elements are: culture, environmental, language, content, and learning. Educators teach learners knowledge of culture and how to communicate interculturally. Educators attend to the linguistic needs of the local community with the goal of internationalization. They may teach Italian artists language needed to present their work in Sweden. In CLIL, meaningful learning is a priority. Educators present and provide learning experiences that connect the content and language through activities in order to acquire the grammar, vocabulary, and pronunciation for communication in the field. Educators teach the content learners need explicitly. Finally, educators integrate a variety of instructional techniques, activities, and tasks into lessons to actively engage learners with the content, language, and communication strategies (Reynolds, 2015).

Guided Language Acquisition Design

The Guided Language Acquisition Design (GLAD) model was developed in the 1980s and 1990s by Orange County Department of Education in California to integrate the content and language learning of ELLs. It is a popular model on the West Coast of the United States, because the model has outlined many practical instructional activities they can implement immediately in their classes to support ELLs. The GLAD strategies, which are instructional strategies/activities, are differentiated for grade level and proficiency level and can be infused into any content lesson.

The GLAD model is built upon a foundation of literacy instruction for ELLs and native speakers, context-rich interaction, knowledge of vocabulary, grammatical patterns, syntax, and other linguistic features of English. It encompasses 35 instructional strategies within 5 component areas: focus/motivation, input, guided oral practice, reading/writing, and closure.

Project GLAD

GLAD provides teachers practical instructional strategies for implementation in their content courses to support ELLs' content and language learning. The instructional strategies have been categorized into five areas.

1. Unit planning pages:
   a. Teacher explicitly articulates the purpose of the lesson.
   b. Activate background knowledge.
   c. Create shared knowledge.
2. Focus and motivation strategy:
   a. Anchor charts.
   b. Inquiry charts.
   c. Teacher-made big books.
3. Comprehensible input:
   a. Use pictorial, comparative, narrative input charts.
   b. Intentionally chunk lectures (e.g., about 10 min).
   c. Actively participate when the teacher is lecturing (e.g., repeat words/phrases, call and response, use gestures with the teacher).
   d. Support meaning with realia, visuals, movement (i.e., pictorial input charts, graphic organizer input chart).
   e. Make texts accessible.
4. Guided oral practice:
   a. Plan for peer interaction/small-group or paired interaction and team tasks arranged throughout the lesson.
   b. Sentence patterning charts.
   c. Chants and poetry.

d. Mind maps.
e. Expert groups.
5. Reading and writing:
   a. Focus on language through cooperative strip paragraph, ear-to-ear reading, reading logs/journals, interactive journals, portfolios, big books, and sentence patterning charts.
   b. Develop students' learning strategies.
   c. Bridge both languages.
   d. Use a cognitive content dictionary to introduce vocabulary.
   e. Conduct word study by analyzing word parts, parts of speech, patterns, spelling.
   f. Ask learners to retell a story while teachers write their contributions on a chart, which is similar to the LEA.
   g. Focus on writing with writers' workshops.
   h. Attention to reading through paired read-alouds, focused reading and teacher read-alouds.

(Adapted from Education Northwest, n.d.)

Many GLAD strategies are ESL instructional strategies and techniques, but some, such as anchor charts, come from general education.

Research studies by Cawthon (2005) and Hahn (2009) on the effectiveness of GLAD instructional strategies have found that when educators put the strategies into practice properly, the model is effective at developing both content knowledge and second language learning for ELLs. Another study by Deussen et al. (2014) had mixed results.

Questions for reflection

- Which model do you think is the most comprehensive? The most effective?
- Which model would you like to investigate and/or teach in? Why?

ESP

CBI is concerned with teaching academic content (mainly literacy, math, history, science) to ELLs in K–16 while they acquire the new language. CBI is related to English for academic purposes (EAP), which is one area of specialization in ESP. ESP describes the development of tailored coursework, language learning experiences, and assessments related directly to the goals and needs of the learners. Often, but not always, ESP is an approach used for adult learners at community colleges rather than children or teens in the K–12. ESP generally is an approach that can be used worldwide; however, which specialization within ESP may vary according to the context and learners' needs.

Many ELLs seek to learn English to achieve academic, professional, or vocational goals. Each of these areas has been subdivided into specialized instructional fields (see

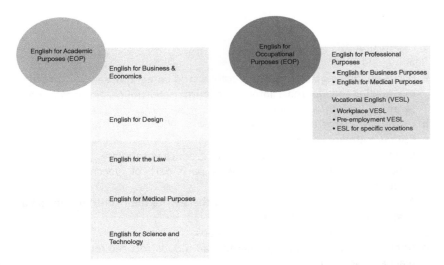

Figure 10.2 English for academic purposes compared to English for occupational purposes.

Figure 10.2). EAP, for example, includes English for medical purposes (i.e., medical English), English for science and technology (EST), and English for the law (i.e., legal English). For individuals studying design, for example, they may also have specific courses using design as the subject in order to develop ELLs' abilities to learn in design courses and communicate about design. Judges in Lebanon may wish to study legal English to be able to read and write about law and precedents with international professional colleagues.

English for occupational purposes (EOP) has two major categories: English for professional purposes, which encompasses English for medical purposes, and English for business purposes; and vocational ESL (VESL), which includes workplace VESL, pre-employment VESL, and ESL for specific vocations.

English for medical purposes may be of interest to nurses, phlebotomists, medics, and ambulance personnel who are already prepared in their field, but need to be able to communicate with English speakers or those who speak English as a lingua franca; for example, Greek medics who need to help international refugees. English for business purposes would be of interest to a person living in China or Chile, for example, who works in international banking, import/export, or manufacturing and sales.

The most common vocational English areas are pre-employment, occupation-specific and workplace ESL. VESL aligns with the English learners' needs in a general preparation for vocational jobs, but VESL also includes occupational-specific English courses; for example, air conditioning repair, welding, electrical, plumbing, or car mechanics. Many individuals need workplace ESL, such as migrant farm workers, factory personnel, or restaurant employees who need to be able to communicate in teams and with employers. One unusual feature of workplace English is that the TESOL educator often goes to the students at their workplace. For example, Kate was once offered a job to teach English to French nuclear physicists who worked at nuclear power stations.

English for business purposes and English for medical purposes are incorporated in both EAP and EOP. The distinction is whether the learners need English for academic study in the field (EAP) or for their jobs (EOP). For example, studying English for pre-med or to become a doctor or nurse is medical English in EAP, whereas studying English to communicate with patients and medical staff in the job is considered medical English in EOP.

The benefits for educators and students of identifying and focusing on these goals are that learning is more personalized, materials more specific and aligned with learners' needs and goals, and the overall lesson is more motivating and meaningful.

Similarities and differences between ESP and CBI

ESP is similar to CBI in that there is the challenge of having two areas of expertise. Some individuals come from TESOL and learn new information about a new field/specialization. Others come to TESOL after years of experience in their vocational/technical or specific academic field, some in their retirement. For example, in legal English, some individuals have a juris doctorate (i.e., law degree) and preparation to teach ESL. They combine their knowledge and skills in both areas to provide learners with authentic, accurate, and meaningful learning experiences in law. They would teach learners to read via legal cases that learners would discuss and debate. Learners would write legal briefs. In these courses, learners may conduct oral arguments in a moot court. Through this narrowed concentration on the topic, learners would acquire the legal vocabulary they needed and the ways that English speakers communicate about the law and to create laws. Often, individuals have expertise in only one area and need to learn the practices of the other. TESOL professionals are often called upon to learn about academic and technical areas far beyond their existing knowledge. Having a growth mindset and a lifelong learning stance helps a great deal with teaching CBI and ESP, as does a solid liberal arts degree and/or vocational preparation; however, sometimes TESOL educators must be a "Jack of all trades" and quickly learn about a new field.

Chapter Conclusions

Motivating learners and providing English learning experiences aligned with their goals and needs are the main catalysts for the development of CBI and ESP. These specializations within TESOL have been developed considerably over time by TESOL professionals, who have contributed to advance the body of research, develop models and programs, and innovate instructional and assessment practices. Having the choice of interesting specializations is one advantage of being a TESOL professional.

Discussion Questions

1 What are the benefits and drawbacks of CBI instruction? How might you lessen the drawbacks?
2 What are the major areas of similarity and difference in CBI by grade cluster (K–2, 3–5, 6–8, 9–12, and 13–16)? How would lesson planning, delivery, materials, and assessments differ at these levels?
3 What are the benefits and drawbacks of ESP instruction? How might you lessen the drawbacks?

4 Which area (e.g., CBI, EAP, VESL, etc.) would you prefer to teach in and why? What would you need to learn to be able to teach in this specialized area? Where would you learn this information? Would it be worthwhile to you to learn in depth about this specialized area? Why or why not?

Tasks

1 Do you feel prepared to teach academics in depth? How about a specific field or vocational area? How might you prepare in advance for CBI or ESP instruction if you had time? How would you prepare if you only had limited time? Outline two or three strategies for each eventuality.

2 Research the CBI model used in an area near you. Interview an educator working in this model to find out why this model is employed as opposed to others. Explore the instructional practices and assessments the educators use to teach in this model. Ask them to share any evidence they can of the effectiveness of the model. Write up your research and share it with your class.

3 Review the legal English example given earlier. Identify a specialization to teach in EOP and outline how and what you would teach. Describe your learner population. Why would this be a meaningful course to them? What topics or themes would you use in a course? What materials? Write up your design and share it with your class.

Further Reading/Read and Discuss

Read about CBI:

Snow, M. A., & Brinton, D. M. (2017). *The content-based classroom* (2nd ed.). University of Michigan Press.

Reynolds, K. M. (2015). *Approaches to inclusive English classrooms: A teacher's handbook for content-based instruction.* Multilingual Matters.

Read about educating adults in workplace VESL:

Anthony, L. (2018). *Introducing English for specific purposes.* Routledge.

Marshall, B. (2002). *English that works: Preparing adult English language learners for success in the workforce and community.* National Center for ESL Literacy Education. http://www.cal.org/caela/esl_resources/digests/Englishwks.html(accessed March 25, 2021).

References

Butler, G., Heslup, S., & Kurth, L. (2015). A ten-step process for developing teaching units. *English Teaching Forum, 53*(3), 2–12. https://americanenglish.state.gov/resources/english-teaching-forum-2015-volume-53-number-3 (accessed March 26, 2021).

Cawthon, S. B. (2005). *Guided Language Acquisition Design (GLAD) training and strategies that enable teachers to successfully help Hispanic English learners accelerate language acquisition and improve academic achievement.* University of La Verne.

Chamot, A. U. (2007). Accelerating academic achievement of English language learners: A synthesis of five evaluations of the CALLA model. In J. Cummins & C. Davison (Eds.), *International handbook of English language teaching* (pp. 317–331). Springer.

Chamot, A. U., & O'Malley, J. M. (1994). *The CALLA handbook: Implementing cognitive academic language learning approach.* Addison Wesley Longman.

Cline, Z., & Necochea, J. (2003). Specially designed academic instruction in English (SDAIE): More than just good teaching. *Multicultural Perspectives, 5*(1), 18–24. https://doi.org/10.1207/S15327892MCP0501_4

Deckert, G. (2004). Guidelines for the selection of topical content in ESL programs. *TESL Canada Journal/Revue TESL du Canada, Special Issue,* (Special Issue 4), 73–88. https://doi.org/10.18806/tesl.v0i0.1041

Deussen, T., Autio, E., Roccograndi, A., & Hanita, M. (2014, April). The impact of Project GLAD on students' literacy and science learning; Year 1 results from a cluster randomized trial of sheltered instruction. *Paper presented at AERA Conference,* Portland, Oregon. https://educationnorthwest.org/sites/default/files/Deussen%20Handout%20Impact%20of%20Project%20GLAD%20on%20Literacy%20Science.pdf (accessed March 26, 2021).

Díaz-Rico, L. T. (2018). *The cross-cultural, language, and academic development handbook: A complete K–12 reference guide.* Pearson.

Echevarría, J., Short, D. J., & Powers, K. (2006). School reform and standards-based education: A model for English-language learners. *The Journal of Educational Research, 99*(4), 195–211. https://doi.org/10.3200/JOER.99.4.195-211

Echevarría, J., & Short, D. (2010). Programs and practices for effective sheltered content instruction. In California Department of Education (Ed.), *Improving education for English learners: Research-based approaches.* CDE Press.

Echevarría, J., Vogt, M. E., & Short, D. J. (2013). *Making content comprehensible for English language learners: The SIOP model* (4th ed.). Pearson.

Education Northwest. (n.d.) *Classroom observation protocol: Project GLAD study.* http://projectgladstudy.educationnorthwest.org/#5 (accessed March 26, 2021).

Hahn, S. L. A. (2009). *Developing the English language vocabulary of native Korean-speaking students through Guided Language Acquisition Design (GLAD).* Unpublished dissertation thesis, University of Oregon. https://scholarsbank.uoregon.edu/xmlui/bitstream/handle/1794/10221/Hahn_Sarah_Leigh-Anne_D.Ed2009sp.pdf (accessed March 26, 2021).

Kareva, V., & Echevarría, J. (2013). Using the SIOP model for effective content teaching with second and foreign language learners. *Journal of Education and Training Studies, 1*(2), 239–248. https://doi.org/10.11114/jets.v1i2.173

McTighe, J., & Wiggins, G. (n.d.). *Essential questions.* Association of Supervision and Curriculum Development. http://www.ascd.org/publications/books/109004/chapters/What-Makes-a-Question-Essential%A2.aspx (accessed March 26, 2021).

Mohan, B. (1986). *Language and content.* Addison Wesley.

Moll, L., Amanti, C., Neff, D., & Gonzalez, N. (1992). Funds of knowledge for teaching: Using a qualitative approach to connect homes to classrooms. *Theory to Practice, 31*(2), 132–141. https://doi.org/10.1080/00405849209543534

Oxford, R. (1990). *Language learning strategies: What every teacher should know.* Heinle.

Reynolds, K. M. (2015). *Approaches to inclusive English classrooms: A teacher's handbook for content-based instruction.* Multilingual Matters.

Short, D. J. (1993). Assessing integrated language and content instruction. *TESOL Quarterly*, *2*(7), 627–656. https://doi.org/10.2307/3587399

Short, D. J. (1994). Expanding middle school horizons: Integrating language, culture and social studies. *TESOL Quarterly*, *28*(3), 581–608. https://doi.org/10.2307/3587309

Short, D. J. (2002). Language learning in sheltered social studies classes. *TESOL Journal*, *11*(1), 18–24. https://doi.org/10.1002/j.1949-3533.2002.tb00062.x

Short, D. J., & Echevarría, J. (1999). *The sheltered instruction observation protocol: A tool for teachers-researcher collaboration and professional development.* Center for Research on Education, Diversity, & Excellence (CREDE)/Center for Applied Linguistics (CAL).

11

How Has Digital Technology Changed Language Teaching and Learning?

Technology has substantially altered the ways TESOL educators engage learners in the learning process both in the classroom and online. Chapter 11 will explore digital technologies to enhance second language learning in face-to-face classes, to extend learning beyond the classroom, and to conduct lessons fully online. Some discussion of effective use of technology to develop learners' four skills and four tools will be included as well as consideration of ineffective applications.

Learning Outcomes

At the conclusion of this chapter, you will be able to:

- combine digital applications with face-to-face learning to increase interaction and provide practice
- apply different approaches to technology integration (e.g., blended learning, flipped classes, and online courses)
- compare and contrast effective and ineffective uses of digital tools for SLA

In the upcoming vignette, two educators working with ELLs in higher education prompt you to consider how digital technology has changed teaching and learning. How has it changed the ways you learn?

TESOL Voices

Digital Engagement in Our Classes

The days of learners writing letters to pen pals or even participating in overseas email exchanges have been replaced by smart watches and Snapchat. Today, learners can send messages to hundreds or even thousands of followers around the world instantly via Twitter or TikTok; they can use Instagram to post a digital photo to several social networking sites simultaneously, or use Zoom to have a live video chat with someone half a world away. In short, learners today have access to information and people around the world like never before. Digital technology has not only changed language teaching and learning practices; it has shaped the way we communicate.

Introduction to TESOL: Becoming a language teaching professional, First Edition. Kate Mastruserio Reynolds, Kenan Dikilitaş, and Steve Close.
© 2022 John Wiley & Sons, Inc. Published 2022 by John Wiley & Sons, Inc.

As an educator, you've probably lost count of how many times you've asked learners to put their cell phones away during class. We all know that our learners are technologically savvy; however, our learners often don't know how best to utilize digital technology tools and resources to learn English. Perhaps, instead of asking our learners to put away or turn off their technology in the classroom, we ought to empower learners to hone their technological skills to reach their English language educational goals. While our learners have the technology proficiency, we have the linguistic and educational expertise. Our job is to bridge the gap in order to increase their language competency and cultural knowledge.

Currently, as educators, we are beginning a new school year and educational institutions from K–12 to higher education are adapting to online teaching platforms. It's uncharted territory not only for teachers, but also learners. Incorporating technology into our classroom enhances the four language skills, provides additional time on task, addresses a variety of learner needs and styles, and increases student motivation and engagement. As educators, we must adapt to enhance learning opportunities for learners.

Recently, we've utilized technology in our classrooms in new and exciting ways by asking an author to join our class via a Zoom discussion of their work, asked our learners to go on virtual museum tours to places they wouldn't normally have had access to, and increased student engagement using mobile phone apps. It's our job as educators to provide opportunities for learners to harness their skills to best utilize these resources to increase English language knowledge. While there are multitudes of digital technological tools and resources, you don't have to use them all—you just have to find what works best for you and your learners.

Mari Bodensteiner and Ami Christensen
Instructors
University of Wisconsin Eau-Claire

What Is the Influence of Technology on English Language Teaching?

Gradually, since the advent of technology in 1980s, English language teaching has progressed in various ways. The opportunity for recording and disseminating the human voice led to increased exposure to authentic human communication. Learning from cassettes developed into learning through digital resources that are accessible and can be improved and multiplied over time. Exposure to the recorded communication and resources has even been replaced by real-time interaction, which has led to increasing opportunities for online intercultural communication. People began to interact with others online for real purposes including business, education, games, and cultural exchange, which has changed the way learning might take place.

Real-time audio/video interaction has accelerated the pace with which people acquire second languages. Through these technologies, learners could acquire language rather than learn it, owing to the availability of this authentic language and opportunities for interaction. Audio/video interaction allows for discourse in English, in real time, with other speakers. Even the millions of videos online can have closed captioning attached, so learners can more fully comprehend the speaker's message. Exposure to systematic comprehensible input based on reading too has now included audio/video format, which constitutes an enriched exposure to comprehensible input. The input has also been transformed into situations where learners can participate in real-time interaction with others for meaningful authentic purposes rather than just "practice." Technology has made accessibility to the abovementioned relevant human resources and materials more possible and has led to an abundance of opportunities for people to develop their language knowledge and skills.

The haves and have nots concern

With all these new opportunities that educational and communication technologies allow, educators need to be mindful of the *digital divide*. The digital divide is a term describing the gap between populations with ready access to technologies and those who do not. Educators should anticipate potential problems around technology ownership and internet access. Not all learners will have a mobile phone to use in class or at home. Some learners may have a mobile phone that is not a smart phone or that lacks internet access. Not all learners have a computer or tablet to use at home. Not all learners live in a household with internet access or with high-speed internet. For some households with internet, there may only be intermittent access.

Some schools ensure that learners have access to computers or tablets by assigning them to learners, yet not all schools or school systems can afford this. Even asking learners to participate in a class game using their mobile phones can highlight differences in ownership. Often, educators partner learners with one another to share mobile phones for activities. The context of learning is a big factor in expectations of technology availability and use. TESOL educators endeavor to anticipate potential issues and equalize learning opportunities so as not to advantage one person over another.

Digital Literacy

Digital literacy refers to the ability to use digital resources including tools, platforms, and digital materials to find, create, and communicate information. Spires et al. (2019) define digital literacy as comprising skills that rely on speaking, listening, reading, writing, and researching; finding, reading/viewing, and vetting information; creating digital content; interacting with others digitally; and sharing digital information through writing or speaking. Digital literacy skills align easily with instructed language learning through particular learning outcomes. Going beyond substituting course materials with the digitalized forms, which involves uploading course documents as PDFs, Word documents, or PowerPoints that can be shared as handouts, digital literacy requires knowing how to digitalize materials, develop engaging courses, and create learning outcomes for higher levels of student engagement in learning, and prolonging task engagement in and beyond the classroom. The main aim in developing a mindset of digital literacy is to create a learning environment and opportunity that transform learning into a relatively more active, interactive, and creative process by integration of multimodal input exposure and output creation including digital media.

Several natural connections exist between teaching/learning practices and digital resources. For example, deeper critical thinking is activated since multiple views are shared and evaluated in online communities. Individuals often engage with multiple sources and synthesize the information. Other critical thinking skills include transformation, analysis, or processing of meaning through questioning and continuous evaluation. Additionally, individuals can promote the depth and breadth of the discussions and offer alternative views that broaden the perspectives. Richer collaboration can occur since individuals can craft objects together from wider distances. Digital resources have been tailored to the ways humans interact, so they allow for the meaningful sharing of knowledge, which can be aligned with SLA practices of comprehensible input, interaction, and pushed output. Finally, digital resources also promote comprehension of enhanced and transformed written texts through media, visuals, audio, and hypertexts.

Digital resources that are currently available can help:

- build networking that continuously interact and develop;
- promote constant dialogic interaction;
- grant autonomy to learners to work interdependently and independently;
- develop agency for learners to self-regulate their learning process;
- create joint developmental tasks; and
- offer process-based review, practice, and assessment opportunities.

Questions for reflection

- Can you identify issues that are relevant to you regarding the meaning of digital literacy?
- How digitally literate do you think you are? Think about what you can and can't do when teaching?
- How might you teach a class with individuals who have access to technology and those who do not?

Computer-assisted or Computer-aided Language Learning

The use of any computer/device, technology, or application in language teaching and learning is referred to as *computer-assisted or computer-aided language learning* (CALL) or *technology-enhanced language learning* (TELL). The acronyms are commonly employed by TESOL educators. The terms encompass all aspects of technology use in language learning from computer software, internet games, chat rooms, applications, and audiobooks online. As new technologies emerge, the CALL/TELL community of TESOL professionals has embraced them. These TESOL professionals also research how CALL/TELL affects L2 learners' SLA, motivation, and engagement.

Blended learning and teaching

Blended learning is described as the modality for course delivery that is achieved as a result of engagement of learners in face-to-face and online modes within the same course. The major rationale behind such course designs is to prolong the time in which learners can work on tasks that are assigned. By, for example, blending some of the tasks and assigning them online to be completed after the class, teachers might compensate for any lost class time or incomplete work in class.

The blending process can be systematically and purposefully organized to engage learners in individual and independent study. Some types of tasks lend themselves to different modalities and digital tools. ELLs need space and time to work individually and strengthen their autonomous learning and develop independence, so educators may choose online or digital learning for individual work. Interactive tasks, projects, or communicative activities would be more appropriate for face-to-face meetings.

There might be some logistical and technical issues in the implementation of the blending process. Therefore, the degree to which any portion of a class will be digitally/online or face-to-face is carefully planned, depending on the available course hours and the objectives that are to be attained by the learners. There are general principles that are recommended in deciding what, how, and why to blend learning with online work.

The modality to be employed to teach the content (i.e., what learners will learn) is chosen based on (a) the best manner to teach and learn the concept(s) and optimize opportunities for language skills/interaction, and (b) the most resourceful use of class time. The common practice is to create online or digital tasks for what can be learned individually or in collaboration with others without needing expert help. These might include practice of what has already been learned in ways that might require student creativity or responding to the assignments. Some tasks might require longer to complete than the allotted class time, such as drafting an essay, so it would be wise to offer longer for individual learner work. Also, tasks that are designed to integrate technology, for example, presentations using visuals and media, require more time and access to the internet so learners can find resources. Information that requires attention and support from the teacher, or that learners might not be able to address and process alone, is assigned to face-to-face meetings. This is not to say that it is necessary to abandon tools like sustained silent reading, drafting a paper, or preparing a presentation in class. These clearly still have their place, but educators need to make these decisions based on their learners and contexts.

Course management/learning systems

An easy definition of course or learning management systems (CMSs) is software that creates an online classroom. CMSs allow educators to create a learning space to share information, encourage interaction, and assess learners' knowledge. CMS software includes Blackboard, Canvas, Desire2Learn, Moodle, Google Classroom, Schoology, Top Hat, and ItsLearning.

CMSs are designed for fully online, blended, or flipped learning. Educators are provided tools for use in their classes, but not all the tools are employed for every class by every teacher. For example, when Kates teaches online she uses the university's CMS, Canvas. In Canvas, there are features that allow her to post threaded discussion topics; share readings, PowerPoints, videos, and URLs; record and share lectures with Panopto; hold synchronous online class meetings with Blackboard Ultra; and set quizzes. Her students see a fully developed series of modules with directions and sequences of learning tasks.

Individuals who are not enrolled in the CMS cannot participate in the course, so it is considered a closed environment. Having a closed environment is important for students' comfort and safety. Open-environment courses exist too; they are called massive open online courses (MOOCs) (for more on MOOCs, see https://www.mooc.org).

Today, many ESL/EFL/ELT instructors tutor online using only Skype or Zoom too.

The online portion of a blended course could aim to improve interaction among learners beyond class time, to prolong the on-task engagement time, or to integrate some facilitating tools such as discussion over scenarios, reading tasks, discussion boards, online collaborative critical/reflective reading and writing, and synopsis writing through video watching or podcasts. These digital facilities could enable learners to initiate interaction followed by reflective discussion and writing, or to engage in a digital simulation followed by a discussion. The online portion of blended courses may need to be monitored and evaluated depending on the learning population and the task. Some closed-network online tools help protect K–12 learners on the internet when doing course discussions and activities, such as Google Classroom and Schoology, which provide interactive platforms that are closed to outside internet traffic. Many educators use online portions of blended courses for evaluation through online quizzes and tests. Many tools have been developed that reduce the possibility of cheating too, such as lockdown browsers and timers.

Synchronous versus asynchronous learning

When educators discuss online or blended learning, they often refer to online meetings with learners as either:

1. *synchronous* in which teachers and learners are present at the same time; or
2. *asynchronous* in which learners participate at different times from each other and their teacher.

Synchronous online meetings have the advantage of immediate interaction, feedback, and support. Synchronous learning also allows participants to convey information much faster via speaking. Learners who are socially motivated or extroverted may prefer synchronous learning.

Asynchronous online instruction is trickier in those areas, since students and teachers may comment on a written post at different times. Asynchronous instruction often relies heavily on learners' ability to comprehend information from reading and listening/video passages without support, and share their thoughts and perspectives in written form. It does have the advantage of allowing learners to learn at their convenience. Learners who are reflective, introverted, or shy may prefer interacting asynchronously.

Educators should also consider the digital divide when making choices about the degree of synchronicity in their online or blended courses. To elaborate, if an educator is in the Philippines, for instance, where learners must pay expensive rates for data and internet access, asynchronous courses are more desirable for learners, because they cost considerably less.

Adult language learners who have jobs and/or families may also prefer asynchronous online instruction owing to the flexibility it offers.

Finally, the online portions of blended classes might include the following course objectives that are promoted in active digital learning:

1. To support learning by interacting.
2. To encourage self-regulated and/or collaborative critical engagement.
3. To stimulate interaction followed by reflective writing.
4. To practice forms and patterns through gaming.

Face-to-face portions in blended learning classes

The face-to-face portion of a blended learning course, on the other hand, can be designed to allow teachers to share concepts and learners to discuss and collaborate, in methods such as task-based language teaching or communicative language teaching, for example. The face-to-face portion is then allocated to introducing new topics, issues, and concepts, which could be challenging for learners to learn by themselves without systematic instruction. Face-to-face courses could help facilitate the exchange of peer feedback, develop class rapport, and provide social and emotional support. The face-to-face portion of the course may also align with the online portion. Based on the reflective discussions and writing, the face-to-face portion might focus on assessing and discussing the online experiences and reflections, thereby complementing the targeted topics and skills under discussion.

Synchronously, the face-to-face portion might have the following objectives:

1. To meet, discuss, reflect, and learn together in a meaningful social environment.
2. To complement the online sessions.
3. To introduce new topics, issues, and concepts used in the online activity.
4. To focus on assessing and discussing online experiences and reflections.
5. To offer a more in-depth discussion of the topics.
6. To provide social (and emotional) ongoing support.

Both portions would be organized to synchronize, to lead to, and to promote active learning while taking the course. Digitalization of content inherently offers active learning and your digital literacy development plays a key role in that of your students. Learners will acquire not only the language skills you are teaching, but also digital literacy skills.

Questions for reflection
• Have you taken blended courses before? If so, what were your experiences in these courses with blended learning?   • What could be new ways you can adapt in the integration of face-to-face and online opportunities?   • What could be the challenges you might have in the blending process and how might you overcome them?

Flipped learning

Flipped learning, as the name implies, assigns new roles to the teachers and learners through the use of technology. It refers to a learning design where learners are supposed to read course materials and watch the lectures, videos, or podcasts before attending the face-to-face meetings in the classroom. The course time is designated for improving dialogic and critical interaction on the content learners have already encountered in the course readings, lectures, and podcasts. The idea is that time spent in the face-to-face meeting would not focus teacher and learners' attention on the delivery of new material; rather, that time would be focused on discussing learners' knowledge and understandings, deepening their understandings, tweezing out misunderstandings and misconceptions, and engaging in pair or group work.

Philosophical and theoretical underpinnings of flipped learning

Flipped learning is mainly designed to grant more autonomy to learners in the learning process and offer an opportunity for the teachers to use class time more efficiently. It also changes the instructional model from a knowledge transmission format to a co-construction of knowledge format. When educators lecture, in many cases, learners expect them to transmit knowledge without the learner needing to do more than grasp a surface-level understanding of the material, remember the material, and restate the material on an assessment. In this model, learning is not necessarily deep, meaningful, or lasting. To allow the material to be learned in a more profound and lasting way, educators can engage learners' brains in the co-construction of knowledge. While learners initially take in different perspectives through readings, videos, podcasts, lectures, etc. prior to the class meeting, when the class convenes educators design learning experiences to prompt learners to enhance their knowledge collaboratively (i.e., co-construct their knowledge) through interaction. This learning perspective is called *social constructivism* or simply *constructivism* (Fosnot, 2005, 2013; Fosnot & Perry, 1996). The links between technology, education, and constructivism have been investigated extensively by Jason Ravitz (https://evaluationbydesign.com).

In moving from teachers having the exclusive role of generator of information to guiding the learning process and causing learners to think critically and participate actively in their own learning changes, many facets of the teaching and learning process are transformed. The workload is shared in time and space. Prior to face-to-face meetings, teachers produce and share digitalized content. Learners work toward understandings and thinking about the material. All of these activities are performed in space outside of the classroom.

Benefits of the flipped design

The "flipped" classroom as a pedagogical design increases the time spent on learning content and engaging in tasks, which are key factors in the quality and amount of learning. It also strengthens learners' sense of responsibility and boosts a sense of confidence, such that they attend the lesson with a great deal of knowledge needed to participate in discussions and generate critical ideas during the courses. In this way, class time is no longer used to introduce new knowledge, but discuss how new knowledge can be built, interpreted, and used.

Despite the pedagogical benefits of a "flipped" classroom, there are some practical challenges for both teachers and learners. Flipping classes in this manner requires a different type of preparation for teachers; sometimes this preparation is more time-consuming. Teachers, for example, need to work harder before the course to prepare the whole course and all the materials. They need to prepare the digital course content by scripting and video recording themselves in order to make them available online. The workload increases for both teachers and learners, which necessitate the course credits to be increased for courses delivered in this mode.

The "flipped" style also requires learners to learn differently, which does not always appeal to all learners. Some learners do not want to read course material outside of class or watch a lecture and take notes. They simply want the teacher to tell them information during class time. They may feel that the only time they have allocated to learning the material is during class time. Another disadvantage could be that some learners may avoid attending class meetings if they have not prepared beforehand, thinking that they will not be able to engage in the discussions built on the content presented in the digital materials.

Educators need to weigh the benefit of more profound and lasting learning against the need to prepare differently or educate learners on how to learn in this format. This requires that teachers use flipped course designs cautiously considering their learners' capacity, commitment, and engagement levels. One suggestion to teachers regarding this concern could be that they flip the course content for certain weeks where they make sure all learners attend to the flipped materials.

Digital tools for flipped classrooms

Finding prerecorded content that aligns with your instructional goals and is appropriate for your learner population is challenging. Whether searching for videos, lectures, or podcasts, we want them to be engaging, succinct, clear, and brief. While YouTube.com may offer videos, the site requires the educator to watch and vet many to ensure they are appropriate for the proficiency level and topic of study. Some reliable sources of high-quality streaming videos that you can use in your ESL/EFL/ELT courses include:

- ESLvideo.com provides video shorts that contextualize a grammatical form and vocabulary in four skills instruction on social topics at each proficiency level. (free)
- Myenglishclub.com includes videos on how to perform common speech acts and grammar forms. It has videos on vocabulary sets and pronunciation points in addition to videos on art, culture, science, nature, news, and history. Some videos have subtitles, but others do not. (free)
- FluentU.com offers a collection of videos and podcasts featuring English speakers all over the world using English authentically to share a wide variety of topics. It also offers music videos, movie trailers, and news so educators can alter genres. A helpful feature is that they are sorted by proficiency level and annotated to support learners' comprehension. (subscription required)
- Podcastsinenglish.com includes hundreds of downloadable listening and video resources on social and academic topics arranged by proficiency level. Transcripts and vocabulary activities are also included. (free)
- Manythings.org, ESL Videos includes a wide range of video content on topics from winemaking to building airplanes. Some videos on grammar, slang, pronunciation, and spelling are included. Many videos include subtitles and transcripts. Some videos may be out of date since the most recent ones are from 2011. (free)
- Teachertube.com provides thousands of videos on English language arts, science, math, history, social studies, and educational songs for K–12. (free)
- TED-Ed (ed.ted.com) makes available hundreds of short 5–6 min videos that investigate academic questions (e.g., can we bring back an extinct species?) for K–16. (free)
- Discoveryeducation.com offers many thorough K–12 content videos, experiential videos, and virtual field trips in social studies and STEM fields. (subscription required)
- Khanacademy.org includes online videos, courses, lessons, and practice on topics ranging from art and reading, to life skills and computing for K–14. (free)
- Learner.org—Annenberg Learner provides a good selection of educational videos arranged by grade level on many academic topics. (free)

Recording information can be challenging because the recording tools offer too many options, which makes them difficult to use. Or they only record the presenter speaking over a PowerPoint or other presentation tool. Kate has long wanted a producer for her recordings to make them more succinct and engaging with multilayered illustrations, visuals, and sounds, so she can avoid being the "talking head" on the screen. Some commonly used recording tools for recording lectures or explanations are:

- Panopto—A tool offered by many universities and some K–12 schools to record lectures of any duration. It is not a free tool, though. Recordings can easily be shared with Canvas CMS.
- Screencast-o-matic—A free tool that allows educators to record up to 15-min talks and share them via a link or on YouTube. Educators can download and save

them as well. This tools is useful for illustrating how to use online technologies, because you can grab everything on your screen.

- Camtasia Studio—Another tool that allows educators to add visual effects and place videos, music, flashcards, quizzes, annotations, animations, and games into PowerPoint presentations. This tool is widely used, but a bit more intricate to use, owing to the number of options it provides. It is a great tool for educators who are more experienced in creating digital recordings. Camtasia offers a basic, free version, but for some of the more advanced options, it requires payment.
- Flipgrid.com, Shorts feature—An online community of educators who share the content and resources they create and curate. The Shorts feature allows educators to record their own video and embed it into the Whiteboard feature for presentation to learners. It requires a free membership and contributions to the community.

Questions for reflection

- What are the advantages and disadvantages of a flipped class arrangement for ELLs?
- How might your teaching in this manner compare to face-to-face L2 classes? What modifications would you need to make, so the course is interactive, supportive, and engaging?

Online instruction

As an alternative to classroom instruction where the teacher and learners are present in a classroom setting, the introduction of internet facilities has allowed new instructional course delivery modes to emerge. Full online courses, for example, can be delivered by tutors who are offering the course online every week without meeting face-to-face in classroom setting.

Some digital education platforms allow online interaction with learners offering opportunities to stream live courses, assign homework, initiate discussions, and grade learners' learning. In such classes, the platform functions like a classroom where the teacher and learners interact and run the courses. This format is call *synchronous*, meaning that the teachers and learners are meeting online at the same time. On the other hand, such a course can be delivered *asynchronously*. In this format, the teacher and learners interact over the course assignments and discussions in written form without meeting in real time. There are also hybrid or blended instruction modes where most courses are synchronously or asynchronously delivered online and a small portion is offered face-to-face. The idea behind face-to-face meetings is to keep learners active and address their questions and concerns with regard to the course content and delivery. It also helps with building learning environments that have good rapport between the teacher and learners, and providing social and emotional support for the learners.

There are several pedagogical as well as logistical advantages of delivering online courses. Pedagogical advantages include:

- They encourage reflective thinkers and more introverted or shy learners.
- They reduce the potential threat of face-to-face classroom encounters (i.e., embarrassment).
- They provide opportunities for learners' simultaneous written responses in the chat box; as opposed to a classroom environment where learners can only talk one after the other.
- Learners can contribute to the discussion as much as they want and read others' comments as they listen to the lecturer.
- They ensure sustained attention to the flow of the session.
- The learners share responsibility during the course with the instructor.

There are also several logistical advantages, which might include:

- Learners can participate in the course in their own location: home, office, via mobile phone, etc.
- Learners can watch the course as it is recorded and note-take comfortably as well as rewatch
- Learners and teachers can enjoy the comfort of home and attend the courses without commuting, which could be challenging particularly in big cities.

In addition to the advantages of such courses for the teacher and learners, some challenges of online coursework need to be highlighted. Teachers have to be much more meticulous in their course preparation since the materials become a digital property available to and accessible by learners even after the courses. There is a higher degree of teacher involvement in delivering the content, responding to the instant comments and questions, promoting and sustaining interaction, etc. Teachers also need to encourage learners to contribute and maintain their motivation in the course.

Along with the potential disadvantages for teachers, learners may find that there are aspects of learning that cannot be effectively implemented in online learning. In such classes there will be relatively few opportunities for group work. Students may feel they do not receive enough of the teacher's attention and feedback. Learning online requires learners to remain focused and active in reading, listening, and writing, which can be demanding. Information that can be shared in an instance in spoken form takes a good deal longer to share in written form. ELLs are further challenged because they may not have the support of teachers or peers to help them express an idea. Finally, they may become mentally overwhelmed because of the need for metacognition.

Having highlighted the advantages and disadvantages to consider, online instruction could be improved for ELLs by attending to the following:

- Establish interpersonal relationships with learners and between learners.
- Create a learning environment that ensures equal and sustained participation.
- Develop different ways of participating, for example, individual, in pairs, or groups.
- Create opportunities for verbal and written communication before, during, or after the courses.
- Integrate new tools for assigning group studies that learners can jointly manage online.

- Include ways for learners to take a brain break or become energized.
- Use other tools to ensure sustained communication about the course content.
- Provide sustained support as some learners are not comfortable with the absence of the physical context of a lecture.
- Use student-sensitive language in written or verbal communication to minimize misunderstanding.

How does teaching English online differ from in-person teaching?

Online instruction differs from in-person teaching in several, significant ways. As an illustration from the United States, Kate taught online via a learning platform, Talk Bean, in the summer of 2008 (the company no longer exists). She taught one-on-one lessons to children and adults learning English in South Korea. She had worked with both children and adults ESL in person prior to that experience, so she had a good deal of experience to bring to online ESL teaching. A detailed description of this platform can provide some clear examples of both the advantages and disadvantages of online learning.

The Talk Bean platform allowed for the seamless integration of visual, audio, instant messaging, and PowerPoint lessons. The PowerPoint lessons consisted of paragraph-long readings on general interest topics and discussion questions. The student and Kate could read the passages, see each other while they discussed the topic, and write questions and examples in the chat box or on the PowerPoint slides. Kate would provide feedback on pronunciation, grammar, or vocabulary throughout the lesson since the emphasis was on oral language and the adult learners wanted correction and feedback. Technically, the platform was excellent in that it allowed for the integration of the four skills in synchronous interaction. It was not designed to allow for a variety of activities, because of the one-to-one nature of the format. All the interaction occurred between Kate and the student, but the interaction was good quality and supported for the student.

Kate found that working in this format was both effective and efficient. However, there were a few notable drawbacks. First, the time difference was 12 hours and needed to be accounted for. Classroom management was a challenge too: not for the adults, who had motivation and maturity, but for the children who would speak only in Korean, wander away from the computer, pound on the keyboard, or write nonsense on the PowerPoint slides or in the chat box. Children need engagement beyond speaking, listening, or learning their alphabet, so the premade curriculum and the format were not workable for them. Furthermore, Kate noted that she needed more movement activities (i.e., kinesthetic activities) with children, and to be able to use tangible, concrete items, such as manipulatives and realia.

From this example, you can see that the platform, format, and synchronicity are important differences between face-to-face and online instruction. How you teach is constrained by the CMS or other digital tools.

Other significant differences are communication, interpersonal relationships, motivation, accountability, classroom management, and types of activities and materials the platform allows. Communication differs between face-to-face and online contexts in whether four skills will be used or only sets of either speaking/listening or reading/

writing. Online instruction that relies too heavily on one language skill may be taxing on learners. Communication may be more easily confused or misinterpreted in online instruction if it is written, so educators need to be mindful of the clarity of their comments. Finally, teachers cannot gauge learners' confusion or frustration in asynchronous online learning because we do not necessarily have access to their nonverbal cues. It is for this reason many educators expect learners to keep their cameras active throughout synchronous meetings.

Advantages and disadvantages of online learning

Online learning also poses advantages and disadvantages for students based on their personal characteristics. For some, online interaction is a threat just as face-to-face interaction is for others. Thriving in an online environment could therefore be a matter of preference for a particular personal communication style that needs to be considered, just as face-to-face interaction might bring with it issues that divert the attention of learners while learning.

Interpersonal relationships develop differently in online environments than in person. Even when cameras are on, we only see the person's face. In person, we understand a great deal more about others, based on their body language alone. Learners do not have many opportunities to socialize in online learning environments as they would before, during, and after a face-to-face class, even though educators strive to develop the learning community. Learners need to trust their peers in ESL classes, so they can take risks without fear of embarrassment. Developing techniques and activities to help learners build interpersonal connections with their peers and the educator is indispensable. Having lived through 2020 and taught online throughout it, we can attest to the pressing need to spend extra time building rapport and developing community.

Motivation and accountability do not look the same in face-to-face and online learning. When a learner attends a class and has not first prepared by reading the dialogue or doing the homework, they may be embarrassed. The social pressures to be prepared and stay on top of work are palpable in a face-to-face class. Online, it is not always obvious if peers have not done their homework or submitted their discussion comments, and such issues often go unnoticed. Educators attempt to encourage learners to keep up with their assignments, but it is simple to postpone it for another day when it is online. Synchronous class meetings tend to help educators hold learners accountable and motivate them in their coursework.

Educators' classroom management in online learning has recently been confronted by Zoom-bombing (i.e., when an uninvited student attends without permission to derail a lesson). This sort of disruption is not the only challenge. Learners' internet connections may be intermittent, which can cause disruption and frustration. This was also seen in the earlier example, which explained that children can be disruptive in an online learning setting, but may also tune out or become distracted. Educators of online ESL classes need to be prepared for the unique classroom management issues that occur in this modality. If you are scheduled to teach young learners (i.e., preschool, K–3), one way to avoid some distractions is to ask a caregiver to be nearby during instruction. Providing some guidelines to the caregiver for how they can help keep their child focused is also a good strategy.

Finally, when comparing online classrooms to face-to-face ones, the types of activities and materials that can be conducted or employed, respectively, may vary. In face-to-face learning, the TESOL educator can use a wide range of exercises, activities, tasks, and projects, and use tangible and concrete items. In online learning, depending on the CMS or learning platform, options for activities are more constrained. For example, some kinesthetic activities, such as "Find someone who...", an icebreaking activity in which learners walk around and chat with multiple peers, would not be effortless to conduct. Material use is substantially curtailed unless all the learners have access to the same materials onsite and have them ready when necessary. It takes planning and coordination to arrange for all learners to have the identical materials at their locations. Organizing multiple learners to interact in pairs or small groups in face-to-face classes is clear-cut, but doing so online takes the right technology and the technological know-how to arrange. Some online tools, such as Zoom and Blackboard Ultra, make it easy to move students into small groups and pull them back when they are finished.

In order to align online language instruction with the macrostrategies and SLA and learning principles, educators must learn the technology well and make the extra effort. Likewise, educators need to anticipate differences between modalities and make back-up or contingency plans to reduce the number or intensity of problems.

Questions for reflection

- Have you taken online courses before? If so, what were your experiences in these courses with online learning?
- What could be the challenges you might have teaching L2 online and how do you think you can overcome them?
- What tools and resources do you think you would need so your course is interactive, supportive, and engaging?

How Can Digital Technologies Enhance L2 Courses?

One definite reality is that digital technologies enhance the learning of a new language. They provide visuals and videos, listening passages with different English accents, interaction with others, and opportunities to collaborate in writing. Chapter 9 explained the University of Iowa's Sounds of Speech app, which helps learners visualize the movement of articulators during pronunciation. Many digital technologies promote active engagement in learning through races, games, and simulations, while others help learners focus on close-ended practice of vocabulary, grammar, and spelling. This section will highlight some of the current digital technologies you can employ in face-to-face, blended, or online L2 classes to engage learners, build comprehension and interaction, and enhance their learning experience.

Integrated content and engaging presentations

- Flipgrid.com is an interactive tool that allows educators to share content focused on a topic. This free program allows educators to record a video in the program or upload one. Media such as Vimeo videos, GIFS, emojis, or images can also be added into discussions. Other digital tools can be linked to the topical flipgrid, such as MS and Google products, Kahoot, Wakelet, Nearpod, Newsela, Adobe Spark, Wonderopolis, and Buncee.
- Nearpod allows educators to transform their PowerPoints/Google Slides and videos into interactive or self-paced lessons or borrow from teacher-created materials. Tools within the site include web content, three-dimensional images, simulations, virtual field trips, BBC video, audio, PDFs, and MS Sway. It links to Zoom too.
- Padlet is a versatile online, virtual bulletin board that allows for the creation of bulletin boards with content, such as vocabulary, and includes visuals, readings, audio recordings, and annotated maps.
- Socrative.com is an online interactive tool for gauging learners' comprehension during synchronous meetings. The free version includes quizzes, races, multiple choice, true/false, short answer, and exit tickets (i.e., cards, slips of paper, or a ticket-shaped sheet—exit tickets are provided by each student upon exit of the classroom and show evidence of students' learning).
- Trackstar facilitates the connection of website readings together on a theme and facilitates annotation, which is helpful for narrow, intensive reading and contextualized vocabulary development.
- Wakelet allows educators to curate content on a topic by including articles, videos, blogs, tweets, songs, PDFs, and visuals. Learners can collaborate, present, create digital stories, compile portfolios, and develop mixed media newsletters.

Developing and practicing four skills and tools

- Buncee allows teachers and learners to develop presentations to narrate, explain, and describe their content creatively.
- Edmodo is a private social platform for education. It can be used to encourage interaction among your learners.
- Empatico links classes of learners around the world through videos, activities, and messaging. Middle school learners can share their lives and experiences with their peers while learning about their peers.
- ePals is an online K–12 penpal arrangement so learners can instant message, write emails, vlog, or blog together.
- English Club offers free ESL chat rooms for learners to communicate with other ELLs on social topics through instant messaging.
- ESL Games World includes close-ended games (e.g., memory games, matching, Snakes and Ladders, Spin the Wheel, Billionaire, word searches, crossword puzzles, cloze activities, and quizzes) for grammar, vocabulary, pronunciation, listening, phonics, and spelling. The games are appropriate for all levels of proficiency: beginner,

intermediate, advanced, and various grade levels including adults. Topics are social language concepts (e.g., animals, jobs, countries/cities, days of the week, clothes, chores, travel), but they have practice on communicative phrases.

- ESL Pages offers chat rooms for learners to practice their social writing and reading skills with peers.
- Flashcard Stash lets educators make their own digital flashcards with images, select definitions, and sentences in context for independent or group practice. It includes three types of matching games.
- iEARN is a digital network of schools, classrooms, and youth organizations who are focused on collaborating on project work. Projects include sharing cultural traditions and insights, researching solutions to world problems, discussing economic, social, and political issues, and creating and discussing art.
- International Children's Digital Library offers free access to thousands of books in many different languages.
- Kahoot is a student favorite for interactive class games that educators can make using true/false, quiz, polls, puzzles, and short-answer formats.
- Lit2Go includes hundreds of free audiobooks, but many of the books and poems have free PDFs to download and print so that children can read along, highlight, and mark up the passage being read. Many of the readings are historical.
- Loyal Books includes many classic readings in audio format for middle to high school learners. Some of the readings may appeal to university-level learners as well.
- Newsela offers tens of thousands of English language texts in over 20 genres. The readings are leveled, so teachers can differentiate readings on a topic.
- Project Gutenberg offers more than 50,000 free ebooks, but not all of them are audiobooks.
- Seesaw is a digital portfolio tool that allows learners to draw, make collages, record audio or video, and annotate their portfolios.
- Storybird.com is a website to develop learners' writing skills through visual storytelling, prompts, courses and tips, projects, and activities.
- Storyboard That allows both educators and learners to create stories with different settings, characters, and plots.
- Storyline Online offers hundreds of kindergarten to third grade picture books brought to life in readings by famous actors.
- StoryNory offers free audio downloads of classic fairy tales, world fairy tales, fables, 1001 Nights, etc.
- Taking it Global is a resource for engaging globally in solving world problems. Action guides teach learners to take action on a topic or issue. They include other resources that would encourage authentic interaction: blogs, conversations, toolkits, and petitions.
- Thinglink permits the labeling and annotation of visuals, maps, or graphics with text, images, audio, or video, or the creation of infographics. The program is useful for showing key concepts in a sentence, paragraph, or essay (e.g., discourse markers, main ideas, etc.).
- Vocabulary Spelling City is a platform for creating or using spelling lists of high-frequency words. Learners can practice with different activities: in spelling, writing, phonics, and vocab word meanings.

- Voice Recorder is an app by Canomapp that allows teachers opportunities to record listening passages or allows learners to record their voices and annotate the recording with notes, images, and pins to highlight key parts.
- WriteReader is a digital tool for learners to write and share their own multimedia and hypertext books.

These digital resources are only a fraction of what is available. As digital technology advances, there will be even more digital resources that can be used in TESOL. When checking out new digital tools, it is important to vet them for face-to-face, blended, online or flipped classes, and educators should consider several points. The digital tools should be reliable and easy to use. Safety and privacy are considerations as well. Some public-facing tools, such as blogs or vlogs, may expose the learners to the public. For adults that may not be a problem, but it should be avoided with children. Educators also need to balance the amount of time required to teach learners how to use the digital tool against the learning outcomes of the course. Cost is another consideration. On a practical note, how will these tools fit into existing lessons, and assess learners' language development? However, even more importantly, we want to be conscious of how the digital tool supports the learners' SLA. Does it provide authentic, contextualized interaction? Or does it promote isolated, decontextualized learning as many online games do. Which language skills does it allow learners to utilize? What is the quality of the input? Is it comprehensible? Are the opportunities for oral or written communication meaningful? Being intentional about our technology choices in our planning will help us focus on the learners and learning and make informed decisions that align with SLA principles and macrostrategies.

Chapter Conclusions

Our learners are 21st-century learners and they expect engagement in their classes with digital technologies. Four major course delivery modalities (i.e., face-to-face, blended, online, and flipped classes) are widely employed by TESOL educators to work with individual learners one-on-one, with small groups, or with classes. In each of these modalities, TESOL educators employ digital tools to engage learners in the four language skills and tools. Knowledge of your learner population and context will help you make informed decisions about appropriate digital tools to use in your classes.

Discussion Questions

1 Which course delivery modalities (i.e., face-to-face, blended, online, and flipped classes) have you participated in? How would you rank the modalities in terms of your learning? Which modality is best for your learning and which is worst? Why?
2 Why is it important to engage ELLs in language learning through digital technologies? What are the benefits and drawbacks for learners?
3 Of the digital tools presented, which ones have you used as a student or educator? Which were the most and least effective for your learning? How effective do you think they would be for learning a new language?

Tasks

1 How do you envision implementing one of the digital tools into your class? Choose one and plan your implementation from introducing it to the learners, and teaching them how to use it, to providing time for them to use it while they continue to learn the language. What challenges do you foresee in implementation? How will you ensure that learners focus on language learning?

2 Investigate the digital tools offered at your school or one where you would like to work. What are teachers using? Do these tools seem effective for language learning? Why or why not?

3 Interview a TESOL educator who teaches online, blended, or flipped classes. What do they like about teaching L2 in the modality? What do they dislike? What do their learners think about learning another language in the modality? What do the educators do to keep the learners motivated and comfortable?

Further Reading/Read and Discuss

Read about digital literacy and second language learning:

Byfield, L., Shelby-Caffey, C., Bacon, H., & Shen, X. (2016, January). Digital literacy and identity formation in 21st century classrooms: Implications for second language development. *International Journal of Applied Linguistics & English Literature, 5*(1), 39–45.

Read about online discussions around ELLs' writing:

Roose, T. M., & Newell, G. E. (2020). Exploring online discussions through an academic literacies approach. *ELT Journal, 74*(3), 258–267. https://doi.org/10.1093/elt/ccaa027

Read about digital tools online for teaching English pronunciation:

Cox, J. L., Henrichsen, L. E., Tanner, M. W., & McMurry, B. L. (2019). The needs analysis, design, development, and evaluation of the English Pronunciation Guide: An ESL teachers' guide to pronunciation teaching using online resources. *TESL-EJ, 22*(4), 1–24.

References

Fosnot, C. T. (Ed.). (2005). *Constructivism: Theory, perspectives and practice* (2nd ed.). Teachers College Press.

Fosnot, C. T. (2013). *Constructivism: Theory, perspectives, and practice* (2nd ed.). Teachers College Press.

Fosnot, C. T., & Perry, R. S. (1996). Constructivism: A psychological theory of learning. In C. T. Fosnot (Ed.), *Constructivism: Theory, perspectives, and practice* (2nd ed.) (pp. 8–33). Teachers College Press. http://rsperry.com/wp-content/uploads/2015/10/Final-CHAPTER-2.pdf (accessed March 26, 2021).

Spires, H. A., Paul, C. M., & Kerkhoff, S. N. (2019). Digital literacy for the 21st century. In M. Khosrow-Pour (Ed.), *Advanced methodologies and technologies in literacy science, information management and scholarly inquiry* (4th ed.) (pp. 2235–2245). IGI Global.

12

What Are Ways of Planning for Second Language Instruction and Assessing Learning?

Practical skills of curriculum and lesson planning based on goals and assessments will be outlined in this chapter. TESOL educators' approaches to the development of classroom-based assessments are discussed. Information about standardized tests and test accommodations will be shared.

Learning Outcomes

At the conclusion of this chapter, you will be able to:

- outline a curriculum for a course with or without a textbook
- plan a lesson to integrate the four language skills and tools
- provide constructive feedback on learners' use of language
- describe how assessments are used in the L2 classroom and how they shape ELLs' educational experiences

Curriculum planning is a creative process that requires educators to vary between the global planning perspective and specific details. How do educators develop curriculum? In this vignette, observe how one educator undertook a curricular challenge in her teaching context.

TESOL Voices

Engaging in Curriculum Development and Professional Development Activities

About 15 years ago, I was working as a consultant for a school district in Georgia and was asked about the best way for ESL teachers and content teachers to collaborate. One administrator wanted ESL teachers to "push in" to content teachers' classrooms to support the learners. I had questions, though. How would the ESL teachers utilize their expertise best in this situation? Would they take on the role of a paraprofessional or would they co-plan and co-teach bringing their mutual expertise together? I did not have all the answers, so I began reading through the literature, but at the time, there wasn't a lot of information on

---

Introduction to TESOL: Becoming a language teaching professional, First Edition. Kate Mastruserio Reynolds, Kenan Dikilitaş, and Steve Close.
© 2022 John Wiley & Sons, Inc. Published 2022 by John Wiley & Sons, Inc.

collaboration in TESOL. It became my mission to answer these questions. This situation exemplifies the importance of sharing our knowledge and engaging in professional development in order to answer our questions to improve our practice.

Fast forward a few years. I was completing research for my dissertation, still seeking to find answers to my questions on effective TESOL collaboration. While observing and interviewing teachers who collaborated to ensure English learners needs were met, I became particularly interested in a partnership between an ESL teacher and a third-grade teacher at one of the schools. The ESL teacher shared that their collaboration started when they had both attended a writing workshop one summer. The two were so enthusiastic about the teaching ideas they learned, they, along with several other colleagues who attended the summer workshop, decided to model mini-lessons for other third-grade teachers. The school was set up in pods, where there was a common area in between the grade levels' classrooms. They decided to pull their kids out into the pod to teach, where other classes could join them. These "pod sessions" became so popular other teachers decided to share their successful strategies from their classrooms. They also chose books and articles related to what they were working on or wanted to know more about to improve their practice.

Interestingly, my research investigating how ESL and grade-level teachers worked together to support English learners revealed teachers developing professionally by collaborating and sharing research, book talks, lessons, strategies, and ideas with each other. Now, it was my opportunity to share my findings with other TESOLers; my TESOL convention proposal was accepted. I also attended all of the sessions dedicated to teacher collaboration at that convention, and I began networking with other presenters whose interests aligned with my own. From these new partnerships, we have published several articles, a book chapter, and have presented at TESOL conventions. The colleagues I have connected with through TESOL live in different states and countries, yet we come together to share knowledge. Coming full circle back to the introduction of this story, a year or two later one of the last sessions at a TESOL convention I attended was on how school districts in Georgia were implementing collaborative practices. When I sat down and started listening to the presentation, the information seemed very familiar. And then I noticed it ... my research being shared from districts in the state where my questions started a few years before.

Angela B. Bell, PhD
Visiting Assistant Professor, TESOL
Missouri State University

Seeing the Big Picture

Planning for a lesson starts with organizing the big picture, known as *curriculum planning,* and moves downward to planning individual lessons (Figure 12.1). TESOL educators take into consideration several competing priorities when planning their

Figure 12.1 Curriculum planning.

courses: the goals and needs of learners, the content to be learned, the available materials and resources, the contextual expectations, and constraints.

Graves (2014) defines curriculum as "a dynamic system of interconnected, interrelated, and overlapping process. The three main curricular processes and planning, enacting, and evaluating...These processes are in play at every curricular level, whether it is a lesson, unit, course, or program. They are carried out by people and may result in an array of curriculum products such as syllabuses, lesson plans and assessment instruments" (p. 49).

Curriculum planning simply means taking all the competing priorities, making choices about what will be taught and for how long, and organizing the topics in a coherent and sequential plan.

Curriculum planning begins as a linear process, but educators engage reflectively with it. An example of this would be drafting a robust plan with colleagues or independently, but not knowing if this plan will meet the learners' goals and needs, questioning whether the time spent on differing areas is enough or too much, or allowing for the depth of learning in the L2. An educator, either alone or working as part of a team, will enact the plan in teaching. In classes and afterward, it's necessary to think about if and when the learners can speak, listen, read, write, and use the vocabulary, grammar, intelligible pronunciation, and spelling. Planning involves watching and observing learners' performance on the learning outcomes of the class and sharing insights with other members of the team. Doing so makes it possible to learn from them what they observed in their classes. Collaboratively, the team may refine the plan for the following day and the next time the course is taught. Each time that we teach a course again, we modify our syllabus to mirror what we have learned the last time we taught it.

When lesson planning, educators often refer to the *scope of learning* and *sequence of learning* in lessons over time. *Curricular scope* describes the breadth of the content. For example, the content could be a course on world history for high school students, pronunciation for university-level ELLs, survival English for adult refugees, social language for newcomers, or English for restaurant employees. Often, educators are assigned to a course with a particular content, but in some situations, they are expected to determine what content they need to include in the course.

Curricular sequence concerns the order of the topics within the content. Using the example of survival English for adults, educators may include in this course topics such as introducing themselves, asking for and giving personal information, asking for directions, ordering a meal, going to the doctor or dentist, going grocery shopping, using the local currency, renting an apartment, and using the library or the post office. These topics would need to be sequenced from easiest/most approachable and of greatest immediate need to most difficult/complex. Of the survival English topics, it would be easiest to teach introducing themselves, but going grocery shopping and using local currency would be of equal initial importance, whereas going to the doctor or dentist and renting an apartment would be more complex. Within these topics, the vocabulary, sentence patterns, and grammar structures learners need to communicate ideas are often embedded, and they, too, move from easiest to hardest. They are cumulative as well. The sequence of topics and tools thus transforms into a map, also known as a curriculum map.

Who designs curriculum?

In some cases, the curriculum educators are expected to employ originates from a national ministry of education, a publisher, or other educators. Depending on the context, educators may have complete control over what, when, and how information is taught and how long for, or they may have no control over these aspects of the teaching, learning, and assessment processes. Consider the degree to which educators have control and responsibility for their curriculum as a continuum on which a slider can move to describe the degree of control and responsibility (Figure 12.2).

In contexts where educators have no control of the curriculum, they may not be allowed to modify any aspect of scope, sequence, topics, goals, etc. That may even extend to daily lesson plans, which the educators must teach without modification for the learners. In this situation, the educators also do not have much responsibility for the curriculum. Kate's former brother-in-law taught EFL in Beijing, China for a couple

Complete Control   No Control
Complete Responsibility   No Responsibility

Figure 12.2   Teacher control over the curriculum.

of years and found that in his specific instructional setting he was not allowed to stray from the provided curriculum at all. A classroom monitor was present to ensure he did not stray from the curriculum and textbook provided. The problem was that the curriculum was designed for teaching speaking to learners in a class size of 25 or fewer students, so they had opportunities to speak, listen, and receive feedback. His class had 75 students in it, which made the curriculum unworkable. In "low-control" contexts, educators need to make realistic choices about what is achievable. They can develop effective learning experiences within the constraints, though, if they are flexible in their thinking. It also depends a great deal on the quality of the curriculum and materials they are given.

Textbook as curriculum

In some cases, educators are handed a textbook and are told to teach using it without any sort of curriculum plan or map outside of it. In these situations, the educators have little sense of how the content and topics from the textbooks fit into the bigger curricular picture. While this may seem a simple approach to organizing a course, the textbook is merely a tool, not the curriculum. Byrd and Schuemann (2014) echo this sentiment, stating that "Textbooks should not replace the curriculum plan, but embody core ideas" (p. 381). The textbook may not suit the learners' goals and needs, include all the necessary content, structure lessons to integrate the four skills and tools, include enough interaction opportunities, provide formative and summative feedback, or meet the expectations of the context in terms of what the learners should know and be able to do with the L2. While this situation may be acceptable for some educators, it may be frustrating or disorienting for others.

Kate had an instructional experience that demonstrates the issues that emerge owing to too little or too much external control over curriculum when she was in an EFL context to teach second-year translator/interpreter students at university. She was shown a list of 12 topics for the course including: politics, environment, border crossings, and occupations. None of the topics had any development of them to elaborate what exactly to teach within the topic, nor were there any textbooks. Kate was expected to use her knowledge of ESL/EFL/ELT and language teaching/learning to create opportunities for learners to acquire enough information about each of the topics while developing their language skills. For her, this was a welcome challenge that stimulated her creativity. For others, it may have been overwhelming.

In "high-control" instructional settings (where educators have complete control of the curriculum), educators bear more responsibility, but they are also afforded the chance to bring about powerful, transformative learning for the learners. In high-control settings, educators are expected to be knowledgeable and informed educators who can employ their knowledge of the learners, learners' goals, needs, and interests, SLA, teaching and learning of ESL/EFL/ELT, and assessment within the planning process. They have opportunities to be creative in the development of a curriculum tailored to their specific population. However, it is easy, as Kate learned, to go too deeply into a topic and not do enough on the basics.

Questions for reflection

- How do you envision the curriculum development process working?
- What tasks would you do at the global level?
- How might you handle a low-control and a high-control instructional setting when it comes to curriculum development? Which do you prefer and why?

Identifying Learners' Linguistic Needs

When educators start working at a new school or in a new context, they need to learn as much as they can about the students. They need to learn about the learners' culture(s), first language(s), interests, goals for learning, and language learning needs, for instance. Many teachers enjoy gauging learners' interest in topics using *interest inventories*. In some scenarios, educators walk into a class on the first day with very little knowledge of these areas. However, in other scenarios, educators have a mentor or peers to share with them basic information about the learners. It is often a good idea to ask for a mentor and develop collegial relationships with other educators in the school or program.

Even if we have guidance about the learners from administration, mentors, or peers, we will want to learn more specifically about the learners in our particular class. We can learn more about them from program records (if available) (e.g., home language surveys, standardized test scores/results) and needs assessments. Home language surveys are informational forms that caregivers complete and submit about the languages used in the home, exposure to English, and academic study in English. A quick search online will yield many examples.

Needs assessment

A needs assessment, or needs analysis, is similar to a pretest. We design or make use of various tools to gather information about learners' abilities in the four skills, grammar, syntax, pronunciation, and spelling, and language learning strategies, among other areas. What we gather should align with the purpose of the course (academic, professional, survival, ESP). When teaching an integrated language skills class, an educator might solicit examples of their speaking and writing, and gauge their comprehension of listening and reading passages appropriate to the age(s) of the learners. If learners are old enough to tell us, we may also want to learn which language skills learners find the easiest/hardest, and what they would like to work on most/least.

The format and design of a needs assessment are often just like the exercises and activities we use to teach language. We employ close-ended and open-ended activities/tasks. For example:

- close-ended exercises and open-ended activities, such as question and answer formatted interviews, information gap, role-plays;
- listening/reading passages with comprehension questions and cloze exercises for listening, reading, grammar, and vocabulary; and
- writing and speaking activities that require extended discourse, appropriate to the proficiency level.

We also want to conduct activities that require spontaneous, impromptu language production and more reflective activities since learners will respond differently in these two scenarios. Finally, we want to gather information about learners' language abilities by offering multiple opportunities in each skill area. This allows us to have a truer sense of their abilities.

It may sound as though getting settled into a class would require that weeks are spent gathering data, but that is not the case. In the first week of class, it is possible to get to know quite a bit about the learners, help them become familiar with each other, and establish class routines, rules, and expectations. It is also a good idea to intertwine the needs assessment tasks with these goals by systematically gathering data. Learners do not need to know they are being assessed; they just need to give their best effort.

Once data sets have been gathered, it's time to analyze the learners' abilities in the targeted skills and other areas. At this point it's possible to identify where their strengths and weaknesses lie and other information that will help determine what needs to be taught. A profile or checklist can help with the compilation of goals for the whole class. For more on needs assessments/analysis, see Brown's (2009) "Foreign and Second Language Needs Analysis," Long's (2005) *Second Language Needs Analysis*, and the Center for Applied Linguistics/Center for Adult English Language Acquisition's *Needs Assessment and Learner Self-Evaluation*.

Planning with the End in Mind

Another consideration when planning what to teach in a course is the ways that learners will be assessed on their learning. For example, they may be assessed by a standardized language exam, a teacher-made test, a test from the textbook, or a performance assessment (see the section on "Types of Assessments"). If ELLs need to take any standardized exam, TESOL educators identify the knowledge and performance areas the learners need for success on the exam. These knowledge and performance areas are then built into the instruction of the course. Likewise, if schools, programs, or educators intend to assess learners' language learning via textbook tests, teacher-made tests, or performance assessments, the knowledge and performance expectations on these tests and assessments are analyzed, so that instruction can prepare learners to succeed on them. This approach to course preparation is called *backward design* (Wiggins & McTighe, 2005). Figure 12.3 shows how the backward design approach works with textbooks.

As you can see in Figure 12.3, the first step is to identify the standards to be met during instruction based on the learners' needs, which may focus on language, content, or strategies. The second step is to analyze the end of term assessments and *draft* course or unit student learning outcomes (SLOs) that would meet the standards and prepare learners to be successful on these assessments. The third step is to drill down to the lesson SLOs by analyzing the book for the objectives present in the text. From this analysis, the educator can identify any SLOs needed to build skills not found in the text. It is in this way that the educator can identify lesson-level SLOs while being mindful of the textbook strengths and weaknesses. SLOs may be developed for 2–3-day sequences or for a module if online. Kate usually encourages her students to develop lessons not based upon course meeting time; rather, to design lessons based on the SLOs and then factor in the time needed for the lesson.

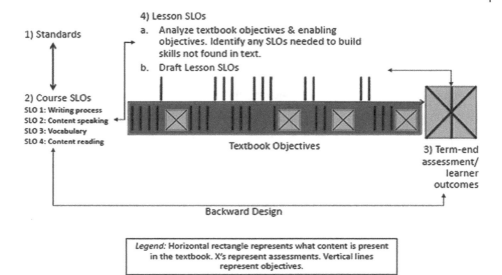

1) Standards

2) Course SLOs
SLO 1: Writing process
SLO 2: Content speaking
SLO 3: Vocabulary
SLO 4: Content reading

4) Lesson SLOs
a. Analyze textbook objectives & enabling objectives. Identify any SLOs needed to build skills not found in text.
b. Draft Lesson SLOs

Textbook Objectives

3) Term-end assessment/ learner outcomes

Backward Design

Legend: Horizontal rectangle represents what content is present in the textbook. X's represent assessments. Vertical lines represent objectives.

Figure 12.3 The role of textbooks in curriculum development in backward design and lesson planning.

Questions for reflection

- How do you envision the backward design process working? How could you use it effectively?
- Which resources do you need to plan using the backward design process?

Standards, goals, SLOs, can do indicators, and success criteria

Based on the specific information we gleaned from the assessments learners will take and the needs assessment, we will craft goals, SLOs/can do statements, and success criteria, and align them with the appropriate *standards*.

Standards are guidelines educators use to ensure consistency in learning across grades in a system or as benchmarks in the process of learning a new language. Standards can be general or exceedingly specific, which influences how easy or difficult it is to use them. Professional organizations, governmental agencies, and consortia develop standards/guidelines for their unique population of learners. They may focus on the grade, age, content, or context. See the "Standards and guidelines for language learning" textbox. Many standards have identifiers of numbers and letters that pinpoint which one is being mentioned (e.g., A.1.d. or 2d). These identifiers can be combined with the course goals to illustrate which standards are being linked to which goals in the course. For example, WIDA Standard 2 is:

> **Standard 2—Language of Language Arts**
> English language learners communicate information, ideas and concepts necessary for academic success in the content area of language arts. (WIDA, 2012)

Standards help educators determine what to teach or include in a course, unit, or module. They help ensure that our work is professional and relevant. Courses can be fun, but there is a problem if there is very little learning.

Standards and guidelines for language learning

Some notable and influential language learning standards and guidelines are included here, but many others exist. Make sure you check with your school or the professional organization in your context to determine which are most appropriate for you.

ACTFL Proficiency Guidelines https://www.actfl.org/resources/actfl-proficiency-guidelines-2012

Common Core Standards and English Language Learners (ELLs) https://www.colorincolorado.org/common-core-and-english-language-learners

Council of Europe Common European Framework of Reference for Language (CEFR) https://www.coe.int/en/web/common-european-framework-reference-languages/the-cefr-descriptors

TESOL Standards include:

Pre-K–12 English Language Proficiency Standards;

Adult Education Standards; and

Guidelines for Developing EFL Professional Teaching Standards https://www.tesol.org/advance-the-field/standards

World-class Instructional Design and Assessment (WIDA) Standards Language Development Standards 2019 https://wida.wisc.edu/teach/early/elds https://wida.wisc.edu/teach/standards/eld

Which standards or guidelines seem the most appropriate for your context?

Goals are general targets the educator thinks are appropriate for the learners. They tend to be written in a general manner for the term. For example, "To compare/contrast the formats, motifs, and unique features of the literature genres: fairy-tales, tall tales, fantasy and myths", "To practice the four language skills with content from the genres of study," or "To learn and use the writing process." These goals link directly to WIDA Standard 2 (above) since they are part of the study of language arts. Goals serve to guide the educator initially, but they will be further specified.

In the past, educators wrote objectives, which were similar to goals. These days, once they have identified the course goals, educators write SLOs/can do statements, and success criteria.

Writing SLOs

SLOs describe what the learner will have learned and be able to do as a result of their learning. SLOs are effective when they are written to be specific, focused on the learning to occur in the course or lesson, and measurable.

SLOs may be written for an entire course, unit/module, and/or for individual lessons. Course SLOs are more general and the lesson SLOs are highly specific. A course SLO may resemble this one: at the end of the course, learners will be able to distinguish between types of news stories (e.g., straight news/hard news, features, editorials, community interest) and their purposes (e.g., objective, interpretative, investigative, and crime). This example shows the types of news stories that will be explored in the course, and the various purposes for new stories to be discussed.

Unlike objectives, which focus on what the *teacher is doing*, SLOs focus on what the *students are learning*. For example, lesson SLOs for a low intermediate integrated language skills class may resemble the following:

Students will be able to:

1. Use regular past tense (-ed ending) when writing their family history with 80% accuracy.
2. Employ vocabulary words to describe their family members with 95% accuracy (i.e., mother, father, grandmother, uncle, brother, sister, cousin).
3. Write transition words (such as first, second, next, then, after, etc.) appropriately to show time changes in stories.
4. Write their family history using complete simple sentences and three to five-sentence paragraphs.

At this point it should be clear that SLOs are written formulaically. They are typically written in this pattern: the students will be able to [action verb that demonstrates something] in [instructional context/activity] with [degree of accuracy, when appropriate].

SLOs should describe learning outcomes that can be measured. This should be an overt, observable activity, even if the actual learning is covert or mental in nature, such as comprehension and understanding. If it can't be seen, heard, tasted, touched, or smelled, there is no way to be sure an audience really learned it. Often with reading and listening, TESOL educators will ask learners to demonstrate their comprehension in some manner so it is measurable. For some concepts, we can measure the degree of accuracy. This is only necessary when a specific set of criteria should be met. In those instances, it's generally a good idea to give a benchmark for accuracy. For example, is the goal total mastery (100%) or to respond correctly 80% of the time? Often, educators will use a nonscientific benchmark of 80% accuracy, owing to performance issues.

Can do indicators

Can do indicators are the SLOs transformed for learners and are used mostly at the lesson level. At the beginning of lessons, educators are encouraged to state (orally and/or in writing) what students will be learning. These statements need to be comprehensible to the learners, so educators write them as statements of what learners can do as a result of learning in the class. For example, "I can write my family history using three to five complete sentences," or "I can write my family history using correct regular past tense verbs."

Success criteria

Finally, success criteria describe what products and processes look like when learners successfully accomplish lesson SLOs. They clearly indicate how learners can successfully demonstrate their learning at the end of the class meeting. They are often co-constructed or negotiated with learners through inductive processes, so students take ownership of their own learning during lessons. If we take the SLO example of writing a family history, we can provide an exemplar paragraph and engage learners in a discussion of formatting by asking them questions about key transitions, etc. We can develop anchor charts with learners to summarize what a first-rate family history looks like; for example, we would not want it to be too detailed or not detailed enough.

Differentiating SLOs by proficiency level

One area in which TESOL educators can *differentiate* instruction, or tailor the learning to specific learners' needs, is in the lesson SLOs. During planning, lesson delivery, and assessment an educator can modify:

- the language use when presenting new information;
- the length and complexity of listening and reading passages (see oral and written production below);
- the length of oral and written production (speaking and writing) of ELLs:
  - word level (WIDA ELP Level 1);
  - sentence level (WIDA ELP Levels 1 and 2);
  - paragraph level (WIDA ELP Levels 2 and 3); and
  - essay level (WIDA ELP Levels 3 and 4);
- the complexity of ideas that are required (higher-thinking skills) and language combined;
- the number of new vocabulary words;
- the complexity of new vocabulary and ideas combined;
- the supports provided (e.g., graphic organizers, word banks, etc.); and
- complexity of the products learners create, or processes they follow.

For more on differentiating instruction and assessment, see Fairbairn and Jones-Vo's (2019) *Differentiating Instruction and Assessment for English Language Learners: A Guide for K–12 Teachers*, 2nd edition.

Questions for reflection
<ul><li>How do you differentiate between standards, goals, SLOs, and student success criteria?</li><li>Why do you need standards, goals, SLOs, and student success criteria in your planning? How do they help educators?</li></ul>

Ways to Organize Curriculum

Once the overall sense of what needs to be taught is established, the planning process will move downward from the big picture (year-long or whole term). One factor that influences the organization of a year or term is the amount of time. Goals must be set regarding what must be taught, what should be taught, and what can be taught if time permits. Setting a hierarchy of this type ensures that time is managed effectively in the classroom, and reduces the chances that essential material will be bypassed owing to lack of time. This is the most general level of the planning process. Building flexibility into a course timeline is an often-overlooked facet of teaching, but a course with no "wiggle room" is almost certain to fail when the "unexpected" occurs.

The grade level in which teaching takes place will have influence on how curriculum is organized, because it also implies what is available in terms of the time period and lesson duration. The way that time for learning is allocated varies considerably by country and region (see Robb, 2013). Similarly, the time of year within which a lesson takes place can strongly affect how it is received by students. One of the intriguing features of international public education is when the school year begins. In Brazil, for example, the school year begins in January. In South Korea and Peru, the school year starts in March. In the United States, it commences in August or September. The beginning of the school year coincides with the beginning of autumn, so it varies according to northern or southern hemisphere.

Planning an overall course involves dividing the material into segments (lessons). However, different patterns of organization within schools will affect the number of class meetings available, and thus how long each lesson must be. The duration of the school year fluctuates, with some countries holding school for anywhere from 9–10 months a year and others, such as Australia, Japan, and South Korea, with year-round school. Breaks within the year differ, with some countries planning 2–4-week breaks between terms. The school year in Kenya is broken up into three 13-week terms with 1-month breaks between, for example.

Private language schools and private schools may or may not follow the pattern of the academic year of the public school system. Private language schools tend to offer variable, shorter duration courses of between 4 and 8 weeks for the convenience of the learners. Knowledge of the educational system of a country and what their pattern is for academic years is important for TESOL educators as is the ability to adapt and adjust to another country's pattern.

Educators assess the amount of time available in the term to determine how much time they deem necessary to spend on each unit, module, or week. Units tend to be the term employed in K–12 for a thematic or topical concept to be explored, whereas module is mainly used to describe online units. University educators often refer to weeks, because they have a new topic/theme for each week. In some cases, educators will refer to a chapter from the textbook as their unit of instruction. Teachers estimate the length of time for the unit or module by the amount of content and depth of learning.

What is a syllabus?

With the knowledge of content and time, it is now possible to start drafting a plan. A *syllabus* is one way that educators organize their course or term. A syllabus is a plan for what is to be taught, and a rough time frame. It may be an unrefined sketch of topics to discuss/teach over a course of a couple of days or a week. A syllabus, whether a copy is given to the learners or not (depending on age), serves as a guide for the educator, and works in tandem with the textbook (if one is being used).

Years ago, a syllabus was one or two pages long. Today, they are several pages long. Whether handing out the syllabus or posting it online, it includes information about the course, such as:

- instructor affiliation and contact information;
- the course title;
- the instructor's goals and learning outcomes for the course, which are often tied to the standards to be addressed;
- materials and/or technology that are required/optional for the course;
- class rules and procedures;
- assignments, due dates;
- assessment, rubrics, and grading policies/grading standards; and
- a time schedule with information about readings, assignments, and due dates.

At universities, syllabuses become part of the university's curriculum and accreditation process, so they are public documents that may be gathered regularly. Learners will use a syllabus even after the course, if they transfer to another university or they seek another degree later. Therefore, the abovementioned information is critical for assessment of university programs and students' learning experience. A syllabus will often include "boilerplate" paragraphs that describe policies or information deemed necessary by administrators. For example, a typical college syllabus includes information on plagiarism policies and services for learners with exceptionalities. Most schools also require that the syllabus include set pieces of information that affect course organization such as late work policies and grading standards.

Organizational tools for a syllabus are typically Microsoft Word or Excel. In many online courses, though, educators organize their syllabus in a course learning/management system. Some educators use binders and cognitive maps. Which tool an educator employs is really a matter of what works best for that individual, but it is also a good idea to plan around sharing to any others, such as a students, parents, grade-level or subject-specific team, co-teacher, instructional/curriculum coordinator, principal, department chairperson, etc.

Types of L2 syllabuses or curricular approach

In the field of TESOL, syllabuses take on another definition in addition to the one above. They indicate an approach to the content that relates to the school's and educators' instructional philosophy and belief system about SLA. In this sense of the word, it is closer to the idea of a curricular approach.

Penny Ur (2009) and Kathleen Graves (2014) outlined the types of syllabuses present in the field of TESOL. Some of the most common today are:

- Grammatical—A grammatical syllabus is a list of grammatical structures (e.g., present tense, adjectives, relative clauses) to be learned in a course. They are usually arranged from easiest to most difficult and by importance. A grammatical syllabus is often found in beginning-level EFL courses.
- Skills-based—These syllabuses are based on the development of a specific language skill, such as speaking in a conversation management class.

- Procedural (or task-based)—These syllabuses specify the learning tasks to be done rather than the language itself (e.g., reading maps, writing stories, developing a marketing plan, conducting a scientific experiment).
- Genre or text-based—The genre- or text-based based syllabus focuses on the study of spoken or written texts. For example, learners may study novels, poetry, or movie critiques. Depending on the choices of genre/texts, this approach is adaptable for almost any ELL population.
- Project-based—Learning activities in a course with a project-based learning syllabus revolve around a series of distinctive projects in which the learners will engage. This type of syllabus would work well with a group of designers who would design different projects in their field and learn the language to discuss, develop, and share their project design.
- Content or ESP—These types of syllabuses are typically structured around the content to be learned or the integration of content and language in content-based instruction (CBI), content and language integrated instruction, or ESP.
- Mixed or multi-strand—Syllabuses that combine different aspects of all the other types in order to be comprehensive are called mixed or multi-strand. Often mixed-strand syllabuses combine elements, such as grammar, vocabulary, skills, with functions and notions from the Functional/Notional syllabus. Functions are "things learners can do with language" (e.g., explaining, denying, promising). Notions are concepts that language can express (e.g., time, place, color, number). These are one of the most common syllabuses in textbooks today and it is easy to see the various elements organized in a grid of interconnecting concepts.

It has become a fairly standard practice to include a sample syllabus in the table of contents of a textbook, and these samples demonstrate what the text's authors see as the backbone or blueprint of the textbook. In this way, individual educators can compare and contrast their approach to that of the author(s).

Textbook selection and evaluation

Evaluation of textbooks and materials is an important skill of TESOL educators. Jack Richards (n.d.) describes the process that educators can follow to evaluate a textbook as having three phrases: pre-use, in-use, and after use (i.e., reflecting upon its use). In other words, we evaluate it prior to using it. We may be part of a selection team or have the opportunity to choose the book independently for our classes. Richards indicates that educators should analyze these areas:

- aims and objectives of the book;
- theoretical framework and methodology the book is based on;
- target learners; proficiency level of the book;
- language content (i.e., themes, topics covered, skills addressed, quality and authenticity of four skills materials, etc.);
- situations it is intended for;
- time required;
- components and ancillaries (i.e., additional resources, such as digital or web-based tools, listening/reading passages, teachers' book, workbooks);
- number and length of units;

- organization of units (i.e., coherent, consistent, gradual increase in difficulty);
- appeal to learners and teachers; and
- price.

Within Richards' framework, the "fit" of the textbook outlined by Byrd and Schuemann (2014) is helpful. They indicate that when evaluating textbooks for selection to use in a course, TESOL educators should consider whether it fits with:

- the curriculum (e.g., standards, curriculum/syllabus type, standardized tests and assessments);
- the learners (e.g., age appropriate, culturally congruent, proficiency level, content and explanations, examples, exercises/activities/tasks, and presentation/ format); and
- the teacher(s) (congruent with the educator's teaching philosophy and style, content and explanations, examples, exercises/activities/tasks, and presentation/format).

When TESOL educators analyze a textbook in a thorough and thoughtful manner, the analysis will help them identify the areas of the textbook that the educators need to supplement, skip, reduce, or elaborate. All of these tasks take time, so the analysis helps us manage our planning time more effectively.

Educators often wish to know what others think of a textbook, so they read text reviews. Writing text reviews is a professional development activity where an educator can share their evaluation of a text. It is an easy first step to start engaging with the TESOL professional community (read more about sharing professional knowledge in Chapter 13).

Questions for reflection

- Will you develop a syllabus for your courses? If so, why? If not, why not?
- Why does the type of syllabus matter to TESOL educators?
- Why is it important to thoroughly review your textbook and materials? How might it benefit you and/ or your instructional team to do this well?

Ins and Outs in First-year Curricular Planning

The curriculum development process continues narrowing the focus on progressively smaller units from curriculum and syllabus planning to unit/module and lesson planning.

Unit or module planning involves organizing the course goals and SLOs by topic or theme into a cumulative, scaffolded plan and allocating the time necessary for achievement of the goals and SLOs. If a lesson were arranged around teaching the theme "Justice," the theme could be broken down into subtopics/subthemes.

Justice:

1. What is justice? What is injustice?
2. How do we know whether something is just or unjust?

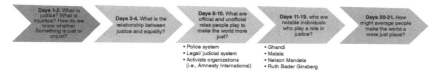

Figure 12.4 Thematic unit subtopics/subthemes.

3. What is the relationship between justice and equality?
4. What are official and unofficial roles people play to make the world more just?
   a. police system;
   b. legal/judicial system; and
   c. activists' organizations (i.e., Amnesty International).
5. Who are notable individuals who play a role in justice?
   a. Gandhi;
   b. Malala;
   c. Nelson Mandela; and
   d. Ruth Bader Ginsberg.
6. How might average people make the world a more just place?

Each of these six subtopics/subthemes can be developed into integrated skills lessons that may last anywhere from 1–4 days (Figure 12.4).

Units typically span anywhere from 1 to 21 days depending on the topic/theme, learners' ages, and duration of class meetings. Educators estimate the amount of time for each subtheme with wiggle room, and are ready to adjust as necessary.

How long are typical class meetings?

The answer to this question is not straightforward. The duration of class meetings in private language schools will vary considerably as will the duration of online lessons. Mostly, private language school classes will run for 1 hr though.

If you are teaching elementary grades, you may have self-contained or rotating classes. A self-contained class means that you have one group of students all day for all academic subjects, whereas rotating classes means that teachers specialize in one subject and the students rotate between classes. The duration of elementary classes may be very short, with as little as 20 min per lesson.

The ordinary duration for a class period for middle and high school is 50 min. Universities offer 50-min class meetings twice a week, but may also offer longer, but fewer, class meetings per week. For university, it depends on the number of credits being earned in the class. Credits represent the time per week the course will meet for either a quarter (10 weeks*) or semester (16 weeks*) (*depending on the country and university).

The next step of the unit design process is one that helps build coherence and comprehensibility for the learners. We should intentionally build in threads that connect the subtopics (Stoller & Grabe, 2017). They explain how threads function, "They are, in general, not directly tied to the central idea controlling each theme unit. Rather, they are relatively abstract concepts (e.g., responsibility; ethics, contrasts, power) that provide natural means for linking themes, for reviewing and recycling important content and language across themes, and for revisiting selected learning strategies" (Stoller & Grabe, 1997, p. 6).

When planning a unit, it is a good idea to consider which assessments will be used and when they will occur in the unit. Some assessments may gather feedback on how the learners are progressing in their second language learning through teacher-made tests, textbook assessments, or performance assessments (see the section on "Types of Assessments"). Educators often design the goals and criteria for assessment at this stage of curriculum planning.

Questions for reflection

- What tools might you use, digital or otherwise, to design your unit(s)?
- How will you make sure that your unit is cohesive between lessons?

Lesson Planning

Once the unit and assessment plans are in place, it is time to narrow the focus to lesson planning. Lesson plans help educators organize the learning and engage the learners. They guide the instructional process, so educators do not overlook a key component and can avoid potential problems. They also assist educators to reflect on the lesson and learning after the class session.

When lesson planning, educators will want to think through how they will assist ELLs in developing their communicative competencies in the process of meeting or mastering the lesson's learning goals and SLOs. They will want to prethink how the integration of the four skills and tools will occur and how activities/tasks and instructional sequences will aid learners. The instructional sequences or routines for teaching content and the four skills and tools (see Chapters 7–9 on teaching the language skills) are thought through.

They will want to ponder how they will know learners have met/mastered the goals and SLOs and what the criteria for success are; they would ultimately connect these to the lesson assessments. Ideally, lessons should be linked to the learning of the previous day and the following day through intentional transitions, so these transitions should be anticipated too.

Formats of lesson plans

Formats of lesson plans vary considerably among educators. Experienced educators may follow a rough outline since they have internalized many instructional practices and patterns, whereas new professionals may need to use a standard format and spend more time on lesson planning.

It is important to remember that lesson plans are not always written for the educator. Other audiences who would use them include substitute teachers, peers, administrators, or program evaluators. In some instructional contexts, though, educators may be required to submit the lesson plans for approval prior to lesson delivery or afterward for program records. For these reasons, it is important to (a) write down a lesson plan, (b) make it clear for others, and (c) use a comprehensible format or one sanctioned by the school or program.

Lesson plans often include:

- basic course information (i.e., school, course title, time of lesson, and instructor information);
- a description of the learner population (i.e., L1s, proficiency level(s), socioeconomic status, specific needs);
- equipment needed;
- lesson SLOs (with standards noted) and success criteria;
- the lesson theme, topic, and essential question;
  - the procedures to be followed in a stepwise manner, for example;
  - initiation (i.e., warm-up/energizer), lesson overview/preview with daily SLOs and success criteria mentioned;
  - presentation of new material in either a deductive or inductive approach;
  - discussion questions/prompts;
  - types of activities and directions with any materials, manipulatives, tools, or supplements needed;
  - lesson closure (i.e., summation of learning, preview of next day);
- timing/pacing;
- interaction formats, such as pairs, small groups, whole class;
- contingency plans;
- the assessments (e.g., exit tickets, observations of oral interaction or reading, student in-class work, or quizzes/tests); and
- a space for reflection on lesson delivery and student learning.

A simple lesson plan format can be seen in Figure 12.5.

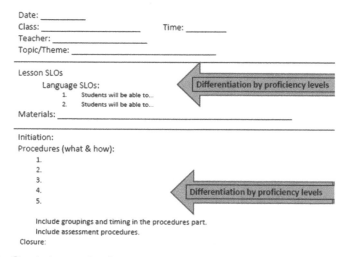

Figure 12.5 Simple lesson plan format.

Moving through the process of writing a lesson plan, it is a good idea to pause to identify, find, or create the necessary activities, word banks, visual vocabulary lists, presentations of new material, readings, tools, or assessments. Kate consistently encourages her teacher candidates to write up discussion questions and prompts so they can avoid telling learners about a topic instead of facilitating a discussion with learners on the topic.

Questions for reflection

- What process do you think you will follow to develop your lessons?
- Will you design your own activities and materials?
- Which type of lesson plan format do you prefer, and why?

Lesson planning takes time, but it will pay off in students' learning and educators' professional development over time. The ability to reflect on students' learning as well as upon the original explanations, linguistic modifications, and groupings that were part of the initial design helps educators to become more effective in all teaching-related tasks.

Assessing Learning

Curriculum planning is interrelated to assessments in an intricate, nonlinear fashion. In the backward design discussion in the section on "Planning with the End in Mind," you saw how SLOs were linked to assessments. Knowing the available options about assessment and evaluation is key for a TESOL educator. In the next vignette, glimpse how one educator uses formative assessment in her ESL classroom to help guide her instruction.

TESOL Voices

Reassessing Assessments

While teaching a middle school ESL class, instruction was planned after consulting the assessment data on hand, but then I would also start a new unit with some sort of additional pre-assessment. Often, I would choose a picture or a brainstorming web for students to discuss, write, or draw ideas they knew about the topic on a large piece of butcher paper or self-stick chart paper. They could each add what they knew in any language they were comfortable with, including words in English, which gave us a multilingual concept wall that was prominently displayed for the duration of the unit. It also gave me the opportunity to build on their background knowledge.

Each day, as I walked around the room monitoring students during activities, I had a clipboard with a checklist of standards, goals, and objectives. I would document how students were progressing toward each of the targets while noticing, supporting, and documenting when a concept was too challenging for a learner. When in a rush, I would use a sticky note to add it to the students' portfolios where I kept data and evidence of how each child was performing. Then, I would use the data to create mini-lessons to teach a concept if students were struggling. Students were assigned to flexible groups that changed often, depending on the concept being taught. By using these small teaching groups, I could focus on an area where a learner needed explicit feedback and teaching, giving the students opportunities to practice collaboratively and apply the information.

I have always understood the value of observation, formative assessments, and using the data from informal assessments as well as formal assessments in order to adjust my instruction. What I was missing, however, was giving students more of a voice in the assessment process. In a course I took in graduate school, we read *Classroom Assessment Techniques* (Angelo & Cross, 1993). I began using many of their ideas. For example, I asked students to provide feedback on our class, "What is going well? What is not? What can you do better? What can the teacher do better?" Sometimes we relied on translations, depending on the English proficiency level of the learners. I took students' anonymous responses and created a slide that showed their aggregated responses and then I told them what I, the teacher, would do based on their replies. Not only did this kind of assessment help me to make the class a better experience for the students, it also helped me in establishing a trusting relationship. My students knew I had their best interests at heart and would work to make sure the conditions were appropriate for their learning needs to be met.

After formatively assessing students via checklists, observations, assignments, discussions, and self-assessments, and guiding instruction based on these data points, it was time for the summative assessment. I was always careful that I taught the way I was assessing, that there were no tricks, and that rubrics and criteria were clear. I loved using performance-based and project-based assessments with options. Depending on the ELL's level of proficiency, the target might be the same, but the criteria may look a little different, and so will the grading. Of course, students also took local and state assessments. As summative data was gathered, it was analyzed, reflected upon, and used to inform instructional decisions, as we started the process all over again.

Angela B. Bell, PhD
Visiting Assistant Professor, TESOL
Missouri State University

In the curriculum development process, it is necessary to consider how to gather data about students' learning systematically at the lesson, unit, and/or course levels. Two approaches to assessment are employed by educators for different purposes: formative and summative assessment.

Formative assessment: Assessments that inform instruction

Formative assessment is when an educator gathers information on learners' performance during to guide learning and instruction. TESOL educators engage in daily, ongoing formative assessment by observing students' language use when working in pairs or small groups, gathering students' self-assessment on their learning or reading students' dialogue journals, for instance. They can compile the data to see areas of need for individuals, groups of students, or the whole class. For example, a TESOL educator may form writing groups at differing proficiency levels so as to provide differentiated instruction for each group. From these sources of data, the educator can also make choices to teach a particular form, check learners' comprehension and re-explain a concept, or to skip an activity.

Summative assessments: Assessments that show learners' achievement of SLOs

Summative assessment is when an educator gauges the degree of student achievement in a unit or course. Summative assessments are known to every student everywhere as quizzes, tests, essays, or oral presentations. They have a role within the language classroom too. They provide feedback to learners in addition to the more informal formative assessment and are the basis for unit or course grades.

Whether we use a formative or summative assessment, we will want to provide constructive and kind feedback to learners on the specific SLOs and their overall progress. When we provide feedback we want to make sure it is comprehensible to the learner, meaning we use language they can understand. This is particularly true for learners at lower proficiency levels. We try to raise students' awareness first and provide hints prior to moving to recasts (see Chapters 9 and 12). If these practices do not yield results, we can move to more explicit feedback. We may try to explain what was incorrect and why, and provide examples of the incorrect and corrected forms (e.g., grammar, syntax, idioms, vocabulary, pronunciation, or spelling). We coach them to try the corrected forms in practice too. While these approaches may seem only applicable to spoken feedback, they are employed in written feedback as well. One practice that helps facilitate feedback on written forms is one-on-one writing conferences.

Grading, scoring, and grading systems

Grading systems have evolved distinctively all over the world. For example:

- In China, in most of the top-level universities, the grading system is divided into five categories:
  - you-xiu ("优"): Excellent (85–100%);
  - liang-hao ("良"): Good (75–84%);
  - zhong-deng ("中"): Satisfactory (literally, "middle"; 65–74%);
  - ji-ge ("及格"): Pass (60–65%); and
  - bu-ji-ge ("不及格"): Failure (0–60%).
- In Egypt, the grading system has six tiers:
  - 100–85% is Excellent (Arabic: ممتاز);
  - 84–75% is Very good (Arabic: جيّد جدًا);
  - 74–65% is Good (Arabic: جيد);
  - 64–50% is Acceptable (Arabic: مقبول);
  - 49–30% is Weak (Arabic: ضعيف); and
  - 29–0% is Very weak (Arabic: ضعيف جدًا).)

- In France and Tunisia, a scale of 1–20 is the standard: 20 is the highest, but rarely achieved, 10 and below is failing, 12 is roughly "B" work, and 17 is exceptional.
- In Germany, they employ a 6-point scale with 1 being the highest and 6 the lowest.
- In Japan, they use a 1–100 scale with 30 and below as failing.
- In Romania, in primary schools, a 4-point grading scale is used:
  - Foarte Bine (FB, very good);
  - Bine (B, good);
  - Suficient/Satisfăcător (S, pass);
  - Insuficient/Nesatisfăcător (I, fail).
- In Turkey, secondary schools use a 6-point grading system (e.g., 5 = excellent, 4 = good, 3 = satisfactory, 2 = passing, 1 = failing, and 0 = failing), and many universities use a 1–4, 1–5, 1–10 (maximum), or 1–10 (minimum) scale. Degrees are graded on a 50–100 scale: 85–100 pekiyi, 65–84 iyi, 50–64 orta, 50 geçer, and 0–49 geçmez.
- In Ukraine and countries from the former USSR, they use a 12-point scale:
  - 12 perfect;
  - 11 excellent;
  - 10 almost excellent;
  - 9 very good;
  - 8 good;
  - 7 fairly good;
  - 6 above satisfactory;
  - 5 satisfactory;
  - 4 below satisfactory;
  - 3 above unsatisfactory;
  - 2 unsatisfactory; and
  - 1 unacceptable.
- In Vietnam, they employ a 5-point scale ranging from 0.00–3.49 very poor, 3.5–4.99 poor, 5.00–6.49 average, 6.5–7.99 good, to 8.00–10.00 excellent.

TESOL educators may be expected to learn new or different grading systems for courses if they travel internationally for work.

On any type of assessment, educators identify or develop the grading/scoring system while they create their assessment. They establish how many points will be awarded for different questions on a multiple choice test, or how they will score an oral presentation using a rubric (see section on "Rubrics to assess performance in English"). It is important from the outset to identify total number of points or percentages and how these points/percentages work within the overall points for the course or unit. For an examination of how to make grading more effective, see "Grading Student Work" (https://cft.vanderbilt.edu/guides-sub-pages/grading-student-work).

When developing assessments, educators need to have a clear sense of the criteria upon which the grade will be based. Criteria may be anything related to language learning. Take, for example, the SLO, "students will be able to write two or three simple sentences using irregular past tense forms with 80% accuracy." The assessment criteria for this SLO may include that they write two or three simple sentences that are

(a) comprehensible and (b) accurate in word order and (c) other grammatical forms (identified specifically), and they can use the (d) correct form of the irregular, past tense verbs. In this case, too, the 80% accuracy level means that there would be "wiggle room," so they could still receive a high score even if they were not accurate 100% of the time. When educators have a clear sense of the criteria upon which the grade is based, it helps them grade more efficiently and fairly.

Questions for reflection

- How might you systematically gather information about learners' four language skill use in the classroom for formative assessment? How about for summative assessment?
- What grading system do you anticipate using? What would you do if your school or program required a different one?
- How would you allocate points on different items of a teacher-made test?

Types of Assessments

While there are many ways to assess learners' knowledge and performance in a L2, we will only mention four main types. These types of assessments are common for the L2 classroom.

Teacher-made tests

Educators may need to make quizzes or tests in situations where they are not provided or do not assess SLOs of the course, unit, or lessons. Educators often start the test design process by identifying their assessment goals and all the instructional concepts that have been taught using a list called a test specification list. The assessment goals should align with the course, unit, or lesson SLOs. For example, if a course's learners need to develop conversation management strategies, the educator will develop an assessment to evaluate their abilities to use the conversational management strategies that were taught. Test specifications lists are a broad outline of the test with the skills and concepts that are to be assessed and ideas of the types of items on the test (items are questions, activities, etc.). Using the test specifications list ensures educators do not overlook any key area.

A recommended assessment practice is to develop quizzes or tests comprising close-ended exercises or open-ended activities that mirror the instructional practices employed in teaching. For example, to address learners' reading, educators provide them a reading passage comparable with ones they read in class and ask them comprehension and inference questions. To assess learners' writing, educators may ask them to write about the topic of study. Vocabulary (productive) and grammar can be assessed through speaking and writing, but receptive vocabulary can also be assessed via listening and reading for understanding the words in context.

Educators may develop all aspects of the test from designing/finding the exercises and activities, listening or reading passages, writing or speaking prompts, rubrics to score production activities, to the test directions. While this may appear to require much effort, it is sometimes easier to create these assessments than find one premade that works for a given learner population, theme/topic, proficiency level(s), and instructional practice. However, teacher-made tests are not necessarily valid or reliable, so we should be mindful of this when grading. A common practice to ensure that our grading decisions are accurate and reliable is to gather more than one set of data on a language skill or concept, so educators may combine a quiz with a performance assessment, for example.

Three helpful texts on developing tests are:

- Brown, H. D. (2004). *Language assessment*. Pearson.
- Hughes, A. (1989). *Testing for language teachers*. Cambridge University Press.
- Madsen, H. S. (1983). *Techniques in testing*. Oxford University Press.

Textbook assessments

Supplemental resources provided by textbook authors and publishers that often accompany an ESL/EFL/ELT textbook are quizzes and tests. Commonly, there is a teacher's manual that contains instructional suggestions, transcripts, reading passages, and quizzes or tests and their scoring guides. The item formats (i.e., kinds of questions, exercises, and activities) on textbook quizzes and tests usually align with the topic and methodology in the textbook. While textbooks assessments are convenient and comprehensive, they may not include everything that was taught in the unit and they may not be valid or reliable for assessment purposes. One strategy that Kate uses is to adapt textbook assessments to the unit of instruction by borrowing useful items, modifying others, and creating some that are not present. For her, they may only stimulate her thinking on how to assess the unit.

Performance assessments

One of the most informative types of assessments for TESOL educators is performance assessment. Performance assessment is a method of evaluation that requires learners to perform a linguistic task so their teacher can see how they use the language. For example, if an educator wants to know if a student can engage in an oral conversation by asking and answering personal questions, the educator would design a task in which learners would ask and answer personal questions in a conversational format, for example, in an oral interview with the educator or a role-play with a peer. Performance assessments are considered authentic assessments because they require learners to participate in linguistic tasks that mirror real language usage. They are considered a type of alternative assessment that differs from traditional multiple choice tests, which require learners to select an answer from a list.

Some examples of performance assessments are telling a story from picture prompts, giving directions, explaining a recipe, writing a blog post or editorial, listening to a podcast or news report and summarizing it for a classmate, or reading a biography to create a timeline poster of key events in the person's life.

The Center for Advanced Research on Language Acquisition (CARLA) outlined integrated performance assessment for language learners with a step-by-step process to design them for classroom use (https://carla.umn.edu/assessment/vac/CreateUnit/p_2.html). Its outline guides educators through nine steps:

1. Reviewing standards.
2. Selecting a theme and essential question.
3. Identifying instructional and assessment goals.
4. Designing performance tasks.
5. Identifying standards.
6. Connecting the integrated performance assessment to Common Core standards.
7. Identify can do statements, structures, and patterns.
8. Identifying vocabulary.
9. Determining key activities.

It should be clear that many of the steps are intertwined with the curriculum development process itself.

Rubrics to assess performance in English

Performance assessments require the use of rubrics for scoring, so that the educator is more objective. Rubrics describe levels of performance (i.e., scale) on the area(s) of the assessment (i.e., performance criteria). For example, for a speaking performance assessment, the educator may wish to include fluidity (i.e., appropriate pausing/hesitations, fluidity, clarity of the message, oral grammar, oral vocabulary, or intelligible pronunciation) and the scale may range from lower to higher degrees of performance. Some systems that educators use to describe the scale are listed below, but other grading scales can be employed as well:

- novice, intermediate, advanced (with low, middle, and high indicators used too);
- needs improvement, meets expectations, exceeds expectations;
- novice, emerging, developing, approaching, proficient, advanced; and
- emerging, progressing, partial mastery, mastery.

Rubrics help educators systematically, equitably, and quickly score performance assessments. They also provide more detailed feedback on the performance criteria for learners so learners understand how they are performing and where they can improve. An excellent instructional practice is to provide the scoring rubric to learners and discuss it with them when the assignment is provided. This practice helps learners understand the assignment expectations so they may target them in their work.

Rubric-making tools

Many online rubric-making programs are available to help educators quickly create rubrics to match their assessments. Some noteworthy examples are:

- Annenberg Learner (custom-design your own);
- Essay Tagger (based on Common Core Standards);
- iRubric (custom-design your own);

- PBL Checklist (custom-design your own rubrics for project-based learning);
- RubiStar (custom-design your own using templates);
- RubricMaker (custom-design your own templates);
- Teachnology (premade and custom-design your own); and
- ThemeSpark (based on Common Core Standards).

To learn more about performance assessments and rubrics, you may want to read:

- Abedi, J. (2010). *Performance assessments for English language learners.* Stanford University, Stanford Center for Opportunity Policy in Education.
- Blaz, D. (2013). *A collection of performance tasks and rubrics: Foreign languages.* Routledge.
- Brookhart, S. M. (2013). *How to create and use rubrics for formative assessment and grading.* Association for Supervision and Curriculum Development (ASCD).
- O'Malley, J. M., & Valdez Pierce, L. (1996). *Authentic assessment for English language learners: Practical approaches for teachers.* Addison-Wesley Publishing.

Portfolio assessments

Portfolios are also an alternative assessment to traditional multiple choice type tests. Learners compile samples of their work in a portfolio, which is graded using rubrics and self-assessments. The use of portfolios help learners and educators to see the learners' linguistic progress over a course, term, or year; however, they may be unfamiliar or difficult for learners, so class time may be spent on organization. Oral language abilities can be included in portfolios too, with some thought and planning. Digital portfolio tools may also aid learners and educators in organization and inclusion of each of the four language skills.

Questions for reflection

- Out of teacher-made tests, performance, and portfolio assessments, which do you prefer and why? Which do you think would be the easiest to implement? Which would be the most informative? Which would be the quickest to grade and provide feedback on? Why?
- How might you design a portfolio system for an ELL you teach?

Placement tests or screeners

When a language learner enters a new school or program, they are assessed on their second language abilities to determine placement into a level in a language school, a grade in K–12, or a course in a university. These types of tests are called placement tests or screeners. The only difference between a placement test and a screener is that screeners tend to be of shorter duration. The reason for using placements and screeners is to identify the ideal level for instruction for their abilities, whether it is a level in a program, grade, or course, so they can receive appropriate instruction that is not too difficult or too easy for them.

Placement tests differ from achievement tests and diagnostic tests: placement tests indicate a general or composite level of ability in the four skills, vocabulary, and grammar; achievement tests indicate if learners have learned the required information; and diagnostic tests indicate specific areas of strength or weakness in a subject. Each different purpose requires a different assessment design and system of results.

When starting work in a new school or program, it is important to learn about the system of placement and the assessment. Since placement tests do not diagnose what the learner needs, but only give a general or combined score of a learner's four skills to arrive at a level of ability, it is vital for educators to be mindful of their limitations. An ELL may perform strongly in reading and writing, for instance, but struggle in oral language skills; their placement may seem dissimilar to others who are stronger in oral language skills, but assigned in the same general level. Owing to differences in performance on the four skills, all TESOL educators teach multiple proficiency levels in the same class, even though the learners may be placed within the same proficiency level.

Standardized exams

Standardized exams are tests that are used to determine a learner's achievement in a subject. They are considered standardized because they are proctored and scored in a consistent and reliable manner. They are also designed to be highly accurate and valid with statistical tests used to assess accuracy of particular test items/questions.

Individuals, programs, schools, and corporations often wish to know an individual's knowledge and performance in a language for personal recognition, academic advancement, or hiring/promotion purposes. Often, standardized exams are crucial for learners because they distinguish those who may advance academically, obtain a job, or receive a promotion from those who do not. For this reason they are labeled "high stakes."

In the field of TESOL there are many standardized exams, which are designed for particular populations. International students wishing to study in an English-medium university take the International English Language Testing System (IELTS) (https://www.ielts.org/en-us) or Test of English as a Foreign Language (TOEFL) exams (https://www.ielts.org/en-us). Individuals seeking to obtain a job or promotion often take the Test of English for International Communication (TOEIC) (https://www.ets.org/toeic). Students in the K–12 take the WIDA ACCESS for ELLs test (https://wida.wisc.edu/assess/access).

In some educational settings, ELLs may not be familiar with how to take a standardized exam, since they have had no previous experience with it. In these situations, TESOL educators teach ELLs the formatting of the exam, what to expect in terms of test items and answer formats, and strategies for taking the exam. This practice is not considered teaching to the exam, because it does not teach only the concepts that will appear on it. Teaching to the exam is generally considered a poor instructional practice.

Proctoring standardized exams

When learners take a standardized exam, educators are often called upon to proctor and/or score it. Proctoring, or conducting, summative assessments requires the educator to establish a quiet, uninterrupted classroom setting, provide oral and/or written directions, answer questions about directions, provide test accommodations, and monitor for cheating. The roles and responsibilities of TESOL educators vary considerably when proctoring depending on the instructional context. In some schools, TESOL educators are required to participate in proctoring the university-wide placement or achievement tests at the beginning or end of terms, respectively. In some contexts, the notion of cheating is defined differently, so all educators need to be aware of how it is defined and what a particular institution requires an educator to do if they catch a student cheating.

Accommodations on standardized exams

Accommodations on assessments, standardized or other types, are modifications to the test environment, tools, or services so that ELLs can demonstrate their knowledge and abilities to the best degree possible. Offering accommodations during assessments is a common TESOL practice. Accommodations to the test environment may include using headphones in private cubicles so learners can hear better or individually testing in a separate location. Some tools that are common test accommodations for ELLs are bilingual dictionaries (without definitions), thesauruses, word banks, or visuals. Modifications to services include having the test read aloud, simplifying or repeating test directions, additional time for the test, having periodic breaks in testing, or having translations of directions. For more on accommodations, see Young and King (2008) or Kieffer et al. (2009). Accommodations may be used on any summative assessment from teacher-made to standardized tests.

The field of assessment has developed substantially over the past 50 years. Individuals can specialize in evaluation for an entire career and there are even scholarships and fellowships for study of text development and evaluation through the Educational Testing Service, for example. More material about second language learning and assessment is available in the following.

- Brown, H. D. (2004). *Language assessment*. Pearson.
- Coombe, C., Stoynoff, S., O'Sullivan, B., & Davidson, P. (2012). *The Cambridge guide to second language assessment*. Cambridge University Press.
- Flores, G. S. (2016). *Assessing English language learners: Theory and practice*. Routledge.
- Gottlieb, M. (2006). *Assessing English language learners: Bridge from proficiency to academic achievement*. Corwin.
- Law, B., & Eckes, M. (2007). *Assessment and ESL: An alternative approach*, 2nd ed. Portage & Main Press.

Questions for reflection

- How might you find out what criteria are being assessed on a standardized exam?
- How might you prepare your learners for a standardized exam through your lessons without teaching to the test?
- How might you integrate a standardized exam into your overall assessment array for a course or year?

Chapter Conclusions

The process of curricular development is a circuitous and recursive process that involves gathering information, establishing priorities, organizing the curriculum, writing engaging lessons, and assessing learning. The process can be informed by needs assessments, textbooks, standards, and assessment criteria. Educators may collaborate or work independently in the development of a curriculum. Curriculum development begins from a global perspective and narrows successively to specific lessons. Without the global curricular perspective, educators cannot guide their learners through material in a coherent and connected manner and may not know what to do the next day. When designing curriculum, educators will review standards and assessments through the backward design process to ensure that educators include all the concepts and skills learners need to be successful on their assessments. Six types of assessments were discussed in terms of how they impact the L2 classroom and how teachers could use them.

Discussion Questions

1. How would you describe the curriculum development process? What do you think would be the easiest and hardest parts?
2. What are the pros and cons of collaborating with a colleague or team to develop a curriculum for ELLs? Which would you prefer and why?
3. Compare and contrast teacher-made and textbook-provided tests in terms of pros and cons for using each. How might you make them more valid and reliable?

Tasks

1. Evaluate a publisher-produced curriculum for ELLs. What does the curriculum say about the producer's beliefs regarding second language teaching and learning? What is included that is effective/ineffective for ELLs? What is missing that should be included? Remember to look at how the communicative competencies, four

language skills and tools, and content address the level(s) of proficiency and age(s) of the learners.

2 Draft a curriculum plan for a class you are teaching or plan to teach from the curriculum goals and the unit goals and SLOs to lesson goals and SLOs. Be sure to review the standards and assessments and link to them. Share your plan with a peer or colleagues for feedback. Reflect on the curriculum process (e.g., What did you like/dislike? What was most easy/challenging, how might you do it differently in the future?).

3 Make an assessment for a class you are teaching or plan to teach. It can be a teacher-made test or performance assessment. Write your assessment goals, test specifications, and types of items to be included. Provide a rationale for your choices.

Further Reading/Read and Discuss

Read about curriculum design:

Macalister, J., & Nation, I. S. P. (2010). *Language curriculum design*. Routledge.

Read about curricular design for ESP:

Campbell, C., MacPherson, S., & Sawkins, T. (2014). Preparing students for education, work, and community: Activity theory in task-based curriculum design. *TESL Canada Journal, 31*(8), 68–92.

Read about oral and written feedback for ELLs:

Sheen, Y. (2010). Differential effects of oral and written corrective feedback in the ESL classroom. *Studies in Second Language Acquisition, 32*(2), 203–234. https://doi.org/10.1017/S0272263109990507

References

Angelo, T. A., & Cross, K. P. (1993). *Classroom assessment techniques: A handbook for college teachers*. Jossey-Bass.

Brown, J. D. (2009). Foreign and second language needs analysis. In M. H. Long & C. J. Doughty (Eds.), *The handbook of language teaching* (pp. 269–293). Blackwell.

Byrd, P., & Schuemann, C. (2014). English as a second/foreign language textbooks: How to choose them—How to use them. In M. Celce-Murcia, D. M. Brinton, & M. A. Snow (Eds.), *Teaching English as a second or foreign language* (4th ed., pp. 380–393). National Geographic Learning/Cengage.

Center for Advanced Research on Language Acquisition (CARLA). (2019). *Create a standards-based integrated performance assessment unit step-by-step: Integrated Performance Assessment (IPA)*. https://carla.umn.edu/assessment/vac/CreateUnit/p_2.html (accessed March 26, 2021).

Fairbairn, S., & Jones-Vo, S. (2019). *Differentiating instruction and assessment for English language learners: A guide for K–12 Teachers* (2nd ed.). Caslon.

Graves, K. (2014). Syllabus and curriculum design for second language teaching. In M. Celce-Murcia, D. M. Brinton, & M. A. Snow (Eds.), *Teaching English as a second or foreign language* (4th ed., pp. 46–62). National Geographic Learning/Cengage.

Kieffer, M. J., Lesaux, N. K., Rivera, M., & Francis, D. J. (2009). Accommodations for English language learners taking large-scale assessments: A meta-analysis on effectiveness and validity. *Review of Educational Research*, *79*(3), 1168–1201. https://doi.org/10.3102/0034654309332490

Richards, J. (n.d.) *Evaluating a text book*. https://www.professorjackrichards.com/evaluating-text-book (accessed March 26, 2021).

Robb, T. (November 23, 2013). School calendars around the world. TESOL International Association. https://www.tesol.org/connect/tesol-resource-center/search-details/teaching-tips/2013/11/23/school-calendars-around-the-world (accessed March 26, 2021).

Stoller, F. L., & Grabe, W. (1997). A six-T's approach to content-based instruction. In M. A. Snow & D. M. Brinton (Eds.), *The content-based classroom* (pp. 78–94). Addison-Wesley Longman.

Stoller, F. L., & Grabe, W. (2017). Building coherence into the content-based curriculum: Six T's revisited. In M. A. Snow & D. M. Brinton (Eds.), *The content-based classroom* (2nd ed., pp. 53–66). Michigan University Press.

Ur, P. (2009). *A course in language teaching: Practice and theory*. Cambridge.

Wiggins, G., & McTighe, J. (2005). *Understanding by design* (expanded 2nd ed.). Association for Supervision and Curriculum Development (ASCD).

World-class Instructional Design and Assessment (WIDA). (2012). 2012 *amplification of the English language development standards: Kindergarten–grade 12*. University of Wisconsin System and WIDA Consortium.

Young, J. W., & King, T. C. (2008). *Testing accommodations for English language learners: A review of state and district policies* (research report no. 2008-6). College Board.

Part Four

Where Do We Go From Here?

13

How Does TESOL Develop Its Body of Knowledge and Share Professional Knowledge?

Thus far, this text has shown how TESOL professionals draw from a set of knowledge, which guides their teaching and assessment. We have explained the academic disciplines that TESOL and Applied Linguistics bring together in instruction and assessment. Where did this knowledge originate? Who are the individuals who study all the variables related to teaching and assessment of ESL/EFL/ELT? Where is the information shared? Why is sharing our knowledge important? This chapter will address these questions from global and local perspectives.

Learning Outcomes

At the conclusion of this chapter, you will be able to:

- describe the origins of the knowledge set that serves as a foundation for ESL/EFL/ELT instruction and assessment
- connect to the ways that educators working in settings ranging from preschool to university, university faculty, school district personnel, administrators, and educational leaders have participated in developing the knowledge that guides English language instruction
- determine which venues of professional knowledge are credible and accessible to you
- identify ways you can become involved in sharing your professional knowledge

When entering a new profession, many educators take courses/programs or obtain a degree. Once they have completed their program or degree, they often engage beyond their classroom to continue to develop their knowledge and skills.

TESOL Voices
Teachers' Research Makes a Big Impact
The Reading Intervention Program of Quezon City Science High School is a school initiative research program of the Department of Education in the Philippines. It addresses the country's goal to make every Filipino child a reader and is known as the 3Bs "Bawat Bata Bumabasa" (i.e., Every Child Reads).

Introduction to TESOL: Becoming a language teaching professional, First Edition. Kate Mastruserio Reynolds, Kenan Dikilitaş, and Steve Close.
© 2022 John Wiley & Sons, Inc. Published 2022 by John Wiley & Sons, Inc.

The teacher-led research program used the Philippine Informal Reading Inventory (Phil-IRI), which is composed of literature-based passages to determine a student's performance in oral reading, silent reading, and listening comprehension. These three types of assessments aim to find the student's instructional preferences, independent reading abilities, and frustration levels. Data from the 12-session program was used to design or adjust classroom instruction (i.e., small-group or individualized instruction) to fit the students' needs and abilities.

The skill sets became part of the 2020 school entrance exam for incoming grade 7 students. After the program, teachers learned that instilling confidence in students was more important than giving the techniques in reading comprehension. Later, teachers discussed and showed examples to students of the skills needed in noting details, inferred learning, and even the basics—topic sentences and title suggestions. Exposure to the type of questions and choosing a correct answer gave more confidence to students.

To develop skill sets in oral reading, teachers made a suggestion that a 5-min random, inspirational student reading activity should be encouraged as part of classroom routine activity. Flashcards also played an important role in developing these skill sets. We know that reading interventions have their limitations, just like this experience of a Philippine public high school teacher's reading research is limited. Beyond the demands of teaching in a Philippine public school system and of family life, this teacher researcher believes that commitment and dedication to our oath remains the same whether we are in Asia, Europe, or the Americas, or in this case a small science school in Bago Bantay, Quezon City.

Bernardo Tupas Panzo
English teacher
Quezon City Science High School (Regional Science High School for NCR)

A Rationale for Ongoing Professional Development

To be effective, ESL/EFL/ELT educators need an extensive knowledge base. This knowledge base includes information about:

- cultures: intercultural/cross-cultural communications, culturally responsive teaching, critical race theory;
- language systems: English language syntax, phonology, lexicon, semantics, morphology, pragmatics, orthography;
- language use, processing, and acquisition: sociolinguistics, psychology, child development, first and second language acquisition research and theories;
- instruction and assessment: methods of instruction and assessment appropriate for the learners and the learning context, content-based ESL instruction, sheltered content instruction, English for specific purposes; and
- educational systems.

Furthermore, ESL/EFL/ELT educators need to be able to organize a curriculum, plan lessons, make and modify materials, deliver lessons, employ technology, manage learners, assess learning, and reflect upon the teaching and learning. Collaboration with other educators and parents is important too. The list is extensive, yet each topic can be further unpacked and explored.

The knowledge and skills within TESOL came from many individuals who shared their knowledge. Each of these individuals most likely started out as a TESOL educator rather than a researcher. It may appear, for example, that the research on many of these topics came from researchers who work at universities, in governmental institutions, or for nonprofit organizations. Researchers, however, can be anyone with curiosity or a problem to solve. Educators research when they grade students' papers to see if students met the learning targets. Educators investigate when they try a new technique to see if the students would learn the topic more easily than another similar class, or when they analyze students' conversational management strategies to determine which strategies to teach. Research is just an activity that we all do every day, but it is often considered a scary activity done by only some people.

The importance of teacher research

Educators can and should conduct research to generate practical knowledge that could inform their present and future teaching. Research can help them explore the context of the classroom, understand learners, explore and improve their own teaching practices, examine or revisit their beliefs, and keep learning about their profession as an individual or collaborative investment. It is often suggested that educators can best learn when they collaborate meaningfully with their students and jointly engage in research with their direct contribution. Learners are the key beneficiaries from the instructional process and can offer first-hand evidence for educators to justify or discredit practices that might require modification, and change or deepen understanding of the practices to enable them to teach with awareness in an evidence-informed way. Research also offers space for meaningful critical reflection on teaching practices, which allows educators to feel empowered and self-confident since they have underlying relevant and supportive knowledge to help them improve their teaching. Research-based reflection also offers contextual evidence that strengthens pedagogical thinking and planning. Such a process nurtures and cultivates educators' criticality and mindset since research findings might contradict their already existing teaching practices raising awareness of potential pragmatic gaps and pedagogical inappropriateness. Sometimes even a small amount of feedback from learners can show how much we take for granted that we offer very effective teaching, but that this might not always be the case. Research in this sense is also a means to adopting a self-reflective stance on our own practices. It empowers our self-evaluation process without a gatekeeper who keeps an eye on our practices (Senaydin & Dikilitaş, 2019) and awakens us when there is need for a change. Investing and engaging in research in the classroom:

• put educators at the epicenter of their own learning;
• position them as knowledge generator rather than as knowledge transited;

- assign them new roles such as researcher, author, and presenter, thereby nurturing a new identity;
- connect practice to theory rather than vice versa;
- transform power relations in the classroom: co-researching and co-learning;
- shift the lens through which learning is perceived;
- bring learners closer to the center of learning;
- help educators and learners problematize the issues together;
- balance learner and educator issues rather than focusing only on the latter;
- allow for learner-driven educator learning that situates professional development in a specific context; and
- initiate a realistic self-evaluation of teaching rather than looking at pedagogical issues simplistically without adequate and deep reflection.

Educators become potentially autonomous when they discover contextual knowledge and learn further about their practices (Dikilitaş & Griffiths, 2017). Autonomy is a self-regulatory process of how best to learn as an educator that is supported by the critical lens developed though the researching initiative.

In education today, it is commonly recognized that educators in K–12 schools have many situated insights into teaching, learning, and assessment activities (North, 1987; Cochran-Smith & Lytle, 1993, 1999a, 1999b). Educators are creative and often develop new materials and techniques. They also have insights into working with learners and the challenges that learners experience. This practical knowledge helps their students, but if shared it can benefit many other ELLs. Orienting yourself to share your knowledge, whether research or practical, may be a step you take further down the road, but it will help you continually grow as an educator as well as helping you along your professional development journey (Johnson & Golombek, 2016; Dana & Yendol-Hoppey, 2019).

Educators can begin sharing their knowledge locally at their schools. It is possible, with some effort, to develop a reputation for possessing knowledge and abilities among coworkers and administrators. Administrators often ask teachers who are recognized as participants in "thinking about teaching" to co-teach, coach a colleague, or present a workshop for their peers. Over time, any teacher who is interested in advancing the field can share a new technique or material at a district training seminar or a regional conference. Farther afield, even relatively inexperienced educators can share their knowledge online or in different locations worldwide through grants, such as on the English Language Fellows program.

Questions for reflection

- Would you want to engage in classroom-based research? What would you need to learn or do to be able to conduct classroom-based research?
- How would professional engagement help you develop your professional knowledge?
- When do you think professionals should begin to engage in professional development?

Venues for Sharing Professional Knowledge

Educators can share their knowledge and learning in communities of practice (COPs). COPs are groups of individuals with common goal or focus who learn together. "Communities of practice are groups of people who share a concern, a set of problems, or a passion about a topic, and who deepen their knowledge and expertise in this area by interacting on an ongoing basis" (Wenger, 2002, p. 4). A team of fifth-grade teachers or university EFL instructors are examples of COPs. The fifth-grade team can collaborate to distribute and discuss materials they develop in weekly meetings. The EFL instructors may confer to develop a rubric for writing assessment that would allow for appropriate and valid placement into the program.

A research team established at schools can also be an example of a COP. In research teams, educators collaborate to understand, explore, and challenge their established teaching practices. COPs can be small or large. They can be face-to-face or online. They can meet regularly or intermittently. Chapter 2 explained several professional organizations; these are also COPs. These COPs are large with an international reach, offer face-to-face and online interaction opportunities, and they meet regularly. In this section, we will explore types of COPs in which any educator can share their professional knowledge while receiving feedback and guidance in their professional development process.

COPs in schools

At their individual schools, educators can share their knowledge with colleagues in weekly meetings or professional development sessions. In these school-based COPs, many educators offer material they develop to their colleagues for use. Materials that educators create for use in their classrooms are diverse; these materials include graphic organizers, anchor charts, mnemonic devices, strategy posters, and language learning games and activities. Some educators even translate vocabulary sets or readings. For example, educators may make infographics to help explain a grammar point (e.g., present simple of "to be" in affirmative or negative, idioms of love or money, or collocations of the word "break") or a poster of a concept with visuals (e.g., body parts, weather words, classroom objects, or landscapes). Infographics can be made online at Piktochart.com, Venngage.com, or Canva.com. PowerPoint or Prezi presentations on topics of interest to the team are also useful tools to aid sharing of knowledge. Other professional knowledge that educators share in COPs includes tips for working with learners at a specific proficiency level, teaching a concept, or engaging with parents. This knowledge is practical and unique to the school and community context.

Developing materials

This week in Kate's TESL Methods course, future ESL specialists are creating visual vocabulary lists. Visual vocabulary lists are several words (8–10 words depending on grade level) with definitions, a visual to illustrate the concept, and an example sentence. Educators can use these visual vocabulary lists to teach a set of topical or thematic words learners need for their reading, writing, speaking, or listening. This is just one example of the kinds of materials that educators develop for their classrooms. Educators write mini stories targeting a specific reading proficiency level, draw illustrations of settings from history or books, develop bookmarks with word attack or reading strategies, and compose songs and chants around the topic of study, just to name some of the materials educators have created. The materials that can be developed for classes are only limited by creativity and funding. In the next section, we will explain more about the types of materials that can be shared, and with whom they can be shared.

Materials that educators develop are often used in collaboration with other educators to help them engage learners. Other reasons to develop materials are to facilitate the learning of the language, fill a void where a material does not exist on the topic for the grade and proficiency level, and improve the quality of materials available by making materials relevant and authentic.

When we develop materials and share them, our peers and their ELLs benefit from their use. Many educators have developed materials and shared them over the years, and we borrow and adapt them often. One of the most pervasive materials employed is the K-W-L chart (*know, what to know, learned*). It is a resource that helps learners and educators to connect to learners' background on a topic, build interest, predict what they will learn, and reflect on their learning. It allows learners to compare what they thought they would learn with what they actually learned. K-W-L charts are graphic organizers that enhance the learners' awareness of their own knowledge and learning processes while providing insights for educators. It has since been adapted to K-W-H-L to include *how* students learned the information. What most people do not know is that Donna M. Ogle developed the first K-W-L chart. Ms. Ogle, a reading teacher, shared her graphic organizer in *The Reading Teacher* in 1986.

Sharing our materials is an important way we contribute to the profession of TESOL. We also benefit from sharing if we receive feedback on them. For more information about developing materials, check out *Materials Development in Language Teaching* (2001) edited by Tomlinson or *EFL Magazine's* "A no-nonsense guide to writing materials" (https://www.eflmagazine.com/3458-2).

Teacher book study

Educators can learn together on a topic of mutual interest by participating in a teacher book study. The goal of a teacher book study is established based upon members' professional interests. Group members identify what they hope to learn from the book study (e.g., to make language learning classes more interactive, or to identify ways to improve ELLs' reading comprehension), and identify professional texts, journal articles, white papers, or other reading material to help them answer their questions.

When we join book studies with our general education peers, we can help them glimpse more about ELLs and provide ideas and materials for collaboration, co-teaching, or their classroom use. Book studies can be organized to learn more about a topic in depth, enhance professional knowledge, remain up to date in knowledge and practices, or glimpse other perspectives. It is important in a book study group to choose high-quality professional material and to read critically.

Book study groups usually meet in person, but they may also meet online to discuss the text(s) they wish to study. Often materials can be obtained from professional publishers who print texts for teacher education or professional development. Some reputable publishers of teacher education books in TESOL are organizations such as the British Council, IATEFL, and TESOL. Publishers who specialize in or have extensive resources for teacher education in TESOL and Applied Linguistics include Cambridge University Press, Cengage, John Benjamins, Multilingual Matters, Oxford University Press, University of Michigan Press, and Wiley. Each of these organizations and publishers approaches publication of teacher education or professional development materials in a more or less practical, theoretical, or accessible manner. Finding a text on a topic is a start, but making sure it is applicable, comprehensible, and useful are other important considerations when starting a book study. A good rule of thumb is to choose texts that are current, so not older than 5 years.

An effective way to structure book study meetings applies the Rule of 3 Protocol developed by Southern Main Partnership with Camilla Greene (as cited in UFT Teacher Center, n.d.), which deepens the members' comprehension of the text. The Rule of 3 Protocol suggests groups should be formed with three to five members and a designated facilitator and timekeeper. Members should be encouraged to read in advance, but if they do not have time allow members to read the material and identify key passages that have significance to their work. Each participant takes 3 min to (a) read and discuss the literal meanings of a passage, (b) indicate each reader's interpretation, opinion, and connections to past experiences, and (c) connect this passage to their work. The others in the group have 2 min to respond to what is striking to you. After all members have discussed their thoughts, the group members would discuss their "aha" moments, ideas, and learning for 5 min.

When we read professional writings, we want to keep an open mind about the new material. One of the challenges encountered by teacher educators is when newcomers to the field dismiss new information without first pondering it. Elbow (2000; Belanoff et al., 2002) encourages educators to engage in "the doubting and believing games" in which the educator suspends their disbelief about a new technique or approach (i.e., believing), so they do not dismiss it out of hand. In effect, this allows the educator to ponder the new technique or approach and possibly to try it before arriving at a judgment about it. The opposite effect is the doubting game. The doubting game is when educators discover a new idea they love and, instead of quickly embracing it, they critically look at the idea and analyze it from different perspectives. In our book study groups, it is important to read critically, objectively, and reflectively.

Conducting investigations

At schools of different levels, there are opportunities to conduct research and to share learning and materials. Many instructional techniques are employed in instruction based on tradition, but have no research to support their use. Educators need to employ evidence-based techniques and practices. The evidence can be developed through simple investigations that are reasonably conducted by educators. In some cases, educators can collaborate to investigate a topic of shared interest, which makes teacher inquiry less daunting and burdensome while increasing the quality of the inquiry (Dana & Yendol-Hoppey, 2019).

Teachers, or teams of educators, can compare methods or techniques of instruction to learn which method or technique works more effectively with their unique population of ELLs. For example, one topic Kate is interested in exploring is how effective round robin/popcorn reading is with ELLs. Round robin reading is a technique in which students take turns reading a sentence or paragraph aloud and going around the room. This is a technique often employed in classrooms, but how effective is it for ELLs' comprehension of the material? Is the ELLs' lack of oral language proficiency a hindrance or too great a challenge in this reading format? Is there a better technique?

An educator can investigate using different approaches or techniques to teach vocabulary; for example, using vocabulary lists derived from a reading or a thematic list to see whether students retain the vocabulary better using one approach over the other. One can investigate explicit instruction of grammatical concepts or which memorization games aid in recall. The research model to compare approaches or techniques is a comparative study. Many other areas of investigation are available to educators.

One type of investigation that can be done by educators is a case study. A case study could be conducted to follow the learning process of a student over time to chronicle the successes and challenges the learner experiences when learning language in a pullout model for 5 hr weekly and being in the general education classroom for the remainder, for example. One could investigate using a case study approach the learning of first-grade Japanese students when immersed in the language through songs, games, and projects. The topic does not need to be a specific instructional or assessment practices or a particular case. Educators can investigate problems to better understand the nature of the problem and possible solutions to the problem. For example, educators may want to investigate issues such as:

- finding effective ways of working with learners who have experienced interrupted learning;
- identifying strategies of supporting language learners who are refugees and have experienced trauma; or
- helping learners to read if they come from a first language that is not written.

A research model that educators can use to investigate a problem is action research. Anne Burns (2010) noted that action research is a valuable tool to enhance our instructional skills and gain insight into our students, instruction, and ourselves (p. 1). Action research is a research method in which educators identify a problem and possible solutions to learn more about and plan ways to gather information (i.e., data) to gain insight into the problem and potential solutions. The cyclical series of steps an educator takes in action research, according to Burns, is planning, putting the plan into action, observing the results of the plan, and reflecting upon the learning and plan. Following this model, action research can be employed within the lesson plan structure to affirm and help educators serve ELLs in the best manner possible. For more in-depth learning on action research, read Burns' approachable and easily read book *Doing Action Research in English Language Teaching*.

Language learning is influenced by many different factors, such as cultures, individual experiences, language exposure, patterns of classroom instruction, and assessment. Because of this, one research methodology would not serve to help us answer all of our questions. To learn about other research models for the various types of studies, look for our upcoming volume on research methodologies in TESOL. Other useful texts are *Research Methods in Second Language Acquisition* by Mackey and Gass or *Doing Second Language Research* by Brown and Rodgers.

Local and regional communities of practice

Beyond the school, educators may share their knowledge and materials in local school districts or regional gatherings. Since these COPs tend to be smaller, there are often opportunities for individuals within the COP to share their ideas and materials. This sort of contribution is often viewed as more realistic and beneficial for other educators in the COP, because the individual presenter has an insider's understanding of the dynamics of the local/regional context.

The type of local or regional community of practice gatherings may be formal, such as a conference, or informal, such as a workshop or a book study. The events may be mandatory for all school personnel to learn about a new curriculum approach or optional for individuals wishing to develop their skill sets in a distinct direction, such as improving guided reading practices. Topics for these events target the goals of the educators and their ELL in that area.

Here are some examples:

- A school district in Illinois has a face-to-face and online COP doing a book study of "Special Education Considerations for English Language Learners" (Hamayan et al., 2013).
- A school district in Washington State has workshops on racial equity and cultural responsive instruction.
- An upcoming conference in Hilo, Hawaii, emphasizes English literature, linguistics, globalization and policy, and assessment.
- In Buenos Aires, Argentina, another regional conference focuses on practical activities and tools for teaching EFL to Spanish speakers in K–12 classes.
- Africa TESOL is hosting a conference on topics such as teaching large classes, education policy and World Englishes, computer-assisted language learning, student-centered practices in the African ELT classroom, and teaching in low-resource contexts.

Each area has its unique perspective and interests.

Questions for reflection

- In your area, what do you anticipate are the topics of interest for the COPs?
- How might you contribute your knowledge within your local or regional COP?

Online COPs

Online opportunities to share one's knowledge are plentiful, yet the give and take of sharing and feedback are not present in the same way as when one is working with a face-to-face school-based team. Moving to an online environment makes any submitted work more public, which presents distinct positives (e.g., a larger audience) and negatives (e.g., lack of anonymity, public criticism). We will explore some of the options for educators wishing to share their professional knowledge online.

Professional development organizations often have online discussion forums or list-serves for interaction among their members, such as Washington State ESOL Online or TESOL's MyTESOL. Educators can ask questions to others who may be experiencing a similar situation. They can ask for ideas or resources. It is often the case the new educators need a recommendation for a textbook or a way to teach a tricky topic. Learning and sharing in these forums tends to be collegial, informed, and supportive, so they are a welcoming venue to interact with peers.

Educators can record videos of instructional techniques and post them at YouTube. Videos to teach how to make a request or a tricky phrasal verb are examples of topics educators share. Some examples of educator-developed videos posted on YouTube are:

- Elemental English;
- Mad English TV;
- JenniferESL; and
- Learn English with Steve Ford.

These videos cover a range of practical topics for English learners. The benefits of sharing knowledge through short videos are that you can reach a wide audience, focus on one concept at a time, and get creative. One does need to know a bit about video recording and editing, but many tools are available today.

Another similar venue for sharing professional knowledge is a vlog (i.e., a video blog) to demonstrate patterns of English use. Video recordings and vlogs both share the use of video. Vlogs differ from videos, however, because vlogs chronicle a slice of teaching life. For example, a teacher, with proper permissions, may record themselves conducting a lesson with their students to demonstrate a technique. Other vloggers record themselves going shopping or to the library to demonstrate the use of English in these environments. Julian Northbrook's YouTube channel has many examples of vlog-type recordings.

Webcasts are increasingly becoming an important professional learning venue for many educators who cannot attend conferences. Webcasts have the advantage of being live, so that participants can interact with the presenter. They may also be more intimate with a limited audience, which helps to avoid the public exposure that videos and vlogs experience. Since webcasts are presentations, a participant would present their information to educators in the school district. Afterward, participants could ask that participant questions about the topic. Some of the webcast software has a chat box for participants to ask questions during the presentation. Educators often work through a professional organization to conduct webcasts, but some venues for broadcasting a webcast exist. For example, educators can use online software for webcast, such as ezTalks, GoToWebinar, WebinarJam, Click Meeting, or iMeetLive. Using a webcast to share knowledge and engage in discussion on the topic is a good solution for locations that are spread out or where travel is not an option.

Educators also share many resources on Pinterest. Pinterest is one venue for sharing a blog, vlog, infographic, visuals of materials, or website. People use it as an electronic bulletin board for posting all kinds of personal and professional information. Many TESOL educators use Pinterest as an electronic filing cabinet for ideas and tools related to teaching ESL/EFL/ELT. For example, an educator could post items that they created for use in your classroom such as creating models of cells out of "Shrinky Dinks," using effective conversation starters, showing visuals of vocabulary sets, demonstrating bilingual books made for a class, posting rubrics for ELLs' writing, and describing sight word games. While Pinterest has ample resources for instruction, it does not provide a forum for interaction among its members. When sharing your professional knowledge this way, there may not be much feedback from those who see or use the material that was provided.

Grant programs to work with international COPs

Grant and fellowship programs allow educators to share their knowledge to COP internationally, while developing their expertise. There is a reciprocal exchange of information when one participates in these programs. We have learned so much from interacting with colleagues on grant programs. For instance, Kate participated as an English language specialist with the U.S. State Department and was welcomed by colleagues in Colombia. Her task was to provide workshops on task-based ESL/EFL instruction. During the workshops, educators asked great questions. For example, what is the difference between a task and a project? This question prompted some in-depth readings for Kate. She grew as a result of the question.

International COPs can go beyond language teaching, and into detailed aspects of cultural exchange, adaptation to the pace of life in a new country, and expectations when living in a nation where the dominant language is not the speaker's first language. Steve participated in a Training of Trainers in Ukraine, designed to educate Peace Corps volunteers about the various stages of adaptation to life in an unfamiliar place. His chief task was to cover the basic "curve" of living overseas, using a planned curriculum that predicted what each of the Peace Corps volunteers would experience during their time in Ukraine. The goal was to teach them about the "culture shock" model, noting that they would begin with excitement and enthusiasm, gradually become homesick and perhaps even alienated by the unfamiliar culture in which they were living, and gradually level out into a true appreciation of Ukrainian culture. Trainings like these can literally save lives, and they demonstrate why COPs are so important.

This section will demonstrate some prominent grant and fellowship programs, but they are only some of the public and private grants offered. Location, emphasis, and experience are factors that would influence which opportunities are available to a particular educator. The grant programs mentioned were chosen because they allow educators to participate in an exchange of professional knowledge.

Professional organizations offer grant programs, for example, travel grants to attend a conference or to develop materials. The British Council is one such organization, offering a variety of grants for educators' professional development and exchange (https://www.britishcouncil.org/school-resources/funding).

Publishers and assessment groups, such as Kagan, offer grant programs to further their interests, too. For example, Educational Testing Service (ETS), who developed the standardized Test of English as a Foreign Language (TOEFL), has the English-Language Researcher/Practitioner Grant program (https://www.ets.org/toefl/grants/el_researcher_practitioner_grant) to help educators learn about the complexities of English language learning and teaching.

Governments also offer grants and fellowships. For example, the Japanese government offers the Japan Exchange and Teaching Program (https://jetprogramusa.org), known as the JET Program. It is for individuals worldwide who would like to work in Japanese schools, boards of education, and government offices. Participants may assist Japanese educators in K–12 settings to teach English, often by providing examples of authentic language use.

The Fulbright Teaching Excellence and Achievement Program (https://www.irex.org/project/fulbright-teaching-excellence-and-achievement-program-fulbright-tea), known as the Fulbright TEA grant, is a 6-week teacher exchange sponsored by the U.S. Department of State. This grant is available for teachers from international settings to visit the United States for programs that include observation of courses, collegial collaboration, and sharing of best practices in education. The Fulbright program offers many other grant opportunities to TESOL professionals at all stages of their career. You may want to investigate their other programs at https://eca.state.gov/fulbright.

The English Language Fellow Program (https://exchanges.state.gov/us/program/english-language-fellow-program), sponsored by the U.S. Bureau of Educational and Cultural Affairs, is a 10-month program in which TESOL specialists can share their expertise with educators in selected countries. English Language Fellows (ELFs) may teach language classes or teacher education classes, but they may also collaborate in the development of curriculum, materials, or workshops for their school. ELFs are typically experienced educators who also hold a Master's degree in TESOL.

English Language Specialist Program (https://exchanges.state.gov/us/program/english-language-specialist-program) is a shorter duration program of 2 weeks to 3 months. TESOL educators apply to the pool of specialists. The organization in the target country requests an expert on a professional development topic of interest to them. The U.S. State Department discusses the topic of interest with them and aids in the choice of the appropriate specialist. Specialists tend to have a Master's or higher in the field with considerable experience.

Sharing Professional Knowledge in Written Form

A traditional manner to share professional knowledge and to become an active participant in the TESOL COP is to share work in written form. While it is traditional, it does not have to be complex or intimidating. There are several edited books that include English language teachers' research reports (see Barkhuizen et al., 2018; Dikilitaş & Hanks, 2018; Dikilitaş et al., 2019).

Newsletters, magazines, and blogs

Many TESOL educators start sharing their materials and instructional tips in newsletters, magazines, or blogs. The formality and accessibility of newsletters, magazines, and blogs make them an approachable place to begin. Winston-Salem/Forsyth County Schools' ESL department publishes a newsletter for parents, teachers, and students of ELLs. In their volume from the first quarter 2019, they share information about their program, language proficiency levels, language objectives, and tips for welcoming ELL newcomers to general educators' classes (Winston-Salem/Forsyth County Schools, ESL Department, n.d.). This information has real-world practicality and is valuable for the teachers and parents, so they know better how to support English learners.

Magazines for TESOL professionals offer hands-on, applicable information that teachers can employ in their lesson planning and delivery, and assessment too. Some notable magazines for teachers of ESL/EFL/ELT are *British Council Voices*, *EFL Magazine*, *English Teaching Professional*, *IATEFL Voices*, *Language*, and *Modern English Teacher*. Magazines are more informal and not typically based on research.

Teacher blogs can allow the writer a wide and diverse online audience, so may have an impact on many TESOL professionals. An example of a teacher-written blog, which is widely known and respected, is by Larry Ferlazzo, who is a high school teacher in California (http://larryferlazzo.edublogs.org). He writes on practical topics related to teaching in general and tips and techniques for teaching ELLs in English and social studies. His blog titled "5-Minute Film Festival: 7 Videos for ELL Classrooms" provides video resources to teach language topics, such as asking for an opinion (Ferlazzo, 2015, November 20).

Suggestions to make publishing practical for teachers:

- Submit articles to a program or affiliate newsletter.
- Get involved with organizing a program or affiliate newsletter. Write for *EFL Magazine*, for example (you can volunteer at https://www.eflmagazine.com/write-for-us).
- Start a blog or vlog with colleagues. Donaghy (2016) offers a step-by-step guide for setting up a blog for sharing ELT materials (https://members.iatefl.org/projects).
- Contribute your materials to Pinterest, What Works Clearinghouse (https://ies.ed.gov/ncee/wwc), or TESOL's Resource Center (https://www.tesol.org/connect/tesol-resource-center).
- Apply for a mini grant.

Journals

As an educator grows in their professional knowledge, their discussion of their practices and research becomes less anecdotal (i.e., based on their personal experiences). These educators move to other venues, such as articles on practices and research. Journals specialize for their audience. In TESOL International Association, they offer an online, practice-oriented journal, *TESOL Journal*. It is peer-reviewed, meaning peers review the articles and give recommendations on which to accept for publication. In many instances, reviewers' suggestions are shared with the authors so they may improve their article. The emphasis of *TESOL Journal* is on teaching practices that are supported by research and theory. An upcoming special edition is only incidental and informal vocabulary learning, but they accept articles on any topic related to teaching and learning of English.

Another respected practice-oriented journal is *TESL-EJ*, which is an electronic, peer-reviewed journal that publishes articles and reviews of textbooks, software, or websites. With topics ranging from "Demotivation and dropout in adult EFL learners" to "A practical guide to integrating technology into task-based language teaching" and

"The effect of input enhancement and consciousness-raising techniques on the acquisition of lexical and grammatical collocation of Iranian EFL learners," all the articles encompass worldwide venues and are free to access online. For both journals, *TESOL Journal* and *TESL-EJ*, submission guidelines are available to assist potential authors in the formatting expectations of their contributions, which makes the process a great deal less intimidating.

Books, white papers, and reports

With many years of experience and/or unique instructional understandings, educators collaborate and write books, white papers, and reports. Educators often adapt the materials they develop and employ in the classroom into language textbooks. Language textbooks are often focused on a skill or integrated skills (speaking, listening, reading, and writing), but they may be focused on developing language abilities in a specific academic content area. For example, language textbooks may be on writing academic essays for university students, survival English for adults at community college, or integrated language and social studies for middle school ELLs. Professional books can be on practical topics about teaching any of the myriad aspects of learning English as a second language. They may be situated in the instructional practices of a specific location too.

Another category of publication is called white papers or reports. These reports are longer investigations of topics of interest to nongovernment agencies, professional organizations, or governmental institutions. Often an institution will determine a need for better understanding of a language teaching or assessment practice, and they will solicit professionals to volunteer in the research and writing of a white paper. One such project undertaken by TESOL International Association was "Changes in the expertise of ESL professionals: Knowledge and action in an era of new standards" by Guadalupe Valdés, Amanda Kibler, and Aída Walqui (2014, March). The goal of this white paper was to, "explain the challenges and the possibilities associated with the new Standards for the ESL profession in the K–12 context and to examine the ways in which their implementation raises important questions about our long-established views on the teaching and learning of English as a second language." These three knowledgeable colleagues researched the ways that new standards were influencing the instruction of ELLs in the United States. Their analysis and recommendations helped inform teachers and educational leaders about SLA principles and instructional practices for teaching ELLs, so that they would be included and accommodated into academic content lessons.

The British Council's professional materials include another example of a research report (ELT Research Papers 18.04) entitled "From English language learners to intercultural citizens: Chinese students sojourners' development of intercultural citizenship in ELT and EMI programmes" by Will Baker and Fan (Gabriel) Fang. This report is centered on a particular population—Chinese students who study abroad in ELT and EMI programs. The paper reports on how they transitioned from learners of English into citizens who could communicate interculturally. This information is valuable to educators wishing to determine if and how study abroad experiences transform learners' language abilities.

Questions for reflection
• Which type of sharing of professional knowledge is most appealing to you at this time in your career? Why is this type of engagement appealing to you? Do you think this may change over time?

To become involved in these sorts of collaborations, the first step is to volunteer in professional organizations and on institutional task forces. Participation in professional organizations on a regular basis provides opportunities for sharing knowledge and abilities, and this inevitably opens doors for participation in various projects. World-Class Instructional Design and Assessment's (WIDA) assessment project started as a state task force and blossomed into a reputable, international organization. The work to create standards has been done by committees through professional organizations, ministries, and governmental institutions.

Benefits of Sharing Professional Knowledge

Helping others solve problems, figure out new approaches or techniques, and understand the dynamics of working with ELLs within a context is personally rewarding in the short term, and has a longer-term, more widespread impact. Consider the impact of Elizabeth Kitzmann's support of K–12 educators in the vignette below. How would her support change the lives of ELLs in her school district?

TESOL Voices
Sharing Your Knowledge Starts with a Need
I was hired as a K–12 ESL teacher in a small school district in northwestern Wisconsin, a district that comprises five elementary, a middle, and a high school. The ESL population fluctuated between 10 and 15% and the primary native language within this group is Hmong. Only "newcomer" students (i.e., students who only recently arrived in the United States) were in sheltered classes; the remainder of ESL students were all placed into grade-level mainstream, general education classes. Although I was based out of the high school (student population of ca. 1,000), for several years, I also traveled to three/four elementary schools daily. When I started, the ESL program was little more than a "safe space" or study hall where content area teachers (i.e., teachers of math, English literature, science, or history) sent test copies to be completed with the assistance of the ESL teacher and, more often than not, with open textbooks, notes, peer input, etc. I needed to bring about a change in how the content area teachers viewed their role and responsibility in teaching ELLs. I frequently found myself in the role of liaison or mediator between nonnative English-speaking students and content area teachers, who had little inclination to

or experience in collaborating with a state-licensed ESL teacher. There was a fair amount of resistance and "I don't have time" comments. So, instead of relying solely on chance meetings in hallways coupled with the distribution of my organizers and color-coded binders filled with tips and resources to each staff member, I approached my high school principal and requested time to address the entire staff at once. It was a slow process, from 10 min during a twice-monthly staff meeting to eventually a 2-hr professional development seminar twice a year. During this time, the state mandated ACCESS Testing for ELLs that produced individual student reports, which gave me the opportunity to interpret data, combine it with students' academic transcript information, and prepare a profile sheet for every ESL student. I then shared these reports with the ELLs' content area teachers. I was careful to focus on student strengths that an individual math, history, or art teacher might see, in addition to offering instructional strategy suggestions to attend to student challenges.

Getting teachers on board to examine their instructional craft and to be willing to make the required modifications necessary for our ELLs is a very delicate dance indeed. As a 40-year veteran teacher, I know all about overworked and underappreciated, so beating them to death with Lau v. Nichols was not going to send the right message. Using a multimodal and rather interactive approach, I focused primarily on including the big three objectives in every lesson: content objectives, language objectives, and learning strategy objectives. I highlighted the importance of instructional strategies including the sacred seven: speaking, listening, reading, writing + vocabulary, grammar, and pronunciation. I thoroughly explained social language and academic language using relevant examples, even going so far as to show current test items from the faculty that not only needed modification for ELLs, but probably for the native English speakers as well! In addition to strongly emphasizing modification, modification, modification, I also included linguistic (contrastive analysis) and sociocultural information about both the native languages and native cultures of our ESL students that teachers needed to be aware of while making the effort to build relationships with our culturally and linguistically diverse students.

Speaking of relationships, because I consider this to be at the very heart of teaching, I knew I had to develop a good working relationship with each staff member if I expected them to feel comfortable collaborating with me. I brought humor and feeling into my professional development sessions in an effort to facilitate empathy on their part. For staff members to walk away with even a small sense of what the academic/educational experience might be like for non-native English-speaking kids in *their own classes* is a strong positive step. I hoped they could relate and want to make some instructional changes to support ELLs. One activity I employed was to show a few scenes from the movie *The Terminal*, pausing and asking small groups to share reflections. A second activity was sharing vocabulary size of different languages in the activity "So What?!" I presented the approximate total number of words in several modern languages faculty might know, such as English, French, Spanish, and German. Then I gave the approximate number of words in Hmong (primary first language of our district's ELLs), and compared Hmong to English, which comes to approximately 167

English words for every single word in Hmong. I then asked them to take notes in English as I give a 335-word lecture in French with only two words in English. Fun and powerful.

   The evidence I have of the impact of my professional development sessions was divided between the immediate positive comments from staff members during and after the sessions and the steady rise in student ACCESS test scores. I definitely had more content area teachers seeking out collaboration opportunities and demonstrating the adoption of various modifications in their instruction and assessment. Admittedly, there were still a few who refused to work with modifications for ESL students. Yet, while continuing these professional development efforts along with my own content-based instruction, not a single ESL student dropped a WIDA proficiency level, and almost 90% steadily increased in their English language proficiency as measured by the annual ACCESS testing.

Mrs. Elizabeth Kitzmann
ESL Instructor and teacher educator

Developing a professional sharing mindset

How does an educator arrive at the desire to share their professional knowledge? Perhaps this desire comes from a sense of gratitude to others who have shared their knowledge and allowed us to build upon it. It could come from a wish to be recognized among peers in the field as being knowledgeable and authoritative. Some individuals are required to share professional knowledge through publications or presentations in order to secure contracts, tenure, or promotions. Some professionals earn additional income from their publications. Many individuals simply wish to improve educational quality for English learners.

   Whatever form of motivation an individual educator might have, we all benefit from sharing professional knowledge. First, of course, whenever knowledge is shared in a professional manner we benefit from the development of our field. We benefit from learning better ways to teach and assess language. We benefit from the recognition of the field through professional acceptance, hiring practices, and professional treatment. For instance, educators with professional credentials in TESOL earn more money than those without them. They are also treated better in their positions, with formal contracts and fringe benefits.

   We all grow professionally in our knowledge when we put our thoughts and understanding into the professional forums. The interactions we have with colleagues enhance our understanding of the material. This is why many individuals attend professional conferences; the interaction with fellow professionals causes us to see the material from other vantage points. We also benefit from the subsequent discussion after sharing our professional knowledge. For example, sharing instructional and assessment knowledge like Elizabeth Kitzmann did in the vignette facilitates effective interaction with peers. It also promotes better understanding of the material while presenting the welcome challenge of developing concrete examples or making new connections between ideas and concepts. Kate can think of many occasions when she has extended her professional knowledge through discussion with a student teacher or a peer. Recently, on one of her online courses, she was asked to give an example of the intersection of multiple discourses (discourse communities of history, math, science, scuba divers, or hair stylists, for example) and communicative competencies. She needed to show that you would have differing linguistic, discourse, sociocultural, and strategic competence patterns depending on the discourse community. She had never been challenged to consider the language of hair stylists, but the ideas of multiple discourses and communicative competencies can be applied to any discourse community. As she explored this idea for her students, her knowledge of the concept expanded in a novel and unanticipated direction.

For us, the greatest benefit is the knowledge that we are contributing to making education better and the world around us a better place. We help the hotel receptionist be able to greet a customer when checking in. We cause computer technicians who do not share a native language to be able to create a transnational communication software. We are helping make learning more equitable or opening doors for individuals to attend English-medium universities.

Why would educators not share professional knowledge?

At the early stages of professional learning, it would be understandable if a prospective TESOL professional did not feel comfortable sharing their professional knowledge right away. This feeling is called impostor syndrome; people who are new teachers, for example, might feel that they have only just learned how to teach, much less share their knowledge. With time, each of us develops our expertise and hones our skills to the point that we are comfortable and recognized for our abilities.

Another challenge to participating actively in sharing professional knowledge is limited time. Planning to spread professional development over 3–5 years, which allows for the inclusion of bigger projects into a professional plan, is an effective avenue toward growth. Many schools now require a professional development plan for new educators, so they continue as lifelong learners.

As educators, we will continue to deepen our understandings of learners and the material while honing our skills over time. Experience in teaching matters. We welcome a new generation of language learners with unique abilities and needs, which causes us to expand our worldview. We encounter unexpected occurrences or problems, and we figure out how to meet challenges and succeed in communicating course material. We create and pilot original activities to facilitate learning. Educators are expected to engage in continuous professional learning throughout their lives (Day, 1999; Cochran-Smith & Lytle, 1999a, 1999b; Richards & Farrell, 2005; Casteel & Ballantyne, 2010; David, 2014), or to be lifelong learners. If we embrace lifelong learning and engaging in professional development and sharing, our knowledge of our language learners and practices in learning, teaching, and assessing will grow exponentially.

Chapter Conclusions

Throughout this chapter, we have discussed many venues for continual professional development along with a rationale for engaging in professional development that benefits not only educators, but also learners and the academic community. We have shared educators' stories of their professional engagement and how rewarding they find it in this chapter and others.

Discussion Questions

1   What types of professional opportunities have you participated in? What led you to do so? What were the benefits and drawbacks of participating?
2   What book would you recommend for a professional book study? Why this book? Who do you think would be interested in reading this text?
3   What kinds of professional materials would you like to create? Where do you think you would share these materials?

Tasks

1   Would you be likely to volunteer for an organizational committee to undertake a project or investigation? If so, why? If not, why not?
2   Identify two publications that welcome presentations or publications from emerging professionals. What are these opportunities and what sorts of presentations or publications are they seeking?

Further Reading

Read about professional sharing of knowledge:

Rismark, M., & Sølvberg, A. (2011, October). Knowledge sharing in schools: A key to developing professional learning communities. *World Journal of Education*, *1*(2), 150–160. https://doi.org/10.5430/wje.v1n2p150

Read about developing your professional skills:

Coombe, C., Anderson, N.J., & Stephenson, L. (Eds.). (2020). *Professionalizing your English language teaching*. Springer.

Read about how to develop second language learning materials:

Mann, S., & Copland, F. (2015). *Materials development*. TESOL International Association.
Tomlinson, B. (Ed.). (1998). *Materials development in language teaching*. Cambridge University Press.

References

Baker, W., & Fang, F. (2019). *From English language learners to intercultural citizens: Chinese students sojourners' development of intercultural citizenship in ELT and EMI programmes*. ELT Research Papers 18.04. British Council. https://www.teachingenglish.org.uk/article/english-language-learners-intercultural-citizens (accessed March 26, 2021).
Barkhuizen, G., Burns, A., Dikilitaş, K., & Wyatt, M. (2018). *Empowering teacher-researchers, empowering learners*. IATEFL.

Belanoff, P., Dickson, M., Fontaine, S., & Moran, C. (Eds.). (2002). *Writing with elbow.* University Press of Colorado. https://doi.org/10.2307/j.ctt46nxbc

Burns, A. (2010). *Doing action research in English language teaching: A guide for practitioners.* Routledge.

Casteel, C. J., & Ballantyne, K. G. (Eds.). (2010). *Professional development in action: Improving teaching for English learners.* National Clearinghouse for English Language Acquisition. http://www.ncela.gwu.edu/files/uploads/3/PD_in_Action.pdf (accessed March 26, 2021).

Cochran-Smith, M., & Lytle, S. L. (Eds.). (1993). *Inside/outside: Teacher research and knowledge.* Teachers College Press.

Cochran-Smith, M., & Lytle, S. L. (1999a). The teacher research movement: A decade later. *Educational Researcher, 28*(7), 15–25. https://doi.org/10.3102/0013189X028007015

Cochran-Smith, M., & Lytle, S. L. (1999b). Relationships of knowledge and practice: Teacher learning in communities. *Review of Research in Education, 24*(1), 249–305. https://doi.org/10.2307/1167272

Dana, N. F., & Yendol-Hoppey, D. (2019). *The reflective educator's guide to classroom research: Learning to teach and teaching to learn through practitioner inquiry* (4th ed.). Corwin.

David, H. (Ed.). (2014). *Innovations in the continuing professional development of English language teachers.* British Council.

Day, C. (1999). *Developing teachers: The challenges of lifelong learning.* Falmer Press.

Dikilitaş, K., & Griffiths, C. (2017). *Developing language teacher autonomy through action research.* Springer.

Dikilitaş, K., & Hanks, J. (Eds.). (2018). *Developing language teachers with exploratory practice: Innovations and explorations in language education.* Springer.

Dikilitaş, K., Wyatt, M., Burns, A., & Barkhuizen, G. (2019). *Energizing teacher research.* IATEFL.

Donaghy, K. (2016, April 14). *Setting up an ELT materials website.* https://mawsig.iatefl.org/mawsig-blog-guest-post-setting-up-an-elt-materials-website (accessed March 26, 2021).

Elbow, P. (2000). *Everyone can write: Essays toward a hopeful theory of writing and teaching writing.* Oxford University Press.

Ferlazzo, L. (2015, November 20). *Five-minute film festival: Seven videos for ELL classrooms.* https://www.edutopia.org/blog/film-fest-ell-video-resources (accessed March 26, 2021).

Hamayan, E., Marler, B., Sánchez-López, C., & Damico, J. (2013). *Special education considerations for English language learners: Delivering a continuum of services* (2nd ed.). Caslon.

Johnson, K. E., & Golombek, P. R. (2016). *Mindful L2 teacher education: A sociocultural perspective on cultivating teachers' professional development.* Routledge.

North, S. M. (1987). *The making of knowledge in composition: Portrait of an emerging field.* Boynton/Cook Publishers.

Ogle, D. M. (1986). K-W-L: A teaching model that develops active reading of expository text. *Reading Teacher, 39*(6), 564–570. https://doi.org/10.1598/RT.39.6.11

Richards, J. C., & Farrell, T. S. C. (2005). *Professional development for language teachers: Strategies for teacher learning.* Cambridge University Press.

Tomlinson, B. (Ed.). (2001). *Materials development in language teaching*. Cambridge University Press.

Şenaydın, F., & Dikilitaş, K. (2019). Action research for self-evaluation of teaching. *European Journal of Applied Linguistics and TEFL, 8*(2), 61–75.

UFT Teacher Center. (n.d.). Professional book study. https://www.uft.org/files/attachments/professional-book-study.pdf (accessed March 26, 2021).

Valdés, G., Kibler, A., & Walqui, A. (2014, March). *Changes in the expertise of ESL professionals: Knowledge and action in an era of new standards*. TESOL International Association. https://www.tesol.org/read-and-publish/newsletters-other-publications/tesol-professional-papers-and-briefs (accessed March 26, 2021).

Wenger, E. (2002). *A guide to managing knowledge: Cultivating communities of practice*. Harvard Business School Press.

Winston-Salem/Forsyth County Schools, ESL Department. (n.d.). Many tongues, one voice. English as a Second Language/ESL Newsletter. https://www.wsfcs.k12.nc.us/Page/107823 (accessed March 26, 2021).

14

What Are the Current Situations in TESOL and New Directions To Be Taken?

This chapter concludes the text by sharing areas that teachers may want to ponder about becoming a highly effective educator. New ways to develop teachers' professional knowledge, skills, and dispositions will be revealed.

Learning Outcomes

At the conclusion of this chapter, you will be able to:

- justify collaborative instructional arrangements
- evaluate the role of creative and critical thinking in teaching
- envision how to develop into an autonomous, self-efficacious, and transformative educator
- rationalize the need for teachers to be active readers, writers, and researchers
- discuss new directions in teacher learning

In the upcoming vignette, an educator describes her process of reflection upon teaching with respect to her courses and lessons and her professional engagement. She discusses the directions that would help her grow professionally in the future. How might you handle change and modify over time? What do you need from the profession to help you?

TESOL Voices

Reflecting Back, Thinking Forward

I can say I've never delivered the same course or lesson twice. I may teach the same course or lesson topic, but I have grown in my thinking and knowledge between each session and the learners are different people from the previous groups. As a result, every course and lesson are modified in planning, delivery, and assessment. It's like the Heraclitus quote, "No man ever steps in the same river twice. For it's not the same river and he's not the same man."

I see this more and more with every new year of teaching. Every year, I open a particular syllabus for a course I've taught 10, 15, 18 times and commence modifying it.

Introduction to TESOL: Becoming a language teaching professional, First Edition. Kate Mastruserio Reynolds, Kenan Dikilitaş, and Steve Close.
© 2022 John Wiley & Sons, Inc. Published 2022 by John Wiley & Sons, Inc.

I will do so in the next couple of days, actually, since the new school year will begin in 2 weeks, and all my courses will be online. How I will plan to teach these online courses will differ from the ways I just taught them in the spring and fall. I've learned from each of the courses and students, I've read more professional literature, I've participated in webinars, and I've grown professionally. Furthermore, I'm grappling with a new population of learners unlike any I've seen before. They are from a different generation that didn't play kick the can outside in the dark and they have had smart phones in their hands from birth. I'm not judging the differences. This new generation is different, because of the social, cultural, economic, and technological changes and influences. Yet, it is my responsibility as an educator to grapple with these differences and understand the students in order to connect with them in the most constructive and productive manner possible. With the movement of time, the river has changed.

I continue to learn so much every day even in my 24th year in the profession. On any given day, a student will ask a question or share a perspective that prompts me to think differently about the material. Colleagues share their research and practices or continue to develop standards for our work, which cause me to change how I think about language, cultures, content, language learning, teaching, or assessing. This year, I reviewed a research article for *TESOL Journal* and a textbook going into press. In doing so, I bring the knowledge I have to the review and learn from the authors. My colleagues also collaborate with me on projects at my university, in the State of Washington, or internationally. For example, I am currently collaborating to design a symposium about creating welcoming environments and learning opportunities for LGBTQ learners with professionals from the East Coast and south in the United States and Japan, respectively. Through this collaboration, I will be extending my understandings while striving to make the world a more equitable place; I hope to contribute my knowledge, abilities, and perspectives as well. Through these collaborations, I change, so I am not the same woman.

I'm glad to see where the profession is going currently as colleagues strive to make the field more international and diverse. Having diverse perspectives on L2 planning, teaching, learning, and assessing is critical to better understanding all the variables and processes as well as creatively problem-solving issues we collectively face.

I hope too that the profession will revisit research into the role of interaction in SLA. I would like to see more classroom-based research on interaction in the classroom and its impact on specific areas in language learning, for example.

I would greatly appreciate more research on content-based curriculum, instruction, and assessment for ELLs. As a field, we need more research on classroom practices of instruction and assessment, particularly in content-based instruction. The newly emerging paradigm of content and language integrated learning with its dual focus on content and language fully integrated is an important step to equalizing the importance and instruction of content and language; however, it could be more formalized through modeling and methodology.

Recently, we have had productive professional discussions about SLA in text, for example, with translanguaging, but those discussions have yet to integrate into existing approaches or manifest in comprehensive planning, instruction, and assessment practices. These would be beneficial steps for instructors.

It is my sincerest hope that we can better facilitate collaborations between researchers and teachers, so that we can generate and refine theory and practices. This would reduce the burden on the teacher-researcher, provide much-needed access to the L2 classroom for university researchers, and offer opportunities for fruitful collaboration and learning. Furthermore, the field could benefit from the development of consortia of researchers working in collaboration in different locations.

Finally, I hope the field will head in the direction of creativity and innovation. We witnessed so much creativity in the field with the approaches and "designer methods" of the 1970s. While these methods are no longer considered comprehensive methodologies for the classroom, they were early and important explorations into the dynamic variables involved in L2 teaching. We need to extend our understandings and spend more time home-growing our innovators, so we develop new and stimulating ways to teach and assess L2s.

Kate Mastruserio Reynolds
Professor of TESOL and literacy

Where Do We Go From Here?

Becoming a teacher in the field of TESOL requires a long preparation in the educational programs to receive certificates of teaching from authenticated accredited companies. However, being credited as a teacher through documents does not qualify one as a skillful teacher; rather, developing a positive learning environment, working with diverse learners, curriculum, and lesson planning, delivering lessons, and assessing learning are skills that need to be nurtured and cultivated over time. Professional development through engagement with the profession and interaction with colleagues help us to nurture and hone these abilities. In doing so, we contribute in developing and sustaining the profession.

The field of TESOL has entered a new chapter where educators need to perfect their abilities, self-regulate their learning and development process, and adopt 21st-century skills which include critical thinking, creative thinking, communicating, researching, and collaborating. These skills are closely connected to the sustainability of the profession and the development of quality teaching that supports student learning. It is often argued that without developing these skills, educators may not be able to cultivate them in their students. One of the aims of the teacher education in TESOL is to develop these 21st-century skills in educators early in their career. We argue that there are two overarching processes that drive teacher learning in this framework of 21st-century skills.

Communicating and collaborating

Learning, regardless of profession, takes place in social environments where people are connected and interactive in order to achieve a particular purpose or produce a particular task or material. Although individual learning is often valued and recognized as a modality of learning, learning with and from others has been a powerful and relatively more accelerated and accountable since there is immediate validation while constructing and reconstructing knowledge.

Deeper understanding of how interaction and collaboration provide essential input and output and/or allow for the co-construction of knowledge would advance our instructional practices. Moreover, it would be helpful to have additional examinations of the Long's interaction hypothesis (1981) as it pertains to different individuals and proficiency levels within different task types (Ziegler & Bryfonski, 2018).

Critical and creative thinking

Analytical thinking and creative processes are the potential outcomes of the kinds of communication and collaboration that we engage in when we are fully committed to our teaching. This critical thought process has the potential to boost individuals' learning process. To become critical, an educator needs opportunities to subject their own ideas to the social influence of others, and to train their mind to assess and compare others' ideas to their own. To become critical, we need to know what other views exist and to compare and contrast them insightfully. Similarly, creativity is pushing the boundaries of thought in real life, experimenting with new ideas, and creating new ways of using existing practices. Generating new perspectives and actions might also require close collaboration (i.e., working equally with the utmost commitment) and deeper collaboration (i.e., working equitably with the utmost contribution).

Educators have already started to think and teach in accordance with the framework of the 21st-century skills. However, there is still a dearth of such vision in teacher education programs where educators are provided with codified knowledge from books, which they often are barely able to transfer into their teaching context. There are some principles to follow in order to enable such learning, which have been interwoven within this text.

1. Developing meaningful dialogue.
2. Offering collaborative tasks.
3. Increasing joint work.
4. Team-teaching and co-teaching.
5. Supporting joint reflective practices.
6. Encouraging learner-inclusive reflection and research.
7. Teaching educators to design materials and work with curriculum.

The key to developing 21st-century skills is interaction through multiple dialogues and collaboration. One challenge to this sort of collaboration is the isolated nature of teachers. Most of an educator's time is spent working alone, answering to challenges as they arise in the process of teaching. The best educators know how to use a "seat-of-the-pants" approach when teaching. However, some "food for thought" from the theoretical domain is often needed to support theory-informed reflection and evidence-based learning. Teachers today can be characterized by the following qualities, which impact their students too.

Question for reflection
• How might you collaborate in your school setting? With whom? On what topic or issue?

The Empowered, Autonomous Teacher

Educators are often said to need agency, which describes empowerment to use their knowledge and insights to problem-solve in their immediate context, the classroom. New teachers may expect they will be empowered to make decisions and problem-solve in their immediate environments, but this is not always the case. Having agency as a teacher and empowering learners to have agency in their learning are significantly valuable though to promoting quality teaching and learning.

Autonomy is not exactly what individuals may think it is. To clarify the meaning, autonomy does not only mean doing something alone without others, but doing something in the best possible way with regard for the needs of others. An autonomous teacher solves problems and answers to challenges without having to seek constant input from others or placing responsibility or blame outside of the classroom. Autonomy and responsibility must build on one another.

Autonomy lies in the decision-making process of teaching. A teacher should be able to understand the context, including students, materials, and social culture, to make informed decisions on what and how to teach. These decisions and preparations can be made independently, interdependently, and dependently. Autonomy in this sense implies referring to others *and* making contextualized and situated final instructional decisions. One can, for example, become autonomous while actively engaged in a collaborative work where one offers help to others and learns with and from others.

Autonomy is important in that the teacher possesses the contextualized realities for which they can tailor the instruction by exercising agency over their teaching. For educators, "agency means acting purposefully and constructively to direct their professional growth and contribute to the growth of their colleagues" (Calvert, 2016, p. 52).

Autonomy can be developed well within the 21st-century skills, which urge educators to work together by collaborating and communicating to engender critical and creative thinking. Educators working autonomously in the ways described above can also inspire their students to behave similarly while learning, which is critical to their development as a person too. Educators' modeling for their own learning and teaching can nurture students' skills in unpredictable ways.

The self-efficacious teacher

Educators have a socially critical role in society. Being self-efficacious, believing in their own ability to produce an intended result (Bandura, 1982), about what they do, and how they provide educational service often helps them act more responsibly and effectively. Therefore, as a professional community, we should strive to build and support educators' self-efficacy.

Being too self-efficacious is, however, not recommended since this can curb the desire to learn and develop more, and might lead to unsubstantiated satisfaction with teaching. This type of teacher may not increase student learning or help them develop a learner identity that fosters their learning. Consequently, in teacher preparation and professional development, we need to embrace a lifelong learning mindset.

Question for reflection

- How do you envision autonomy and self-efficacy influencing your future instruction and collaboration?

Developing teachers' efficacy is also related to the 21st-century skills that facilitate their learning vicariously in social and professional environments by monitoring others' learning process. They can also be provided with positive feedback on what they know, think, and share, which might boost their confidence. Communicating and collaborating, then, are key processes that can support the development of self-efficacy, particularly when teachers start to think and behave critically and creatively. This is another area in which communities of practice play a key role.

The transformative teacher

Teachers need to seek better teaching practices continuously as they teach in different contexts and with different students. Being in quest of better teaching often brings with it the desire to be transformative. Transformation implies an irreversible shift in the work being done and in the students being taught. It also implies building on the existing knowledge and evolving it in ways that address the new needs, interests, and expectations of students. Transformation does not mean changing practices from A to Z, but giving a new shape and vision to practice A, which would create a new form of teaching and learning. For example, we can be aware of the weaknesses of practice A and reflect on how to turn them into strengths through new ways of thinking. Some ways to change our instructional practices may include reversing the roles of teachers and learners, giving new responsibilities or expectations to students, or integrating digital tools to enhance the functionality of the existing exercises. More specifically, a transformative teacher would try to create new tasks and activities previously inconceivable with the existing mindset.

A transformative teacher, in sum, is one who can and should lead to transformation in the students' minds and the processes of learning. A teacher capable of continuously transforming ways of working, thinking, and knowing can potentially compel the same from students through the use of specific instructional decision and action. Such a process often creates empowerment not only in teachers, but also in learners, with the increased confidence in their own abilities and sustainable supports offered in the learning process.

Teachers as Critical Readers and Writers

Teacher development is potentially enabled in various ways. Some position teachers as consumers of others' views such as in books, articles, magazines, and blog writing. Reading and understanding published knowledge forms a critical basis of teacher learning, particularly when it is systematic. However, being practitioners, teachers often lack conceptual understanding of academic arguments, which might lead to exhaustion and avoidance owing to the theoretical complexity, lack of practical relevance, and over-language (Borg, 2013, p. 82). Alongside these cognitive challenges, they may also have limited time to engage in reading and seeking practical knowledge that could be relevant and useful to them.

The teacher-researcher approach, on the other hand, positions them as producers of practical knowledge (Hargreaves, 1999) through the composition of reflective accounts or classroom research reports. Generating practical knowledge requires systematic reflection and note-taking as well as an ability to write in English. Writing can invariably improve teachers' language skills and thinking processes since the act of writing is a catalyst for further and deeper thinking as well as for creating permanent knowledge that can be useful to others as it is publicly shared and accessible.

Writing also deepens educators' understanding of how other teachers teach and how their own students learn since writing also becomes a process of rethinking and revisiting their own beliefs when trying to formulate the ideas emerging from their experiences. In this way, teachers process their experiences and reinvigorate their perspectives of teaching and learning. Writing gives shape to their thoughts in the form of putting them into meaningful words, which nurtures thinking and cultivates professional identity (Goodnough, 2010).

Teaching is a constantly developing skill, bolstered by theory and practice, but theory and practice can only be passed on if they are described effectively. Therefore, becoming a critical reader and writer promotes teachers' ability to use language, which in turn empowers their skills to teach, enriches their self-efficacy, and boosts their autonomy in various ways.

Teachers as Researchers

Engaging in research is often a challenging process for teachers in that they lack knowledge of how to do research and feel it may not offer them practical ideas that inform their teaching. However, in recent years there has been a general surge in teacher research projects (Dikilitaş & Wyatt, 2018), especially in contexts where there are limited resources for externally hired mentors and trainers. Teachers are guided to become researchers so they can explore and create the practical, context-specific knowledge that they need.

Teachers' engagement in research can offer a number of benefits which help them develop skills that have recently been incorporated into the 21st-century skills framework. Research as a professional development strategy can be well aligned with the 21st-century skills in that it offers opportunities to communicate and collaborate with learners, other teachers, and university researchers.

Research as a solitary activity is possible, but collaborating with learners about issues, concerns, and questions could increase communication, which in turn might help develop relatively more relevant knowledge for teachers to draw on. In addition, such a process of exploration with learners can make them more critical as they might notice learner-sensitive issues that they may have skipped unknowingly. They might also become creative when learner perspectives are reconsidered. Learners might come up with interesting learning designs and viewpoints, which might make research more learner-centered and meaningful for teachers.

Teachers who engage in research also take on various identities, such as critical thinker, problem poser and solver, analyzer and knowledge generator, and insightful interpreter. These roles help them cultivate and transform their identities (Yuan & Burns, 2017) from a traditional teacher into a relatively more critical teacher who can regulate their own learning and that of students. Such teachers influence their students' learning process positively (Dikilitas & Yayli, 2018) and leave students more free thinking and learning, with questioning and reflecting as part of their researcher mindset. Research becomes a joint activity between teachers and learners where they mutually understand each other, develop rapport (Edwards & Burns, 2016), and create instruction that addresses their interests, needs, and expectations. Learners become active participants in co-investigations of classroom issues and experience an attitudinal and behavioral change (Roll & Browne, 2017).

Research on learners that simply observes them, without their engagement, will lack depth and breadth as well as relevance. Learners' awareness of the issues that make learning challenging will also activate their metacognition and self-regulatory skills while learning. We suggest here that teachers engage in research particularly involving their learners (Kinsler, 2010) in the process of seeking evidence for the phenomena they are investigating to increase learner responsibility in the efforts to understand (Hanks, 2019) and improve lessons. The knowledge that might potentially be generated might not only help teachers teach with more confidence, but also help students to learn in a comfortable way.

Teacher-friendly Research Publications

As we mentioned previously, teachers can become writers of publications in different modalities including magazine commentaries, blog posts, reflective papers, and research accounts. These publications not only improve teachers' use of language to express and elaborate on their practices and profession, but also become meaningful and relevant content for other teachers to read. The latter is particularly significant since teachers often do not like to read academic articles that are hard to understand owing to their complex language. However, teacher-generated publications often sound more familiar to teachers and might include arguments that they can relate to. Publishing might look prestigious for teachers, but it actually goes beyond that. It helps generate a community of writers and readers unique to teachers where they can speak each other's language and where practical exchange of relevant knowledge is possible.

In Dikilitaş and Mumford (2019), teachers who read other teachers' research accounts highlighted several positive effects on their abilities to understand what the author means as they found commonalities and similarities with their own pedagogical challenges. With these teacher-authored publications, writing also becomes more accessible not only in conceptual terms, but also in the practicality it offers to teachers. Research written and authored by teachers is then presented in practical terms and is soundly applicable to instruction.

When teachers share their accounts of instructional practices that are effective in their classroom in their writing, they provide key insights into teaching and learning L2 with the specific population and context, but also mentor other teachers who will be entering similar contexts.

Questions for reflection

- How might you participate in the profession through research and writing? What topics or issues would you like to investigate?
- How might you collaborate on these research topics?

New Directions in Teacher Learning

Teacher learning in the context of teacher preparation and in service has been changing from transmission-based learning models to more interactive and community-based models where teachers can be socially active in access to knowledge and in generation of it (Hargreaves, 1999) with others in professional communities. New identities of teachers have emerged recently, some of which include teachers as lifelong learners, as researchers, as digital experts, and as designers. These new roles are still not commonly possessed. We suggest that in teacher preparation programs, courses, assignments, and activities should be adapted to encourage and form these identities. We believe that in-service teachers should be offered professional development that helps them nurture their new perspectives and cultivate new identities over time.

We recognize that there are hurdles to overcome to implement these suggestions fully. First, there is the ever-present issue of time. Teachers and teacher-educators are pressured to teach more, grade more, interact with learners, parents, and communities more, and professionally develop more. Educational systems, specifically administrators, can help learners and teachers by being thoughtful and intentional about issues of time and workload. Overcommitment of the time resources of teachers frequently threatens to preclude the previously described means of participating in the larger world of teaching that exists outside of the classroom. These issues can be ameliorated with thoughtful, intentional, and creative planning. For example, in high-incidence school districts, teachers with dual licenses in a content and ESL can be hired, which would reduce the need for hiring two separate educators, and yield better instructional results for the ELLs. Then, administrators could plan schedules better, resulting in more planning and thinking time for teachers. This is just one radical suggestion, and it is simply intended to spur creative thinking to cope with the issue of time. Smaller class sizes would also yield better learning and more time for educators.

Second, some preservice teacher candidates have preconceived notions of how they will teach and what good teaching looks like when they enter their teacher education programs. Many of the notions come from the instructional and assessment practices that worked for them. Owing to these beliefs, they are not always open to new ideas and approaches as they appear incongruent with their own beliefs. Teacher-educators need to meet this issue head on early in programs through problem-based learning discussions and by exemplifying the kinds of practices they hope their teacher candidates will exhibit later. The challenge here is that there is very little programmatic space beyond the dissemination of knowledge to engage teacher candidates in this manner. This challenge, like others, can be overcome through creative and collaborative problem-solving.

We argue that it is not teachers' sole responsibility to transmit knowledge, but also to help students discover knowledge and hone their language skills. These perspectives and processes for L2 learners mirror how individuals learn to become teachers. Teachers need to be supported to develop autonomy in communities rather than isolated, foster their self-efficacy about teaching and learning, and learn to transform not only themselves, but also their learners. TESOL programs have the potential to contribute to teacher development with new reunderstandings and reinterpretations by enthusiastic strategic educators and innovative curricula.

Question for reflection

- How might you innovate and change teacher education programs to transform the teacher candidates' teaching and learning?

Chapter Conclusions

In this chapter, we have attempted to illustrate the current discussions around L2 teaching and learning that we think will influence future instruction. Collaboration among colleagues, critical thinking, creative thinking, and utilizing our 21st-century skills will help us innovate and extend our understandings and transform our instructional practices. If we have a balanced perspective on our autonomy and self-efficacy, we can become open-minded and empowered. Engaging in our professional communities of practice through reading and writing, professional organizations, and research, our knowledge can transform understandings of teaching and learning. Teacher education programs can lead the way.

Discussion Questions

1 How might you collaborate with educators at your school or in your community/region to transform teaching and learning of L2s? Would you develop communities of practice or participate in a professional organization to collaborate on these topics?

2 How might you help build your sense of self-efficacy in your teaching? How would you help support and build colleagues' self-efficacy?

3 Research plays a big role in innovation and professional development. What do you think of this? What skills or resources (human, technological, or other resources) would you need to engage in L2 research? What topics or issues would be of most interest to you?

Tasks

1 Interview an ESL/EFL teacher to see how they collaborate, innovate, and transform teaching and learning in their schools and classrooms. Share with your colleagues.

2 Research self-efficacy surveys to determine one that would work for your context. Use the survey with your community of practice, whether that is within your class, school, or professional organization. Share your findings in a blog or in class.

3 Research 21st-century skills to identify how you can best connect the skills to your ESL/EFL students learning. Outline a plan of how you will implement them in your ESL/EFL teaching.

Further Reading/Read and Discuss

Read about novice teacher self-efficacy and preparedness:

Faez, F., & Valeo, A. (2012). TESOL teacher education: Novice teachers' perceptions of their preparedness and efficacy in the classroom. *TESOL Quarterly, 46*(3), 450–471. https://doi.org/10.1002/tesq.37

Read about being a teacher-researcher:

Borg, S. (2013). *Teacher research in language teaching: A critical analysis.* Cambridge University Press.

Herrenkohl, L. R., & Kawasaki, K. (2010). Inside and outside: Teacher-researcher collaboration. *The New Educator, 6,* 74–92.

Read about the knowledge-creating school:

Hargreaves, D. H. (1999). The knowledge-creating school. *British Journal of Educational Studies, 47*(2), 122–144.

References

Bandura, A. (1982). Self-efficacy mechanism in human agency. *American Psychologist, 37*(2), 122–147. https://doi.org/10.1037/0003-066X.37.2.122

Borg, S. (2013). *Teacher research in language teaching: A critical analysis.* Cambridge University Press.

Calvert, L. (2016). The power of teacher agency. *Learning Forward*, *37*(2), 51–56. https://learningforward.org/wp-content/uploads/2016/04/the-power-of-teacher-agency-april16.pdf (accessed March 26, 2021).

Dikilitaş, K., & Mumford, S. E. (2019). Teacher autonomy development through reading teacher research: Agency, motivation and identity. *Innovation in Language Learning and Teaching*, *13*(3), 253–266. https://doi.org/10.1080/17501229.2018.1442471

Dikilitaş, K., & Wyatt, W. (2018). Learning teacher-research-mentoring: Stories from Turkey. *Teacher Development*, *22*(4), 537–553. https://doi.org/10.1080/13664530.2017.1403369

Dikilitaş, K., & Yayli, D. (2018). Teachers' professional identity development through action research. *ELT Journal*, *72*(4), 415–424. https://doi.org/10.1093/elt/ccy027

Edwards, E., & Burns, A. (2016). Language teacher action research: Achieving sustainability. *ELT Journal*, *70*(1), 6–15. https://doi.org/10.1093/elt/ccv060

Goodnough, K. (2010). The role of action research in transforming teacher identity: Modes of belonging and ecological perspectives. *Educational Action Research*, *18*(2), 167–182. https://doi.org/10.1080/09650791003740725

Hanks, J. (2019). From research-as-practice to exploratory practice-as research in language teaching and beyond. *Language Teaching*, *52*(2), 143–187. https://doi.org/10.1017/S0261444819000016

Hargreaves, D. H. (1999). The knowledge-creating school. *British Journal of Educational Studies*, *47*(2), 122–144. https://doi.org/10.1111/1467-8527.00107

Kinsler, K. (2010). The utility of educational action research for emancipator change. *Action Research*, *8*(2), 171–189. https://doi.org/10.1177/1476750309351357

Long, M. (1981). Input, interaction, and second language acquisition. In H. Winitz (Ed.), *Native Language and Foreign Language Acquisition: Annals of the New York Academy of Science*, *379*(1), 259–278. https://doi.org/10.1111/j.1749-6632.1981.tb42014.x

Roll, S., & Browne, R. (2017). Students as co-researchers to inform student learning: Findings from a poverty simulation. *Action Research*, *18*(2), 1–21. https://doi.org/10.1177/1476750317723966

Yuan, R., & Burns, A. (2017). Teacher identity development through action research: A Chinese experience. *Teachers and Teaching*, *23*(6), 729–749. https://doi.org/10.1080/13540602.2016.1219713

Ziegler, N., & Bryfonski, L. (2018). Interaction-driven L2 learning: Advanced learners. In P. A. Malovrh & A. G. Benati (Eds.), *Handbook of advanced proficiency in second language acquisition* (pp. 94–113). Wiley. https://doi.org/10.1002/9781119261650.ch6

Acronyms in TESOL/Applied Linguistics

AAAL	American Association of Applied Linguistics
ACTFL	American Council of Teachers of Other Languages
AILA	Association de Linguistique Appliquée (International Association of Applied Linguistics)
ALM	Audiolingual Method
ALT	assistant language teacher
AMEP	Adult Migrant English Program
ASCD	Association for Supervision and Curriculum Development
CAEP	Council for the Accreditation of Educator Preparation
CAL	Center for Applied Linguistics
CALL	computer-assisted/aided language Learning
CALLA	Cognitive Academic Language Learning Approach
CARLA	Center for Advanced Research on Language Acquisition
CBI	content-based instruction
CEFR	Council of Europe Framework
CELTA	Certificate in Teaching English to Speakers of Other Languages
CLIL	content and language integrated learning
CLT	communicative language teaching
CMS	course or learning management system
COP	community of practice
CVC	consonant, vowel, consonant
EAP	English for academic purposes
EFL	English as a foreign language
EGP	English for general purposes
EIL	English as an international language
ELD	English language development
ELF	English as a lingua franca
ELD	English language development
ELL	English language learners or English language learning
ENL	English as a new language
ESL	English as a second language
ESOL	English for speakers of other languages
ESP	English for specific purposes

Introduction to TESOL: Becoming a language teaching professional, First Edition. Kate Mastruserio Reynolds, Kenan Dikilitaş, and Steve Close.

ETS	Educational Testing Services
GLAD	Guided Language Acquisition Design
GT	grammar-translation method
IATEFL	International Association for the Teaching of English as a Foreign Language
IELTS	International English Language Testing System
IEP	intensive English program
IPA	International Phonetic Alphabet
JALT	Japanese Association for Language Teaching
KSAALT	Kingdom of Saudi Arabia Association of Language Teachers
L1	first language
L2	second language
LAD	language acquisition device
LAUSD	Los Angeles Unified School District
LEA	language experience approach
LGBTQIA +	lesbian, gay, bisexual, transgender, queer/questioning, intersex, asexual/ally
MLA	Modern Language Association
MOOC	massive open online course
NABE	National Association for Bilingual Education
NCELA	National Clearinghouse for English Language Acquisition
NL	native language
NNEST	nonnative English-speaking teachers
NNS	nonnative speaker
NP	noun phrase
NS	native speaker
OELA	Office of English Language Acquisition, part of the U.S. Department of Education
PBI	project-based instruction
Phi-IRL	Philippine Informal Reading Inventory
RP	received pronunciation
SDAIE	specially designed academic instruction in English
SIG	special interest group
SIOP	sheltered instruction observation protocol
SIT	School for International Training
SL	second language
SLA	second language acquisition
SLO	student learning outcome
TBLT	task-based language teaching
TEFL	teaching/teachers of English as a foreign language
TELL	technology-enhanced language learning
TESL	teaching/teachers of English as a second language
TESOL	Teachers of English to Speakers of Other Languages
TL	target language
TOEFL	Test of English as a Foreign Language
TOEIC	Test of English for International Communication

TPR	total physical response
TPRS	total physical response storytelling
VESL	vocational English as a second language
WAESOL	Washington Association for the Education of Speakers of Other Languages
WIDA	World-class Instructional Design and Assessment
ZPD	zone of proximal development

Index

Introduction to TESOL: Becoming a language teaching professional, First Edition. Kate Mastruserio Reynolds, Kenan Dikilitaş, and Steve Close.
© 2022 John Wiley & Sons, Inc. Published 2022 by John Wiley & Sons, Inc.